nuts

Linda and Fred Griffith

nuts

Recipes from Around the World

That Feature Nature's

Perfect Ingredient

ST. MARTIN'S PRESS

NEW YORK

www.stmartins.com

Design by Kathryn Parise

LIBRARY OF CONGRESS CATALOGING-IN-PUBLICATION DATA

Griffith, Linda.
    Nuts : Recipes from around the world that feature nature's perfect ingredient / Linda and Fred Griffith.—1st ed.
        p. cm.
    ISBN 0-312-26624-3
    1. Cookery (Nuts)   2. Nuts.   3. Cookery, International.   I. Griffith, Fred.   II. Title.

TX814b.G75 2003
641.6'.45—dc21

2002033286

First Edition: April 2003

10   9   8   7   6   5   4   3   2   1

As we continue to appreciate the extraordinary creativity
of cooks past, as well as those the world over, it is
our hope that our own progeny and theirs will
continue to celebrate the legacy that we leave.

Madison Newman Myers

Forrest Jennings Drucker

Mackenzie Weller Hanauer Myers

Sydney Tate Drucker

Amanda Kim Myers

Alexandra Dove Castillo Griffith

Paige Nicole Myers

Sophia Rose Drucker

Jacob Hanauer Myers

John Graham Castillo Griffith

May they find pleasure in the books we have written,
and may they also understand the importance of the family meal.

contents

Recipes with Nuts
39

CONTENTS   viii

acknowledgments

Once again we are indebted to culinary historians Jan and Dan Longone in Ann Arbor. As dear friends, they have been enthusiastic about this project long before there was ever a word in writing. Jan could always lead us to the right source every time we ran into a wall. They introduced us to Barbara Larrimore, a University of Michigan professor, who told us to "call my cousin Chop in Georgia. He's gone from peaches to pecans." We did. He invited us to visit and we learned a lot. And we thank her for that. The Longones had praised the Circassian Chicken she had served them, but she hadn't made it. She sent us to the person who did—Ann Arbor restaurateur Ayse Uras. So, thanks again to Professor Larrimore.

Generous friends here in Cleveland have a stellar collection of rare herbals and cookbooks. Bobbi and Bob Pincus have been enthusiastic researchers whenever called upon. Being able to see a reference on the original five hundred-year-old page is truly a privilege.

We thank John and Lynn Baritelle of the California Press for their gracious hospitality; and managers Chuck and Gayle Schutte for making sure we never run out of fabulous nut oils.

We've been able to learn firsthand about nuts in many regions where they are grown and celebrated. Nucci and Flavio Russo opened Piedmont to us. We experienced the richness of the hazelnuts and chestnuts. Marco Falco, the fine chef of Osteria della Rosa Rosso, just down the street from the Russo's beautiful Cherasco home, showed us how to use these nuts in the kitchen. We visited the legendary pastry and candy shop Pasticceria Barbero, famous for more than a century for Baci di Cherasco, the world's greatest hazelnut and chocolate sweet. We spent a whole day watching owner/chef Giancarlo Torta work in the kitchen, and tasting everything in the shop!

We thank Roberta Ceretto. Our tour of her family's famous vineyards led, serendipitously, to their *torrone* kitchen, where a small number of confectioners are producing an artisanal-quality hazelnut nougat. We met Alberto Rosa Brunet, who purchases hazelnuts the world over for Ferraro's Nutella, the world's most popular hazelnut product.

With the kind assistance of Air India's Andy Bhatia and Don Buckley, we made a last-minute trip to India to learn about the cashews and coconuts in southwest India. We thank Maya Kaimal, author of the stellar book *Savoring the Spice Coast of India*, for her generous help.

In India, our thanks go to Maya for introducing us to Nimmy Paul. And to Nimmy and her husband, Paul, for opening doors for us and showing us how to cook Kerala style. To Sonny Matthew, cashew farmer; Denny and Anthony John, cashew and coconut processors; P. Gangsadharan Pillai, chairman, and Indira U and K. A. Venkiteswaran of the Cashew Export Promotion Council of India; Dr. R. K. Singh and Mr. Sreekumar of the Coconut Development Board. Thanks to Moosa and Fazia of Ayesha Manzil in Tellicherry for having us in their home, taking us to the spice markets, and showing us more about how to use these wonderful ingredients. Thanks also to Moosa for taking us to meet Dr. Venu V, the brilliant thirty-year-old physician turned public administrator for this part of India. And of course to D. C. Sudhir for travel help.

Closer to home, we thank American Spoon Food's Justin Rashid; Ted DeJong, Chairman of Pomology at UC Davis; Barbara Bowman, one of the founders of USA Slow Food; California nut farmers John Lagier, Craig McNamara, and Kevin Herman; Chop Evans, the pecan king of Fort Valley, Georgia, and Harry Willson and J. B. Easterlin, pecan processors; Susan Brauner and Sam Cunningham, Blue Diamond Almonds; Greg Miller, Empire Chestnut Company; Christina Gerlach, black walnut buyer in Wheelersburg, Ohio; Susan Zartman and Dave Steinmuller of Hammon's in Stockton, Missouri; Kristen G. Elliot of the Peanut Institute; Rick Vidgen of MacFarms in Hawaii; Greg Gorang, Diamond Walnut; Darryll Corti of Sacramento's Corti Brothers; and to Professor Parman Green for telling us who to ask.

The Schlesinger Library's Kathy Herrlich and Barbara Haber, who helped us look for the first pecan pie; the maven of things both musical and Italian, celebrated author Fred Plotkin; the kind librarians at The Cleveland Public Library; David Van Deusen, of *The Walnut Times*; Kathy Dawson, for reminding us of the walnut episode on the Van Dyke show; Donna Stone and Polly Owen of the Oregon Hazelnut Commission; Angela Hopkins, Willard Public Library, Battle Creek; L .J. Grauke, of the National Germplasm

Repository; food and travel writer Janet Podolak; Dr. Peter Gail, ethnobotanist; Ray Gallucci, importer and retailer of wonderful things Italian; Amazon (as in Brazil) expert Jeff Moats; Cleveland television legend Del Donahoo; Stephen Kenyon of Peterson Nut Co., which is lucky enough to be located next to the world's most wonderful ball park, Jacobs Field. Still more thanks to Rich Grossman, Nut of the Month Club, and James Liston, pine nut guy.

We thank Chris Tracy, whose Calphalon cookware has made us forget about our copper. And thanks also to Patrick Martins, Director of Slow Food USA for opening doors all over the world.

We appreciate our many friends who have come for meals good and not so: Sandy and Bob Lontkowsky, Joe Santosuosso, Paul Anthony, Sandy and Peter Earl, David Klausner, Sanford and Frances Herskovitz, Mario Vitale, Lisa and Paul Minnillo, Lisa and Michael Symon, Vid and Anne Lutz, Brandt and Kristen Evans, Dorrie and Merv Sopher, Heidi and Brad Friedlander. And as always we thank organic farmers Molly and Ted Bartlett.

We could not travel without knowing that our four-legged creatures were happy. Cindy Glazer calls herself their nanny—everyone should be so lucky. Donna McCaughtry provides daytime backup while making certain the house runs well. Linda Luria keeps our organic garden blooming; and in times of computer hell, we thank gurus Carolyn Javitch and Larry Mittman. We call and they come. And of course we thank our children and grandchildren for understanding why we are nose to the grindstone so much of the time.

Without Jane Dystal this project would not have happened; no one could have a more supportive agent. Nor could we dream of a better editor than Marian Lizzi. We thank them both, as well as our wonderful copy editor Judith de Rubini, designer Kathryn Parise and all others at St. Martin's Press who have been so helpful.

introduction

Joseph's brothers carried pistachios to Egypt, King Solomon's garden was laden with walnuts, and almonds were part of the ornamentation on the Tabernacle's candlesticks. You only have to look in the Book of Genesis to see how important nuts were in man's early history.

Even in prehistory, there is ample archeological evidence that nuts played a major role in the diets of early humans. In fact, anthropologist Michael Rosenberg at the University of Delaware makes the strong case that edible nuts were the key factor in the beginnings of settled village life. Whenever a population finds an edible nut, that nut is eaten. If a certain nut grew in quantity in a certain place, nomadic people invariably would find it and learn that they could gather and store it for future use. That meant that they didn't have to be always on the move in quest of food. Once they were settled, the way was open for the development of small villages with solid dwellings. Agriculture, cuisine, art, and religion then followed.

If nuts had not been a nearly perfect food, basically providing everything humans need for survival and health, this might not have happened. They were high in protein and packed with nutritional elements. In those early encounters when our ancestors found an area rich with nuts, they found a truly life-sustaining food. As centuries passed and prehistoric man became an entry on a time chart, and agricultural practices evolved, nuts became less important by themselves and more an important accompaniment to the main dish. But there can be no escape from the idea that nuts helped make civilization possible.

What Is a Nut?

It is most often defined as the dry, one-seeded fruit of any of various trees or bushes, consisting of a kernel, often edible, in a hard and woody or tough and leathery shell, more or less separable from the seed itself. The kernel, or meat, of such a fruit can be called a nut. Strictly speaking a peanut is not a nut, a sunflower seed is not a nut, a water chestnut is not a nut, a coconut is not a nut, and a pine nut is not a nut. There is a common denominator: a shell that encloses an edible and tasty substance, a kernel, seed, or even coconut water and copra. Loosely, any hard-shelled fruit that will keep a long time without decaying can be called a nut. Some argue that the soybean should be called the soy nut, and dried, toasted, and salted, the soybean has a good taste, but it grows in a pod, like a pea, and not in a shell.

In his new magnum opus, *The Oxford Companion to Food*, Alan Davidson writes, "Nuts are impossible to define in a manner which would be compatible with popular usage yet acceptable to botanists. In this book popular usage is preferred, so the groundnut (a legume, also called peanut) and the chufa nut (a tuber) are allowed to shelter under the umbrella word." He points out that in some languages there is a lack of any such umbrella word. "*Noix* in French looks like one," he writes, "but just means walnut."

The tree nut people, growers of such nuts as almonds, pistachios, and cashews, don't include three of the twelve that we have chosen for this book under their definition, but the world recognizes chestnuts, coconuts, and peanuts as nuts.

Nuts in History

While world history has been packed with stories about early explorers who sailed in search of the spices of India, we were surprised to learn that there were similar explorations in the search for nuts.

Global migrations moved crops and agricultural practices along with religion and culture. Early practitioners of Islam moved across the world carrying cooking styles in which various nuts played a prominent role. Irrigation systems brought to Sicily and Spain by the Moors helped them establish their orchards of almonds, hazelnuts, and other crops.

The Portuguese were the most daring and successful in moving agriculture about. Very early they took the cashews of Brazil to India where it is now a dominant agricultural crop. They took peanuts to China and India, which together now produce half of the world's number one nut. The South American peanut also was taken to Africa. When West African slaves were brought to the Eastern United States in the eighteenth century, they brought these same peanuts with them, for the first time establishing them in the American South. (The slave trade was particularly selective; slave traders dealt with African merchants for the most skilled farmers available. They wanted expertise in growing and handling rice and cotton.)

American farmers, as they explored new land in the middle part of the country, carried along the hardwood nuts of the South. Even the English, rarely noted for their culinary skills, tried to introduce the European filbert into the Massachusetts colony. The macadamia came to Hawaii when a traveler thought they would be good shade trees for plantations.

One of our sons was working with a team of archeologists and anthropologists in Georgia, searching an area that would soon be covered by the building of a dam. He discovered a planting pattern in the big pecan trees of the doomed forest. Some were very old, and there was a second growth of pecans. He and his colleagues concluded that an orchard had been planted there probably before the Civil War. The farmers were most likely displaced by the war and they never got back to what they had started. That work told us that the planting of pecans in Georgia took place somewhat earlier than anyone thought.

Early in the last century, the case was made that forests and forest crops are good for the environment; therefore nut crops are good for the environment. J. Russell Smith, the Columbia and University of Pennsylvania economic geographer, made the case in his 1929 book, *Tree Crops*. Strange to say, now, in an environment of despair about the world, some experts are optimistic. They feel that with the gradual reestablishment of forests and forest crops around the world, the corner can be turned on environmental degradation. Carbon dioxide can be reduced and global warming turned around.

Nuts in Today's Cuisines

This book will focus on a dozen nuts and how to use them in the kitchen. They are mostly tree nuts, but we are including the maverick coconut and the groundnut or peanut. Some, like the macadamia, are niche nuts—small production, high prices, specialized markets. Others, like the almond, cover the world. Where did each nut come from? How did it get from here to there? Was it a culinary hit? How was it used? There are thousands of stories.

"Nuts are gastronomy's sine qua non. For centuries, they have played an indispensable role in the great cuisines of the world: they thicken sauces both subtle and crispy, and they provide incomparable flavor and texture to pastry and confectionary and non-sweet dishes, which also call on them for crisp garnishes." Martha Rose Shulman, in an Oldways monograph, says it in a nutshell.

Originally nuts were widely used in cooking simply because they were there. People used what they had back in the old days—and they had nuts.

Nuts are delicious by themselves and wonderful in combination with other foods. They are high in protein and packed with a host of important nutritional elements. Nuts can have a variety of personalities and play a range of roles.

Whole, out of the shell, they add texture, crunch, and flavor. Coarsely chopped they add more subtle contrasts to a dish. Finely chopped, the texture is less, but the flavor is often greater. Used this way, they often are also a thickening agent. Nuts can be pressed for oil or can be ground into paste. They can also be dried and ground into flour. They can be utilized in savory dishes as well as in sweet.

As we gave thought to the twentieth century, and the changes made in the way Americans eat, we realized just how much people wanted to add items to their culinary repertoires. First, serious American cooks took on the French, integrating their ideas into what they cooked for their families. The influences of the Italian cuisines are everywhere. We discovered the wok and learned how to cook like the Chinese. Today, Indian food is hot, and so is Japanese. The dishes of Thailand and Vietnam have hit the scene. Mexican cooking weaves in and out. The cuisines of the Iberian Peninsula are here. Everyone has heard of fusion and Pacific Rim.

Creative chefs in America have pioneered and still lead the way. Today in our homes, with a treasury of modern cookbooks available to us, we can go from the Western Mediterranean to the Black Sea, from North Africa to the Fertile Crescent, as we cook for our families and friends.

Cooks everywhere are exploring cuisines that a quarter century ago they hardly knew existed. Hispanic, Asian, and Middle Eastern food markets are now common even in Middle America. Significantly, nuts play an important role in all of these cuisines.

Nuts and Health

Nuts are good for you. Today we state that flatly and without fear of contradiction, but as recently as twenty years ago, we probably couldn't have.

In the 1980s, consumption of nuts in the United States started to slide. By then there had been so much fear generated by the perceived relationship between fat and heart disease that people just started turning away from any food that contained fat. There wasn't an antinut campaign. It's just that nuts were high in fat. Fat was bad. Therefore nuts were bad—but now nuts are back.

It wasn't until the middle of the 1900s that the medical establishment started to understand the role of cholesterol in heart disease and stroke. We were told that there is a connection between a high-fat diet, especially a diet rich in animal fats, and health. The Framingham study in Massachusetts and the work of Ancel Keys at the University of Minnesota helped make the case. That was just the beginning. It was vastly more complicated than it first appeared.

Food pyramids hit the scene, telling us what to eat, how much, and how often. In an early one from the USDA, nuts were in the meat/meat alternate group, which encouraged people to stay away from nuts. Things changed when Keys's famous seven-country project was reported in 1970. That led directly to the Mediterranean Food Pyramid. As with earlier pyramids, red meat is at the top, meaning it should be eaten rarely. Vegetable fats, however, were vindicated; thus we could eat as much of them as we wanted—and nuts were placed at the same level as fruits, vegetables, and legumes.

Then, there were scores of studies of specific diet components, many of them involving nuts. One of the earliest and most persuasive was done at Loma Linda University in California. The Seventh-Day Adventists study there involved thirty-four thousand men and women, mostly vegetarians. Results published in 1992 showed that those who ate an ounce or so of nuts five times a week had a significantly reduced risk of heart attacks. Some researchers thought it was the high level of Vitamin E in nuts that made the difference, but later studies showed that it was the high percentage of monounsaturated oils in nuts. Other Loma Linda studies found that of sixty-five foods they checked, nuts had the most positive relationship to the reduction of the bad fats.

The Nurses Health Study was another very important key to the nut revival. At Brigham and Women's Hospital and the Harvard School of Public Health in Boston researchers followed the histories of eighty-six thousand nurses. They found out that nurses who ate five ounces of nuts per week had one-third fewer heart attacks than those that didn't. Even those who ate nuts only one to four times a week decreased their risk of heart attacks, compared to the non-nut-eating population.

A study of forty thousand postmenopausal women showed that the more nuts they ate, the less the risk of heart attacks. Eat nuts five times a week and, according to that study, you cut the heart attack rate in half. Even eating nuts once a week led to a 25 percent reduction, and the nuts seem to lower the bad LDL cholesterol without affecting the good HDL.

Another comparative study of three diets, one based on olive oil, another on almonds, and the third on dairy products, showed that the almond diet gave the best results. A Loma Linda study of walnuts showed that a diet with 20 percent of daily calories from walnuts reduced heart problems. More good news for the walnut growers—a new study in France showed that "beneficial blood lipid levels were associated with walnut consumption." Another set of trials in Europe showed that diets with a lot of almonds reduced total cholesterol and the so-called bad cholesterol significantly. Further study of the Boston data also shows that the risk of type 2 diabetes in women is substantially reduced by nuts in the diet.

In spite of these studies, many people were still reluctant to eat nuts because of their calorie content. As caloric as they are, nuts won't necessarily make you gain weight. Nuts satisfy. Satiety is the term for it. Eat just an ounce or so of nuts, and the edge is taken off your hunger. So you tend to eat less.

Other experts have made the case for nuts' ability to fight not only heart disease, but cancer as well. Specifically cited were two studies that showed a decreased risk of prostate cancer among men forty-five to seventy-four when they ate a lot of nuts. But researcher Paul Davis at UC Davis warns that there is much more to be learned before you can just eat a tree nut or two and diminish your chances of cancer.

There is one essential caveat. As many as three million Americans are allergic to peanuts, but tree nuts also trigger allergic reactions in thousands of people. An allergy can manifest itself in a number of ways—wheezing, sneezing, and difficulty in breathing. There can be hives and intestinal problems. At their worst, allergens can be fatal, triggering what is called anaphylactic shock. Most people who are allergic to nuts already know it and know to keep their distance.

So, unless you have an allergy to them, eat nuts, reduce heart attacks, and enjoy one of nature's most nutritious, delicious, and complete health foods.

NUTRITION CHART

The amounts of basic nutritional elements found in one ounce of the twelve nuts covered in this book. This information is from the USDA Nutrient Database.

	CARBOHYDRATES-G	CALORIES	PROTEIN-G	TOTAL FAT-G‡	FIBER-G†
ALMONDS	6	167	6	14	3
BRAZIL NUTS	4	186	4	19	2
CASHEWS	9	163	4	13	1
CHESTNUTS	15	70	1	1	4
COCONUT, RAW	4	99	1	8	2.5
HAZELNUTS	5	179	4	17	3
MACADAMIAS	4	299	2	21	2
PEANUTS	6	166	7	14	2
PECANS	5	189	3	20	3
PINE NUTS	4	161	7	14	1
PISTACHIOS	8	164	6	13	3
WALNUTS	4	162	4	18	2

*Specifics on vitamins, minerals, and types of fat in the individual nuts are available at *www.usda.gov*.
† Grams.
‡ On average, of the fat in these twelve nuts, only 14 percent is saturated. Nuts are generally strong in most of the essential vitamins and minerals.

Into the Woods

On a beautiful fall morning, we walked through the nearby woods with our great dog Sanford. He is a fancier of squirrels, but he doesn't pay much attention to them if they are high in the tree.

We were approaching the three shagbark hickories that grow at the edge of the lower Shaker Lake. As we drew closer, we heard, on a bright sunny morning, what sounded like rain. Fragments of husk and shell were falling from the seventy-five-foot-high canopy of the slender trees.

Squirrels were at work, and Sanford didn't even notice. There were plenty of whole nuts on the ground, and we gathered a few of them to take home for drying, and perhaps, down the line, cracking and eating. We wanted to see how much work it takes to get a handful of nutmeats from a wild source. We wanted to know how hard our farming ancestors had to work to lay in a batch of nuts for Thanksgiving and Christmas.

Beechnuts abound in these woods, which are virtually unchanged since John D. Rockefeller deeded this land to Cleveland with the stipulation that it would never be disturbed. We discovered firsthand what kind of a commitment it takes to work through the prickly husks before you can taste the delicious tiny kernels they produce.

We made another discovery in a museum field at a busy intersection in Shaker Heights. On the site of one of the first Shaker settlements still stands a tall black walnut tree, probably well over a hundred years old. It was having a very good season. The squirrels hadn't done much with its heavy yield, and we easily gathered a few to take home for drying. In a deep part of the forest, we found an American chestnut tree. It was not clear if it is one that survived the blight that destroyed virtually all of them by 1950, or something that had been planted since.

So, black walnuts, beechnuts, shagbark hickories, and chestnuts, all part of the larder of the early settlers in this region of Ohio, were still there, and we learned what they had to do to get the treasures that were in those tough shells.

It has been more than twenty years since Frederic Rosengarten published *The Book of Edible Nuts,* the best on the subject ever published. His emphasis was more on botanical, technical, and historical information and not so much on the use of nuts. Since it came out, so much more has been learned about the value of nuts in our diet. Great breakthroughs have taken place in integrating nuts in our cooking, not just here, but across the world. Our emphasis here is on recipes that deal not only with traditional uses of nuts but also new ways of getting the most out of the taste and quality of some of the world's most perfect foods.

notes on nuts

almonds

Family: Rosaceae

Scientific name: *Prunus dulcis*

In A.D. 79 an entire culture was frozen in time. With the eruption of Mt. Vesuvius that year, the intense heat, coupled with the huge amounts of smothering ash, carbonized and preserved houses, kitchens, farm sheds, gardens, and all of the things that were in them. We know that onions and garlic grew just outside the kitchen door. Inside, in storage jars and baskets, were olives, grains, and fruits of the region—and there were nuts. Filberts, walnuts, chestnuts, pine nuts, and almonds were clearly important in the daily diet of the people who lived and died under the shadow of the great volcano.

That there were almonds was no surprise. Sam Cunningham, chief scientist at the Blue Diamond almond cooperative in California, says that humans were using almonds fifteen thousand years ago. They likely first grew in Central Asia and made their way to the Mediterranean through early travel and trade. Mythologies of the Mediterranean have often taken note of almonds, and there are written almond references that are four thousand years old. They have often celebrated the beauty of the trees as they produce their first buds of the early spring.

For example, the Greek word for almond is *Phylla*. It came from the story of Phyllis, who so missed her gallivanting lover Demophon that she died of grief and was turned into a little tree. When her man finally came home and learned what had happened, he burst into tears, producing so many that they brought the tree to life and full blossom.

The Old Testament is full of almond references—more than for any other nut. In Numbers, for example, we have the story of Aaron's famous rod, which, while ostensibly a walking cane, suddenly sprouted branches, bloomed, and produced almonds.

Almonds were first and foremost a food that provided much of what people need for a healthy life. They were eaten whole, but more often crushed and used to thicken and enrich other dishes. At some point, cooks learned how to make almond "milk," grinding the nuts, soaking them in water, and pressing out the rich white fluid. Eventually they were grown all around Southern Europe, and over the centuries, traders found markets for them all over the continent. There are records that document their sale in England eight hundred years ago, and it is likely that they were traded there as early as Roman times.

California got its first plantings along the foggy coast in the 1700s. They failed. In 1850 ranchers planted almonds in the drier regions of the north-central part of the state. This time they flourished, and at last there were American almonds. Today there are about six hundred thousand acres of almonds grown in the Central Valley of California, making that state far and away the world's biggest producer. Almonds are still an important crop around the Mediterranean, but California rules.

The almond is a part of a major food family. Eat a delicious peach and what is left is a pit that looks like an almond, and in fact it almost is. The peach is the almond's first cousin. So are the apricot and the plum. The difference is that the pits of those ripe fruits are hard, and the seeds, once extracted, are not very tasty. The almond is a polar opposite. The flesh that surrounds the almond seed is not tasty, juicy, or sweet; it is pithy and bitter. No one eats an almond like a ripe freestone peach. On the other hand, the seed is delicious. So most members of the family have taste invested in their flesh. In the almond, the taste is in the kernel of the seed.

There are two kinds of almonds—the bitter or the sweet. Eat enough bitter almonds, and you could get sick. The bitterness is from a compound that breaks down to yield cyanide. Bitter almonds are grown for the oil that can be extracted and used in flavorings and cosmetics. The cyanide dissipates in the extraction process.

There are a number of varieties of sweet almonds that have been developed by tree scientists for the California growers. The thin-shelled Nonpareil is the most popular. The Mission, with a harder shell, is number two. Other California varietals include Merced, Carmel, Ne Plus Ultra, Peerless, and Thompson. The Jordan (probably from *jardin*), also grown there, is from Europe.

There are few scenes more beautiful than the great sweep of blooming almond trees you can see on a spring day from a hillside above the Central Valley. The beehives are ready, and when the temperature is just right, billions of bees will start their work of cross-pollinating the flowers. In the fall the almonds are mechanically harvested—

shaken from the trees, swept up, dried, hulled, cleaned, shelled, packaged, and shipped.

According to the International Tree Nut Council, the almond is the world's number one tree nut. It is conservatively estimated that five hundred and seventy thousand metric tons of shelled almonds go to market every year, a much bigger crop than hazelnuts and cashews.

Finally, no report on almonds would be complete without addressing that nut's reputation as a curative. Pliny and Plutarch both wrote about how good they are for you. John Gerarde in *The Herball* of 1597 writes that almonds are "a mitigator of all manner of aches," and among other things, "good for women who are newly delivered." The idea of serving roasted almonds at the bar to counteract your martinis or wine has its roots in the same history. "It is reported," writes Gerarde, "that five or six being taken fasting keepe a man from being drunke."

Gerarde was onto something. Maybe they won't keep you sober, but there is no doubt that they are good for you. Almonds are close to being a complete food, with most of what we need in our diet. They are high in fat, but it is the unsaturated fat that can actually help reduce your cholesterol level. The almond establishment is always happy to tell you about it.

brazil nuts

Family: Lecythidaceae
Scientific name: *Bertholletia excelsa*

Most of the world's edible nuts are cultivated, but the biggest of our best-loved nuts is a wild thing. Brazil nuts are the seeds of a major evergreen in the Amazon forests of South America. The trees grow naturally in a range of over a million and a half square miles of Brazil and neighboring countries, including Peru, Bolivia, Colombia, and Venezuela. The trees are slow growing and huge. They are greedy for the equatorial sun and have long slender trunks and a spread of branches and leaves that can tower as high as two hundred feet above the forest floor and the lesser trees below.

Botanists have tried to domesticate this wild tree, but it takes years for a tree to mature. They are unlikely to be really productive until they are thirty years old—hardly a recipe for a profitable enterprise—but researchers are still at it, looking for some kind of breakthrough.

Seed or nut development is unique. The trees grow large seed pods—called *castanhas* in Portuguese—but they would hardly be recognizable by a nut lover. At maturity, they can weigh as much as five pounds. When they ripen, usually from February to June, they fall to the ground. The collectors, the *castanheiros*, need to be careful. The pods, ripe and hard, falling from a tall tree can deliver a lethal blow. But the collectors have to be there, otherwise the agoutis and other forest creatures will eat them. There are dangers aloft too, but there isn't much the collector on the ground can do about it. When the pods are still green and growing, the macaws of the forest cut them open and eat the still tender nuts.

The pods are spherical with a pithy covering over a thick shell. When this covering is stripped away, the pod looks like a coconut. When it is cracked open, the nuts are revealed, perhaps as many as two dozen arranged around a center stem like the sections of an orange.

About half a million trees are available to regional collectors, and there are probably millions more in the inaccessible parts of the forests. In a good year, a full-grown tree might yield five hundred pounds of nuts. Usually after gathering them, the collectors lighten the load by breaking away the big outside covering and only carry the unshelled nuts to the market. The buyers at the trading stations need to handle them carefully and quickly to protect against mold and decay.

They will soak some of the nuts in water for twenty-four hours, and then boil them just briefly to soften the shell. They are usually shelled by hand, then packaged. For shipping they are often vacuum-packed in nitrogen. Broken nuts are pressed for their rich oil. Some say that if you light the inside of a Brazil nut, it will burn like a candle.

Most Brazil nuts are still shipped in the shell, to confound Dad when he addresses the bowl of Christmas nuts and has to deploy the nutcracker to get to the tasty treasure. It is one of first nuts that people go for when someone puts a bowl of shelled toasted salted nuts before them. For a while in the 1950s, "Kernel Nut of Brazil," decked out in a uniform and medals and holding a bayonet-equipped rifle, appeared in ads and recipe booklets and helped market the product in the United States. Today no soldier is needed; the Brazil nut pretty much sells itself.

The nut collectors, in earlier times, would trade the nuts for other foods, household supplies, tools, clothing, and other things they needed. Now they are paid in cash for what they have gathered and brought to the traders. By the late 1990s about ninety million pounds of Brazil nuts were being exported, bringing in $50 million a year to the regional economies.

There are other ideas for making money from the Amazon. Wherever there are forests there are people who want to cut them down and take the timber to market. There are also developers who want to turn what is left into farms or towns. If the nut collectors opt to work with the timber interests, they could make decent money until the trees are gone, but that would be it. It would take generations for the Brazil nut trees to reestablish themselves, if ever.

On the other hand, if the forests can be kept natural (that is what conservation interests in South America are trying do), and if the market for Brazil nuts remains strong, the nut gatherers will be on the job, waiting for the pods to fall, instead of laying to waste the forest with a chain saw.

So the Brazil nut is at the center of yet another developing country struggle between those who would cut and slash and the interests who want things to stay as they are. Lovers of that famous wild nut had better hope for the victory of the conservationists. Otherwise the much loved Brazil nut could fade from the scene.

cashews

Family: Anacardiaceae

Scientific name: *Anacardium occidentale*

What an odd duck is the cashew! It only grows in very hot climates on ungainly, unruly evergreen trees that have resisted domestication for eons. It is unlike any other nut; the crescent-shaped nut grows to full size and then the stem just above it develops into the plump and fleshy "cashew apple."

The cashew has some strange relatives: It is a cousin of poison ivy, poison sumac, the pistachio, and the mango. Cashews grow to maturity in a thick porous shell that contains a powerful and pungent resinlike compound that is collected and used in polymer-based industrial processes. Freshly picked cashews are dried, shelled, washed, and dried again before they can be eaten.

Although its share of the market has slipped in recent years, India leads the world in cashew production, but the cashew is not native to India's south coasts. It first grew in the hot equatorial forests in Brazil, where it was part of the larder of the native peoples. The early Portuguese settlers in Brazil ate cashews, too. They called them *caju*, an approximation of the local Indian word for this nut. It was the Portuguese who took it to India, East Africa, and Mozambique.

The cashew also made its way to Central America, Indonesia, and the Philippines. In all of those places it found a foothold in the forests and today it still grows wild in those tropical environments.

For a long time, most of our cashews came from wild trees, but now they are grown on tropical plantations across the world. Scientists, especially in India, have developed many new varieties. The National Cashew Gene Bank was started in India in 1986. At last report there was genetic material from more than four hundred varieties stored there. While in the United States, six thousand farmers grow all of our almonds, in India, hundreds of thousands of growers are involved in producing that country's cashews.

In India, Kerala cashew grower Sonny Matthew took us through the process. The bloom begins in the dry weeks of November or December. Pollination is by the wind, although local bees sometimes get into the act, and surprisingly, red ants that live in the trees help with the process. The tiny buds start to metamorphose into the crescent-shaped nut. Each branch of the tree will hold nuts at various stages of development. When the nut has grown to its full size, probably an inch and a half long, the stem elongates and the other part of the equation, the cashew apple, starts to grow. It is ripe when the apple is oval shaped, two or three inches long, and red or yellow in color. That is when the cashew apple and the nut hanging below it fall to the ground.

The cashew apple is a juicy but bitter and fragile fruit that must be used within twenty-four hours after ripening. Its juice is sometimes extracted and fermented into an inexpensive alcoholic drink, but mostly, it is considered expendable and is left on the ground after the nut is taken. The first batch of nuts will be gathered perhaps as early as January. The yield will ebb and flow, peaking and declining for the next several weeks. In mid-March most will have matured and fallen. (Farmers do not pick the nuts from the trees; since each branch will have nuts in various stages of development, pulling a cashew from the branch might damage the immature nuts.) There will be a few more in April, then a final small yield in May, just before the summer rains.

It is a tough enough nut that it does well without much attention. Weeds in the orchard need to be kept under control. Some farmers will spray insecticides, but that adds to the cost. The trees are usually fertilized with manure, animal or green. Cashew processing facilities buy the farmer's crop and make it ready for the market.

The nuts, in their hard dark shells, are usually spread out in the sun to dry for a couple of days. They get a quick roasting to facilitate the removal of the pungent and corrosive CNSL, the cashew nut shell liquid. There are several processes used to do that. Most usually they are bathed in a solvent that dissolves and draws out the liquid. Then the skilled and patient women who work the processing lines carefully cut the cashews open, one by one. In one facility we visited, there were more than four hundred employees, cracking, cleaning, and sorting the nuts. The Indian crop had already been processed and to keep the plant working, managers had brought in cashews from Benin in West Africa.

CNSL is today still a profitable byproduct of cashew processing, showing up in paints and varnishes, or as an element in friction linings, such as clutch facings and brake linings. One of the workers pointed to a huge Indian-made Tata truck. "It uses the cashew two ways," he said. "There is CNSL in the clutch to get it going and in the brake linings to make it stop." We also learned that it is sometimes used, unprocessed, by the fishermen to treat the wooden hulls of their boats.

About 90 percent of the world's cashews are consumed as a snack food. In India, however, especially in the south, cashews are used widely and creatively, often ground to thicken and give flavor to dishes, cooked or roasted as an integral part of a recipe, and often added as a tasty and attractive garnish.

Because of the intensive labor it takes to get them to market, the cashew is one of the more expensive nuts—but clearly the world thinks they are worth it.

chestnuts

Family: Fagaceae (includes oak and beech)

Scientific name: *Castania dentata*

"When chestnuts were ripe, I laid up half a bushel for winter." Henry David Thoreau, living on Walden Pond, knew a good thing. It would have been no major challenge; chestnuts were everywhere back in the nineteenth century.

There were millions of acres of hardwood forests in the eastern part of the United States, and perhaps a quarter of the trees were chestnut. In fact, some claim that there were patches of woods where the tree count was up to 80 percent chestnut. There were as many as three and a half billion chestnut trees at the turn of the last century. The nut undergirded the forest ecology. In earlier times, farmers allowed their pigs to roam the woods where they were fattened by the "mast of the forest," meaning mainly the chestnuts. It was by far our most important tree.

The chestnut was sometimes called "bread of the mountain," nut grain, or corn tree. With its heavy carbohydrate content, it was much more like rice or corn than other nuts—and they were there for the taking. The settlers gathered them from the woods, dried and shelled them, and ground them to make a useful flour. They could be roasted or boiled. Some people made pasta with chestnuts. They could be stored as part of the winter's larder. There was also no more important lumber than that cut from the chestnut trees.

In 1917, Julia Rogers, in her book *Trees Worth Knowing*, wrote that "The nut of this tree is hung high aloft, wrapped in a silk wrapper, which is enclosed in a case of sole leather, which again is packed in a mass of shock absorbing, vermin proof pulp, sealed up in a waterproof, iron-wood case, and finally cased in a vegetable porcupine of spines, almost impregnable. There is no nut so protected; there is no nut in our woods to compare with it as food." She sadly noted in her classic book that something had gone terribly wrong; the trees were falling by the millions to a blight. As tough and good as the American chestnut was, it was doomed.

That blight, in fact, probably arrived on these shores in 1904 when some Asian chestnut trees were planted in New York. The Asian trees were resistant to the blight, but the American trees were not. The forests were changed forever; by 1950 the American chestnut, which had provided so much food and half of all of the sawn logs used in America in the nineteenth century, was gone.

The wood rat, the black bear, and scores of other animals of the eastern forests were hit hard by the decline and death of the chestnut forests. It had been called "the greatest ecological catastrophe to hit the continent."

In recent years the American Chestnut Foundation has been working to reestablish a once great tree. Using the few surviving American chestnuts, scientists have been crossing it with Asian varieties. The idea was to keep the resistance of the Asians to the blight but get more and more of the American characteristics into the hybrids. Scientists are now at $\frac{1}{16}$ Asian and $\frac{15}{16}$ American, trees that are strong and tall like the original American, but, so far, resistant to the blight. The next goal is to reestablish the chestnut in American forests. In 2002, the American Chestnut Foundation was given an international biodiversity award for its work by Slow Food in Italy.

That doesn't mean you can't enjoy a chestnut or two. You will find them in stores and there are always people roasting and selling chestnuts from pushcarts in New York at holiday time. Most are from Asia or Europe. A few American farmers are now growing and selling the Asian varieties. Annual consumption in the United States is less than two chestnuts per person. So it looks like a market with growth potential.

Some of our tastiest chestnut treats come from Europe. We watched a confectioner in Italy soak local chestnuts for a week in warm honey. We can buy them, along with the marrons of France, in jars, especially at holiday time, at specialty food stores.

We know that chestnuts were in wide use six thousand years ago. In fact, some archeologists say they have found chestnut evidence that is fifteen thousand years old. The chestnut helped sustain the human population through long stretches of time.

Now in America, determined scientists and farmers are working to revive a once great nut. We may never be able to walk into the woods as Thoreau did and gather half a bushel for the winter, but it now appears that the American chestnut can again be a player in the ecology of our hardwood forests. Chances are good that someday we will again be able to roast them by an open fire.

coconuts

Family: Palmae
Scientific name: *Cocos nucifera*

In the movie *Castaway*, Tom Hanks, in his first frightening dark night on the little island that will be his home for the next four years, hears the sound of something crashing through the underbrush. The next day he learns it was a coconut falling from one of the high trees along the shore. In fact, with this castaway, as with others who have faced a similar challenge, the coconut growing fifty feet above his head would provide the bulk of his sustenance during his time on the island. He will catch a fish or two, perhaps, but the falling coconuts would give him everything he needs to live—protein, fat, vitamins, minerals, and carbohydrates. Each one holds a quantity of fresh, sweet, clean water. It might get boring after four years, but at least neither thirst nor hunger would put him down.

Not only does the coconut palm feed him; he uses the leaves for shelter, the logs for the raft he builds to escape the island, and the fibers to make rope to lash the raft together. Thus did the contemporary cinema pay tribute to the biggest of our nuts.

No one knows for sure where coconuts grew first. Many think it was India. In fact the *Oxford English Dictionary* reports that for a thousand years they had been called the "nut of India" in historical writings.

The name we know came much later. A book on *The Indes* from 1555, speaks of "the cocus" and makes reference to the three holes on the India nut, "which altogether, doo represent the gesture and figure of the cattes called Mammone, that is Munkeys when they crye: which crye the Indians call 'coca.'" So this great favorite nut is named for an unhappy monkey.

Sometimes you will see it spelled "cocoanut." That extra letter is a mistake. Samuel Johnson in his 1755 dictionary confused coco with cacao and its alternate spelling, cocoa. British customs authorities finally started using the Dutch word *koker-noot* to avoid confusing coconuts with the stuff we use to make chocolate.

Western explorers found coconuts in almost every tropical region they visited, as far away from India as the east coast of Africa and the west coast of the tropical Americas. It is believed that most of this dispersal of the species came through the nut's ability to stay alive and float in the salt water of the oceans and move with its currents. When they washed up on some beach, they would grow. So there are coconuts in coastal areas throughout the tropics. Only in the eastern parts of the Americas is there evidence that it was traders, and not ocean currents, who gave the coconut a new place to grow. The Portuguese took them to Brazil and the Spanish delivered them to the Caribbean.

India, appropriately enough, leads the world in production; fifteen billion coconuts grew there last year. Worldwide, there are at least twenty-five million acres of coconuts, managed by several million farmers. It is hard to know the exact amounts, but total world production is close to forty-seven million tons, or about ninety-four billion pounds (including the shells). After India, the Philippines, Indonesia, Malaysia, and Sri Lanka all have flourishing coconut plantations and processing facilities. And of course local populations harvest them wherever they grow.

The coconut palms grow quickly and as early as six years old may start growing both male and female flowers. A batch of the nuts can start to develop from either self or cross-pollination. In the fourth month the small coconuts start to fill up with a sweet "coconut water." In the next couple of months, the shell hardens and the gelatinous coconut meat begins to form around the inside of the shell. These "green" or "tender" coconuts are sometimes harvested in the seventh or eighth month to meet the demand for the sweet and refreshing "water." (Fly Air India and you will be offered "coconut water" along with tea and soft drinks.) After twelve to fourteen months the nut is mature and nutmeat has formed and firmed. At this point, the nut may be eight to twelve inches long and weigh five or six pounds, and the mature nuts (perhaps five or six will have survived to maturity in each clump) are ready for harvest. If not taken by the gatherers, they will usually fall within another month or so. The coconut meat and coconut water comprise about half the weight of the harvested coconut. The rest is husk and shell, and there are good uses for that material as well.

In the meantime, the coconut palm will have started other batches of nuts, and they follow the same timetable. The result is that the trees are producing nuts regularly around the calendar. There is always a supply coming in for processing, and the workers on the plantations and in the factories can count on full-time employment.

In the West, when we think of coconuts, we think Mounds bars or coconut cream pie. What we use is the shredded and sweetened white flesh of the ripe coconut. In places where the coconut rules, however, the cooks have figured out all kinds of uses. In southern India, green coconuts (they like the term "tender coconuts") are cut down, and the coconut water is quaffed through a straw, or sometimes packaged like a soft drink. The gelatinous young flesh is mixed into many complex dishes. If the coconut is more mature, its firmer flesh will be shredded for use in other dishes, or soaked to make coconut milk, which also finds a place in the kitchen.

The coconut meat is rich with oil, and some coconuts are sent to processing plants that extract it and market it for use in the kitchen. The hard shells are also used as fuel in the furnace that heats the flesh before pressing begins.

While we were in India, we saw evidence of a disturbing blight that is affecting the trees. It has happened before and so far it does not seem to be as threatening as the chestnut blight, for example, was in America, but it is a cause of concern and agricultural scientists are working to understand the problem.

There may be as many as three thousand species of palm trees, but all of the world's billions of coconuts come from just one species, *Cocos nucifera*. No single tree looms as large in the lives of so many people around the world as the coconut.

hazelnuts

Family: Corylaceae
Scientific name: *Corylus avellana*

"This kernell is sweet and pleasant unto the taste." So wrote John Gerarde about the hazelnut in his classic *Herball*, published in London in 1597. It is an important nut whether you call it a filbert or a hazelnut, and people still call it both.

The word "hazel" comes from an old English word *haesel*, meaning "bonnet," which in turn comes from the shape of the short husk that partially covers the nut. (The word *Corylus* in the scientific name comes from the Greek word for that hood, *korys*.) Other varieties had a long husk that completely covered the nut, and that may have lead to the word, filbert, after the German word *Vollbart*, or "full beard." Some say it was named after St. Philbert, whose feast day is celebrated at about the time that the nuts are harvested. In the United States, because of Oregon's hazelnut marketing board, hazelnut is gaining. "No matter what you call the tree," they tell us, "what comes off that tree is a hazelnut." If you don't like either, you can call it a "cobnut," another popular name for this good nut.

Oregon growers probably have the right to call it whatever they want. They produce almost all of America's hazelnuts. They claims that they are the best in the world, tastier, even, than the nuts of Italy's Piedmont, so widely used in top-quality candies. As with most nut crops, there is a wide variation in production from year to year. In the past decade Oregon's production has been as low as thirty million pounds and as high as eighty-four million.

Of the tree nuts of the world, the hazelnut ranks second behind the almond in the amount of shelled nuts produced. World output is about four hundred and fifty thousand metric tons of shelled hazelnuts and Turkey produces as much as 80 percent of the total. It has the right kind of soil, but, most important, mild winters, warm springs, rarely a late freeze, and cool summers. The Turkish farms are still small labor-intensive operations along the Black Sea shore. Over three hundred and eighty-five thousand farmers grow them, compared to only eight hundred in Oregon. Italy also ranks ahead of the United States, producing some nuts in Piedmont but most in Sicily. In some recent years Spain has slipped to fourth, just behind the United States.

The Turkish farmers still tend to plant their filbert trees in clumps and harvest them by hand. In Oregon, they are planted in orderly rows which allow growers to do a complete machine harvest.

Hazelnut trees start producing at the age of about six. The trees bloom in the late winter. Wind carries the pollen from the male catkin to the tiny female flower. The fertilized flowers stay dormant until late spring. Then the nuts start to form. They mature slowly and are not ready for harvest until October when they fall to the ground. In Turkey they are usually gathered by hand; in Oregon machines sweep them into windrows, gather them into bins, and load them on trucks that carry them to the processing plant. Then they are washed, dried, sorted, graded, cracked, shelled, and shipped.

In postglacial Europe, ten thousand years ago, the hazelnut's ancestor trees were everywhere. Botanists checking peat bogs have found fossil pollen in quantity, indicating that it was the most widespread tree as the glaciers retreated and the forests moved north. There is also evidence that the hazelnut was widely used by the prehistoric people of Europe. There are written records of hazelnuts being used in China five thousand years ago. Carbonized shells were found in Pompeii, and there is documented commerce in hazelnuts before the time of Christ.

While there were hazelnut cousins in the Western Hemisphere, they were not valued as food. As early as 1629, the Massachusetts Company included filberts in the seed package prepared in England for the early settlers, but the climate wasn't right; spring freezes always seemed to nip the plants in the bud. In retrospect, we now know that the soils of New England just weren't suitable.

Oregon's first hazelnut tree grew from a seed planted in 1858 by a retired English sailor. In 1876, David Gernot, an immigrant farmer from France, sent home for seeds of a thin-shelled hazelnut variety. He planted them as a windrow between the fields of his farm. In the twentieth century, George Dorris of Springfield, Oregon, put in America's first hazelnut orchards. Some of those trees are still productive today, over a century later.

As with so many traditional foods, there are stories of the filbert's efficacy as a medicine. Some Greek texts two thousand years ago held that ground filberts would help cure a cough or cold. There is an ancient recipe for filberts made into a paste with animal fat to be used to fight hair loss. Even today, some people in Spain still believe that the way to cure a bedwetter is to have the child eat a dozen filberts just before bedtime.

There are at least two ways branches from the hazelnut tree have been put to good use. For dowsers looking for water, a forked filbert stick was the divining rod of choice, and the fleet-footed Mercury had the two snakes of his caduceus, that famous symbol of healing, twine around a piece of neatly carved hazelnut wood.

macadamias

Family: Proteaceae

Scientific name: *Macadamia integrefolia*

The macadamia nut was a key part of the larder of the indigenous tribes in the semitropical regions of Australia, but the immigrant European farmers didn't notice; they paid no attention to it. In fact, it wasn't until the late 1850s that the botanist Ferdinand von Mueller first took note of the tree and named it after John Macadam, a young doctor and friend of his who had come to Australia in 1855 to teach chemistry. It is unlikely that Dr. Macadam ever tasted the nut that was named after him; he died in an accident at sea while sailing to New Zealand in 1865. At about that time, some brave Australians, noting that Aboriginal tribes ate the nuts of that tree, tried a few and started waxing rhapsodic about how good they were. Still, it took years before the first real macadamia orchard was planted in Australia in 1888.

By that time the macadamia had already been taken to Hawaii. A few years earlier, William Herbert Purvis planted a few seeds he had brought from Australia. The trees grew well, but the nuts were not harvested. They were used in reforestation projects or grown as shade trees on plantations and along city streets.

However, early in the twentieth century, a few growers started collecting the nuts. They did not roast well. As early as the 1930s tree scientists at the University of Hawaii started developing new cultivars that were more appropriate for the soils and microclimates of Hawaii. Their work was very successful and the first plantings yielded marketable nuts. For a while, Hawaii led the world in production. By the late 1950s, those varietals were taken back to Australia where they have again made Australia the leading producer of this coveted nut. Today, Australian scientists have developed still other cultivars for specific places there.

The macadamia is self-pollinating, although growers prefer the cross-pollination of closely planted orchards. The nuts are not shaken from the tree. They fall when they are ripe. They are swept up, taken to the processing plant to be husked. The in-shell nuts are then dried.

The macadamia is the hardest of all commercial nuts. Tapered turning steel drums provide the three hundred pounds of pressure required to crack the shell. The empty shells are then used as fuel in the furnace that gives the freshly harvested nuts their first drying. There are special crackers for home use for those who buy the nut in its shell, but most macs are shipped shelled so that the customer doesn't have to worry about it.

Remove the husks from one hundred pounds of Hawaiian macadamias and you have fifty pounds of nuts in the shell. Open and discard the shells and you have between twelve and a half and fifteen pounds of shelled nuts. In some other places where macadamias are grown, the yield is as low as seven pounds of kernels from one hundred pounds.

Hawaii is an ideal place for the macadamias due to the lack of indigenous insect pests that can require a lot of expensive control measures. In the Hawaiian orchards, no spraying is needed.

In the past decade, however, drought conditions have hurt the harvest and challenged the scientists. Rick Vidgen, president of MacFarms, one of Hawaii's leading growers, says such a problem "makes us better farmers. People set to work developing better ways to maximize the available water, and develop cultivars that can handle the drier conditions." Like the nut he grows, Vidgen is Australian. He is the chairman of the nutrition committee of the International Tree Nut Council, and he is happy with scientific studies that give the rich nuts he grows a good report card.

World production of macadamias is between thirty-five and forty million pounds, a relatively minor nut when compared to almonds and pecans, cashews, and coconuts. Australia produces about 45 percent of the world's supply and Hawaii is second with 35 percent. In recent years, orchards have been established in Kenya, Costa Rica, Guatemala, and other tropical countries. A few macs are also grown in California.

The Hawaiian macadamias have had some high-profile champions. Julie Andrews and James Stewart were both early investors in orchards there. Jim Nabors, who was TV's Gomer Pyle, discovered, early on, the beauty of both Hawaii and macadamia orchards. In the 1970s, Anita DeDomenico, who gave up a career as a ballerina to develop macadamias in Hawaii, created the first macadamia cookbook. "It is the rarest and noblest of all nuts," she wrote.

peanuts

Family: Leguminosae

Scientific name: *Arachis hypogaea*

It's the world's hottest nut—and yet it is not a nut at all. The peanut is a legume, closer to the pea and the bean than to the pecan or the pistachio.

People eat more of this humble groundnut than all of the tree nuts of the world combined. In the United States, we consume one and a half billion pounds of peanuts a year, with about half of that in the form of peanut butter.

Peanuts are a major world crop with production approaching twenty-nine million metric tons. It ranks in the top twenty-five foods of the world. India and China each grow about nine million tons. The United States and Nigeria vie for third place, followed by Indonesia and Senegal. In the United States, peanuts are the twelfth largest farm product, worth more than $2 billion a year. The average American eats six pounds of peanuts a year. (We eat our share at Jacob's Field, while watching baseball.)

Peanuts need heat, sandy soil so that the deep roots can grow easily, and plenty of water at the appropriate times. They are planted when there is no risk of frost. In the United States, four main varieties are used—Runner, Virginia, Spanish, and Valencia. As a legume, peanuts take nitrogen into the soil, and the peanut crop is an important player in crop-rotation practices. They grow fast and flower early. They are self-pollinated. After fertilization, a spike grows from the flower and goes straight down into the soil where the nut forms.

In the United States, the harvest is mechanized. The nuts are undercut, pulled up, shaken, dried, and then either stored in their shells (for up to six months) or shelled and put in refrigerated storage. A tiny part of the peanut production is bought right out of the field, boiled, and sold at once. All the rest are processed as needed, either in the shell or shelled. Because of the high fat content, rancidity is a possible problem. In-shell peanuts are often soaked in brine and then roasted. These are what you eat at the ballgame.

Peanuts are shelled, sorted, sized, and packaged by machine. Each nut is inspected by light-sensitive screeners. A blemish gets the culprit banished. If they are to be blanched, they get a roasting or a boiling, and the dark skins are brushed off. After this processing, they are packaged for the snack market, bakers, candymakers, peanut butter factories, or oil mills.

Actually, while in the United States the peanut butter industry is the major consumer, worldwide well over half of the peanuts grown are pressed for oils for cooking and for industrial processes. The compressed nuts left over after pressing can be used as livestock food or fertilizer. The shells can be used industrially as well.

The peanut is one of the near-perfect foods. You could probably get by on peanuts alone. They have protein, lots of fat (most of that unsaturated), plenty of carbohydrates, and several essential vitamins and minerals.

In the United States there are about three million people who are allergic to peanuts. Peanuts are probably the number one allergen. If you are allergic to them, you probably already know it. Food processors that use peanuts need to label their products carefully to avoid problems. Although rarely seen in the United States, aflatoxins, which can cause severe health problems, can contaminate peanuts through certain molds. Proper processing and handling can minimize the risk.

Where did peanuts come from?

Originally from South America, according to most authorities. From the lower-lying hills of Bolivia, perhaps. Then later Peru and Brazil. To back this up, archeologists will tell you that there is evidence of peanuts in South America as early as 3000 B.C. They found fossilized peanuts shells in excavations, Inca necklaces with gold peanuts, and pre-Incan pottery shaped like a peanut. Anya von Bremzen, a food writer and university lecturer, says the Incan diet had a "miracle combination of carbohydrates from corn and protein from peanuts and other beans." It was an agricultural economy based on the ability to store things—dry them out, put them aside, then reconstitute them as needed—and there, peanuts fit right in.

Historian Diane Spivey, in her book on the global migration of African cuisine, argues that the peanut originated in Africa. She describes how Africans took wonderful food traditions with them as they were carried across the globe in the slave trade. She says there is documentation of the use of peanuts in Mali by the Mandingo peoples as early as A.D. 1300. We were unable to learn about this from agricultural officials in Mali.

There are, however, indigenous groundnuts in Africa and they were used by the local populations. The Bambara groundnut (*Voandzeia subterranea*) is similar to the peanut. It grows edible seeds underground, one to a pod, all over temperate and tropical Africa, and is an important player in regional subsistence agriculture. There is another one called Kersting's or Hausa groundnut (*Kerstingiella geocarpa*), but it has not spread very much on the continent. Neither of these groundnuts has taken as important a role in feeding a continent as the common peanut, and neither is even a close relative of the peanut, *Arachis hypogaea.* H. G. Baker, one of the authorities quoted by Spivey, studied plants that might have been domesticated by West African farmers. He mentions only Kersting's groundnut and makes no case that it was important. Ethnobotanists now say that genus *Arachis*, the common peanut, was only found in South America.

The Portuguese had a habit of carrying food around the world. They took the cashews to India. They took cassava (tapioca) to Africa. So why wouldn't it make sense that they also took peanuts to places on their trading itinerary? India's enormous peanut production can be traced directly back to Portuguese traders and explorers in Goa. And although some botanists thought there were groundnuts native to China, peanuts were almost certainly introduced through the Portuguese colony of Macao on the China coast. By the sixteenth century, the peanut was everywhere, including Africa.

The peanut became very important there, and there is good evidence that when African slaves were brought to Virginia and the Carolinas in the eighteenth century, they carried with them their own food traditions, which, by that time, included mastery of the South American peanut. They brought their own name for them as well— the Bantu word *nguba*. From this came the common southern word, "goober," as in "goober peas."

The Cambridge World History of Food laments the lack of creative uses of the peanut in the Western Hemisphere. It says that the Indians, Indonesians, Chinese, and Africans all understood the peanut's potential. Except for West African cookery in Brazil's northeast, you will not find inventive uses of the peanut anywhere in the hemisphere where it first grew.

Still Spanish colonists in South America did their best. They devised ways to thicken a sauce with ground peanuts, and they invented sweet nut confections. Later they took New World foods to Spain, where they were not embraced with much passion. For a while, peanuts were roasted, ground, and used as coffee by the Spanish. Later, after the Civil War, Americans would do the same thing. Some in Spain thought peanuts could cause afflictions—quite the reverse of what we now know to be the truth. A Frenchman named Condamine, who had lived in Ecuador in the eighteenth century, praised the peanut when he got home, but to no avail; the peanut had a slow start in Europe. It wasn't until the middle of the nineteenth century that French cooks, taking advantage of its abundance, cheapness, and ability to withstand high heat, started frying things in peanut oil.

Von Bremzen says that as the colonial society developed in the Americas, the wealthy moved in the direction of almonds and walnuts for their cooking, leaving the cheap peanut for the poor. For decades in this country the peanut has carried the stigma of its budget price.

George Washington Carver, in his legendary work on peanuts, changed agriculture in the southern United States. At Tuskegee Institute in Alabama he pioneered at least three hundred uses for the peanut and peanut byproducts. Peanuts became a major crop, and made the agricultural diversification of the South inevitable. It was all the more important as the boll weevil ruined cotton crops.

Still, it was only in recent times that it has been used in upscale foods. That may be because chefs and food writers finally found that many Asian cuisines used peanuts in a forward and creative way. For example, after Arab traders brought the peanut to Indonesia, cooks there created the now classic satay (saté). It is dazzling to see and taste the scores of ways peanuts are used across the continent.

We now know beyond dispute that peanuts are good for you, can help lower cholesterol, and reduce the chance of heart trouble. They hold an important spot on the latest food pyramid as a food we can eat often, even regularly.

As Anya von Bremzen says, the power of the peanut is in its taste. That has made this humble groundnut one of the truly universal foods, a player in virtually every cuisine of the world.

pecans

Family: Juglandaceae.
Scientific name: *Carva illinoinensis*

The pecan is an all-American nut. It and its hard-to-crack cousins grew in profusion in the mid-South, from Georgia to Texas, and as far north as Nebraska and Iowa and as far south as Mexico. The name is derived from the Algonquin word *paccan*, which referred to all of the hard tree nuts of their region that had to be cracked with a rock. It was French settlers in Louisiana who gave the word its present form, "pecan." The Algonquins and others gathered and stored these nuts for winter use. Then, when they were needed, they cracked the shells, crushed the kernels to make a "nut milk," and used the leftover pulp to thicken broths and enrich other foods. They also used hickories, walnuts, and other forest nuts. Early settlers saw how important these nuts were to the local people and they were quick to adapt them to their own needs.

The range of the pecan and these other nuts grew as farmers, hunters, and traders carried them to their newer settlements farther north, usually planting a few around their farmhouses. At least two of our presidents, Washington and Jefferson, did the same thing on their plantations in Virginia. It was then, and is today, the most important tree nut native to North America.

Eventually so many were growing in Illinois that botanists assumed it was a native there and named the pecan *Carya illinoinensis*. This set off a scientific squabble when some tree people in Texas demanded that the name be changed to *Carya texana*.

The Texan love affair with the pecan goes back to the nineteenth century. Teddy Roosevelt, hunting along the Llano River in 1885, wrote about "the grand old pecan trees along its banks." A few years later, James Stephen Hogg became the governor of that state. (He obviously had a sense of humor; he named his daughter Ima, no doubt accelerating her interest in finding a husband.) When he died in 1906, he chose as his grave marker, not some piece of carved rock, but a pecan tree and a walnut tree with instructions that the nuts "be given out to the plain people of Texas so that they may plant them and make Texas a land of trees."

Louisiana could make a legitimate claim for the scientific name as well. It was on a plantation near New Orleans called Oak Alley that the first grafting experiments with pecans took place in 1846. Dr. A. E. Colomb, a friend of J. T. Roman, the plantation owner, had identified a pecan tree that had been particularly fruitful. He enlisted a slave gardener named Antoine to cut scions, or branches, from that tree and graft them onto rootstock of the ordinary pecan trees. That first season Antoine produced a small orchard of sixteen trees. By the time of Roman's death in 1848 Antoine had grafted one hundred and ten trees. At the end of the Civil War, there were one hundred and twenty-six highly productive pecan trees on the property. The young trees produced more and better nuts and set off botanical work with the species that continues to this day.

In 1876 at the World's Fair in Philadelphia, Antoine's pecan was given the name "Centennial," and by 1882 a tree nursery in Louisiana was selling the budded and grafted trees through a farmer's catalog. Eventually a new owner of Oak Alley took out most of the pecan trees to plant sugar cane, but there are three trees still there that could be from Antoine's original planting. Professor L. J. Grauke of the USDA is checking that possibility. He is certain that the Centennial pecans still being grown today in southern orchards are what Antoine created all those years ago. Today Oak Alley is an important historical museum with part of the mansion used as a luxurious bed-and-breakfast.

While people valued and enjoyed the pecan for centuries, it was not until the twentieth century that it really hit its potential with huge investments in new varietals and new orchards, efficient processing equipment, and skillful marketing. Today, through the work of tree scientists, there are over four hundred varieties. Trees are vastly more productive. The nuts are bigger with thinner shells, which are easier to harvest, crack, and process. They taste better and last longer. They have more resistance to blight and rust, and there are cultivars designed to work well in specific climate and soil conditions.

Georgia grows the most by far, but there are substantial plantings in Texas, Alabama, Louisiana, New Mexico, and Arizona as well. Now pecans are grown in Australia, South Africa, Brazil, and Israel. Among the ruling cultivars are the Schley, Stuart, Success, and Wichita.

The sex life of this great tree is different from other tree nuts. It matures in from six to ten years and starts monoecious flowering, meaning that each tree has both male and female components. Still, most pollination is from other nearby trees. (You give me your pollen and I'll give you mine.) The trees need a warm climate, but some winter chill. They need careful orchard management to make sure that some opportunistic pest does not come in and ruin the harvest.

The harvest is remarkably automated. On October 10, workers, using big machines, start shaking the ripe nuts from the branches. They are swept into rows and gathered up for an initial drying. They are cooled for storing (and sometimes frozen) until it is time for processing. Then they are shelled, cleaned, graded, and packaged. They turn up in a thousand different delicious treats. Pecan growers celebrate their nut's new prominence as a curative, a nut whose high fat content is unsaturated, and a nut that could reduce the chance of heart disease.

In the 1999–2000 production season, the United States produced three hundred and ten million pounds of in-shell pecans, most of the world's supply. The following year would probably show a smaller yield, owing to the pecan's alternate bearing cycle—one year good, the next year not so good.

We don't know how the tax people got into it, but the Internal Revenue Service figures a pecan tree will live and produce for about fifty years. No big problem for the farmer or the government, but pecans live a lot longer than that; we are told that there are pecan trees in Georgia that are a thousand years old, and still producing an edible nut from time to time.

pine nuts

Family: Pinaceae

Scientific names: *Pinus pinea*, **the Italian pine called pignolia**

Pinus edulis, **the piñon of the southwestern United States**

Pinus koraiensis, **the Chinese species**

When we first started using pine nuts in our cooking, we didn't have much of an idea of where they came from. We had never been aware of anything edible on the pine trees we knew. Pine nuts may have lurked in the pine cones that we found in our yard, but they were certainly not big enough to bother with.

Pine nuts are the seeds of the pine. There are more than a hundred different pine trees across the world, and all have seeds, but only about a dozen species yield a nut worth collecting—one that is tasty and big enough. All of them grow in the Northern Hemisphere—Europe, Russia, Siberia, Central Asia, China, Korea, and North America.

In fact, just three species yield most of the world's commercial production. The European pignolia is number one, while some pine nuts from the Western piñon will come to market in the United States, and the Chinese pine now yields a substantial and marketable crop. These are often found in U.S. markets.

A lot of nuts were found in the ruined kitchens of Pompeii and pine nuts were among them. There is evidence that the first Roman soldiers to explore England carried stashes of pine nuts among their provisions. Pliny looked into pine nuts, too, but it's no surprise, he checked out everything. In his era, they were sometimes preserved in honey.

The very early Greeks sometimes put pine nuts in their stuffed grape leaves. There is a Chinese tradition of making sweets with them.

We know that they were widely consumed by the Native Americans of the West. They were carefully gathered and shelled, often ground into meal and stored in crocks or baskets for the winter. Ethnobotanists have found evidence of their very early pine nut consumption through carbon dating of materials found in anthropological digs, some from as long ago as six-thousand years.

In European folk medicine, people thought pine nuts were good for gout and cataracts. In the Balkans, they were said to make one who dines on them bulletproof. (They probably know by now that it isn't true.)

A possibly more exciting attribute of the pine nut is its ability to perk up a sagging libido. It was Roman and Greek Viagra. The food writer Apicius recommended a stew of pine nuts, cooked onions, white mustard, and pepper. The poet Ovid told us to eat "the nuts that the sharp-leaved pine brings forth." Galen, the Greek chronicler of medicines, advised taking a mixture of pine nuts, honey, and almonds for three consecutive nights. An Arab herbal a while later was more specific—a glassful of honey, twenty almonds, and one hundred twenty pine nuts. Three nights of this, they wrote, will help a man "acquire vigor for coition."

Like other tree nuts, the pine nut has lately been absolved by modern medicine of the charge that they contain too much fat to be good for you. We now know that, while they have a lot of fat, it is the good stuff, and not the bad.

Harvest techniques are labor intensive, difficult, and primitive. In the United States, collection of the native piñon is haphazard and unorganized. The piñon is slow to produce, often not yielding seeds until the trees are twenty-five years old. It can take up to three years for a growing pine cone to mature. It just isn't feasible to try to create orchards. There are actually two varieties of this western species. A hard-shelled nut grows in New Mexico, Arizona, and Utah. They have to be cracked to collect the tender kernel. There is also the more popular and easier to handle soft-shelled nut that grows in Nevada. Our friend, food writer Janet Podelak, told us that if you gather these nuts, be prepared to be coated with a virtually insoluble pine tar. Her experience collecting for a day made her understand why she has to pay $20 for a pound of them at the specialty food market.

Even at that kind of a retail price, foragers often find it is simply too costly and time-consuming to collect them. The crop is unpredictable. One year there could be a lot of pine nuts and the next year almost none. During the ad-lib harvest, between two and four million pounds will be gathered annually in the United States. In Nevada collecting the nuts is often a family hobby. You can gather twenty-five pounds without a permit. If you take more than that, you are considered a commercial collector.

The mature pine cones are usually picked from the trees in the fall and winter.

(Since the fall is hunting season, the Nevada Bureau of Land Management warns collectors to "wear bright clothing" since people can sometimes be mistaken for deer.) The cones are allowed to dry until the scales open and the seeds are loosened. They are shaken out and dried some more. Then they are cracked and the kernels are brushed to get rid of the thin brown covering. Finally, the white kernels are ready for pine nut lovers who are always ready to pay whatever price the market demands.

pistachios

Family: Anacardiaceae
Scientific name: *Pistacia vera*

Anyone over thirty may remember those bright red pistachios. Back when most of the world's pistachios came from Iran, red dye was a big feature of the processing. It was an aesthetic issue; the importers had the processors dip the nuts into a red dye to hide harmless blemishes. Besides, they believed that the red nuts would stand out in a store and attract customers. For a while the red dye days were gone. Pistachios then came to market from Iran, California, Spain, India, Turkey, Sicily, and Australia in their clean white shells, but recently, probably for nostalgic reasons, some California producers are once again dying theirs pistachios red.

For an eon, Iran ruled the pistachio world. Although there had been some pistachio trees in California from the middle of the nineteenth century, there was little commercial production. When the Iranian crisis of the late seventies blocked pistachio imports to the United States, scientists and farmers sped up their trials with Iranian trees. Eventually they found or developed varietals that were perfect for the California environment.

Venture capitalists saw an opportunity in pistachios. They invested in big pistachio farms in California's Central Valley. While it took time to get the orchards established, the judgments were right. The varietals worked and no major nut enemies have shown up. It is a hardy nut that handles heat and doesn't need much water. The California trees took seven to eight years to become productive, and they are unlikely to run out of steam anytime soon. (As a matter of fact, there are productive pistachio trees in the Middle East that are seven hundred years old.) There are a few pistachio trees in Arizona and Texas, but almost all of America's pistachios are grown on one hundred thousand acres in California. About a third of the California crop is exported.

Kevin Herman is the farmer-partner in the Valley Pistachio Company. He manages three thousand acres of pistachio orchards. He took us through the process. Unlike almond trees, the pistachios need no bees. In fact, the growers discourage bees, which can carry away the pollen that is needed where it is. There are male trees and female trees, and pollination is by the wind. The trees bud in the spring, grow in the summer, and ripen in the fall. The nuts grow in profusion, in clusters like grapes.

At harvest time, machines are used to shake the ripe nuts loose. If the pistachios hit the ground they can get a destructive mold. So a kind of upside-down umbrella is put beneath the trees to catch the nuts. The pithy hulls are removed right away. They are then gently washed and dried. By this time the shells have split. Then there is a second drying, low and slow, to reduce moisture and get the nuts ready for sizing and packaging. About 85 to 90 percent of the world's pistachios are shipped to the snack market in their split shells. Those that don't open are culled, cracked, and the nut-meats sold to food processors for use in cookies, candies, pastries, ice cream, baklava and, surprisingly, in pork sausages and pâtés.

Like other nuts, pistachios are nutritious and delicious, and they are low in saturated fats.

The pistachio is a cousin of the cashew, mango, and poison oak. The sap of the pistachio tree has the smell of turpentine. In some places farmers score the bark on these trees and collect the sap. Like the strong resin produced by the cashew, it can be used industrially in paints and varnishes. Some resin has even been used to make chewing gum and liquor. Of the dozen or so species of pistachios, only one, *Pistacia vera,* grows a marketable nut.

The pistachio most likely originated in southwest Asia. There is archeological evidence that they had been collected and used by people in Jordan and Turkey 9,000 years ago. The earliest writings about pistachios were found in Syria. They are among the few nuts noted in the Bible. Jacob's sons carried nuts to Egypt, and scholars believe they were pistachios. They were taken to Europe in the reign of Tiberius. By the twelfth century, Arab traders and travelers had taken them all around the Mediterranean.

Raw pistachios, picked from the trees while the hull is still tender and green, are considered a delicacy in Turkey, Iran, and Lebanon. Some people believe that they are an aphrodisiac. So understandably, there is a constant if small market for them, a natural Viagra that requires no prescription.

walnuts

Family: Juglandaceae
Scientific name: *Juglans regia*

Bacchus, the Greek wine god (and god of other worldly pleasures), fell in love with a princess named Carya. She had sisters who were jealous of the relationship and tried to keep Carya away from him. Bacchus was vexed. In his anger, he turned the sisters into stones, and then transformed his lover into the first walnut tree. It doesn't make much sense, but that is what he did.

Carya's name, by the way, lives on in the scientific name of several forest nuts, including the pecan.

If this story is true, Bacchus created one of our most valuable trees, a provider of great wood for furniture and construction, an array of tasty nuts that have sustained populations in time of need, and the ancestor of the successful walnut of commerce.

Almost all of the world's marketable walnuts today are *Juglans regia*, the Persian walnut. Men lived on acorns, it was said, and Bacchus's fellow gods ate the best walnuts; *Juglans* means "Jupiter's acorns" and *regia* means "royal."

Ultimately mythology must yield to archeology. This species of walnut is so widely scattered over the globe that it is hard to know exactly where it originated. South-central Asia seems most likely. We are not sure of Bacchus's dates, but we know that archeologists have uncovered walnut shells 9,000 years old. Walnuts were found in the ruins of Pompeii, indicating that they had come as far as southern Italy as early as 2,000 years ago.

Over the centuries the Persian walnut was taken to and established in almost every temperate area visited by traders and explorers. Traders brought such quantities of them to England that they were sometimes called the English walnut. It is popular everywhere because it is hardy, grows well, and is easy to crack. There may be as many as a dozen other species of walnuts around the world, including the rough, tough, and tasty black walnut that is native to North America. No other species, however, lends itself to commercial cultivation.

The Persian walnut came to California with Franciscan priests probably in the late eighteenth century. It became a significant crop in the middle of the nineteenth century, and by 1900, scientists were at work developing hardier and more productive cultivars. In 1912, the Diamond Walnut cooperative was established in Stockton, California.

To start new trees, nurseries often use a rootstock from a northern California black walnut species. It is a tough, hardy, and disease-resistant tree, and cuttings from the Persian trees grow well on that stock. In the orchards, the trees are planted thirty feet apart. They produce when they are six to eight years old. When they get too big, the orchard is thinned. Mature trees need a spacing of fifty feet. The trees live a long time, with century-old trees still producing good crops.

Today walnut growers in California are about as high tech as you can get. The nuts are ready for harvesting when the hulls start to split, usually starting as early as September and continuing on until November. The nuts are shaken from the trees by big machines. Mechanical sweepers make windrows. Another machine gathers them and takes them to the processing plant. They are mechanically hulled as soon as possible and then quickly machine-dried to reduce the chance of spoilage. Then other machines sort, crack, size, scan, and package them.

California productivity is very high. While the world average is about one ton of nuts per acre, many California growers get as many as three tons per acre.

Annual world production is at about a billion and a quarter pounds. The United States grew nearly half a billion pounds in 2000. China has developed tens of thousands of acres of new orchards in recent years, and is now threatening America's role as the walnut king of the world. Turkey, which for years was number two, has slipped to third place in world production.

Walnuts, they say, will make you fecund. For that reason, in some places they were often thrown at weddings in the interest of insuring an early pregnancy. If you think someone may be a witch, and that person is sitting, slip a walnut under the chair and they will not be able to get up. Chew walnuts if a mad dog bites you. A walnut looks like a brain, and in the Middle Ages it was thought to be a good brain food or even a brain medicine. Walnut husks would be ground into a paste and applied to a head wound. Additionally, the mentally ill and people with epilepsy were advised to eat lots of walnuts.

The primary reason that so many are grown and sold is that walnuts are delicious, perhaps our most desired nut for confections and quality baked goods.

"Holidays are walnut days." This statement in a *Ladies' Home Journal* ad in 1923 picked up an American tradition. The wild walnuts of the woods were routinely gathered in the fall and hulled and shelled for Thanksgiving and Christmas. The walnut establishment wanted to keep the tradition alive as people moved to the cities and away from nature. Wally Walnut, a cartoon character whose head was a walnut, became a fixture in walnut publicity well into the 1940s.

The American growers of this great nut face the problems faced by so many other American farmers. Costs are high. Labor is hard to find and expensive. The equipment needed puts a fierce burden on a farmer's budget. The people who market walnuts have to face the competition of cheaper products from third world countries. Walnut growers continue to do what they do because they love doing it, and the consumer benefits by having access to Bacchus's great walnut, the direct descendent of his transformed lover.

other nuts

Besides the dozen we have written about in this book, there are scores of other nuts, nut kin, and seeds that have been consumed around the world. Some of them, like black walnuts, butternuts, hickory nuts, and beechnuts, we have used in recipes. There are sources for them listed in the back of the book. If they seem too costly for use in a recipe, a less expensive commercial cousin will work just fine.

Acorns are abundant, a true nut, but as nut expert Frederic Rosengarten says, they are "too astringent for human consumption except in times of famine." After we tried them, we agree. Another wild nut is the chinquapin. They are a chestnut relative, but, while delicious, they are too small to be worth gathering.

A nut is a seed, of course, but a seed isn't necessarily a nut. Some, like pumpkin seeds and sunflower seeds, have nutty characteristics and could play a main role in the kitchen. Most other culinary seeds—caraway, sesame, cardamom, poppy, cumin, and celery—are used for seasoning dishes.

recipes with nuts

introduction to using nuts in recipes

Some General Tips

- In freezing nuts, keep in mind that those already ground tend to lose some flavor when frozen.
- Don't be afraid to use your nut oils as a garnish. Drizzle some over grilled fish and poultry right before serving.
- In baking, use nut oil instead of butter to grease your pans.
- A nut oil in lieu of olive oil in a vinaigrette will please everyone. Finish the salad with a few of the same nuts, finely chopped.

Some General Terms

Coarsely chopped. Nuts are either chopped or crushed, but in a variety of sizes.

Finely chopped. Nuts are cut as evenly as possible into very small, but discernable, pieces.

Medium-sized. Pieces should be chopped about the size of pine nuts.

Crushed. Nuts will be of various sizes as a result of the application of weight (such as a rolling pin) applied to the whole nuts. It is easiest to do this when the nuts are on a dish towel. That way they will not fall to the floor.

Ground. This is also known as nut meal. There should be no discernible nut pieces. This can be done in a mortar, a coffee/spice grinder, a blender, a food processor, or a special nut mill. Most nuts can be purchased already ground.

Shelling and Skinning (Blanching)

It is now possible to easily purchase nearly every variety of nut already shelled, so we will only provide shelling information where it is particularly needed.

Almonds are easily purchased both with the skin on and with it removed, or blanched.

Brazil nuts are usually already blanched when sold out of the shell. One can easily rub away any skin still adhering to the nuts. Just turn the nuts into a rough towel and rub for a minute or two.

Cashews are always sold peeled and skinned. You will really appreciate that fact when you read more about them in this book.

Chestnuts are most commonly (and economically) sold fresh in the shell. To remove the shell: Place chestnuts in a large bowl and soak in warm water for about 20 minutes, then drain. (NOTE: Chestnuts will explode when heated unless they are first punctured.) Slash around the rounded side without penetrating the nut flesh itself, or you can make an **X** on the flat side with a knife. Place the nuts on a shallow-sided baking pan and roast at 300°F, turning occasionally, until the nuts are tender, about 20 minutes. (NOTE: Roasting time may vary depending on a number of factors. You can test for doneness by sticking a fork into the opening made by the knife slash.) Turn the nuts onto a large bath towel, wrap tightly, and steam for 10 to 15 minutes. Carefully, using a sharp paring knife, remove the shell, and try to get as much of the skin as will come off (usually it comes off right with the shell).

If chestnuts are peeled and dried, pour boiling water over them to cover in a large bowl. Let soak overnight, or for at least 6 hours. Then drain and cook in salted boiling water until tender.

Coconuts need to be hulled, shelled, and the skin removed before the flesh is useful. Ripe coconuts are usually hulled before you buy them. There are three indentations on top of the coconut. Puncture two of them with a screwdriver or ice pick and pour out the liquid for later use. Bake the drained coconut for about 15 minutes at 400°F. Let it cool. With a hammer, break it into several pieces. With a paring knife, separate the meat from the shell. Remove the brown skin with a peeler. The coconut meat then can be grated by hand or in a food processor. Excess grated coconut will freeze well.

To make coconut milk, see Basics, page 50.

"Tender" or green coconuts are immature, usually picked in the seventh month. (They are mature at twelve to fourteen months.) Green coconuts are shipped in the hull. Cut it away to expose the indentations. Puncture and pour out the "coconut water." Use it as a drink or in recipes. Crack the shell with a hammer. The white flesh will be gelatinous and can be spooned out for use in recipes.

Hazelnuts are more commonly sold with the skin on. To remove the skin yourself: Spread the nuts on a large, shallow baking sheet in a single layer. Toast at 350°F for 15 minutes. Carefully transfer the hot nuts to a large bath towel and wrap tightly so the nuts may steam some. When cool, start rubbing the nuts with the towel until the skin has been brushed away.

Macadamias are always sold out of the shell. Some are sold as is. Others are already roasted and salted. It is common for the unroasted nut to be sold in bulk. Roasted and salted nuts are usually in jars.

Peanuts are available every way, in the shell plain, boiled, or roasted; out of the shell, plain or roasted. Unless you have a passion for peeling, it is best to buy them already shelled and au naturel, so you can finish them yourself.

Pecans are available already shelled or in-shell. Usually, we buy them already shelled and ready for use. They are sold by size, with the larger ones more impressive (and expensive). Buy complete halves for use in appetizers and for those dishes where handsome, unbroken pecans are needed to dazzle. The broken nuts are less expensive and are just fine for most cooking.

Pine nuts are always sold shelled and ready to go.

Pistachios are sold both shelled and in the shell. We usually buy them shelled for cooking and in the shell for snacking. There may be an insignificant skin on the nuts, but they have no discernible effect on the flavor, so there is no particular need to blanch and peel. Pistachios in the shell are usually simple to remove. So when you are serving the nuts as a snack, leave them in the shell. One tends to eat a few less when the nuts need to be removed one at a time from the shell.

Walnuts are easily available already shelled and peeled. Only if they are to be served as a snack is it worth the time and effort to crack them and carefully remove the pieces using a tiny pick.

Toasting, Roasting

We use the two words interchangeably. Both refer to the browning of nuts in the oven in order to enhance the basic nut flavor, making it more pronounced and pleasurable. (See the essay on the Maillard Reaction, page 236.)

From our point of view low and slow is the best way to achieve the best results. So we roast all nuts on a shallow-sided baking pan, in a single layer, at 325°F. Most nuts will require 12 to 20 minutes, but some might need a bit less time. Be sure to stir them and respread them one time during the process. For example, pine nuts go quickly, Brazil nuts are slow.

Let nuts cool for at least 15 minutes before using them.

We have learned that it is possible to toast and cool and then store in zipper-type bags in the freezer. It is not the very best way to go, but the loss of any flavor is not major.

Frying, Sautéing

You certainly can achieve browning in a skillet, but we have learned in India that the wok really does it better. The only potential for difficulty comes from waiting too long to remove the nuts from the hot oil. Once they start to change color, it happens quickly. You really do need to get them out, so keep your batches small until you are really comfortable with this. Invest a few dollars in a large Chinese frying strainer. It is much better for this than a perforated spoon. We have concluded that the best fat for this is ghee (clarified butter); for recipe, see Basics, page 50. It also has the best flavor.

One should first soak the nuts in water for 2 to 3 minutes, then drain well. Be sure to drain the nuts on several layers of paper towels.

Store all fried nuts in clean, airtight tins. Use them within 2 weeks.

Storing Nuts

Shelled nuts store best when packed in zipper-type bags and are stored in the freezer. Black walnuts, for example, will hold up for a year. Pine nuts maintain their fresh sweetness for less time, about 3 months. If you are going to use the nuts within a week or two, store them in the refrigerator, but take them out of their package and store them in a zipper-type bag as well.

Store nuts in their shells in the refrigerator for up to a month. Let them come to room temperature before you shell them.

in our kitchen

We try to follow the Slow Food belief that one should eat seasonally and regionally, using the freshest organic products possible. If you need help finding organic growers in your region, check with the agricultural extension service and seek out regional farmers markets.

As much as possible we like to know the sources of our food. In the Ohio summer that is not difficult, but in our long winters one does tend to tire of root vegetables, so we admit we are grateful that our local organic market, The Mustard Seed, will have some good tasting fruits and vegetables from California.

In summer we eat whatever is current at Silver Creek Farm in Hiram, Ohio. Our garden is lavishly filled with herbs, tomatoes, and peppers. And baby lettuces, as well as edible flowers. We may even have fresh figs, if our weather allows them to ripen. Whenever possible, we use fresh herbs; the flavor they impart is significantly better than those dried, in most cases.

With Indian dishes, or with those just influenced by those complex cuisines, we prefer to grind our own seasoning blends of spices and herbs, the "masala" as it would be called. However, we realize that not everyone wants to take the time to do that. Therefore, in Americanized recipes, we call for "a good Madras-style curry powder."

Because we like the clean flavor and rough texture, we cook with kosher salt. Then, for special garnishes, we will use some good French sea salt.

Nearly all of our grains are certified organic and stone ground from Arrowhead Mills. We use their unbleached white flour for baking everything from breads to cakes, unless the recipe specifies something else. Their cornmeal has a very lovely flavor; it is also fine in texture.

We do, however, buy the superlative Marino organic polenta, a celebrated organic product from Piedmont. Our milk comes in real glass bottles and our heavy cream is never ultrapasteurized. And we always cook and bake with unsalted butter.

Most of our meats are USDA-graded Prime meats, unless otherwise indicated. We buy hormone-free, cold-water plucked poultry that tastes significantly fresher than ordinary chicken and stays moister during cooking. We are very particular about the freshness of fish and shellfish. Seek the very best purveyors in your region, and keep your fish iced until the moment of cooking.

We use a variety of extra virgin olive oils in our cooking, the top quality for those dishes where olive oil is not to be cooked. The best-quality Parmesan cheese is genuine Parmigiano-Reggiano, from the region of Emilia-Romagna, Italy. We prefer cheese from an organic producer outside of Modena. Otherwise we try to use artisanal cheeses from this country, France, and Italy.

All of the garlic we use comes from Bobba-Mike's and from Filaree Farm (see Sources, page 313). Our sweet onions and very large shallots are all from Robison Ranch.

When it comes to specific ingredients, we try to be consistent in terminology: A plump garlic clove yields at least 2 rounded teaspoons of minced garlic.

We dice onions so they will not be mushy. When we specify "chopped onions," that means that it is OK to use a food processor, since the onions are intended to break down and cook into the sauce.

We call them scallions when they have little or no bulb. We call them green onions when they have a large, fresh white bulb with no dried skin on it and a long, green quill attached. We refer to sizes of onions as Jumbo, Large, Medium, and Small:

Jumbo:	Over 1 pound
Large:	¾ to 1 pound
Medium:	About ½ to ¾ pound
Small:	Below ½ pound

The most important tool in our kitchen is an old scale that had belonged to Linda's grandmother, Mary Weller. In addition there is a digital scale that we use mostly for weighing things like pasta and rice.

We have been blessed with a wonderful collection of splendid cookware, but it is very eclectic. We have many old cast-iron skillets and spun aluminum saucepans. The latter was the ancestor of Calphalon. We also enjoy using Le Creuset casseroles. Then in addition to our old French copper, we now use Calphalon skillets and sauté pans. We only rarely use nonstick cookware. Finally, we must not forget Fred's very old and well-seasoned wok with its battered, but tight, cover.

While most of the recipes in our books are of our own creation, many others are from our families, food notes from travels, and our friends. If the head notes offer no attribution, then it is a recipe of ours. Otherwise its origins will be identified.

Finally, we believe that most recipes are not cast in stone. So feel free to make your own adjustments; we won't object.

"I'm Charley's aunt from Brazil—
where the nuts come from."

A line from Charley's Aunt,
by Brandon Thomas, 1892.

basics

Ghee

Crème Fraîche

Rich Coconut Milk

Pie Crust

Our Tomato Purée

Roasted Garlic

Ghee (Clarified Butter)

While there is a somewhat more complicated way to make ghee, this is the simplest way to do it, and we find that the resulting solid butter, a.k.a. ghee, really tolerates high heat well.

1 pound unsalted butter

Melt the butter in a small saucepan. Pour it into a 4-cup heatproof (Pyrex) measuring cup and chill until the top is solid, at least 4 hours, but preferably overnight.

Scrape any foam from the very surface of the solid. Then remove the solid from the milky liquid at the bottom. Wipe the bottom of the ghee well and store in a covered container in the refrigerator. This will last more than 4 weeks.

MAKES ABOUT ¾ CUP

Crème Fraîche

3 cups heavy cream
  (not ultrapasteurized)

½ cup buttermilk

Blend the cream and buttermilk together in a medium-sized bowl. Cover loosely and let stand at room temperature overnight. The next morning, blend well. Pour into a container that has a tight-fitting lid and store in the refrigerator until needed. This will keep for up to 2 weeks.

Rich Coconut Milk

The Pleasures of Cooking was a splendid magazine published by Carl Sontheimer of Cuisinart fame. In the November/December 1981 issue, the late Copeland Marks wrote a wonderful article about using coconut milk. I've been making it his way for more than two decades. In his introduction he wrote, "When a coconut is heated, the meat pulls away from the shell and is easy to extract. Rich milk can be frozen. To use, let it come to room temperature. The milk will have separated, so stir it well to reconstitute it." It is still the best way to do this that I have found to date. This process is different from what we saw recently in Kerala. There the coconuts are cut in half and grated with an instrument that goes from the outside of the flesh to that closest to the brown skin. The flesh grated first is kept separate from the flesh closer to the brown. This latter flesh will use less water and yield a thicker milk, or cream, that is only used for finishing a dish, because it will curdle if boiled. The other is called "thin" coconut milk.

1 fresh coconut (about 3 pounds)	3 cups hot water

Preheat the oven to 400°F. NOTE: First, puncture two of the indentations on the top of the nut and drain the liquid from the coconut before baking.

Bake the coconut until the shell cracks, about 15 minutes. Remove it and leave it on a rack until it is cool enough to handle.

Put the coconut into a double layer of plastic bags that self-seal. Place the bag on a very hard surface and, using a hammer, hit the coconut very hard in the area of the oven-induced crack. One or two blows should split it open.

Discard any remaining liquid (this is not milk) and carefully separate the meat from the shell. Use a peeling or paring knife to remove the brown skin. Put half the coconut meat into a food processor, then pulse until it is coarsely chopped. Add 1½ cups of the hot water and process for 1 full minute. Pour into a large bowl and repeat with the remaining coconut meat.

Let this mixture soak for 15 minutes. Then strain it through a colander lined with cheesecloth, pressing down on the coconut to extract as much liquid as possible. Discard the solids. The liquid should stand for 10 minutes, then be transferred to a storage container. Discard any sediment.

The milk can be stored in the refrigerator for up to 2 days, or in the freezer for several months.

MAKES **3** CUPS

Pie Crust

This makes a very short pastry that is wonderfully delicious, but the crust is rather fragile, so handle carefully when baked. You can prepare pastry several days ahead, keeping the dough thoroughly wrapped in the refrigerator. If it is that cold, let it stand for at least 20 minutes at room temperature before rolling.

2 cups unbleached flour	13 tablespoons cold unsalted butter, cut into small pieces
½ teaspoon kosher salt	Up to 7 tablespoons ice water

Combine the flour and salt in the bowl of a food processor. Add the butter bits and pulse 15 to 20 times, until the mixture is the texture of cornmeal. Sprinkle evenly with 6 tablespoons ice water. Pulse 15 more times; the mixture will be crumbly and not at all gathered. If it feels too dry, add some more water and pulse 5 times.

Dump the mixture in a mound on a lightly floured work surface. Using the heel of your hand, quickly push small amounts of the dough at a time away from you across the work surface until all of it has been worked. With the help of a pastry scraper, gather the now-blended dough together. Cut into 2 equal pieces. Form dough into disks about 4 inches in diameter, wrap with wax paper, and chill for at least 20 minutes.

Generously flour your work surface and rolling pin. Roll pastry into a 13- or 14-inch circle and carefully fit it into a 10-inch pie pan or an 11-inch tart pan with a removable bottom. Trim the edges to be 1 inch above the top of the rim, fold in half to the inside, leaving a firm ½-inch rim above the edge of the pan. Prick the bottom and sides with a fork, then chill the shell for 40 minutes.

While the shell is chilling, preheat the oven to 425°F.

Line the shell with foil and fill with pie weights or rice so that the sides will not slip down. Bake for 15 minutes, remove the weights and foil, and bake for another 5 minutes, or until nicely browned.

Transfer the shell from the oven to a rack until it's time to fill.

PASTRY FOR **2** 10-INCH SHELLS

Our Tomato Puree

Amish Paste, Blue Beech, Hog Heart, Principe Borghese, and Orange Banana are some of the wonderful heirloom paste tomatoes that we use for tomato puree. They are among two dozen heirloom varieties we plant each summer. We've learned over the years that a very simple handling yields the most marvelous fresh flavors, despite the many months of sitting in our freezer. We add no seasoning, and we do nothing to reduce the puree. We cook the tomatoes very slowly and then put them through a good food mill. When you use the puree in winter you can reduce it, if you wish.

3 tablespoons extra virgin olive oil   About 5 pounds paste tomatoes

Coat the bottom of a heavy 4-quart saucepan with olive oil. Cut the tomatoes crosswise in half and squeeze the seeds and liquid out. Pack the squeezed tomatoes into the saucepan until it is tightly filled.

Place the pan over low heat and cover tightly. Cook, stirring a few times, until the tomatoes fall apart. This will take between 45 minutes and 1 hour and 15 minutes. (We have learned that Blue Beech and Hog Heart cook slowly.)

Remove the saucepan from the heat and let it cool somewhat. Then process the tomatoes in a food mill over a large container. Distribute the puree among 2-cup and quart containers. Cover when completely cool and store in the freezer. This puree is actually fresh and delicious during the second winter—if some lasts that long!

MAKES ABOUT 3 QUARTS

Roasted Garlic

Most of the garlic we use in our kitchen is hard-necked garlic grown by a small farmer. Most of these garlics, as well as the special soft necks, have large cloves. These are especially wonderful when roasted. You will find that the flavors of slowly roasted garlic will all have rounded out into a very mellow taste. You can store roasted garlic for weeks in the refrigerator. Just squeeze it into a small, very clean container that has a tight-fitting lid. A well-rounded tablespoon of roasted garlic is equivalent to about 4 roasted plump cloves.

4 large heads of garlic

4 tablespoons extra virgin olive oil

4 teaspoons water

Preheat the oven to 325°F. Slice off the tops of the garlic. Gently remove the heavier outer papery skin from the sides of the heads. Place the heads in a small ovenproof dish just large enough to hold them. Spoon 1 tablespoon of oil over the top of each head, then drizzle 1 teaspoon of water over each. Cover them tightly with foil. Bake the garlic for 1¼ hours. Uncover, baste with any remaining pan juices, and bake uncovered until golden, about 15 minutes more.

Let the garlic cool, then squeeze the flesh from each clove into a shallow bowl. Add any remaining pan juices, too. Using a fork or potato masher, thoroughly mash the garlic. Then blend the mixture with softened butter and season with salt, pepper, and a dash of Tabasco sauce. Spoon the mixture into a small serving dish and wrap tightly. Store it in the refrigerator. Bring the mixture to room temperature and serve it with crusty bread or warm focaccia.

Taste Memory

For Marcel Proust, it was those cookies, but for many Americans, it is the aroma of roasting nuts. We really don't have to say much more than that. Already both the reader and the writer are back in the past, in a homey, warm, and happier time. Whatever kind of cookies Mom always made, we can smell and taste them now. That little store on Capitol Street wafted the aromas of peanuts cooking in oil or pecans and walnuts roasting in an oven right out onto the sidewalk as we were walking by. You couldn't resist. You bought peanuts if you didn't have much money, and pecans and walnuts if you had more.

Probably Proust would have eventually written *Remembrance of Things Past* even if it hadn't been for the madeleine that his mother brought to him one day as he shivered with a cold. Nevertheless there is no doubt that it gave the project a spark.

Alan R. Hirsch is one of the world's authorities on the power of taste and smell. Dr. Hirsch is the neurological director of the Smell and Taste Treatment and Research Foundation in Chicago. He believes that "the sense of smell has a more powerful impact upon the emotions than any of the other senses. That's because anatomically the nose is connected with the olfactory lobe, which is part of the limbic system, the area of the brain considered the seat of the emotions." An odor can bring back a memory from the past through what he calls an "olfactory-evoked recall." It is a sure-fire trigger for feeling of nostalgia, "the bittersweet yearning for the past."

Businesses are built on the power of those recollections. It is not by accident that the real estate agent suggests you bake some bread before the prospect comes to see your house. People who run a theater make their popcorn in the lobby, and if you are selling nuts, it is wise to waft the aromas of the roasting process out onto the street, into the noses of people walking by.

Dr. Hirsch worries that for young people, having grown up without the wonderful things their elders had in their backgrounds, the smells that trigger nostalgic thoughts are "plastic, VapoRub, Sweet Tarts, and Play Doh." People fifty years from now will be nostalgic for man-made chemicals and not for chestnuts roasting on an open fire.

For now, for most of us, it is still our taste memories, the remembrance of things from the kitchens of our past, that bring back some of the most pleasant elements of yesterday.

appetizers

Candied Walnuts with Heat

Crunchy Indian Cashews with Anise,
Salt, and Pepper

Pistachios Tempura

Hummus Bi Tahini: Chickpeas with
Sesame Paste and Pine Nuts

Caponata: A Sicilian Eggplant Relish
with Pine Nuts and Almonds

Tapawingo's Savory Cheesecake with
Basil and Walnuts

Circassian Chicken

Shrimp and Snow Pea Pod Pot
Stickers with Spicy Peanut
Dipping Sauce

Spanish Meatballs in Tomato Almond
Sauce

Bacalà (Salt Cod) Cakes with
Pistachios and Raisins

Calamari with Pine Nut
Stuffing

Candied Walnuts with Heat

These sweet and crunchy walnuts have a pleasing suggestion of heat. They make a marvelous snack and are splendid as a garnish for salads and stir-fries. These will hold for several weeks in an airtight container.

2 cups sugar

1 tablespoon cayenne, plus more if
needed

¼ teaspoon cream of tartar

½ cup water

¼ cup corn syrup, preferably Lyle's
Golden Syrup (see Sources,
page 313)

2 teaspoons Tabasco sauce

4 cups walnuts

Cover a large cookie sheet with parchment.

In a medium-sized saucepan, combine the sugar, cayenne, cream of tartar, water, corn syrup, and Tabasco. Using a candy thermometer, cook the mixture over medium heat until the temperature reaches 246°F. Add nuts and stir thoroughly.

Pour the nut mixture onto the parchment, spread evenly, and cool. Break the cold nut mixture into pieces. Taste, and if you wish more heat, dust with additional cayenne. Store in an airtight tin.

SERVES 6

Crunchy Indian Cashews with Anise, Salt, and Pepper

There is no limit to the irresistible culinary treasures that come from Kochi, India. There, on the coast of the southern state of Kerala, is a talented young cook who takes the simplest ingredients and makes them soar. Nimmy Paul is her name, and she is an expert at showing visitors the variety and richness of the region's Syrian Christian culinary traditions, a cuisine that enthusiastically incorporates cashews and coconuts in all sorts of ways. These peppery cashews will not last long. While the anise is our particular touch, the technique and simple seasoning come from Nimmy. (Keep in mind that the town of Tellicherry where the peppercorns are grown isn't far away.) These nuts are especially delicious as a nibble before dinner, but they also make a great garnish with many of our Asian dishes. Our Giant Schnauzer, Sanford, likes them at any time. He has learned to open the tins!

3 cups raw cashews

3 cups water

1½ cups vegetable or peanut oil

1 small piece of star anise, more if needed

3 tablespoons Tellicherry peppercorns (available at Asian markets)

2 to 3 tablespoons kosher salt

In a large bowl, cover the nuts with water and soak for 2 minutes, then drain thoroughly.

Heat the oil in a wok over high heat. Working in batches, fry the nuts until golden, only a minute or two. Drain thoroughly on paper towels. Repeat until all of the nuts are browned.

In the bowl of a spice grinder, combine a small piece of star anise with the peppercorns. Pulse until finely grounded.

Place the nuts in a bowl and toss with the pepper mixture and lavish amounts of salt to taste.

When the nuts are cool, taste and adjust seasonings. Store in a tin with a tight-fitting lid. These nuts will keep for up to 2 weeks.

SERVES **6**

Pistachios Tempura

We first had pistachio tempura in the remarkable restaurant, El Bulli, on Spain's Costa Brava. Food lovers from across the world flock there to experience the work of Feran Adria, considered by many to be the most creative chef working in the world today. This recipe is our credible approximation of Adria's pistachio tempura.

1 cup unbleached flour

2 teaspoons baking powder

1 teaspoon salt

1 cup ice cold club soda or seltzer

2 cups organic vegetable oil, plus more if needed

2 cups raw, shelled pistachios

Sea salt to taste

Preheat the over to 250°F.

Cover a large baking sheet with two layers of paper towels.

In a medium-sized mixing bowl, blend together the flour, baking powder, and salt. Quickly whisk in the soda water, whisking until the batter is thoroughly blended.

Pour the oil into a wok and heat until hot enough to quickly brown a cube of bread that is tossed into it.

Turn the nuts into the batter and blend well. Working with about one-quarter of the nuts at a time, drop the well-battered nuts into the oil by scattering them across the wok with a large spoon. Use another large spoon to break up any large clumps of nuts. Using a Chinese frying strainer, keep turning nuts in the oil until they turn golden, 1 to 2 minutes. Transfer browned battered nuts to the prepared baking sheet to drain. Keep warm in the oven until all of the nuts are battered and fried. Allow to stand for about 10 minutes.

Toss generously with sea salt and serve.

SERVES **6** TO **8**

Hummus Bi Tahini: Chickpeas with Sesame Paste and Pine Nuts

Tahini is a oily paste made from roasted sesame seeds. Thinned with lemon juice or a little water, it becomes the basis for a host of tasty dishes served throughout the Middle East. This very popular dip of chickpeas and tahini is piqued by generous amounts of garlic and lemon juice. To be really authentic, you should start with dried chickpeas. Canned ones are not as wonderful, which is why we always have bags of the dried beans all cooked in our freezer. While we like to serve this as a predinner snack, especially in the summer, it is often served as part of the break-fast meal in Middle Eastern countries, as Linda learned from Saudi Arabian graduate students years ago. They served it with a topping of rich olive oil, black olives, and toasted pine nuts.

7 plump garlic cloves, smashed

3 teaspoons kosher salt, plus more as needed

3 cups cooked chickpeas, skins removed

1 cup reserved cooking water or spring water

½ cup extra virgin olive oil, plus more if needed

⅔ cup tahini (sesame paste), available in supermarkets and Middle Eastern markets

½ cup fresh lemon juice, more if needed

1 teaspoon freshly ground black pepper, plus more if desired

⅓ cup toasted pine nuts

Oil-cured black olives

Wedges of pita for dipping

In a mortar, combine the garlic and salt. Pound vigorously until the garlic is creamy. This texture is so pleasing that it would be a shame to press the garlic instead, but if you must, you must. Reserve.

Combine the chickpeas and ½ cup each of the cooking water and olive oil in the bowl of a food processor. Pulse until thoroughly puréed. Add the tahini and lemon juice. Pulse again. Scrape the creamy garlic into the food processor, then add 1 teaspoon of the pepper. Run the processor until the mixture is thoroughly blended. Scrape the sides and taste. Add more cooking water if mixture is too stiff or thick. Adjust all seasonings as desired.

Scrape into a shallow serving bowl. Garnish with toasted pine nuts. And, if you wish, drizzle with several tablespoons of warmed olive oil. Also, if desired, you can scatter olives over the top. Surround with wedges of fresh pita.

SERVES **6** TO **8**

Caponata: A Sicilian Eggplant Relish with Pine Nuts and Almonds

A Sicilian dish, caponata has its roots in Arab cuisine, which not only incorporated nuts in savory foods, but also introduced sweet-and-sour sauces to the Western Mediterranean. There are many versions of caponata, some with and some without nuts. There are also some in which the vegetables are deep fried in olive oil, and others where they are sautéed. The givens are that Sicilian caponata will always be sweet-and-sour and that it is never served hot, but rather at room temperature. It keeps very well for weeks in a tightly covered container in the refrigerator. Finally, you can cut down on the total oil needed for cooking by using a large nonstick skillet.

2 pounds small eggplants, peeled
    and cut into ¾-inch cubes
Kosher salt, as needed
Up to 1 cup olive oil, plus more if
    needed
⅓ cup pine nuts
⅓ cup silvered blanched almonds
2 plump garlic cloves, thinly sliced
1 large red onion, cut in half and
    thinly sliced
2 large celery stalks, trimmed and
    thinly sliced
2 large carrots, peeled and thinly
    sliced

3 large, fleshy vine-ripened
    tomatoes, peeled, seeded, and
    finely chopped
¼ cup superfine sugar
⅓ cup golden raisins
½ cup rich red wine vinegar
¼ cup capers, preferably salt
    packed, rinsed
⅓ cup pitted green olives, sliced
    into rings
¼ cup fragrant extra virgin olive oil
Kosher salt and freshly ground black
    pepper to taste

The day before you plan to serve this, sprinkle eggplants generously with kosher salt and let stand in a colander for at least 30 minutes. Rinse and blot dry.

Heat ¼ cup of the olive oil in a large sauté pan over medium-high heat. Add the nuts and cook until golden, 2 to 4 minutes. Using a slotted spoon, transfer the nuts to a large bowl.

Adding oil as needed, transfer the eggplant to the pan and cook over medium heat, stirring often, until somewhat browned and tender, 15 to 20 minutes. Using a slotted spoon, add the eggplant to the nuts and reserve.

Always adding more olive oil as needed, cook the garlic and onions, stirring often, over medium heat until golden, 7 to 10 minutes. Transfer with a slotted spoon to the bowl with the eggplant.

Cook the celery and carrots in sauté pan until tender, about 7 minutes. Then transfer to the bowl, too.

Cook the tomatoes over medium heat, stirring frequently, until the tomato water has evaporated and the tomatoes are almost a thick sauce, about 15 minutes. Add the sugar, raisins, vinegar, capers, and olives. Simmer over low heat for about 10 minutes. Blend into the eggplant mixture along with the extra virgin olive oil. Add salt as needed and a generous amount of pepper.

Store, tightly covered, in the refrigerator for at least 24 hours before serving. Bring to room temperature and serve in an attractive bowl, accompanied by hors d'oeuvre plates and salad forks.

SERVES **6** TO **8**

Tapawingo's Savory Cheesecake with Basil and Walnuts

We've known for more than fifteen years that Harlan "Pete" Peterson was one of the best chefs in the country. His long-celebrated restaurant, Tapawingo, has made the tiny village of Ellsworth, Michigan, a destination for all dedicated food lovers. We first sampled this tasty appetizer cheesecake early in our friendship with Tapawingo and its staff. More than a decade later, it still is a favorite among our friends and our children's friends.

1 tablespoon butter, softened

¼ cup dry bread crumbs

¾ cup grated Parmigiano-
   Reggiano

¼ cup minced fresh basil

¼ cup coarsely chopped fresh flat-
   leaf parsley

1 plump garlic clove

2 tablespoons olive oil

Pinch of kosher salt

12 ounces soft goat cheese

8 ounces whole-milk ricotta cheese,
   at room temperature

8 ounces cream cheese, at room
   temperature

½ cup sour cream

4 large eggs

¼ teaspoon freshly ground white
   pepper

½ cup roasted walnuts

Preheat the oven to 325°F.

Thoroughly butter the bottom and sides of an 8-inch springform pan. Combine the bread crumbs and ⅛ cup of the Parmigiano-Reggiano and spoon it into the pan. Toss crumb mixture all over to coat the pan well. Shake out excess.

Combine the basil, parsley, garlic, olive oil, and salt in the bowl of a food processor. Process until mixture becomes a smooth paste, scraping sides several times. Reserve.

Combine the goat cheese, ricotta, cream cheese, sour cream, and remaining Parmigiano in the bowl of an electric mixer. Beat well until the mixture is completely smooth. Scrape sides and beat again. With the motor running on high, add the eggs one at a time and beat until the mixture is well blended. Beat in the white pepper.

Transfer one-third of the cheese mixture to a small bowl and set aside for the top. Combine basil mixture with remaining cheese mixture in the bowl and blend well. Scrape filling into the prepared pan and smooth the top. Spread the reserved cheese mixture (without the basil) over the top. Sprinkle evenly with the walnuts.

Bake for 1 hour 20 minutes. Turn the oven off, open the door slightly, and cool for 1 hour; then transfer to a cake rack and cool completely.

Serve the cake at room temperature, or slightly warmed. Garnish with basil leaves and parsley. In summer, serve with edible flowers.

SERVES 12

Circassian Chicken

Circassia is a region in the northwestern part of the Caucasus Mountains, with a western boundary formed by the Black Sea. While the people of the region converted to Christianity in the thirteenth century, sometime in the seventeenth century they became Muslims. The country was annexed to Russia in 1829. After prolonged resistance by the Muslim population, most of them finally emigrated to the Ottoman empire. Today there are Circassians living in Turkey and there is also a very active community in Jordan. Circassian chicken, however, is most often viewed to be a Turkish dish and is very popular. In its best known versions the chicken is always shredded and mixed with a luscious creamy sauce made of ground walnuts, garlic, some rich chicken broth, and thickened with bread. In some regions, however, the chicken is cut into large pieces that are then covered by the sauce. Some versions include minced fresh cilantro, others do not. In season, many garnish it with fresh pomegranate seeds. Regardless of the details, this dish is always greeted with enthusiasm. This particular recipe, except for a few minor adjustments, came to us from Ayse Uras, proprietor of Ayse's Café in Ann Arbor, Michigan. We are grateful to culinary historian Jan Longone and her wine expert husband, Dan, for introducing us.

2 pounds of bone-in chicken
   breast, skinned
1 pound chicken backs
1 medium onion, unpeeled
1 large carrot
1 teaspoon whole peppercorns
1 bay leaf
2 thick slices dry bread, preferably
   a tasty sourdough, crusts
   removed
1½ cups walnuts, lightly toasted

6 to 8 plump garlic cloves
Up to 3 cups chicken broth
Kosher salt and freshly ground black
   pepper to taste
2 tablespoons finely chopped fresh
   cilantro
6 walnut halves for garnish
2 tablespoons walnut oil
1½ teaspoons hot paprika
Seeds from 1 pomegranate
   (optional)

Combine the chicken, onion, carrot, peppercorns, and bay leaf in a saucepan. Cover generously with water. Bring to a boil over high heat. Reduce the heat to a brisk simmer, place the cover somewhat ajar, and simmer until chicken breasts are tender, about 30 minutes. Transfer the chicken breasts to a large cold platter. Strain and reserve the broth. Discard the other pan items.

Pull the chicken apart with the help of two forks. The meat should be thoroughly shredded. When it is, chop it coarsely with a large knife. Transfer the chicken to a large bowl.

Combine the bread and 1 cup of the reduced broth in a bowl and soften.

Combine the nuts and garlic in the bowl of a food processor and pulse until mixture is finely ground. Add softened bread and any remaining liquid in the bowl. Let motor run until mixture has made a thick paste. Season generously with salt and pepper to taste. With the motor running, gradually add more chicken stock to make a creamy sauce. Taste and adjust for salt and garlic.

Pour the sauce over the chicken. Add a generous amount of black pepper and the minced cilantro. Blend the chicken thoroughly. Then slowly add more rich broth as needed to make the mixture very creamy. Taste and adjust the seasonings.

Mound attractively in a shallow serving bowl. Cover with plastic and chill until 1 hour before serving. Bring to room temperature.

Garnish the chicken with walnut halves. Mix the walnut oil with the hot paprika and drizzle the mixture over the top. Scatter the pomegranate seeds on top and serve.

SERVES **6** TO **8**

Shrimp and Snow Pea Pod Pot Stickers
with Spicy Peanut Dipping Sauce

San Francisco's Ton Kiang serves a variety of luscious dumplings. That's where we first had the combination of shrimp and pea pods in various styles. We finally decided to try them at home, but we are most comfortable making them as light and lovely pot stickers. While we have always used an electric fry pan (almost an antique by now), any very large, heavy-bottomed skillet with a tight-fitting lid will be fine. This Thai-style dipping sauce provides just the right counterpoint for our dumplings. You can make the sauce several days ahead, but just let it stand at room temperature for several hours before serving. If you find round Wonton/gyoza wrappers made by Wonton Specialists, Inc., of Brooklyn, New York, grab them; they are superbly thin and easy to handle.

SPICY PEANUT DIPPING SAUCE

⅓ cup roasted peanuts, crushed
    with a rolling pin
4 plump garlic cloves, thoroughly
    smashed and diced
2 teaspoons grated fresh ginger
1 small fresh hot chile, seeded and
    chopped
¼ cup hoisin sauce
½ cup chicken stock
¼ cup freshly squeezed lime juice
2 tablespoons minced cilantro
1 tablespoon nam ploc (fish sauce;
    available in Asian markets or in
    some supermarkets)
1 scallion, trimmed with 1-inch
    green, finely minced

THE POT STICKERS

Up to ½ cup cornstarch
1 cup water
¾ pound raw shelled shrimp,
    chopped into small pieces
1 tablespoon minced fresh ginger
3 scallions trimmed with 1 inch
    green, minced
¾ cup (6 to 8 ounces) finely
    chopped snow pea pods
1 plump garlic clove, minced
1 tablespoon soy sauce
1 tablespoon rice wine
1 teaspoon dark sesame oil
1 package round gyoza wrappers (a
    wrapper made without eggs),
    defrosted

To make the dipping sauce: In a food processor, combine the crushed peanuts, garlic, ginger, chile, and hoisin sauce. Pulse until the mixture is puréed. Add the stock, lime juice, cilantro, and fish sauce. Pulse until the ingredients are well blended. Stir in the minced scallion. Pour the sauce into a small bowl and it let stand at room temperature.

To make the pot stickers: Sprinkle a large flat tray or plate with some of the cornstarch and set it aside. Pour ½ cup of the water into a small bowl and place nearby.

In a large bowl combine shrimp, ginger, scallions, pea pods, garlic, soy sauce, rice wine, and sesame oil. Blend thoroughly. Arrange the wrappers, six at a time, flour-side up, on a work surface. Put a heaping teaspoonful of filling in the center of each wrapper. Dip your finger into the water and moisten the outer edges of the filled wrappers. Then, one at a time, fold each piece in half, making a few pleats in the top. Make certain that the edges are sticking to each other. Place the plump side of each dumpling down on a prepared tray and repeat the process until all the dumplings are made. Cover them well with wax paper until it is time to fry them.

In another small bowl combine 1 teaspoon cornstarch and the remaining ½ cup of water. Mix with a chopstick to blend thoroughly.

With the temperature set to 400°F, heat the electric fry pan with enough oil to coat the bottom. Arrange the dumplings close together in the pan, but without touching; fry uncovered, until the bottoms begin to brown, about 4 minutes. Quickly reblend the water-cornstarch mixture, then pour evenly over the tops of the dumplings and cover the pan. Reduce heat to 375°F and cook until dumplings are golden on the bottom and tops have a nice shine to them, about 4 minutes more.

Carefully transfer the pot stickers to an attractive heated serving platter. Serve with the dipping sauce.

MAKES 3 TO 4 DOZEN

Spanish Meatballs in Tomato Almond Sauce

That almonds make a splendid thickener for soups and sauces has been well known for eons by Spanish cooks. Here we use them along with tomato sauce for a good old-fashioned-style appetizer. On the other hand, the meatballs also can make a tasty supper along with some zesty rice. We usually begin it a day ahead, then heat it on the stovetop and transfer the mixture to an ovenproof casserole to finish baking. Spanish paprika has a distinctive flavor that gives a note of mystery to the sauce.

THE MEATBALLS

1 pound ground beef
1 pound ground pork
1½ teaspoons each sea salt and
    freshly ground black pepper
1 teaspoon ground Spanish paprika
2 plump garlic cloves, minced

⅔ cup minced onion
¼ cup ground almonds
½ cup fresh bread crumbs
2 large eggs
⅓ cup water

THE SAUCE

3 tablespoons olive oil

1 large yellow onion, finely chopped

4 plump garlic cloves, minced

⅓ cup finely chopped blanched
almonds

⅓ cup crumbled country bread
without crusts

½ teaspoon ground cayenne

2 teaspoons Spanish paprika

⅓ cup dry Spanish sherry

4 cups tomato purée (see Basics,
page 52)

1 large fresh ancho or Anaheim
chile, roasted, peeled, seeded,
and chopped

Sea salt and freshly ground black
pepper to taste

Juice of 1 lemon

2 tablespoons minced fresh flat-leaf
parsley

2 hard-boiled eggs, cut into
wedges

To make the meatballs: Preheat the oven to 500°F.

Combine the ground meats, salt, pepper, paprika, garlic, onion, ground almonds, bread crumbs, eggs, and water in a large mixing bowl. Mix vigorously until all the ingredients are thoroughly blended. Form the mixture into meatballs the size of plump walnuts. Place on a large, shallow-sided cookie sheet and bake until well browned, 12 to 15 minutes. Let cool before loosening from the sheet with a metal spatula.

To make the sauce: Preheat the oven to 350°F.

In a large sauté pan, heat the olive oil over medium heat. Add the onion and garlic. Stir the mixture until the onions have wilted, about 3 minutes. Stir in the almonds, bread, cayenne, and paprika; then stir in the sherry and cook for 30 seconds. Add the tomato purée, chopped chile, salt, and pepper. Cook over medium heat until the mixture begins to bubble. Add the meatballs to the pan. Scrape the browned bits from the baking sheet and add that too to the sauté pan.

Transfer the meatball mixture to an ovenproof casserole. Bake, loosely covered, in the preheated oven for 1 hour.

To serve, drizzle lemon juice evenly over the casserole, garnish with parsley and egg wedges.

SERVES **6** TO **12**

Bacalà (Salt Cod) Cakes with Pistachios and Raisins

It is one of the great dishes of the Western Mediterranean. The French call it bran-dade, *the Spanish call it* bacalao *and in Italy it is known as* bacalà. *Common to all is the combination of salt-dried cod, potatoes, and garlic to form some kind of paste, puree, or cake. We add pistachios and raisins to this delicious dish as a salute to the ancient Arab invaders who not only brought this marvelous nut to the Western Mediterranean but who made other distinctive contributions to the region's culinary and cultural traditions that last to this day.*

1 pound salt cod

4 plump garlic cloves, smashed and minced

1 cup mashed potato, preferably Yukon gold

½ cup unbleached flour

½ teaspoon baking powder

¼ cup cream

2 large eggs, lightly beaten

⅓ cup coarsely chopped pistachios

⅓ cup golden raisins

1 teaspoon freshly ground black pepper

½ cup cornmeal or dry breadcrumbs

¼ cup olive oil

Romesco Sauce (page 156) or Lemon Pecan Mayonnaise (page 158)

Begin one day ahead. The day before serving, place the salt cod in a colander under the faucet in your sink. Trickle cold water over the cod for 1 to 2 hours, moving the pieces around (bottom to the top) occasionally. Transfer the fish to a large bowl and cover them with cold water. Keep them refrigerated for 24 hours, changing the water at least 4 times. Drain, rinse, and pat them dry. Place the cod in a large sauté pan and cover them with water. Bring it to a boil, then simmer for 10 minutes. Drain the fish, then remove the skin and bones. Break the fish into pieces and place them in a food processor. Pulse about 4 times, just enough to break them into small pieces.

Turn the fish into a large mixing bowl. Add garlic, potato, flour, and baking powder. Blend somewhat. Then add cream, eggs, nuts, raisins and pepper. Blend thoroughly.

Form the mixture into cakes that are about 3 to 3½ inches in diameter and about ⅔-inch thick. Coat them lightly with cornmeal.

Refrigerate the cakes at least 3 hours and up to 6.

Heat ¼ cup olive oil in a large skillet over medium heat. Add the fish cakes, cover and fry them until the bottoms are crisp and golden, 3 to 4 minutes. Turn the fish cakes and cook, uncovered, until the other side is golden. Drain thoroughly on paper towels. Serve on heated plates accompanied by some Romesco Sauce or Lemon Pecan Mayonaise.

SERVES **8**

Calamari with Pine Nut Stuffing

This is the way grandmothers made calamari! It was taught to us nearly fifteen years ago by Franny Santosuosso, who in turn learned it from her grandmother. We use pine nuts in this version to add a toasty sweetness to the very spicy filling. We eat the calamari as it is, right out of the skillet, with lots of Italian parsley and lemon juice.

5 pounds fresh calamari, cleaned
1½ pounds smoked bacon, chopped
1 large red onion, finely chopped
1 medium green bell pepper, seeded, deveined, and finely chopped
1 medium red bell pepper, seeded, deveined, and finely chopped
7 plump garlic cloves, minced
⅔ cup pine nuts
¾ teaspoon cayenne
1½ teaspoons ground black pepper

1 teaspoon kosher salt
½ cup dry white wine
½ cup dry sherry
½ cup chicken stock
¼ cup lemon juice
3 large eggs
½ cup grated Parmesan cheese
Up to 1 cup soft bread crumbs
⅔ cup unbleached flour
¼ cup olive oil, plus more if needed
⅓ cup minced fresh flat-leaf parsley
3 lemons cut in wedges

Cut the calamari tentacles into pieces and set aside. Place the calamari bodies in a pot of salted water and bring them to a boil. Simmer for 5 minutes to reduce liquid. Drain in a colander and cool to room temperature. Reserve.

In a large sauté pan, cook the bacon, onion, and peppers until the onion is translucent. Add the garlic, nuts, and seasonings and cook for several several minutes, or until the pine nuts brown somewhat. Add the wine, sherry, stock, and lemon juice; cook briskly over medium heat until the liquids are greatly reduced, 10 to 20 minutes. Let it cool and add the eggs, Parmesan, and enough bread crumbs to hold the mixture together.

Using a pastry bag with a large tip, stuff the calamari (don't overstuff) with the mixture. Dredge each piece in flour as it is stuffed and place it on a cake rack.

Heat the olive oil in a large skillet until smoking. Carefully, without crowding, arrange the stuffed calamari in the hot oil. Cover and cook for 2 to 3 minutes on a side to brown. (Be sure to cover the skillet because calamari pop in hot oil.) Remove the calamari from the oil and keep warm. To cook the tentacles, dredge in flour and either sauté in the same pan or deep-fry for several minutes until brown.

Serve on heated plates with lots of flat-leaf parsley and fresh lemon wedges.

SERVES 6 FOR DINNER, 10 AS A FIRST COURSE

soups

Tarator: A Bulgarian Cucumber Yogurt Soup with Walnuts

Chilled Coconut Cucumber Soup with Buttermilk, Yogurt, and Spanish Peanuts

Golden Gazpacho with Hazelnuts

Strawberry Gazpacho Sant Pau with Toasted Almonds

Creamy Peanut Soup

Asian-Style Curried Corn and Crabmeat Chowder with Cashews

Springtime Almond Asparagus Soup

Cream of Hazelnut Mushroom Soup

Chestnut Soup with Madeira

Mushroom Barley Soup with Escarole, Pine Nuts, and Poached Egg

Black Bean Soup with Andouille Sausage, Yams, and Cashews

Out-of-India Chicken Soup with Almonds

Tarator: A Bulgarian Cucumber Yogurt Soup with Walnuts

Linda hosts the food forum for Cleveland.com. A former Clevelander now living in San Francisco was a frequent poster as "Ootch." He told us about making a marvelous yogurt soup with garlic, walnuts, and dill. It sounded so good Linda asked for the recipe, and this awesome tangy cold soup with the walnut crunch and the dill garnish is the result. So we send our thanks to Chad Fox, a.k.a. Ootch, who grew up just a few miles from our house! We also thank his friend Lino's mother, Svetla, formerly a chef and bakery owner in Sophia, Bulgaria. Svetla, by the way, uses an entire bulb of garlic in this! She also wanted us to know that there are many tarators, as each region has its own variation, but this is the best!

2 large English cucumbers, trimmed and finely chopped (not puréed)

4 cups plain whole-milk yogurt, preferably Middle Eastern

4 very plump garlic cloves (more if preferred), pressed

2 tablespoons extra virgin olive oil or vegetable oil

⅔ cup lightly toasted, coarsely chopped walnuts

2 cups cold bottled (spring) water

Kosher salt and freshly ground black pepper

½ cup finely chopped fresh baby dill

In a large bowl, blend together the cucumber and the yogurt. Add the garlic, olive oil, and walnuts. Next add the water and blend well. Then season generously with salt and pepper. Blend thoroughly and chill.

To serve, ladle into soup plates and garnish lavishly with dill.

SERVES **6** TO **8**

Craig McNamara

There are vetches, clover, and fava beans, knee-high among the still-bare walnut trees, as green as Ireland. These vibrant cover crops growing in an orchard are a clear sign that an organic farmer works here.

The farmer's house is sequestered from the ranch by a wooded circle. Nearby a small, open, freestanding office is as comfortable as a living room with chairs, a desk, bookcases, and a collection of beautiful black-and-white photographs above and between the windows.

A couple of lambs and their mother are in an enclosure nearby and a beautiful cow in another, both student farm projects.

Craig McNamara and his family live here. The farm—or to use the California term, "ranch"—is 565 acres and the main crop is walnuts. McNamara grew up in the east among the intellectual and power elite of the nation. His father was the Secretary of Defense in the Kennedy and Johnson administrations. Craig's options in that environment were endless, but early on, he became a farmer, starting out with strawberries and other crops and gradually moving toward an organic and sustainable walnut operation. He has been working his Sierra Farm in the Central Valley for more than twenty-five years.

He is worried about American agriculture. In order to stay competitive in the world market, he says American farmers have to become more and more efficient. In the European Community agriculture is far more heavily subsidized than in the United States.

One of the reasons for this crisis, McNamara believes, is that the farmers have no political clout. They are a continually shrinking percentage of the total population, and it becomes harder and harder to arrest the attention of the broader society, and hence lawmakers.

For McNamara, and many other creative farmers, adding value to their crops on the farm may be a way out of a profitless environment. Someone is trying to develop a red walnut. "Why not?" he says. "They would look great on a salad."

But for Craig McNamara, the key to the future of farming is education. He has formed an organization called Farms that is specifically dedicated to making sure children learn about their food and where it comes from. The Great Valley Farm and Nature Center has been set up to help. Kids come and learn. It is tactile and participatory. They feel the soil, handle the equipment, feed the livestock, harvest the nuts. McNamara would like to see something like this made a part of every school curriculum, and his Web site helps people do that. It can be reached at www.farmleaders.org.

He wants to make sure that farmers survive, that the society they nourish understands who they are and what they do, and why it is so important. He wants to continue to harvest his high-quality walnuts. He also hopes he never has to cut down his trees and sell his land to a developer.

Chilled Coconut Cucumber Soup with Buttermilk, Yogurt, and Spanish Peanuts

English cucumbers are those long skinny, seedless ones. We like them because they are not waxed, so you can eat the skin as well as the flesh. If you grow cukes your-self, you can certainly use yours but remove the seeds first. Cucumbers and coconut milk really compliment each other nicely. The onion adds a lively note, while the Spanish peanuts in our garnish make a very mellow crunch. The flavors and tex-tures of this soup are really quite delightful!

1 English cucumber, grated, liquid retained
½ jumbo sweet onion, finely diced
1½ cups unsweetened coconut milk (see Basics, page 50)
2½ cups plain yogurt
2 cups buttermilk, plus more if needed
Salt and freshly ground white pepper to taste

FOR GARNISH
⅔ cup finely diced cucumber
⅓ cup coarsely chopped roasted Spanish peanuts
¼ cup minced fresh cilantro

Combine the grated cucumber and liquid, onions, coconut milk, yogurt, and buttermilk in a large mixing bowl. Blend thoroughly. Add salt and pepper and mix well. Cover and chill until you are ready to serve it, up to 8 hours. Taste the soup and adjust season-ings. If the soup is too thick, thin with more buttermilk.

Divide the diced cucumber among the soup plates, then pour the soup over it. Sprinkle with roasted peanuts and cilantro and serve.

SERVES 6 TO 8

Golden Gazpacho with Hazelnuts

Gazpacho is a cold soup that tastes like a combination of salad and vinaigrette. While its roots may go back to early Christianity, its more contemporary history is associated with Spain. It is best in late summer, when the tomatoes are right from the garden, but we have found a way to enjoy it throughout the year. Because Linda fills our yard with a vast variety of heirloom tomatoes, we always have a surfeit at the arrival of all, so we prepare pots of both red and yellow tomato purées. Here is our method: Coat the bottom of a very heavy pot with a film of olive oil. Fill the pot with a mixture of quartered tomatoes. Cover tightly and cook over very low heat until the tomatoes fall apart, stirring every 15 minutes. This will take about 1 hour for a 3-quart pot. When the tomatoes are cool, purée them through a food mill. Freeze the purée, unseasoned, in pint and quart containers. It will taste of summer even in the middle of winter!

1 cup toasted hazelnuts

6 plump garlic cloves, peeled and pressed

½ English cucumber, peeled and cut into chunks

½ large sweet onion, peeled and cut into quarters

6 cups tomato purée, plus more if desired (See Basics page 52)

3 tablespoons fresh cilantro leaves

¼ cup extra virgin olive oil, preferably Spanish

Kosher salt

6 drops Tabasco sauce

1 teaspoon freshly ground white pepper

3 tablespoons sherry vinegar

Minced fresh cilantro, chopped hazelnuts, and minced fresh chives for garnish

Place the nuts in the bowl of a food processor and pulse until very finely chopped. Add the garlic, cucumber, and onion and purée. Add 1 cup of the tomato purée and the cilantro. Purée the mixture completely.

Pour the mixture into a large mixing bowl. Vigorously whisk in the remaining tomato purée, olive oil, salt, Tabasco, pepper, and vinegar. Taste and adjust the seasonings. Chill for at least 4 hours.

Just before serving, adjust the seasonings again. Ladle the soup into serving bowls. Sprinkle with chopped nuts and fresh chives.

SERVES 6 TO 8

Strawberry Gazpacho Sant Pau with Toasted Almonds

Our guests love it! While strawberry gazpacho may sound crazy, it's amazing just how well garlic, onion, and cucumber marry with those luscious berries. As in many dishes in Catalonia, toasted almonds are used not only to add depth of flavor but to thicken as well. We have to thank Carme and Toni Ruscalleda, whose celebrated beachfront restaurant in Sant Pol de Mar, Spain, brings visitors from everywhere. Hailed as one of Spain's top chefs, the diminutive Carme has a way with flavor combinations that most of us only hope of developing. She is devoted to the favored ingredients of traditional Catalan cuisine, but her playfulness is apparent when she uses them in unexpected ways. Her lusty gazpacho, for example, celebrates the fact that one of the top agricultural products of the region around Sant Pau are large, luscious strawberries.

1 quart ripe strawberries, hulled

½ English cucumber, peeled and quartered

3 plump garlic cloves, peeled and smashed

1 stalk celery, cut into chunks

¼ very large sweet onion, skin removed

½ cup toasted slivered almonds, plus more for garnish

3 tablespoons fruit vinegar

1 teaspoon kosher salt, plus more if needed

½ teaspoon freshly ground white pepper

¼ teaspoon Tabasco sauce

1 cup apple juice or cider

⅔ cup finely diced cucumber

High-quality almond oil, or extra virgin olive oil, for garnish

In the bowl of a food processor, combine the berries, cucumber, garlic, celery, onion, nuts, and vinegar. Pulse until the ingredients are all finely chopped, then run the motor until the mixture is puréed. Scrape the sides of the bowl, add the salt, pepper, and Tabasco. Pulse again. Add the apple juice and pulse one more time.

Refrigerate the soup for at least 2 and up to 6 hours. Thin the soup, if needed, with some water. Divide the diced cucumber among the soup plates, then ladle the soup over them. Drizzle some oil over the soup and sprinkle with a few toasted almonds.

SERVES 6 TO 8

Timbo's Boiled Peanuts

"I brake for boiled peanuts" read a bumper sticker in Charleston.

We didn't brake when we saw a "Boiled Peanuts" sign, but we took good note of the location. We were on our way to one of the historic South Carolina plantations. But on our way back we stopped for Timbo's Boiled Peanuts. Linda had never eaten a boiled peanut and Fred hadn't tasted one since his Air Force days in Alabama.

Timbo's Boiled Peanuts are meant to be eaten today. They don't travel well and need refrigeration if they are not going to be consumed soon. We tasted all three of Timbo's varieties, and bought the Cajun-flavored style—delicious, and quite different from any other peanut you have eaten.

Timbo runs his little stand all day long after cooking the peanuts at his house in the evening. He works seventy-five to eighty hours a week, cooking and selling five hundred to six hundred pounds per week. He doesn't try to expand the business because he is too strung out to work any harder. (He has been doing this for maybe twelve years and in January of 1999 he was part of a *Travel and Leisure* article on South Carolina country food.)

We asked Timbo about canned boiled peanuts, which you can sometimes find in specialty food stores. He was diplomatic; he talked about the difference between "the edible and the enthusiastically edible."

Creamy Peanut Soup

Like other parts of the world that incorporated the peanut into their cuisines, the southeastern American colonies did, too. According to the late chef and culinary historian Bill Neal, "Peanut soup is a hallmark of eastern Virginia cooking and part of the legacy of African cooks who introduced the legume to North America." There are myriad recipes for such a soup in a host of old cookbooks, but, ultimately, we turned our attention to simply tasting our way through the creation of one that worked for us: not too thick, yet silky on the tongue; richly flavored without being overly sweet and cloying. We concluded that caramelized onions are a perfect match for the peanut butter. Dry Manzanillo sherry adds other flavor notes, creating a delightful mélange of tastes that transform peanuts from a sweet treat to a delicious savory instead.

4 tablespoons unsalted butter

1 dried red chile, crumbled

1 large Spanish onion, halved and thinly sliced

1 cup creamy peanut butter, preferably freshly made

5 cups rich chicken broth

½ teaspoon dried thyme

1⅔ cups heavy cream

¼ cup good quality Manzanillo sherry, or another dry sherry

Kosher salt and freshly ground white pepper

¼ cup coarsely chopped toasted peanuts

¼ cup minced fresh chives

Melt the butter in a 3-quart sauté pan over medium heat. Add the chile and onion. Cover and cook over medium-low heat, stirring occasionally, until the onions have caramelized, 30 to 40 minutes.

Stir in the peanut butter and whisk half of the broth and the thyme into the onion/peanut mixture. Then purée it in a food processor until smooth.

Pour the purée into a large, heavy saucepan. Add the remaining broth and 1 cup of the cream. Cook over low heat just until bubbling, then add the sherry, salt, and pepper. Slowly simmer for another 15 minutes. Adjust the seasonings before serving.

To serve, whip the remaining ⅔ cup heavy cream until it holds soft peaks. Ladle soup into heated soup bowls. Garnish the soup with generous dollops of whipped cream and sprinkle with toasted peanuts and chives.

SERVES **6** TO **8**

Asian-Style Curried Corn and Crabmeat Chowder with Cashews

This light, tomato-piqued crab chowder has a marvelous fragrance and delicious flavor. The mysterious nutty note comes from the addition of roasted cashew butter. For the finish, cilantro and chopped cashews add other satisfying punctuations of flavor and texture.

2 tablespoons vegetable oil

1 dried red chile, crumbled

2 plump garlic cloves, minced

1 bulb lemongrass, trimmed and minced (available in Asian markets and some supermarkets)

½ cup finely diced plump green onions or scallions

½ cup finely diced red bell pepper

2 medium tomatoes, peeled, seeded, and finely diced

1 tablespoon good-quality curry powder, preferably Madras-style

2 tablespoons roasted cashew butter

½ cup dry white wine

2 teaspoons soy sauce

Juice of 2 limes

6 cups rich fish stock

1 cup fresh corn kernels

1 pound lump crabmeat, thoroughly picked

Kosher salt and freshly ground pepper to taste

⅓ cup finely chopped fresh cilantro

⅔ cup chopped roasted cashews

Heat the vegetable oil in a large, heavy saucepan over medium heat. Add chile, garlic, and lemongrass and stir for 1 minute. Add onions, pepper, and tomatoes. Cover, reduce heat to low, and cook for 10 minutes, or until the onions are translucent and the peppers are tender. Be sure to stir from time to time. Add curry powder and cashew butter; stir until fragrant, about 1 minute.

Whisk in wine, soy sauce, lime juice, and fish stock. Cover, raise heat, and cook until mixture begins to bubble, about 5 minutes. Reduce heat to low and simmer briskly for 5 minutes. (This can be made ahead to this point.)

Just before serving, add the corn and crab. Increase the heat and cook briskly for 3 to 4 minutes, until the crabmeat and corn are hot. Stir in salt and pepper. Ladle into heated soup plates and sprinkle generously with cilantro and cashews.

SERVES 6 TO 8

Springtime Almond Asparagus Soup

This is a light and luscious soup. The flavor of almonds add a delightful exotic note to the freshness of the asparagus. It is simple to prepare and goes beautifully with a fish or poultry main course. Process the nuts in a mortar and pestle, or a food processor, and grind as finely as possible to become a pastelike mixture. It's worth looking for the first asparagus of the spring; they are especially delicious and aromatic.

4 tablespoons (½ stick) unsalted
   butter
1 large sweet onion, finely chopped
3 pounds asparagus, trimmed and
   cut into thirds
2 medium-sized Yukon gold
   potatoes, peeled and finely
   chopped
6 cups water or chicken stock
¼ cup fresh lemon juice

2 teaspoons fresh lemon thyme (or
   1 teaspoon dried)
⅔ cup thoroughly ground
   blanched almonds
⅛ teaspoon pure almond extract
1 cup heavy cream
¼ cup dry sherry
Sea salt and freshly ground white
   pepper to taste
½ cup heavy cream, whipped

In a heavy-bottomed saucepan, melt the butter over medium heat. Add the onions, chopped asparagus, and potatoes. Cover and cook over the lowest heat possible, to sweat but not brown them. After 10 minutes, add stock, lemon juice, and thyme. Increase the heat and bring to a boil. Next reduce heat to very low, cover, and cook for at least 20 minutes, or until asparagus stems are falling apart. Stir in the ground almonds and almond extract.

Purée the solids with the liquids in a food processor. Rinse the saucepan well, then return the soup to it. Stir in the cream, sherry, salt, and pepper.

To serve, heat the soup until very hot then ladle into soup plates. Spoon a dollop of whipped cream onto the center of each. Using a fork, draw the cream into a decorative circle over the soup and serve.

SERVES 6 TO 8

Blue Diamond

"Ben & Jerry's" says the shipping label. Two thousand pounds of almonds are packed into a cardboard box on a wooden pallet, bar coded, and readied for Vermont. In fact, six tons of California Blue Diamond almonds are on the platform awaiting shipment to the famous ice cream maker—and that's a small order. California farmers have grown as many as 830 million pounds of almonds in one season and soon will hit the billion-pound mark. Well over half of them are processed in a huge state-of-the-art plant in Sacramento, where the computer, the laser, and the bar-code rule.

Blue Diamond got its start in 1910 as a processing and marketing co-op for California almond growers. Today there are six thousand almond farmers in California and thirty-eight hundred of them bring their product to this ninety-six-acre site. In peak season twelve hundred workers keep the lines running sixteen hours a day.

When the farmer brings a truckload of almonds, a sample is taken and carefully examined. Payment to the grower will depend on its quality. The nuts go from silos to the top floor of a five-story building, where the cleaning, grading, and sorting operation begins. Using lasers or infrared detectors the process knocks out items that seem too dark or too light. Sand, shell fragments, damaged nuts, and, for confectioners, for whom the perfect nut is essential, the imperfectly peeled are excluded. Every line is backed up by people who might see something the process might miss.

Eventually the system produces exactly what the customer wants—whole, blanched, chopped, sliced, shredded, diced, big, or little almonds. To keep the product fresh until the order comes, there is enough cold storage for millions of pounds. No single operation in the world deals with as many nuts as Blue Diamond.

Sam Cunningham is the director of the Almond Research Center, headquartered at Blue Diamond. Nutrition and health are always on his mind. In an instant he can give you chapter and verse on the chemistry of almonds. He speaks of cyanide, glucose, amygdaline, prunasin, mamdelonitrite, and most important of all, benzaldehyde, the key to the basic almond taste. He can tell you how almonds might help fight diabetes, allergies, cancer, heart disease, and high blood pressure. He sees the health food industry as a place to go with almond paste, almond butter, and almond milk for the lactose intolerant. Nut milks, made from grinding, soaking, and pressing the nuts, were widely used in the past as a substitute for mother's milk for children and for cows' milk in cooking. "Tastier than soy milk," he says. His son came up with a slogan and put it on a big sign in the office that says, "Hey. Leave those cows alone!"

Cream of Hazelnut Mushroom Soup

You've never tasted a creamy mushroom soup like this before. When incorporated into a mushroom soup, hazelnuts add an awesome depth of flavor. It's appropriate that our mushroom cooking tips come from someone who is now showcasing his culinary skills in America's hazelnut-growing state. The maven of mushrooms, Jack Czarnecki, taught us the trick of using some soy sauce to facilitate the cooking of fresh mushrooms. He and his wife Heidi now forage for wild mushrooms in the mountains of Oregon and offer the results in their restaurant, The Palmer House near Dundee, Oregon.

1 to 1.4 ounces dried porcini mushrooms, thoroughly rinsed

2 cups boiling water

4 tablespoons unsalted butter

4 plump shallots, coarsely chopped

1 pound cremini mushrooms, thinly sliced

2 teaspoons soy sauce

3 cups chicken or vegetable stock

²⁄₃ cup finely chopped toasted hazelnuts, ground into a paste

1 cup heavy cream, plus more for garnish

A generous pinch of freshly grated nutmeg

Kosher salt and freshly ground white pepper to taste

Juice of ½ lemon

½ cup sour cream

⅓ cup coarsely chopped hazelnuts

2 tablespoons minced fresh chives

Put the porcini mushrooms in a small bowl and cover with boiling water; let them soak for 1 hour. Then carefully squeeze the excess liquid into the bowl and chop the mushrooms; set aside. Pour the mushroom water through a coffee filter and reserve.

Melt the butter in a large, heavy saucepan. Add the shallots, creminis, chopped porcini, and the soy sauce. Cover and braise over very low heat, stirring often, until the cremini mushrooms are very tender, about 10 minutes. Uncover and add the reserved mushroom liquid and the stock.

Bring the liquids to a boil, then reduce the heat to simmer and cook for 30 minutes. Add the hazelnut paste and cook for an additional 10 minutes. Using a stick blender or a food processor, purée the mixture thoroughly.

Stir in 1 cup heavy cream, the nutmeg, salt, and pepper. Reheat until just hot, not boiling. Add the lemon juice and simmer very slowly over low heat for 10 minutes.

Meanwhile blend together the sour cream, 1 tablespoon heavy cream, and the chopped nuts.

Serve in heated soup plates with a dollop of nut cream in the center, sprinkled with chives.

SERVES 6 TO 8

Chestnut Soup with Madeira

We spent a splendid December week on the island of Madeira. The temperatures were balmy and the market filled with exceptional holiday foods. Our stay at Funchal's fabled Reid's Hotel was a perfect way to experience life as it had been when men always dined in white ties and women always wore floor-length evening gowns. Reid's roots are British, but its founders were also deeply involved in the production of the island's most famous eponymous export. What could be better than this luscious, creamy chestnut soup lavishly enriched with fine Madeira wine. It is also a reminder that the good life is still available to all of us.

6 tablespoons unsalted butter, plus
    more if needed
1 large yellow onion, minced
2 pounds fresh chestnuts, roasted
    and peeled (or 1½ pounds
    dried, first boiled for 1 hour)
2 teaspoons minced fresh tarragon
    (or 1 teaspoon dried)
6 cups rich chicken stock

Several pinches ground cayenne
Freshly grated nutmeg to taste
⅓ cup Madeira, plus more if
    desired
Up to 2 cups heavy cream
Kosher salt and freshly ground
    white pepper to taste
1 plump garlic clove, smashed
6 to 8 thin slices French bread

In the bottom of a large, heavy saucepan, melt 3 tablespoons of the butter. Add the onion and cook, covered, over very low heat until the onions are wilted, 4 to 8 minutes. Add the chestnuts, tarragon, and stock.

Bring the stock to a boil, cover, and cook over low heat until the chestnuts are about to fall apart, 45 minutes to 1 hour. Purée the mixture in a food processor. For extra smoothness, put it through a food mill as well.

Return the purée to the saucepan and season it with cayenne, nutmeg, and Madeira. Add enough heavy cream to make a soup and cook it over medium heat until the cream has thickened somewhat. Season with salt and pepper.

Just before serving, combine the remaining butter with the crushed garlic in a large skillet. Cook over medium-high heat until the butter has melted. Discard the garlic and fry the bread slices, adding more butter if needed, until the croutons are golden on each side.

To serve, place a crouton in the bottom of each heated soup plate. Ladle the soup over the croutons and if desired, pour a bit more Madeira in the center.

SERVES 6 TO 8

Mushroom Barley Soup with Escarole, Pine Nuts, and Poached Egg

So, Linda's grandma Weller never quite made mushroom barley soup like this, but Linda's love of that soup did lead us here. The poached egg is a real surprise. But it works wonderfully well with the bitter escarole, or rapini, and the natural sweetness of the mushrooms. The pine nuts add a toasty crunch to the whole.

1 ounce dried mushrooms,
    preferably porcini
1 cup boiling water
5 tablespoons unsalted butter
⅔ cup pine nuts
1 pound portobello mushrooms,
    trimmed and finely chopped
1 cup finely chopped yellow onions
1 teaspoon dried thyme

7 cups vegetable stock or plain
    water
¾ cup medium pearl barley
Kosher salt and freshly ground black
    pepper to taste
4 cups trimmed and chopped
    escarole or rapini
6 to 8 poached eggs
Tabasco sauce

Chop the dried mushrooms finely, then cover with 1 cup of boiling water and soak for 30 minutes.

Melt 3 tablespoons of the butter in a large soup pot over medium heat. Add the pine nuts and sauté until browned, stirring constantly. Using a slotted spoon, transfer the nuts to a small bowl.

Add the remaining butter to the pot and melt over medium heat. Then add the portobello mushrooms and onions. Reduce the heat and cover, cooking until the mushrooms release their liquid, about 5 minutes. Add the thyme, and porcini mushrooms and their water. Then add the stock or water, barley, salt, and pepper.

Bring the soup to a boil, then lower the heat and simmer, partially covered, until the barley is tender, 40 to 50 minutes. Add the escarole and cook for another 10 minutes, stirring from time to time.

Just before serving, poach the eggs. Hold them in a bowl of warm water.

Place an egg into each heated soup plate. Season with a few grains of salt and pepper. Add 1 drop of Tabasco to the top of the egg. Ladle the soup around, then over the egg. Sprinkle lavishly with the nuts and serve.

SERVES 6 TO 8

Black Bean Soup with Andouille Sausage, Yams, and Cashews

Caramelized onions and garlic add a pleasing richness to black bean soup. Then, too, there is the zesty flavor from spicy smoked andouille sausage. We think that the diced sweet potato also adds very satisfying as well as colorful and flavorful counterpoints. The cashews are the perfect final touch. This hearty soup makes a marvelous Sunday supper. Accompany this soup with good corn bread and a big salad.

1 pound black beans, carefully picked over

12 cups water, plus extra for soaking beans

1 bay leaf

½ teaspoon freshly grated nutmeg

½ teaspoon finely ground black pepper

¼ teaspoon ground cloves

2 large yams or sweet potatoes, peeled and cut into ½-inch cubes

3 tablespoons unsalted butter

1 cup finely diced onions

3 pressed garlic cloves

1 pound andouille sausage, sliced into ½-inch-thick circles

2 teaspoons kosher salt, plus more if needed

1 cup dry sherry

Juice of 1 lemon

2 hard-boiled eggs, sieved

⅓ cup minced fresh flat-leaf parsley

⅔ cup coarsely chopped cashews

Combine the beans and enough water to cover them in a large saucepan. Cover and bring to a boil over high heat. Remove the saucepan from the heat and let the beans stand, covered, for 1 hour. Drain thoroughly and transfer the beans to a heavy soup pot.

Add 12 cups water, the bay leaf, nutmeg, pepper, and cloves. Cover the soup pot and bring to a boil over high heat. Reduce the heat and simmer until beans are very mushy, about 3 hours.

While beans are cooking, fill a small saucepan with water and bring it to a boil. Add the sweet potato cubes and cook for 10 minutes. Drain thoroughly and reserve parboiled sweet potatoes.

Also while beans are cooking, melt the butter in a cast-iron skillet over medium-high heat. Add the onions and garlic. Cook, stirring often, until somewhat golden, 10 to 15 minutes. Add the sausage slices and cook until they are are somewhat browned. Reserve.

When the beans are mushy, remove the pot from the heat. With a large slotted spoon or Chinese frying strainer, transfer the beans to the bowl of a food processor fitted with a metal blade. Add 2 cups of bean liquid and purée thoroughly. Return the purée to the soup pot and add enough liquid to make a pleasingly thick soup, about 4 more cups. Add the salt, potato cubes, and sausage mixture. Cook the soup, covered, over low heat until bubbling. Stir in the sherry and lemon juice. Cook until the sweet potatoes are tender, 15 to 20 minutes. Adjust the seasonings, adding more salt, pepper, or spices.

Ladle the soup into heated soup plates. Garnish with some egg, parsley, and cashews.

SERVES 6 TO 10

Out-of-India Chicken Soup with Almonds

This began life as a soup we enjoyed in Spain, but something was missing; it was just not exciting. As a last-ditch effort to rescue it, Linda decided that a good curry powder and some hot chile would give it the oomph we were seeking. Remember, like the Spanish, the myriad cuisines of India also use ground nuts as a flavorful thickening ingredient. The soup is a lusty one that can be made ahead; in fact, it is improved by an overnight rest. Just save the yogurt for almost serving time. If your palate enjoys it, another chile might be in order.

6 tablespoons unsalted butter

2 plump garlic cloves, minced

2/3 cup finely diced yellow onion

1 hot chile, preferably red, minced

1 carrot, finely chopped

1/2 green pepper, finely diced

1 tablespoon minced fresh ginger

1 tablespoon good-quality Madras-style curry powder

1 skinless, boneless chicken breast, cut into 3/4-inch cubes

3 cups chicken stock, plus more if needed

1/2 cup chopped fresh cilantro

3/4 cup ground blanched almonds

1 cup heavy cream

Kosher salt and freshly ground white pepper to taste

1 cup plain yogurt

In a heavy soup pot, melt the butter over medium heat. Add the garlic, onion, chile, carrot, pepper, ginger, and curry powder. Cover tightly and cook over low heat, stirring often, until the vegetables are soft. Add the chicken, cover and cook, stirring often, until the chicken is thoroughly cooked, about 10 minutes. Stir in 1 cup of the stock and 1/4 cup of the cilantro. Increase the heat to medium and stir, uncovered, until the mixture begins to bubble. Remove it from the heat and let it stand for at least 10 minutes.

Purée the mixture either using a wand in the pot, or transferring the mixture to a food processor. Pulse until the mixture is thoroughly puréed. Return it to the pot, add the remaining stock, almonds, cream, salt, and pepper. Cook until the soup is about to bubble. If it's too thick, add more stock. Otherwise, whisk in the yogurt and cook to heat through.

Adjust the seasonings and serve it in heated soup plates, lavishly garnished by the remaining cilantro.

SERVES **6** TO **8**

yeast breads and cakes, tea breads, pancakes, waffles, and coolers

A Rye Bread with Nuts and Currants

Bread with Two Olives and Pistachios

Linda's Challah with Raisins and Hazelnuts

Coarse-Grain Bread with Hickory Nuts and Beechnuts

Provençale Walnut Bread

Kallappam (Coconut Rice Pancakes)

Sweet Crescents with Fruit Preserves and Pecans

Cherry Pecan Ring Küchen

Rhubarb and Almond Coffee Cake with Cinnamon and Cardamom

Sour Cream Coffee Cake with Brazil Nuts

Almond Butter Bread

Lovely Cornmeal and Chestnut Griddle Cakes

Buckwheat Pancakes with Toasted Hickory Nuts

Silky Lemon Pancakes with Buttery Maple Pecan Sauce

Chestnut Waffles with a Hint of Orange

Banana and Cashew Cooler

Coconut Cooler

A Rye Bread with Nuts and Currants

There is a rich mélange of flavors in this earthy, sweet, and crunchy rye bread. It's dense, yet very nutty in texture and flavor. It is also very, very delicious whether it's just sliced and slathered with good butter and served with a pot of thick pea soup or vegetables soup. You might toast it and serve it warm for breakfast.

2¼ cups warm water

1 tablespoon plus 2 teaspoons dry yeast

3¼ cups rye flour

3½ cups unbleached flour, plus more if needed

1 tablespoon sea salt

1 teaspoon ground anise

⅓ cup Lyle's Golden Syrup (see Sources, page 313) or corn syrup

2 tablespoons walnut or pecan oil

1¼ cups mixed coarsely chopped, toasted pecans and walnuts

¾ cup currants

2 tablespoons cornmeal

1 tablespoon melted unsalted butter

Combine the yeast with ½ cup warm water and blend thoroughly. Set yeast aside in a warm place to bubble, about 15 minutes.

In the bowl of an electric mixer fitted with a paddle, combine 3 cups each of rye flour and the unbleached flour, plus the salt and anise. Add the yeast mixture, remaining water, corn syrup, and nut oil. Mix on low speed until blended. Stir in the nuts and currants. Blend in an additional ¼ cup rye flour and ½ cup unbleached flour. If you are going to knead it in the mixer, change to the dough hook and begin kneading, adding more flour as needed. Knead for 10 to 12 minutes. Dough will be rather tacky but not gooey. If you are kneading by hand, do so on a well-floured surface, adding more unbleached flour as needed.

Knead by hand, or with dough hook for 10 minutes, adding unbleached flour if needed, until the dough is smooth and pliable. Turn out onto a lightly floured surface and knead for an additional few minutes.

Lightly oil a large, warm mixing bowl. Place dough in bowl, turning once to coat all surfaces with oil. Cover the dough with plastic wrap and let it rise in a warm place until doubled in size, 1½ to 2 hours.

Place the top rack in the upper third of the oven; put a large baking tile on it. Preheat the oven and baking tile to 425°F. Sprinkle a large pizza pan, preferably one that has perforations in the bottom, with cornmeal.

Punch the dough down. Shape the dough into a large round bread. Place dough on the prepared pan, cover with plastic, and let it rise in a warm place until doubled in size, about 1 hour. Brush top with melted butter.

Bake in preheated oven until done, about 55 to 65 minutes. If the top gets too dark, cover it loosely with a sheet of foil. The bread will sound hollow when rapped on bottom. The internal temperature should be about 210°F.

Remove the bread from the oven and let it cool on a rack.

MAKES A **10**-INCH ROUND BREAD

Bread with Two Olives and Pistachios

This turns out to be one of the most delicious breads we've made. The olives and pistachios both contrast and compliment one another, lending an outstanding flavor to the bread. Its texture is tender, yet with lots of holes. We always try to have a stash of nut flours (see Sources, page 311) available, often storing them in the freezer. If you don't have the pistachio flour, just use regular flour, but you will be missing another layer of delightful flavor.

1 small (³⁄₅-ounce) cake fresh yeast
    or 1 scant tablespoon dry yeast
¾ cup warm water
3½ cups unbleached flour, more if
    needed
3 tablespoons pistachio flour
Sea salt

6 ounces pitted green olives
6 ounces pitted black olives
½ cup lightly toasted, coarsely
    chopped pistachio nuts
2 tablespoons olive oil
2 tablespoons pistachio oil

Proof the yeast by blending together the broken-apart yeast cake with ¼ cup of the water. Place in a warm spot until bubbling, about 10 minutes.

Combine the flours, salt, olives, nuts, oils, remaining water, and proofed yeast in the bowl of an electric mixer fitted with a paddle. Mix until the dough is evenly blended. Change to a dough hook and knead until the olives are thoroughly broken apart (the liquid from the olives should provide enough moisture for the dough) and the dough feels very soft and elastic, about 10 minutes. Add more flour if the dough is too sticky, a bit more nut oil if the dough is too dry.

Thoroughly oil a large bowl, place the dough in it, cover it with plastic, and let it rise in a warm place until doubled, 1½ to 2 hours.

Place a large pizza tile on a rack in the middle of the oven. Preheat the oven to 400°F.

Shape the bread into a large round loaf and place on a pizza pan, preferably one that has a perforated bottom. Let it rise, lightly covered with an inverted plastic bag, for 1 hour, or until doubled in size. Bake the bread for at least 55 minutes, or until the bread sounds hollow when rapped on the bottom and an instant thermometer inserted into the center reads 210 to 212°F.

Transfer the bread to a cooling rack.

MAKES 1 LARGE ROUND BREAD

Linda's Challah with Raisins and Hazelnuts

Linda has been making challah, a traditional Jewish braided bread made with eggs, for more than forty years. It welcomes the Sabbath and is an integral part of nearly every holiday and other ceremonial occasions like weddings and bar mitzvahs. Once in a while, particularly for a holiday, we'll add some raisins, or chopped dried apricots, and nuts. Any leftovers make sublime French toast. By the way, we find that the best way to make this bread is to weigh the whole dough, then divide it into three equal pieces. If you want to make one jumbo braided bread, plan to bake it for about 75 to 80 minutes, and cover the top loosely with foil after 45 to 55 minutes of baking.

1 tablespoon dry yeast

2¼ cups warm water

⅓ cup honey

3 large eggs, lightly beaten

¼ cup hazelnut oil

6 to 8 cups unbleached flour

1 tablespoon kosher salt

1 cup raisins or chopped dried apricots

1 cup coarsely chopped, toasted hazelnuts

1 egg yolk beaten with 2 teaspoons water

In a warm bowl, combine the yeast, ¼ cup of the water, and 1 tablespoon of the honey. Mix it well and let it rest in a warm place until the mixture bubbles, about 10 minutes.

In the bowl of an electric mixer fitted with a paddle, turn the motor on low and combine the remaining water and honey, then add the eggs and oil. Finally add the yeast mixture. Very gradually add 6 cups of the flour, then the salt, raisins, and nuts. Blend thoroughly, slowly adding more flour until the dough pulls away from the bowl. Then let mixture rest, lightly covered with a towel, for 10 minutes.

Turn dough out on a well-floured surface and knead, adding flour as needed, until smooth and elastic, about 15 minutes. Or knead with a dough hook, and finish it by hand for 5 minutes. Place dough in a well-oiled bowl, cover it with plastic, and let it rise in a warm place until doubled.

Punch the dough down. Then cover it and let the dough rise for 1 hour longer. Thoroughly oil 2 10-inch-long bread pans.

Punch the dough down, then divide it into 2 equal chunks. Divide the first in half. Shape 1 piece to fit in the bottom of the pan. Divide the other piece in half and form it into 2 balls that you place over the large piece in the pan. Repeat the process for the second loaf. Place the pans in a warm place, cover them loosely with plastic, and let the dough rise until the bread is slightly above the tops of the pans, about 1 hour.

Meanwhile, place the rack in the top third of the oven and preheat it to 400°F. When the loaves are ready, brush the tops with egg wash and bake them in the preheated oven for 40 to 50 minutes, or until an instant-read thermometer inserted in the center registers about 210°F.

Remove the breads from the pans and place on racks to cool.

MAKES **2** 10-INCH LOAVES

Coarse-Grain Bread with Hickory Nuts and Beechnuts

It's been many years since the very young Justin Rashid, a forager of wild foods, received a call from his partner-to-be, Larry Forgione, the New York chef who inspired Americans to celebrate American food. "Can you get me some beechnuts?" the chef asked. The forager said he could but he warned the chef that they would be very expensive because of the hours it takes to collect them and open the prickly shell for a very tiny kernel. Nearly twenty years later, we sat in Justin's Petoskey, Michigan, office of American Spoon Foods and talked about the once abundant wild nuts in the northern forests. One can still obtain all these wild nuts from American Spoon Foods (see Sources, page 311). They are costly, but you can certainly substitute pecans or walnuts for them in this recipe.

1 cup cracked wheat

½ cup lavender honey

2 teaspoons sea salt

2 tablespoons unsalted butter, plus more

1⅔ cups boiling water

2 tablespoons active dry yeast

1 cup warm water

1 cup whole wheat flour

5 to 7 cups unbleached flour

1 cup chopped mixed hickory and beechnuts, lightly toasted

3 tablespoons melted butter

In a small bowl, combine the cracked wheat, honey, sea salt, and butter. Pour boiling water over them and stir until the butter is melted, then let it cool.

While the mixture is cooling, proof the yeast by combining the yeast with ¼ cup of the warm water. Stir to dissolve the yeast, then set it aside in a warm place.

When the cracked wheat mixture has cooled and the yeast is bubbling, combine the two mixtures. Add the remaining ¾ cup water.

Combine the whole wheat flour and 5 cups of the unbleached flour in the bowl of an electric mixer fitted with a paddle. Pour cracked wheat/yeast mixture over the flour and blend. Then blend in the nuts.

Change to a dough hook and knead for 10 to 20 minutes on the lowest setting, adding flour as needed to make a dough that is a bit tacky but not sticky.

Turn the dough onto a lightly floured board and gently knead by hand for 5 additional minutes. Transfer the dough to a large, lightly oiled bowl, cover with plastic wrap, and let it rise in a warm place until doubled, 1 to 2 hours.

Punch the dough down, divide it in half, and form it into 2 loaves by patting each half into a flat oval. Then fold each oval in half and flatten them down on the seam, tucking the ends under. Place each piece in a well-oiled loaf pan that is 9×5 inches.

Cover pans with plastic and let the dough rise for 1 hour, or until it reaches above the top of pans. At the same time, preheat the oven to 350°F.

Bake loaves for 50 to 60 minutes, or until the internal temperature reaches 210°F. Immediately brush loaves with melted butter and let them rest for 5 minutes.

Then remove loaves from pans and place on racks to cool.

MAKES **2** 9×5-INCH LOAVES

There is a popular cereal called Nut n' Honey. The name worked well in television commercials: A spouse would call out, "What are you eating?" And the response would be, "Nut n' Honey." This cereal actually does contain both nuts and honey.

Diamond Walnut

Shortly after some California almond growers came up with the Blue Diamond almond cooperative, a group of enterprising walnut growers created a cooperative of their own—and they also used the word "Diamond."

Like their almond friends, the walnut people also wanted an image of value and solidity, so although the almond co-op had first dibs on the diamond, the walnut people, way back in 1912, decided to use it too; they just left off the "blue."

While not on the scale of Sacramento's Blue Diamond, this is still a very big place, thirteen acres under one roof, built in 1956. From early September to mid-November, it handles over two million pounds of nuts a day. They are cleaned, cracked, and sorted and then every nut whisks past one of the acoustic or laser sorters, installed at a cost of a over eight million dollars to insure quality. Backed up by sharp-eyed human sorters, every blemished nut, every tiny shell fragment is banished.

Outside, three huge polygons can hold forty-seven million pounds each of unprocessed nuts. Refrigerated "butlers" or silos hold three and a half million pounds each of the processed walnuts. They are kept cool in a low oxygen environment at 45 to 55 percent humidity until they are ready for shipping.

While the almond growers have no major competitors overseas, the walnut people are very nervous about China. That country already has more walnut acreage than the United States, and Turkey is coming on strong as well.

The big difference between the Chinese and the California growers is production and processing. California's yield is vastly greater per tree, per acre. The walnut handlers in China also have nothing to compare with the cutting-edge, hyper-high-tech processing lines of California.

So the walnut farmers have to keep doing more and more of whatever it takes to stay ahead technically and agriculturally. So far, so good. They are keeping their markets.

Provençale Walnut Bread

The French have long known that slices of very nutty walnut bread are the perfect accompaniment for many cheeses, especially those made with goat milk. While we've been making walnut breads for years, this particular recipe is inspired by an especially delicious loaf we found to be totally irresistible in the Tuesday Market in Vaison la Romaine. If you serve this with cheese, cut the bread slices fairly thin. This bread is also excellent when thickly cut and lightly grilled or toasted.

2 tablespoons active dry yeast	2 teaspoons freshly ground black pepper
2 tablespoons honey	1 tablespoon herbs de Provence
1/4 cup warm water	2 cups whole milk, warmed
4 cups unbleached flour	1/2 cup walnut oil
1 cup rye flour	1 1/2 cups lightly toasted broken walnut meats
1 tablespoon kosher salt	

Combine the yeast, honey, and water in a small bowl and blend well. Set it aside in a warm place until bubbling, about 10 minutes.

In a large mixing bowl, combine 3 cups of the unbleached flour, the rye flour, salt, pepper, and herbs. Add the yeast mixture, milk, and walnut oil and mix thoroughly either by hand or with the paddle attachment of an electric mixer. Stir in the walnuts and mix until they are evenly distributed. If the mixture is very wet, gradually add small amounts of flour just until the dough holds together, although it will still be sticky and shaggy.

On a well-floured surface, knead, adding small amounts of flour, until the dough is soft but rather sticky, 5 to 10 minutes. If the dough is too firm it will be too dry after baking. Incorporate any nuts that fall onto the board.

Turn the dough into a well-oiled bowl, cover it with plastic, and let it rise in a warm place until doubled in volume, about 1 to 2 hours.

Grease a large baking sheet.

Punch the dough down and turn it onto a lightly floured surface. Divide it in half. To form loaves: Pat each half into a flat oval, fold the long sides into the middle; then fold the ends over as well. Pinch the seams together.

The bread at this point will be about 7 inches long and about 4 1/4 inches wide. Place the loaf seam-side down on the baking sheet. Repeat with the other loaf, making certain that they are a considerable distance from one another. Using your hands, firmly shape the loaves so they are not too wide. Then cover them loosely with plastic and let them rise in a warm place until nearly doubled in size, about 1 hour.

Meanwhile preheat the oven to 375°F.

Bake the loaves for 35 to 45 minutes, or until the tops are thoroughly browned and an instant-read thermometer inserted into the center reads about 210°F.

Remove the loaves from the pan and cool them on a rack.

MAKES 2 LOAVES

Kallappam (Coconut Rice Pancakes)

These are really very tender flatbreads that are a delicious accompaniment to any of our spicy dishes. They are made with a lightly fermented batter that is blended with coconut paste made from fresh (young) coconut. We first tasted them at the Kochi home of Nimmy Paul, where they were served with a very spicy wet curry. Like so many of her recipes, they are from a glorious book of Nimmy's family recipes, hand-written for her by her very talented mother. If you must work with dried, unsweetened coconut, soak it for several hours with some coconut milk, then drain it somewhat and grind it in a small grinder or food processor.

1½ cups rice flour

1½ tablespoons semolina

¾ teaspoon active dry yeast

3 tablespoons superfine sugar

½ teaspoon ground cumin

¾ cup water

½ teaspoon kosher salt

1½ cups grated fresh coconut,
    ground into a paste

In a medium-sized mixing bowl combine the flour, semolina, yeast, sugar, and cumin. Gradually whisk in the water, making a thick batter. Cover it loosely and set it aside in a warm place for 6 hours, or until the batter smells somewhat fermented. (It will rise and fall, during this period.) Stir in the salt and coconut. Allow the batter to stand at room temperature for another hour. It should be the consistency of cake batter. (If it is too thick, thin it with coconut milk or water.)

To cook, heat a large nonstick frying pan or griddle over medium heat. Ladle ¼ cup of batter onto the pan, gently patting it into a circle that is about 3½ inches in diameter and ½ inch thick. Repeat several times if there is room.

Fry for about 2 to 3 minutes on the first side, or until bubbles appear on top and the bottom is rather golden, then turn and fry the other side until the pancake is springy to a light touch and the bottom is also light gold. Keep them warm until all the pancakes are prepared.

Serve warm, as a bread, with any savory Indian dish.

SERVES 6 (MAKES ABOUT 12 PANCAKES)

Sweet Crescents with Fruit Preserves and Pecans

Plan ahead because this heavenly yeast pastry spends the night in the refrigerator. These sweet and nutty pastries were a part of Linda's childhood. Then they became one of her son Andrew's favorite treats. In the years he was a student at Wesleyan University, his Nana Gert saw him frequently because she'd let him know they had just come out of the oven. They'd be perfectly cool when he arrived at her New Haven door. We happen to enjoy making these with two different preserves, 1 cup of Red Haven peach preserves and 1 cup cherry preserves. Both come from American Spoon Foods (see Sources, page 311).

1 tablespoon active dry
   yeast
¼ cup warm water
1 cup (8 ounces; 2 sticks) unsalted
   butter
1 cup heavy cream
3 egg yolks, beaten
4 cups unbleached flour
1⅓ cups superfine sugar

2 tablespoons ground cinnamon
½ cup raisins
½ cup finely chopped dried
   apricots
2 cups fruit preserves
1 cup finely chopped lightly toasted
   pecans
3 egg whites, beaten to soft
   peaks

Combine the yeast and water in a small bowl, mix, and set aside in a warm place.

Melt the butter, remove from the heat, and whisk in the heavy cream. When the mixture is no longer hot, pour it into the bowl of an electric mixer fitted with a paddle. With the motor on the lowest speed, add the egg yolks and yeast mixture. Then add the flour and ⅓ cup of the sugar. Mix well, scrape the bowl, and mix again. Cover it with plastic and refrigerate overnight.

Remove the bowl from the refrigerator and let it stand until it comes to room temperature. Divide the dough into 6 equal parts.

Preheat the oven to 350°F.

Arrange your "fillings": Blend together the remaining sugar and cinnamon. In another bowl, blend together the raisins and apricots.

On a lightly floured surface, roll the first piece of dough into a circle about 12 inches in diameter. Spread with ⅓ cup of the preserves. Sprinkle with cinnamon/sugar mixture, raisin mixture, and nuts. (Be sure to save some of the cinnamon mixture for topping.)

Slice the circle into 8 pie-shaped wedges. Roll each wedge from the large part to the center. Bend slightly into a crescent shape and place on a nongreased, noninsulated cookie sheet. Repeat until all crescents are made, allowing about 1½ inches between the pastries. Then brush the tops with some egg white and sprinkle with some cinnamon-sugar.

Bake until the tops are nicely browned, 25 to 35 minutes. Transfer the pastries to cooling racks. Store in a tightly sealed container.

MAKES ABOUT **4** DOZEN

Cherry Pecan Ring Küchen

We once spent a morning in a cherry-processing plant in Wenatchee, Washington. It was better than being in a candy factory. That turned us into lovers of fresh cherries, and we buy them anytime they are available. Add pecans to those luscious fruits and you have a perfect marriage. This is a marvelous dough, tasty and delicate. Because it is refrigerated, this is a great recipe for a weekend brunch. Just roll it out a few hours before the guests are to arrive and they can enjoy the küchens shortly after they are baked and glazed.

1 cup milk

½ cup superfine sugar

1 teaspoon salt

1 stick (8 tablespoons) unsalted
  butter

2¼ teaspoons active dry yeast

¼ cup warm water

1 large egg

4 cups unbleached flour

1 cup dark-brown sugar

1½ cup chopped pecans

2¼ pounds (7 cups) fresh cherries
  (preferably tart), pitted

1½ cups confectioners' sugar

2 tablespoons milk, plus more if
  needed

2 teaspoons fresh lemon juice

1 teaspoon pure vanilla extract

To make the küchen: In a small saucepan, scald the milk. Stir in the sugar, salt, and butter. Let it stand until lukewarm.

In a small bowl, combine the yeast with the warm water. Put it in a warm place until the mixture bubbles, about 10 minutes.

In the bowl of an electric mixer, or if you are making it by hand, with a large mixing spoon, combine the milk mixture, yeast, egg, and 2 cups of the flour. Beat until the mixture is smooth. Add the remaining flour and mix until the batter is stiff. Scrape the sides, then cover the bowl with plastic wrap and refrigerate for at least 2 hours or up to 2 days.

Divide the dough into 2 equal pieces. In a small bowl, blend the brown sugar and pecans.

On a well-floured surface, roll the first piece of dough into a rectangle that is 12 inches high by 18 inches wide. Leave a 1-inch border around the pastry, and sprinkle evenly with nut mixture and cherries. Working with the wide side, carefully roll it up as a jelly roll and seal the seam. Move it into a ring or horseshoe shape, then gently transfer it to a large shallow-sided, well-greased baking sheet. Repeat the steps for a second ring. If you are making a horseshoe shape, be sure to press the ends closed, too.

Using a sharp knife, make slashes at 2-inch intervals partway through each ring. Gently twist or pull these slashes open. Put the baking sheet in a warm place, and cover the rings loosely with plastic or tea towels. Let it rise for 1 hour.

Meanwhile, preheat oven to 375°F.

Bake küchens for 25 minutes, or until golden brown.

To make the icing: Shortly before the rings are done, pour the sugar into a small mixing bowl. Add the milk, lemon juice, and vanilla and whisk together until the icing is smooth and creamy. If more moisture is needed (icing needs to be thin enough to run somewhat down the sides), add more milk, a bit at a time, until icing is "saucy."

When the rings are done, transfer them to cooling racks. After 10 minutes, spread the icing over the tops. Place whole pecans in some of the icing around the tops of the rings. Serve warm or at room temperature.

MAKES **2** 12-INCH RINGS

Rhubarb and Almond Coffee Cake with Cinnamon and Cardamom

We happen to live just a few doors down from a Carmelite monastery. Behind the gorgeous serpentine wall is a garden, supervised by Sister Bernadette, who is also in charge of their kitchen. We know that spring is really here when "Sister Bernie" comes to our door with a huge bag of fresh rhubarb. We make a number of these cakes so we can enjoy fresh rhubarb all summer. The tang of rhubarb, the distinctive aromas of almonds and spices all work together to make this a marvelous breakfast cake. It is also simple and absolutely delicious.

1 stick (½ cup) unsalted butter

1½ cups superfine sugar

1 teaspoon salt

2 large eggs

1 teaspoon pure vanilla extract

¼ teaspoon pure almond extract

1 cup sour cream

1 teaspoon baking powder

½ teaspoon baking soda

2 cups unbleached flour

1 teaspoon ground cinnamon

1 teaspoon ground ginger

2 teaspoons ground cardamom

1½ cups finely diced raw rhubarb

⅔ cup toasted and coarsely
  chopped, slivered almonds

Preheat oven to 350°F. Thoroughly oil a 9-inch springform tube pan.

Cream the butter, sugar, salt, egg, and the extracts. Blend in the sour cream, baking powder, baking soda, flour, cinnamon, ginger, and cardamom. Add the rhubarb and almonds; stir well. Pour the mixture into the prepared baking dish and spread evenly.

Bake for 45 minutes, or until a toothpick inserted into the middle comes out dry.

Transfer the cake to a rack and let it cool for 10 minutes. Remove the outer rim and continue cooling.

MAKES A 9-INCH CAKE

Sour Cream Coffee Cake with Brazil Nuts

This is another of those wonderful, not-too-sweet cakes that we love to serve for a weekend brunch. The cake itself is very light and simple; the nutty topping is delicious and crunchy. Brazil nuts take on a very rich, toasty flavor when they are roasted. You can also experiment with other nuts; try macadamias, hazelnuts, or pecans.

THE TOPPING

1/3 cup granulated sugar

1 teaspoon ground cinnamon

1/3 cup roasted, finely chopped
   Brazil nuts

THE CAKE

2 cups cake flour

1 teaspoon baking soda

1 teaspoon baking powder

1 stick unsalted butter
   (8 tablespoons, 1/2 cup),
   softened

1 cup superfine sugar

3 large eggs

Zest of 1 lemon

2 teaspoons pure vanilla extract

1 cup sour cream

Thoroughly grease a 9-inch springform tube pan.

Preheat the oven to 350°F.

To make the topping: Combine the sugar, cinnamon, and nuts in a small bowl and reserve the mixture for the topping.

To make the cake: Sift together the flour, baking soda, and baking powder into a medium-sized bowl and reserve.

In the bowl of a mixer fitted with a paddle, cream together the butter and sugar.

Add the eggs, one at a time, beating vigorously in between. Then add the lemon zest and vanilla. Scrape the sides thoroughly and beat again.

With the motor running on low, add the sifted dry ingredients and alternate them with the sour cream, a third at a time. Scrape the sides and blend briefly. Pour into the prepared pan, sprinkle evenly with the topping, and bake in the preheated oven until done, about 35 minutes.

Cool on a rack for at least 5 minutes before removing the outside ring.

MAKES A **9**-INCH CAKE

Almond Butter Bread

The aroma of roasted almonds is irresistible. This simple tea bread is so easy and addictive you will want to have several of them in your freezer. Meta Given's Modern Encyclopedia of Cooking *was published in 1953. Its nearly two thousand pages are packed with a vast number of recipes and a wealth of information about all things culinary that were deemed to be important to the postwar housewife, including a wonderful discussion of how to switch menus, if your family preferred to have its main meal at noon instead of in the evening. Among the thousand-plus recipes was a simple recipe for a peanut butter bread. We knew we had to adapt it to the roasted almond butter we first tasted when we visited John Lagier at his California farm. If you cannot find it in your region, you can easily order it from John, along with some of his splendid fruit spreads (see Sources, page 312).*

2 teaspoons almond oil	¾ cup roasted almond butter
(see Sources, page 311)	(see Sources Page 312)
1¾ cups unbleached flour	1 egg
1 teaspoon baking soda	1 cup buttermilk
½ teaspoon kosher salt	½ teaspoon pure almond
1 cup packed dark-brown	extract
sugar	

Using almond oil, coat an 8×4×2½-inch loaf pan. Preheat the oven to 350°F.

Combine the flour, baking soda, and salt in your sifter. Sift 3 times and set aside. In the bowl of a mixer fitted with a paddle, beat the sugar and almond butter until it is a uniform soft crumb. Add the egg and beat well. With the motor running, add flour mixture and buttermilk in thirds. Beat in the almond extract. Scrape the sides of the bowl after each addition.

Pour the mixture into the prepared pan and bake until the sides pull away from the pan and a toothpick inserted into the center comes out dry, 60 to 70 minutes.

Transfer the bread to a cake rack. After 5 minutes, turn the bread out of the pan and finish cooling.

MAKES **1** BREAD

Lovely Cornmeal and Chestnut Griddle Cakes

These corn cakes are really tasty. Cornmeal and chestnut flour are a marvelous flavor combination, enhanced ever so gently by chopped freshly roasted chestnuts and some fresh kernels of corn. These make a great treat for Sunday breakfast, accompanied by some outstanding Virginia bacon from the S. Wallace Edwards smokehouse (see Sources, page 313)—and, of course, some butter and lots of warm maple syrup. You can also make the cakes for an appetizer course, topped with some creamy crabmeat. Prepare your chestnuts ahead. If they are not tender after being roasted, boil them in salted water until they are.

1 cup unbleached flour	3 eggs, separated
¾ cup yellow cornmeal	1½ cups buttermilk, more if
¾ cup chestnut flour (see Sources,	needed
page 311)	8 roasted chestnuts, boiled and
2¼ teaspoons baking powder	chopped (see page 42)
½ teaspoon baking soda	¾ cup corn kernels, preferably
1 tablespoon superfine sugar	fresh
A pinch of salt	Unsalted butter for frying
2 tablespoons melted butter	Warm maple syrup

Combine the flour, cornmeal, chestnut flour baking powder, baking soda, sugar, and salt in a large mixing bowl.

In a small mixing bowl, combine the melted butter, egg yolks, and buttermilk. Beat vigorously to blend. Pour it over the dry ingredients and blend thoroughly. Stir in the chopped chestnuts. The mixture should be thick/thin enough to make a good pancake. If it is too thick, stir in a bit more buttermilk. If too thin, add cornmeal 1 tablespoon at a time, and blend carefully.

Beat the egg whites until stiff. Gently fold them into the batter mixture.

Preheat the oven to 250°F.

Generously coat the bottom of a large skillet with butter. Heat over medium-high heat until it begins to sizzle. Pour enough batter to make 3- to 4-inch round cakes; do not crowd. Fry until bubbles begin to appear on the surface, about 2 minutes. Turn and brown on the other side. Transfer the corn cakes to a cookie sheet lined with paper towels and hold in a warm oven until all are made.

Serve on heated plates with more butter and warm maple syrup.

SERVES 4 TO 6 (MAKES 16 TO 20 4-INCH GRIDDLE CAKES)

Buckwheat Pancakes with Toasted Hickory Nuts

These pancakes are rich in Appalachian flavors. Hickory nuts used to be easily gathered in those forests, even in folks' backyards. Buckwheat flour was also commonly available. Today the nuts are not as easily found. You can substitute pecans, but they will not have the hickory's "lemony edge." We began making these pancakes after July Fourth weekends at the Appalachian Folk Festival in Ripley, West Virginia. In addition to stellar crafts, music, and dance, there was a steam-operated stone grinder turning out bags upon bags of fresh buckwheat. We bought enough freshly ground buckwheat to store for a year in the freezer. While we now rely on Fred's sister Sally to keep us supplied, one can buy excellent-quality buckwheat flour from Arrowhead Mills that is available in organic/natural markets.

1 cup freshly ground buckwheat
flour
1¼ cups unbleached white flour,
plus more if needed
3 teaspoons baking powder
1 scant teaspoon baking soda
1½ tablespoons superfine sugar
3 large eggs
4½ tablespoons unsalted butter,
melted

Up to 2¼ cups buttermilk
1 cup coarsely chopped toasted
hickory nuts or pecans
Up to ¼ cup organic safflower oil

Whipped butter at room
temperature, warmed maple
syrup, more toasted nuts,
fresh fruit, and fresh mint for
garnish.

Combine the flours, baking powder, baking soda, and sugar in a large mixing bowl. Add the eggs, butter, and 1¼ cups of the buttermilk. Whisk well to make a smooth batter. Let the mixture rest for at least 15 minutes and up to overnight.

Before frying, check to see if more buttermilk is needed; the batter should be thick enough to hold some shape when it's dropped from a spoon onto a hot skillet. Thin it with more buttermilk if needed. Stir in the nuts just before frying.

Using only enough oil to coat the skillet, pour the oil onto a large and very well-seasoned cast-iron skillet. Heat oil until a drop of water dropped on the surface sizzles. Spoon the batter into the skillet to make 4-inch pancakes and reduce the heat slightly. Fry the pancakes until they are brown on the bottom, then turn and fry them on the other side until browned. Remove to a heated platter and keep in a warm oven until all the pancakes are prepared. Garnish with butter, syrup, more nuts, fruit, and mint.

SERVES 6 TO 8 (MAKES 18 TO 22 4-INCH PANCAKES)

Silky Lemon Pancakes with Buttery Maple Pecan Sauce

These pancakes have become a frequent feature of our Sunday morning breakfasts. Sour cream gives them a beautiful satin-like texture. Our sauce celebrates the satisfying affinity that pecans and maple syrup have for one another. The inclusion of butter is for Fred, who firmly believes that pancakes require a lavish amount of butter, no matter how delicious the sauce! One word of caution: Don't kill them with too much oil during the frying process, or these pancakes won't be very silky. The sauce is quite wonderful. Try it some time with crystallized ginger or fresh mint.

THE PANCAKES

1 tablespoon superfine sugar
1 generous pinch salt
1 cup unbleached flour
1 cup cake flour
2 teaspoons baking soda
3 large eggs
1½ cups sour cream
4 tablespoons melted butter
Zest and juice of 1 lemon
1½ cups buttermilk, plus more if
  needed

THE SAUCE

4 tablespoons unsalted butter
2 tablespoons dark-brown sugar
1½ cups maple syrup
1 cup coarsely chopped toasted
  pecans

Up to ¼ cup organic safflower oil

Preheat the oven to 425°F.

To prepare the batter: In a large mixing bowl, combine the dry ingredients. In another mixing bowl, whisk together the eggs, sour cream, oil, and lemon juice and zest. Whisk in 1 cup of the buttermilk until smooth. Add the liquid ingredients to the dry and whisk well to make a very smooth batter.

Let batter rest for at least 1 hour.

Meanwhile make sauce: Heat the butter in a small saucepan over medium heat. Add the sugar and cook, stirring constantly, until the mixture is smooth and syrupy, about 10 minutes. Add the maple syrup and pecans. Cook until the mixture is thick and well blended together, 5 to 10 minutes. Set aside.

After the pancake batter has rested, add the remaining ½ cup of buttermilk and whisk. Add more buttermilk if the mixture is too thick to drop from the spoon into the skillet.

Using a large and well-seasoned cast-iron skillet, pour only enough oil to coat the skillet and heat it until a drop of water dropped on the surface sizzles. Spoon the batter onto the skillet to make 4-inch pancakes and reduce the heat slightly. Fry the pancakes until the bottoms are brown and the top are bubbling. Turn and fry until the other sides are brown and pancakes are firm to the touch, 3 to 4 minutes. As pancakes are made, remove them from the skillet, place on a warmed ovenproof platter, and hold in a warm oven.

Quickly reheat the pecan sauce. Serve the pancakes on heated plates, and lavishly garnish them with the sauce.

SERVES 4 TO 6 (MAKES ABOUT 28 4-INCH PANCAKES)

Chestnut Waffles with a Hint of Orange

Shhh. Don't let our grandchildren know there is something "strange" in these waffles. We won't say the word "chestnut" because they would instantly make a face and not ask for seconds. We really enjoy our nonstick Belgian waffle iron and like to welcome the fall chestnut season with these waffles for breakfast. These are light and flavorful, with a subtle hint of orange. We add chopped roasted chestnuts to make a lovely sauce.

⅔ pound roasted chestnuts, peeled

1½ cups chestnut flour (see Sources, page 311)

1 cup unbleached flour

1 tablespoon baking powder

½ teaspoon baking soda

½ teaspoon kosher salt

4 eggs, separated

⅓ cup superfine sugar

Zest of 1 orange

½ cup buttermilk

2 cups whole milk, plus more if needed

½ cup (1 stick) unsalted butter, melted

Warm maple syrup and softened butter

Approximately 1½ hours before serving, check on the tenderness of the chestnuts. If they are not really soft, cover them with boiling water and cook at a vigorous simmer until chestnuts are really tender, up to 1 hour. Drain and chop coarsely.

While the chestnuts are cooking, prepare the batter: In a large mixing bowl, combine the flours, baking powder, baking soda, and salt. Whisk lightly and reserve.

In another large bowl, combine the egg yolks, sugar, and zest. Beat vigorously until thoroughly blended. Gradually beat in the buttermilk, 2 cups whole milk, and the butter. Slowly whisk the flour mixture into the egg mixture and then whisk vigorously until they are thoroughly blended. Let the batter rest at least 1 hour before preparing the waffles.

Preheat waffle iron. When you are ready, stir the batter, adding more milk if the mixture is too thick. Beat the egg whites until stiff peaks are formed. Lighten the batter by beating in some of the egg white mixture. Then add the remaining egg whites to the batter by carefully folding the egg whites into the batter.

Combine the chopped chestnuts and maple syrup in a small saucepan. Heat them until hot. Keep them warm while you make the waffles.

Ladle the batter into the waffle iron and bake according to manufacturer's instructions. At the same time, warm the oven. Place the finished waffles on a paper towel–lined baking sheet and keep warm. Repeat until the waffles are all prepared.

Serve the waffles on heated plates with butter and warm chestnut maple syrup.

SERVES 4 TO 6

Banana and Cashew Cooler

It gets pretty hot on south India's western coast, especially just before the monsoon season. Even then, the temperatures don't fall very much, making it very steamy, too. Coolers are very refreshing ways to greet guests. This one was served to us the first time we visited our friend Nimmy Paul. You will notice that the cashews are soaked in water before grinding, a common technique in the state of Kerala, used mostly when the nuts are to become an integral part of the "sauce." Bananas and cashews also really make a great combination. Perhaps it's because they often grow near one another there, too. Nimmy suggests that you may wish to add some crème de banana or white rum, as well.

½ cup broken raw cashews
Water for soaking cashews
4 large ripe bananas, peeled

6 cups cold whole milk
4 ice cubes, crushed

Two hours ahead, combine the cashews with water to cover in a small bowl and soak.

Just before serving, purée the bananas in a blender or food processor. Drain the nuts and add them to the bananas and purée again. Scrape the sides and add 1 cup of the milk. Process for 1 minute, then scrape again. Add the remaining milk and ice cubes. Process until the ice is integrated into the mixture. Pour into glasses and serve.

SERVES 6

Coconut Cooler

The second day of our visit with Nimmy she welcomed us with glasses of this delicious Coconut Cooler. Folks around Kerala make this with pureed "tender," or "fresh," coconut, the name given to those about seven months old, well before the flesh has solidified. First, however, they drain the liquid from the young coconuts. That "water" is sweet, aromatic, and totally delicious. The flesh is so tender it can be easily scooped out with a soup spoon. Unless you have some nearby coconut trees, you may have some difficulty obtaining young coconuts. They are usually available, however, in cities with large Hispanic or Asian populations.

4 cups coconut milk, or the flesh of
   4 tender coconuts
1 cup finely grated, unsweetened
   coconut

½ cup condensed milk
4 ice cubes, crushed

In the bowl of a food processor, purée the coconut mixture or the tender coconut flesh. Then add the condensed milk and ice; pulse until the mixture is smooth. Pour into glasses and serve.

SERVES 6

salads

A Provençale Salad with Nuts and Raisins

Salade à la Chipolata

Green Almond Salad

Fattoush: A Middle Eastern Salad with Pine Nuts

A Classic Salad with Warm Chèvre and Walnuts

Celery Root Rémoulade with Brazil Nuts and Herbs

Salad of Roasted Beets with Walnuts

Hearty Finnish Mushroom Salad with Pine Nuts

Lemon Fennel Salad with Parmesan and Spicy Candied Walnuts

Minted Peas with Goat Cheese and Walnuts

Autumn Salad with Toasted Hazelnuts, Pears, and Gorgonzola

A Special Waldorf Salad with Macadamias

Coconut Raita (Coconut Yogurt Salad)

Spicy Potato Salad with Cashews and Tomato Cucumber Mint Raita

A Provençale Salad with Nuts and Raisins

The influence of ancient Arab traders can be seen in some of the simple dishes served today in the southern part of France—the region where they settled, albeit briefly. This is a simply delicious salad that includes raisins, almonds, walnuts, and hazelnuts—ingredients basic to Arabic cuisine.

1 teaspoon kosher or sea salt

1 small clove garlic, smashed

1 tablespoon Dijon mustard

1 tablespoon fresh lemon juice

¼ cup rich red wine vinegar

⅓ cup extra virgin olive oil, preferably from Provence

6 cups of baby lettuce

¼ pound Gruyère, cut into thin strips

2 tablespoons golden raisins

2 tablespoons coarsely chopped black olives, preferably from Nyons

2 tablespoons toasted, slivered almonds

2 tablespoons toasted, coarsely chopped hazelnuts

2 tablespoons toasted, coarsely chopped walnuts

Kosher salt and freshly ground black pepper

In a small mixing bowl, combine the salt, garlic, and mustard. Whisk thoroughly with the lemon juice and vinegar. Slowly whisk in the olive oil. Reserve.

In a large mixing bowl, combine the baby lettuce, Gruyère, raisins, olives, and nuts. Season generously with salt and pepper. Toss thoroughly with the vinaigrette and serve.

SERVES 6

Salade à la Chipolata

Georgiana Hill was a nineteenth-century British food writer. Among a small soft-cover series of booklets called Household Manuals, *there is "Salads: How to Dress Them in One Hundred Different Ways." This little jewel was first published in London in 1867. While there is no explanation of the word "Chipolata," this little salad was just wonderfully appealing. According to the author, "This is a favorite accompaniment to either poultry or game." She is, in fact, quite right. The salad is a beautiful combination of contrasts: the sweet and earthy chestnut flavor is complimented by the tang of gherkins and onions, while the tender but coarse chestnuts are set apart by the crunch of endive and the silkiness of the butter lettuce. It is so simple and yet absolutely delicious and refreshing.*

16 dried chestnuts

Water for cooking chestnuts

4 Belgian endives, trimmed and
thinly sliced crosswise

2 plump "heads" butter lettuce,
washed, dried, and torn

3 sweet gherkins, minced

¼ cup minced sweet onion

2 teaspoons fresh minced tarragon

¼ cup rich red vinegar

⅓ cup good-quality extra virgin
olive oil

Sea salt and freshly ground white
pepper to taste

The night before, place the chestnuts in a large saucepan and cover with water. Cover with a lid and bring to a boil. Cook for 1 minute, remove from the heat, and let them stand, covered, overnight.

Adding more water if needed, bring the water once more to a boil over high heat. Reduce the heat, move the lid slightly ajar, and cook until the chestnuts are quite tender, replacing water if necessary to keep the chestnuts covered. This should take 1 to 2 hours.

When the chestnuts have cooled, slice them thinly and place them in a salad bowl. Add the endive, butter lettuce, gherkins, onion, and tarragon.

Pour the vinegar into a small bowl. Slowly beat in olive oil to make an emulsion. Season with salt and pepper to taste.

Toss the salad with the dressing and serve.

SERVES 6

Green Almond Salad

This is another irresistible treasure adapted from Georgiana Hill. While we are rarely fortunate enough to have access to green almonds (almonds picked right from the tree about two months past flowering), one can still enjoy the refreshing flavor mature almonds impart to a simple lettuce salad. According to Miss Hill, this is a delicious salad to serve with roast lamb or turkey. If you happen to have access to green walnuts, these, too, are quite delicious.

½ cup blanched and coarsely
chopped almonds

½ teaspoon sea salt, plus more if
needed

¼ cup fresh lemon juice, plus more
if needed

⅓ cup extra virgin olive oil,
preferably from Provence or
Nice, plus more if needed

4 to 5 cups torn butter lettuce

Freshly ground white pepper to
taste

Using a mortar and pestle, combine ¼ cup of the almonds and the sea salt. Pound into a paste, then gradually combine the paste with the lemon juice. Gradually combine this mixture with the olive oil to make a thick emulsion. Taste and adjust, adding more salt, lemon juice, or olive oil as needed.

Combine this almond vinaigrette and the lettuce in a salad bowl. Add white pepper to taste and toss thoroughly. Garnish with the remaining chopped almonds and serve.

SERVES 6

Fattoush: A Middle Eastern Salad with Pine Nuts

This is really a nifty Middle Eastern bread salad. With a simple dressing of lemon juice and good olive oil, it really retains its fresh flavor. While it is at its best in summer, when tomatoes are so delicious, you can also make it in the winter using really good cherry tomatoes. The addition of toasted pine nuts or walnuts gives another crunchy layer of flavor to the whole.

3 tablespoons unsalted butter, melted

3 large pita breads

4 vine-ripened tomatoes, seeds removed and finely diced, or 2 cups very ripe cherry tomatoes, cut in half

2 or 3 large English cucumbers, peeled and cut into medium dice

14 scallions, thinly sliced

4 or 5 hearts romaine lettuce, cut across in about 1-inch widths

⅓ cup lemon juice, plus more if desired

½ cup extra virgin olive oil, plus more if desired

1 teaspoon sea salt, plus more if desired

1 teaspoon coarsely ground black pepper

⅓ cup finely chopped fresh flat-leaf parsley

¼ cup finely chopped fresh mint (or 2 tablespoons dried)

⅔ cup toasted pine nuts or chopped walnuts

Preheat the broiler. Set the top rack to be about 3 inches below the heating element.

Brush the tops of the pitas with melted butter and broil until lightly toasted. Turn, butter, and toast the other side. Remove them from the oven and break them apart into small, but not tiny, pieces and reserve.

In a large salad bowl, combine the tomatoes, cucumbers, scallions, and romaine. Reserve.

In a small bowl, whisk together the lemon juice and olive oil. Add the salt, pepper, parsley, and mint. Taste and adjust the seasonings.

Just before serving, combine the pita with the salad. Add the dressing mixture and nuts. Toss thoroughly, adding more lemon and oil if needed. Adjust the salt and pepper and serve.

SERVES **6** TO **8**

"Nuts!" General Anthony C. McAuliffe to the Germans
who demanded his surrender at Bastogne
during World War II.

The California Press

At the California Press in Yountville, Chuck Schutte was roasting twelve pounds of pecans. From time to time he would reach into the old gas-fired sesame seed roaster to see if they were hot enough to press. When he figured they were at 165 degrees, he lined a twelve-inch steel cylinder with Dacron sail cloth. He put in a third of the toasted pecans, a circle of thick iron, another third of the nuts, another iron disc, and the rest of the nuts. He folded the Dacron over the nuts and put the container into the seventy-five-year-old hydraulic press. He clicked on the power and under twelve hundred pounds of pressure per square inch the oil started to flow into a container below. While the press did its work, Chuck roasted the next batch of nuts. When the flow of oil ceased, he turned off the press, and put the pressed nuts, now totally dry, into a box for later processing into pecan flour.

On this day, he will press pecans only for about five hours before making the change to some other nut, but before he turns to walnuts or almonds, pistachios, or hazelnuts, he will clean the press with vodka. Not Grey Goose or Stoli, just the cheapest kind.

"It's the best, most efficient cleaning agent we can get," he says.

Chuck is a retired general contractor and an old friend of John Baritelle, the owner of California Press. His little nut oil operation has drawn national attention in some important publications.

Baritelle remembers his family using nut oils when he was a kid. He left the family farm and majored in agricultural economics in college. He became a professor, but after twenty years of teaching, he felt it was time for a change. He moved to a sixty-eight-acre Cabernet vineyard and winery that he and his wife, Lynn, own in St. Helena. His memories of the walnut oil from his family kitchen got him to thinking about doing some pressing. He went to France to see how it was done, and in the late 1990s, started his own press. While production is artisanal and small, the company is close to carrying itself.

The quality of what they produce at California Press is so high, and the tastes of the oils so good, that he just wants people to give them a try. (See Sources, page 311) His advice is buy the oil and use it within six months. Heat and light will hurt the oils, so he recommends the bottles be kept in a cool, dark place—but not in the refrigerator.

The nut flours he makes work well as thickening agents in stews and soups. They are delicious added to cereals, pancakes, and waffles.

Now John Baritelle is also making fruit vinegars, doing it the old-fashioned way, going from juice to wine to vinegar. He keeps the vinegars in wood for a year before he bottles them.

He is optimistic. "People are taking time to appreciate quality," he says.

A Classic Salad with Warm Chèvre and Walnuts

Wherever we travel in southwestern France, we find some version of this salad on the menu. Walnuts and chèvre (goat cheese) can be found everywhere. Equally popular is walnut oil. So this combination of nuts and cheese is really a natural. To make things simple, buy your goat cheese in small logs and use a hot knife when making your slices.

¼ cup rich red wine vinegar

⅓ cup walnut oil, plus more if desired

1 teaspoon minced fresh garlic

Kosher salt and freshly ground black pepper to taste

1 tablespoon minced fresh chives

6 cups baby lettuce and mustard greens, washed and thoroughly dried

2 eggs, lightly beaten

¾ cup finely ground walnuts, plus more if needed

¼ teaspoon freshly ground white pepper

12 (⅔-inch thick) slices goat cheese (about a 14-ounce log)

¼ cup olive oil, plus more if needed

24 walnut halves, lightly toasted

Combine the vinegar, walnut oil, garlic, salt, pepper, and chives in a small bowl and whisk briskly to form an emulsion. Set aside.

Place the greens in a salad bowl and set aside.

Beat the eggs in a shallow bowl. Combine the ground nuts and white pepper in another one. Dredge the slices of cheese in egg, then in nuts, shaking off any excess nuts. Place the slices on a cake rack.

In a large skillet, pour enough oil to coat the bottom; heat until hot. Add the cheese slices and cook over medium heat until golden, about 2 minutes per side. Transfer them from the skillet to a warm platter.

Quickly toss the salad with the vinaigrette. Distribute the greens among six attractive plates. Place 2 slices of cheese on each salad. Garnish with a drizzle of walnut oil, as well as some salt and pepper. Scatter 4 nut halves over each plate and serve.

SERVES **6**

Celery Root Rémoulade with Brazil Nuts and Herbs

Anyone who has visited Paris knows the pleasures to be seen in food shop windows. No one offers more enticing salads "to go" than the French. A luscious beet salad, a celery root rémoulade, and maybe something with mushrooms, or carrots, and you will have the perfect beginning to a lovely meal at home—or a lovely lunch with some crusty bread. Since the French know how to enjoy their nuts, we feel comfortable incorporating this new element into a very traditional dish. The addition of a warm and toasty crunch is totally delightful.

THE SAUCE

2 egg yolks

Juice of 1 lemon

1 tablespoon tarragon vinegar

2 teaspoons dry mustard

½ cup vegetable oil

½ cup extra virgin olive oil

1 tablespoon fresh tarragon leaves

1 tablespoon fresh minced chives

1 tablespoon fresh flat-leaf parsley
   leaves

1 tablespoon capers

THE SALAD

3 cups grated celery root

Zest and juice of 1 lemon

Kosher salt and freshly ground black
   pepper to taste

⅔ cup chopped toasted Brazil nuts

To make the sauce: In the bowl of a food processor, combine the yolks, lemon, vinegar, and dry mustard. Pulse several times. With motor running, very slowly pour the oils through the feed tube until a very thick emulsion is made. Add the herbs and capers and pulse until the mixture is smooth. Scrape the mixture into a clean container, cover tightly, and store in the refrigerator until needed.

To make the salad: Several hours before serving, in a medium-sized bowl toss the celery root with the lemon juice and zest. Add enough rémoulade to make a thick coating for the celery root. Cover and store in the refrigerator for at least 2 hours before serving.

Just before serving, remove the salad from refrigerator and stir. Add more rémoulade if desired. Season with salt and pepper. Let stand at room temperature for 30 minutes before serving.

Toss with Brazil nuts and serve.

SERVES 6

Salad of Roasted Beets with Walnuts

Linda happens to adore beets, so Fred has learned to enjoy them, especially when they are lavishly garnished with nuts—any toasted nut will do for him. We are especially fond of combining them with walnuts, then using walnut oil in our vinaigrette. Since slow roasting really brings out the natural sugars in beets, there is a hint of sweet and sour to this salad once the beets are tossed with the vinaigrette. This can be a handsome salad when you are able to get a combination of the chioggia (red and white concentric rings) and golden yellow. Grated nutmeg adds a wonderful flavor surprise!

4 to 5 large beets, preferably a combination of golden and chioggia
Up to 1-cup apple cider, if available
1 teaspoon Dijon mustard
1 plump garlic clove, pressed
1 small shallot, cut up
⅓ cup fruit vinegar, such as peach or apricot

½ cup walnut oil, plus more if desired
Kosher salt and freshly ground white pepper to taste
1 packed teaspoon chopped fresh tarragon
1 hard-boiled egg, grated
½ to ⅔ cup broken toasted walnuts
Freshly grated nutmeg to taste

Preheat the oven to 300°F.

Trim the roots of the beets so they will stand flat in a baking pan. Select a dish that is large enough to just hold the beets without touching. Add about ¼ inch of cider or water in the bottom. Cover them very well with foil and roast them for 2 to 3 hours, or until tender when pierced with a knife.

While the beets are roasting, make the vinaigrette: In the bowl of a food processor, combine the mustard, garlic, shallot, and vinegar. Pulse 10 times. Then, with the motor running, slowly add the walnut oil to make a good emulsion. Add the salt, pepper, and tarragon and pulse to blend well. Reserve.

When the beets are done, let them cool a bit. Then slip off the skins with the help of a small, sharp paring knife. Slice the beets into ¼-inch circles and gently toss them with the vinaigrette. If you make them early in the day, you can store them in the refrigerator but bring them to room temperature for at least 1½ hours before serving.

Arrange the salad attractively on a platter. Garnish with the hard-boiled egg and walnuts. Then grate some nutmeg over them—and, if you like, a little drizzle of some extra walnut oil—and serve.

SERVES 6

Hearty Finnish Mushroom Salad
with Pine Nuts

Linda first sampled this creamy mushroom salad on her trip to Helsinki. There the mushrooms are wild and varied. Here we use button mushrooms and some shiitakes. The addition of toasted pine nuts is for crunch and flavor contrast. The salad is usually served as part of an appetizer plate, often accompanied by a large dollop of good salmon roe.

14 ounces white mushrooms, wiped

3 ounces shiitake mushrooms, stems discarded

1 medium yellow onion, peeled and quartered

3 to 4 large fresh basil leaves

Kosher-salt and freshly ground black pepper to taste

1¼ cups sour cream, plus more if needed

½ cup toasted pine nuts

Baby lettuce leaves

Salmon caviar (optional)

Combine the mushrooms, onion, and basil in the bowl of a food chopper. Pulse until finely chopped. Scrape the mixture into a mixing bowl.

Blend in the salt, pepper, and sour cream. If the salad is not creamy, gradually blend in more sour cream. Chill until serving time.

Arrange mushroom mixture on attractive salad plates, lavishly garnished with pine nuts and leaves of baby lettuces. A generous dollop of salmon roe will be appreciated, too.

SERVES 6

Lemon Fennel Salad with Parmesan
and Spicy Candied Walnuts

This really tart and refreshing salad is perfect to freshen your palate after any garlicky or very rich meal. The sweet and hot crunch of the walnuts is a marvelous companion to the shaved cheese and the cooling, crunchy fennel.

2 very large fennel bulbs, trimmed, cut in half, and cored

Zest and juice of 3 lemons

Kosher salt and generous amount of freshly ground white pepper

⅓ cup shaved parmesan cheese

Minced fennel fronds (optional)

⅓ cup Candied Walnuts with Heat (See Appetizers, page 56)

Cut the fennel crosswise as thinly as possible. Transfer the fennel to a shallow mixing bowl. Add the lemon juice, salt, and pepper. Toss thoroughly and set aside for 30 minutes, or up to 2 hours in the refrigerator.

Just before serving, toss the fennel mixture with the cheese and fennel fronds. Sprinkle it evenly with walnuts and serve.

SERVES **4** TO **6**

"Behind the nutty loaf is the mill wheel; behind the mill is the wheat field; on the wheat field rests the sunlight; and above the sun is God."

—James Russell Lowell (Quoted in a leaflet promoting lectures on food in Grand Rapids, found tucked into an 1899 book on nut cookery.)

Pecan Man

Our work over the years has put us in touch with some of the most creative people in our country—the farmers. Chop Evans in Fort Valley, Georgia, is one of them.

After graduating from the University of Georgia where he majored in "football and fraternities," he entered an MBA program. But the lure of the farm was too great and he started working with his father's farm holdings.

For ages Georgia dominated the peach world. And Chop grew peaches.

But something happened.

Georgia peaches are delicious. But a delicious peach is not a tough peach. And the big grocery companies wanted varieties developed for shelf life and handleability. Ripeness and taste were secondary. So the buyers turned to the California growers who specialized in the rugged varieties. Now, says Chop Evans, you have a whole population in America that has never eaten a tasty, juicy peach. The result: People buy fewer peaches. Chop saw that coming and started moving toward pecans, a crop that is growing in popularity.

(In the north people say pe-CON. The dictionary says pe-CAN is preferred. But in Georgia, Chop says PEE-CAN.)

He started putting pecan trees in the peach orchards, so that when the peach trees ran out of gas, the field was ready with a different crop. The peach man became the pecan man. He keeps buying and leasing land and now grows 4,900 acres of pecans.

Little by little, he is replacing older varieties with his new favorites, like "Cape Fear," "Stuart," and "Desirable." He showed us an orchard he was replanting, pulling out old trees and planting those that produce better and are less trouble to manage. He had chosen to replant this field because last season there had been a big yield and the trees are famous for producing much less after a banner year. But not always. He had to make the call and this seemed the way to go. But if there is a big yield again this year from the veteran trees still there, he will know he guessed wrong. Chop lives and learns, a trial-and-error farmer.

"Pecan trees are moody," he says. "He might just decide that this time, he ain't gonna do nothin'. And there is nothin' you can do about it." (A pecan tree is always a "he.")

Chop always sprays to protect against scab or insects. "You spray to protect, not spray to correct," he says. But the nuts don't require anything like what the peach trees need.

The harvest runs from October 10 to midwinter. The nuts are cleaned and sorted and go out in trucks in batches from 42,000 to 44,000 pounds. He can sometimes get 800 pounds from a 30-to-40-year-old tree. But the usual yield is an average of about 900 to 1,000 pounds per acre with 12 to 14 trees. In 1999, Chop produced 5.6 million pounds of nuts, or about 6 percent of Georgia's production. It takes about 40 full-time employees to do all this work. Chop knows them all and each has a nickname, like Big Foot, an orchard manager. (His kids have nicknames too: Yard Ape, Legs, Tall Man, Lulu, and Meat Head.)

He says he's not comfortable dealing with buyers, which is why he only has two, Easterlin in Mowtezuma and Harry Willson of Sunnyland Farms in Albany. He has never met Willson; they have a simple telephone agreement. Chop just likes to think about the farm, and what he needs to do to do better.

Riding around with him in the pickup for several hours gave us a chance to learn how a modern farmer manages a big operation like this. He was able, with his cell phone and radio, to stay in touch with any job that any worker was doing on the farm, asking and answering questions, making suggestions, giving instructions, and all in a pleasant and cheery way.

At one point he showed us a giant live oak, maybe a thousand years old. When he leased the land, the condition was that he could not cut down that oak. He willingly accepted the condition, even though he could plant several pecan trees in the space it was taking. Perhaps of all that he showed us that day, he was proudest of something under his care that continues to thrive after a millennium of life.

As we were leaving, we noticed a bumper sticker on a worker's pickup: "Eat Pecans. Millions of satisfied squirrels do."

Minted Peas with Goat Cheese and Walnuts

Pretty green peas, green onions, and bell peppers shine in this salad. To make something good wonderful, just add a zesty vinaigrette with lots of mint, crunchy walnuts, and cubes of feta. We've been serving this salad for years, yet our friends are always delighted to see it on the buffet table. Because it is so colorful, we always try to serve it in a cylindrical glass bowl.

THE DRESSING

2 tablespoons Dijon mustard

3 tablespoons rich red wine vinegar

⅓ cup extra virgin olive oil

2 tablespoons dried mint

Sea salt and freshly ground black
pepper to taste

THE SALAD

4 cups shelled peas (or uncooked
frozen ones)

1 red bell pepper, julienned

1 yellow or orange bell pepper,
julienned

½ cup finely diced celery

½ cup diced green onions

1 teaspoon kosher salt

2 teaspoons coarsely ground black
peppercorns

6 ounces 2-to-4-month-old goat
cheese or feta, crumbled

1 cup toasted walnut pieces

Fresh mint leaves and nasturtiums
for garnish in summer

Early in the day, make the dressing: In a medium-sized bowl blend together the mustard and vinegar. Gradually whisk in the oil to make a thick emulsion. Stir in the mint, sea salt, and pepper. Set aside until needed, whisking vigorously before adding to salad.

To make the salad: No more than 4 hours prior to serving, in a very large mixing bowl, combine the peas (or uncooked frozen ones), julienned peppers, celery, and green onions. Then gently blend them with the dressing. Let it stand in a cool place for at least 1 hour. Just before serving, add the cheese and nuts. Toss well and adjust the seasonings.

Carefully spoon the vegetables into an attractive serving bowl (we use a large glass cylinder). Garnish with mint leaves and nasturtiums before serving.

SERVES **6** TO **10**

Autumn Salad with Toasted Hazelnuts, Pears, and Gorgonzola

Crunchy hazelnuts and tender pears with a caramel-tinged sweetness are really harmonious when paired with tangy vinaigrette, baby greens, and some very ripe Gorgonzola cheese. We have to thank Vid Lutz, executive chef of Cleveland's three Johnny's restaurants for introducing this salad to us many years ago.

THE PEARS

4 ripe pears, peeled, cut in half, and cored

Water to cover pears

Juice of 2 lemons

2 cups superfine sugar

THE VINAIGRETTE

3 tablespoons rich red wine vinegar

7 tablespoons hazelnut oil

1 plump garlic clove, pressed

Kosher salt and freshly ground black pepper to taste

1 tablespoon minced fresh chives

THE SALAD

6 cups baby lettuce and mustard greens, washed and thoroughly dried

1 fennel bulb, cut in half, trimmed and thinly sliced

Kosher salt and freshly ground black pepper to taste

½ to ⅔ cup broken-up Gorgonzola cheese

½ cup hazelnuts, toasted and coarsely chopped

To prepare the pears: Place the pears and lemon juice in a sauté pan just large enough to hold the pears. Add enough water to cover the pears, then add 1 cup of the sugar. Stir around the pears to blend, and bring the water to a boil. Reduce the heat and simmer until the pears are tender, 10 to 20 minutes. Carefully transfer the pears to a cooking rack, then pat them dry.

Spread the remaining sugar evenly in a large cast-iron skillet. Arrange the pears flat-side down over the sugar. Cook over medium-high heat until the sugar melts and begins to darken. Turn the pears in the melted sugar sauce, then carefully remove them from the pan and let them cool in a baking dish. Refrigerate them until needed.

To prepare the vinaigrette: Combine the vinegar, hazelnut oil, garlic, salt, pepper, and chives in a small bowl and whisk briskly to form an emulsion. Set aside.

To assemble the salad: Place the greens and fennel in a salad bowl, and season with salt and pepper; set aside.

Place the pears flat-side down on a carving board. Carefully slice them, but leave the narrow end intact. Lightly brush the pears with some vinaigrette. Just before serving, toss the salad with the vinaigrette. Distribute the greens among 6 or 8 attractive plates. Arrange the pears on the greens, fanning the slices somewhat. Sprinkle generously with Gorgonzola and nuts.

SERVES 6 TO 8

A Special Waldorf Salad with Macadamias

Apples, nuts, and a delicate, light-as-air mayonnaise, piqued by tarragon, make this particular Waldorf salad a favorite of ours. We have included a few pears, as well as some very crunchy celery. Even those who never liked Waldorf salad will enjoy this version. Linda can testify to that herself.

THE DRESSING
2 egg yolks
2 tablespoons orange juice
1 tablespoon champagne vinegar
2 teaspoons dry mustard
1/2 cup vegetable oil
1/2 cup extra virgin olive oil
1 tablespoon fresh tarragon leaves

THE SALAD
Juice of 1 lemon
4 lovely apples, preferably heirloom
　　varieties, peeled and cored
2 ripe pears, peeled and cored
2 large stalks celery, thinly sliced
2/3 cup coarsely chopped toasted
　　macadamia nuts
Kosher salt and freshly ground black
　　pepper to taste
Lettuce leaves, cooked shrimp or
　　crabmeat, small grape clusters,
　　and hard-boiled eggs for garnish

To make the dressing: In the bowl of a food processor, combine the egg yolks, juice, vinegar, and dry mustard. Pulse several times. With the motor running, very slowly pour the oils through the feed tube until a very thick emulsion is made. Add the tarragon and process. Scrape the mixture into a clean container, cover tightly, and store it in the refrigerator until needed.

To make the salad: Up to 2 hours before serving, place the lemon juice in a large bowl. Cut the apples and pears into small dice, about 1/2 inch, and toss with the lemon juice. Then toss with the celery and nuts. Add enough dressing to coat ingredients well. Season generously with salt and pepper. Cover and refrigerate for up to 2 hours.

Just before serving, remove the salad from the refrigerator and taste. Adjust the dressing and seasonings if needed. Serve on lettuce leaves, garnished with sliced eggs, shellfish, and clusters of grapes.

SERVES 6

The Brothers John

In American big-time food processing, the human hand is almost never involved, but in India, pressing coconut oil and shelling cashews are almost artisanal enterprises. In a country where a billion people need to earn a living, the emphasis is on jobs and not on the efficiency of assembly lines.

We had gone to the town of Irinjalakkuda in southern India, where we learned first-hand about that from the brothers Antony and Denny John, both of whom are young, intelligent, and articulate. They are fourth-generation members of a family long involved in processing the coconuts and cashews of Kerala state.

Antony manages the Delicious Cashew Company, and, at the nearby KPL Oil Mills, Denny makes a quality filtered coconut oil for Indian kitchens.

Scores of women wearing colorful saris were at work in a huge, well-lit room at the cashew operation. It was a spectacular sight. Each was working on an aspect of getting the nuts ready for market. Most were cracking open the cashews, one nut at a time. Their hands flew as they cleaned, screened, and sorted. Some were soaking the fresh cashews to remove the corrosive tannins. Near a loading dock men were sealing the cashews in big carbon dioxide–filled tins. Outside, on part of a big concrete area for drying the nuts, thirty workers were brushing through broken shells looking for kernels that might have been missed.

"The market is tough right now," said Antony John. "No one can afford to lose any product."

Not far away, at the KPL Oil Mills, Denny John showed us his operation. Colorfully painted trucks bring in tons of shelled, drained, but still moist coconut meat. After a preliminary drying on a concrete platform with a huge mesh screen above to keep out the coconut-loving crows, workers roast the coconut in an oven fueled by burning dried coconut shells.

After it has cooled a little, other workers chop the dried coconut and put it into the press. Within minutes the oil flows like water. They release the pressure, stir the nuts, press them again, and then a third time. Finally the pulp is soaked in a solvent that leaches out the oil that remains. When the solvent evaporates, that oil is mixed with the other and it is filtered. The pleasant-tasting and fresh-smelling coconut oil is ready for bottling. The crushed pulp is used as cattle feed.

Later Antony and Denny took us to meet their parents in the home where they had grown up. The big yard is full of coconut trees, betel nut trees, bananas, pineapples, and peppers. A young man using a short, thin rope climbed one of the sixty-foot trees and sent down green seven-month coconuts—tender coconuts, as they call them. Then at the big dining room table with all of the family we drank delicious coconut water and ate the soft gelatinous immature coconut flesh with a spoon.

Coconut Raita (Coconut Yogurt Salad)

In this yogurt salad the heat of cayenne is a terrific counterpoint to the cool, comfortable yogurt, mint, and cilantro. It is a Keralan raita, the ingredients from a list read to me by cook extraordinaire Nimmy Paul. Toasted coconut not only adds great depth, it is also a pleasing surprise to those who would not expect it to be present in a yogurt salad.

2 teaspoons black mustard seeds (available in Asian markets)
2 teaspoons Tellicherry peppercorns (available in Asian markets)
½ cup unsweetened grated coconut
2 cups plain yogurt, preferably whole milk, plus more if needed

1 medium-sized red onion, cut in half and thinly sliced
2 teaspoons dried garden mint
1 teaspoon cayenne
2 tablespoons minced fresh cilantro

In a small skillet, combine the mustard seeds and peppercorns. Stir until the aromas are released. Remove from the heat and cool; then grind until the spices are powdered. To the same skillet add the coconut. Stir over medium heat until lightly browned. Remove from the heat and cool.

In a medium-sized bowl combine the yogurt, onions, mint, cayenne, cilantro, ground spices, and coconut. Stir thoroughly and spoon into a serving bowl. Cover and chill for at least 2 hours. Just before serving, thin with more yogurt if needed.

SERVES 6

Spicy Potato Salad with Cashews and Tomato Cucumber Mint Raita

This refreshing potato salad grew out of a cooking class where someone suggested combining leftover raita, or cool yogurt salad, with some cooked fingerling potatoes that were just waiting for a dressing. After tasting the marvelous combination, we quickly sautéed a generous handful of cashews to add to the mix. The end result was sublime.

THE RAITA

1 teaspoon cumin seeds

1 teaspoon coriander seeds

1 teaspoon fennel seeds

½ English cucumber, peeled, grated, and drained for at least 1 hour

½ medium-sized Spanish onion, finely diced

2 large tomatoes, seeded and finely diced

2 cups plain yogurt, preferably whole milk

2 teaspoons dried garden mint

1 teaspoon cayenne

1 teaspoon freshly ground white pepper

1 teaspoon kosher salt

THE POTATO SALAD

18 to 24 small fingerling potatoes, scrubbed

Water to cover potatoes

Kosher salt and freshly ground black pepper to taste

1 cup cashews

¼ cup vegetable oil or ghee

Kosher salt to taste

To make the raita: Combine the cumin, coriander and fennel seeds in a small skillet and stir over medium heat until fragrant. Remove them from the heat and let them cool; then grind the spices to a powder. In a mixing bowl, combine the spice powder, cucumber, onion, tomatoes, yogurt, mint, cayenne, pepper, and salt. Blend together well. Cover the bowl with plastic and refrigerate for at least 2 hours.

To make the potato salad: An hour before serving, combine the potatoes and water to cover in a large saucepan. Bring the water to a boil, then reduce the heat to an active simmer. Cook until the potatoes are tender when pierced with a fork. Drain and quickly rinse with cold water.

Carefully cut the fingerlings in half crosswise, placing them in a large bowl. Toss with half of the raita. When cooled, toss with as much remaining raita as you like. Adjust the seasonings, adding salt and pepper to taste. Just before serving, combine the nuts and oil in a small skillet. Toss over medium heat until nuts are just golden, 3 to 4 minutes. Using a slotted spoon, transfer the nuts to paper towels. Blot well, toss with some salt, and add to the potatoes. Serve with anything spicy from the grill.

SERVES 6 TO 8

Mr. Peanut

His name was Amadeo Obici, but few will recognize the name. There is no one, however, who will not recognize the name of the business he started as an immigrant Pennsylvania teenager before the turn of the last century. The whole world knows the wacky trademark he devised in 1914 to sell his product.

Obici was the world's greatest peanut salesman. In the late 1880s in Wilkes-Barre he sold apples and unshelled peanuts on the street and later from a fruit stand. By 1900 he became the first person to shell, roast, and salt the peanuts before selling them. He also learned how to press oil from the peanuts and sell it as a cooking agent.

By 1906 he figured that his growing company needed a new name, and he came up with the word "Planters." The rest is history. He was the first peanut man to prepackage his products rather than having them scooped out of a bin in stores, and he became the first to go to market with chocolate-covered peanut candies.

The marketer in Amadeo Obici caused him to look for a trademark. Business was good, but he wanted something else. In 1916 he had a contest and invited people to suggest a peanut symbol. A teenaged peanut lover from Virginia sent in a drawing of an anthropomorphic unshelled peanut.

Obici loved the idea. He added a top hat, a monocle, a cane, and put some spats on the peanut's shoes—and Mr. Peanut was born. Obici's salesmen drove around in cars that looked like a giant unshelled peanut. America became peanut crazy. His company thrived through the Depression as he sold the idea that peanuts were nourishing and cheap and a perfect "nickel lunch."

For decades Planters was the world's biggest peanut company. Then in 1960, his heirs sold Planters to Standard Brands.

Nearly forty years later, a big New York advertising firm, addressing the old company's position in the ever more competitive peanut world, decided to revive Mr. Peanut—and it worked. Planters' share of the market is increasing. Mr. Peanut is now a hip icon, still selling peanuts at the age of eighty-six, still wearing his top hat and monocle, but now dancing on the Internet and in television commercials, hooking the youth of the world on peanuts.

"Relax," says the modern Mr. Peanut. "Go nuts."

focaccia, pizza, and pasta

Focaccia Dough

Focaccia with a Simple Ligurian Walnut Pesto and Italian Fontina

Focaccia with Caramelized Onions, Pine Nuts, and Gorgonzola

Pissaladière with Red Pepper and Walnut Tapénade

Pizza Dough

Pizza with Hazelnut Sauce, Fontina, and Truffle Oil

Pizza with Tapénade, Pine Nuts, and Basil

Pizza with Tomatoes, Nutty Potatoes, and Anchovies

Marco's Piedmontese Chestnut Flour Gnocchi

Nucci's Potato Gnocchi with Chestnuts

Surprise Tagliatelle with Escarole, Ricotta, and Pine Nuts

Bucatini with Lusty Lamb Ragout

Pasta with Lemon, Walnuts, and Garlic

Focaccia Dough

This is a particularly appealing dough because the sponge, made earlier in the day, adds wonderful flavor and texture to the finished product. It is also comfortable to handle.

SPONGE

1 teaspoon active dry yeast

1 cup warm water

1 cup unbleached flour

DOUGH

1¾ teaspoons active dry yeast

Up to 1 cup warm water

2½ cups unbleached flour, plus
  more if needed

2 teaspoons kosher salt

1 rounded teaspoon freshly ground
  black pepper

3 tablespoons olive oil

1 to 2 tablespoons finely ground
  cornmeal

In the morning, make the sponge: Blend the yeast with ¼ cup of the warm water. Set aside in a warm place until the mixture bubbles, then combine it with the flour and remaining water. Mix until well blended. Cover the bowl lightly and allow it to bubble and rise for at least 4 hours.

To make the focaccia dough: Blend the yeast with ¼ cup of the warm water. When the mixture is bubbling, add it to the warmed bowl of an electric mixer fitted with a paddle. With motor on the lowest setting, add the sponge, ½ cup more of the water, 2 cups of the flour, salt, pepper, and 2 tablespoons of the olive oil. When the ingredients are thoroughly blended, add more flour as needed. If you are kneading in the mixer, change to a dough hook. If you are kneading by hand, turn out onto a lightly floured board.

Knead the dough, adding only enough flour to keep the dough from sticking. When it's smooth and shiny, place the dough into a large, well-oiled bowl, cover it with plastic wrap, and let it rise in a warm place. It should double in bulk in about 1 hour.

Using cornmeal, lightly dust a large pizza paddle or a shallow-sided cookie sheet. Turn the dough onto a lightly floured surface and roll it into a large rectangle. Lift it onto the prepared pan, then gently stretch the dough all around. It should be at least ½ inch thick. We like to make a rectangle that is about 10×15 inches. Cover lightly with plastic wrap, and let it rest in a warm place for 30 minutes. Meanwhile, prepare whatever topping you will be using.

MAKES A 10×15 INCH FOCACCIA

Focaccia with a Simple Ligurian Walnut Pesto and Italian Fontina

Focaccia is really a kind of Italian bread that is usually served with a tasty—but not thick or heavy—topping. This one has a delicious and simple pesto topping. We discovered that not all Italian Fontina cheeses are alike, and we urge you to look for Fontina d'Aosta, made from the milk of mountain-grazing cows. It is one of Italy's greatest cheeses. If you cannot find it in your area, you can order it from Zingerman's Deli in Ann Arbor or on-line at Esperya (see Sources, page 313).

1 recipe Focaccia Dough
(page 128)

TOPPING
Sea salt
3 plump garlic cloves
½ cup coarsely chopped toasted
walnuts

1 cup fresh basil leaves, torn into
pieces
2 tablespoons unsalted butter,
softened
4 tablespoons extra virgin olive oil
1 cup grated Italian Fontina

To prepare the topping: Use a mortar and pestle if at all possible. Smash together 1 teaspoon sea salt and the garlic cloves. Gradually add half the walnuts, smashing and rubbing until the nuts and garlic are well-combined. Then slowly add the basil until it is all blended into the pesto. Finally, add the remaining nuts. When the mixture is quite smooth, blend in the butter and 2 tablespoons of the oil. Reserve at room temperature. (You can, of course, use a food processor. Combine the basil, garlic, and walnuts in the bowl of a food processor. Pulse until the mixture is thoroughly chopped. Add the butter and 2 tablespoons of the oil; blend until a paste is made.)

After the focaccia rests for the 30-minute rising, use the tips of your fingers to vigorously press "dimples" all over its surface. Drizzle the remaining oil evenly over the focaccia. Then use your fingers to lightly spread the oil, even out to the edge. Then carefully spread the pesto. Sprinkle with some more sea salt and the Fontina. Loosely cover the Focaccia with a towel or with plastic wrap and let it rise for 1 hour in a warm place.

At the same time, prepare the oven. Place one rack near the bottom of the oven; place the other in the top third. If you have a baking stone, put it on the top rack. Preheat the oven and baking stone at 450°F for 1 hour.

Just before baking the focaccia, lower the heat to 400° and put 8 ice cubes in a shallow baking pan on the lower oven rack. Place the focaccia on the hot stone. Bake the focaccia for about 25 minutes, or until the top and edges are golden and the bottom has browned.

Transfer the focaccia to a cake rack for a few minutes. Cut it into generous squares or wedges and serve it while still quite warm.

SERVES **6** TO **8**

Focaccia with Caramelized Onions, Pine Nuts, and Gorgonzola

One of the most satisfying flavor combinations for us is that of caramelized onions, Gorgonzola, and toasted pine nuts. It is such a range of exciting tastes and textures. Just remember, though, that focaccia is not pizza; the topping is to enhance, not thickly cover the bread. Serve this one with a lusty onion or tomato soup, or maybe in the summer when you have poultry or steak right from the grill.

1 recipe Focaccia Dough
(page 128)
Up to 1 tablespoon olive oil
2 to 3 tablespoons cornmeal

THE TOPPING

3 tablespoons unsalted butter
4 tablespoons extra virgin olive oil
1 very large red onion, thinly sliced

1 teaspoon freshly ground black
pepper
8 ounces imported Gorgonzola
3 tablespoons heavy cream, plus
more as needed
½ cup toasted pine nuts
Sea salt to taste
⅔ cup freshly grated Parmigiano-
Reggiano

Oil a large baking sheet, and lightly sprinkle on the cornmeal. Turn the dough onto a lightly floured surface and roll and stretch it into a large rectangle or an 11-inch circle. Lift it onto a well-oiled pan, then gently stretch the dough all around. It should be at least ½ inch thick. We like to make a rectangle that is about 10×15 inches. Cover the dough lightly with plastic wrap and let it rest in a warm place for 30 minutes.

Meanwhile, prepare the topping: In a heavy-bottomed sauté pan over low heat, combine the butter and 2 tablespoons of the oil. Add the onions, cover, and cook, stirring often, until the onions start to brown, 20 to 30 minutes. Remove the lid, raise the heat to medium, and stir often until the onions are caramelized, another 10 to 15 minutes. Stir in the pepper.

While the onions are cooking, combine the Gorgonzola and cream in the bowl of a food processor and pulse. When the mixture is very creamy, scrape it into a small bowl.

After the focaccia rests for 30 minutes, use the tips of your fingers to vigorously press "dimples" all over its surface. Drizzle the remaining oil evenly over the focaccia. Then use your fingers to lightly spread the oil even out to the edge.

Carefully spread the Gorgonzola mixture on top. It doesn't have to cover too evenly. Then distribute the onions, including the remaining oil and butter from the pan. Sprinkle with pine nuts, sea salt, and the Parmigiano-Reggiano. Loosely cover it with a towel or plastic wrap and let the focaccia rise for 1 hour.

At the same time, prepare the oven. Place one rack near the bottom of the oven;

place the other in the top third. If you have a baking stone, put it on the top rack. Pre-heat the oven and baking stone at 450°F for 1 hour.

Just before baking the focaccia, lower the heat to 400° and put 8 ice cubes in a shallow baking pan on the lower oven rack. Place the focaccia on the hot stone. Bake the focaccia for about 25 minutes, or until the top and edges are golden and the bottom has browned.

Transfer the focaccia to a cake rack for a few minutes. Then cut it into generous squares or wedges and serve it while still quite warm.

SERVES **6** TO **8**

Pissaladière with Red Pepper and Walnut Tapénade

Which came first—focaccia, pizza, or pissaladière? We all know that the answer depends upon in which country you ask the question. A traditional pissaladière is sold by the piece in bakeries and food shops in Provence and the Côte d'Azur. It is eaten at room temperature, and commonly topped with onions, tomatoes, and anchovies. We've incorporated some of the other toppings we've seen at the Tuesday market in Vaison la Romaine (where we have also found a scrumptious hazelnut-studded sausage). The combination of olives and roasted peppers makes a stunning background for the walnuts. Covered with mellow Beaufort cheese, from the mountains of Savoy, this pissaladière is really bursting with flavor.

THE DOUGH

1 scant tablespoon active dry yeast

2 teaspoons wildflower honey

1 cup warm water

3 cups unbleached flour

2 teaspoons sea salt

2 tablespoons extra virgin olive oil

1 egg, beaten

PEPPER AND WALNUT TAPÉNADE

4 large red bell peppers, roasted, seeded, and peeled

1 medium yellow onion, thinly sliced

1 large ripe tomato, peeled and seeded

4 plump garlic cloves, minced

½ cup pitted ripe olives, Nyons or Niçoise

¼ cup extra virgin olive oil, plus more if needed

⅔ cup toasted walnuts, chopped into medium-sized pieces

1 teaspoon coarsely ground black pepper

Sea salt if needed

1½ cups freshly grated Beaufort (or another semisoft French cheese)

10 whole lightly toasted walnuts

To prepare the dough: Dissolve the yeast and honey in ¼ cup of the warm water and let it stand in a warm place until the mixture begins to bubble.

In the bowl of an electric mixer fitted with a paddle, combine the flour and salt. With the motor on lowest setting, add the yeast mixture, remaining water, olive oil, and egg. If the mixture is too wet, add 1 tablespoon flour.

Once the dough is mixed, turn it out on a floured surface and knead it until smooth, gradually adding only enough flour to keep the dough from sticking. When it's smooth and shiny, although still a bit tacky, place the dough into a large, well-oiled bowl, cover with plastic wrap, and let rise in a warm place. It should double in bulk in about 1 hour.

To prepare the tapénade: Combine the peppers, onions, tomato, garlic and olives in the bowl of a food processor. Pulse to finely chop. With the motor running, add 2 tablespoons of the olive oil. If the mixture is not a spreadable paste, add more olive oil. Scrape the tapénade into a bowl. Blend in the chopped walnuts, pepper, and some salt if needed.

To finish the pissaladière: Place a shallow baking pan on a lower oven rack. If you are using a baking stone, place it on the upper rack. Preheat the oven to 450°F.

At the same time, lightly coat a large, shallow-sided baking pan with olive oil. Generously flour your pastry surface and your hands. Flatten the dough with your hands, then roll to about 10×15 inches. Brush any excess flour off the dough. Carefully fold the dough over a rolling pin and transfer it to the baking pan. Cover it loosely with plastic wrap and let it rise in a warm place for 30 to 40 minutes.

Gently spread the remaining olive oil over the surface. Then spread on the pepper tapénade. Evenly scatter the grated cheese on top of the dough, then the whole walnuts.

Place the pissaladière pan on the hot stone and put 8 ice cubes in a shallow baking pan on the lower oven rack. Reduce the heat to 425° and bake for 20 to 25 minutes, or until the top and edges are golden. Make certain that the bottom is browned, too.

Transfer the pissaladière to a cake rack for a few minutes; then carefully transfer it to a cutting surface. Cut it into wedges and serve it while it's still quite warm.

SERVES **6** TO **8**

Pizza Dough

This dough will keep in the refrigerator for several days before using; just bring it to room temperature before stretching it. If you like your pizzas to be very crisp on the bottom, bake them directly on a pizza stone or bread tile.

DOUGH

¾ cup warm water, plus more if needed

1 tablespoon wildflower honey

1 tablespoon active dry yeast

¼ cup milk

2 tablespoons olive oil

2¾ cups unbleached flour

¼ cup whole wheat flour

1 teaspoon kosher salt

To proof the yeast, blend ¼ cup of the warm water, the honey, and yeast in a small bowl and let it rest in a warm place until the mixture bubbles, about 10 minutes.

In a small measuring cup, combine the remaining ½ cup water, milk, and olive oil. Combine the flours and salt in the bowl of a food processor. With the motor running, pour in the yeast mixture, then the water mixture. Process just until the dough leaves the side of the bowl and forms a ball. If the dough is too dry, add more water, 2 tablespoons at a time. Process briefly again. The dough should be nice and elastic.

Lightly flour a board and knead the dough for a few minutes. Turn the dough into a lightly oiled bowl, cover it with plastic wrap, and let it rise in a warm place until doubled, about 1 hour. Dough can then be placed in a large plastic zipper-type bag and stored, tightly sealed, in the refrigerator for up to 1 week. When you are ready to use it divide the dough into 2 equal parts and bring to room temperature.

MAKES 2 14-INCH PIZZAS

Pizza with Hazelnut Sauce, Fontina, and Truffle Oil

We had already heard that Piedmont was a great hazelnut region when the celebrated food and wine writer Fred Plotkin told us that the region around Alba gives us the world's best examples. That's possibly why some of the world's most delicious hazelnut candies are made in that region, too. Anyway, this pizza celebrates three of the great foodstuffs from the Piedmont: hazelnuts, truffles, and Fontina. Our hazelnut sauce is shamelessly adapted from a Ligurian walnut sauce in Fred Plotkin's marvelous book, Recipes from Paradise.

3 tablespoons cornmeal

½ of the Pizza Dough at room temperature (see recipe, page 133)

½ rounded cup toasted, chopped hazelnuts

1 plump garlic clove

2 tablespoons dry bread crumbs

⅓ cup fresh ricotta

1 tablespoon water, plus more if needed

4 tablespoons olive oil

2 tablespoons grated Parmigiano-Reggiano

½ teaspoon minced fresh thyme

3 tablespoons truffle oil, plus more

⅓ pound Italian Fontina, thinly sliced

Preheat the oven and pizza tile, if you are using one, to 500°F. Evenly sprinkle a pizza peel or pizza pan with cornmeal.

To prepare the pizza: On a lightly floured surface, roll out the dough into a large round. Begin stretching the dough over closed fists to make a thin 14-inch round. Place the round on the prepared pan or peel. Let it stand in a warm place for 20 minutes.

Meanwhile, prepare the hazelnut sauce: In a large mortar, or in a small food processor, grind together nuts, garlic, and bread crumbs. Add the ricotta and grind it until a thick paste is made. Grind in the water. If the mixture is very dry, add another tablespoon and grind in well. Then slowly add the olive oil, cheese, and thyme. The mixture should be very spreadable.

To assemble the pizza: Using your fingertips, dimple the entire surface of the dough. Then gently spread the hazelnut sauce over the surface of the pizza dough, leaving a ½-inch border around the outer edge. Drizzle the truffle oil over the hazelnut sauce. Cover with the Fontina slices.

Place the prepared pizza on the hot tile. Bake for 12 to 15 minutes, until the rim is browned and cheese has melted.

Drizzle a bit more truffle oil over the pizza, cut into slices, and serve.

MAKES A **14-INCH PIZZA**

Pizza with Tapénade, Pine Nuts, and Basil

These are the flavors of the sun-drenched Mediterranean countries—olives, garlic, olive oil, tomatoes, and basil. Adding some golden pine nuts for toasty crunch is just a natural. In summer, you should make this with one pound of fresh tomatoes, peeled, seeded, and finely chopped. It's really delicious!

2 to 3 tablespoons cornmeal

½ of the Pizza Dough (see recipe, page 133)

4 plump garlic cloves, crushed and peeled

1½ cups pitted Kalamata olives

4 oil-packed sun-dried tomatoes

2-ounce can anchovy fillets, drained of oil and rinsed

1 teaspoon freshly ground black pepper

5 tablespoons extra virgin olive oil, plus more if needed

⅓ cup lightly toasted pine nuts

1 cup drained canned tomatoes, preferably Italian plum tomatoes, chopped

1 small onion, thinly sliced

2 tablespoon capers, preferably salt packed, rinsed

12 large leaves fresh basil, stacked, rolled, and cut crosswise into a chiffonade

Preheat the oven and pizza tile, if you are using one, to 500°F. Evenly sprinkle a pizza peel or pizza pan with cornmeal.

To prepare the pizza: On a lightly floured surface, roll out the dough into a large round. Begin stretching the dough over closed fists to make a thin 14-inch round. Place the round on the prepared pan or peel. Let it stand in a warm place while you make the topping.

To make the tapénade: In the bowl of a food processor, combine the garlic, olives, and sun-dried tomatoes. Pulse 10 times. Then add the anchovy fillets and pepper. Pulse until the mixture is puréed. With the motor running, add 3 tablespoons of the olive oil. If the mixture seems too dry, add 1 more tablespoon. Set aside.

To assemble the pizza: Using your fingertips, gently dimple the entire surface of the dough. Then brush with 1 tablespoon of the remaining olive oil.

Gently spread the tapénade over the surface of the pizza, leaving a ¾-inch border around the outer edge. Scatter the pine nuts, tomatoes, onion, capers, and basil over the surface, then drizzle with the remaining oil.

Place the prepared pizza on the hot tile. Bake until the bottom of the crust is nicely browned, 12 to 15 minutes. Serve at once.

MAKES A 14-INCH PIZZA

Pizza with Tomatoes, Nutty Potatoes, and Anchovies

We make this in the late summer, when the twenty-plus varieties of heirloom tomatoes in our garden are at their peak. Potatoes and toasted walnuts make a superb flavor combination, as do anchovies and tomatoes. All baked together, the anchovies melt into an indiscernible but very flavorful topping for them. Best of all are the little hidden pieces of fresh basil beneath the topping—making every bite exciting.

3 tablespoons cornmeal
½ of the Pizza Dough, at room temperature (see recipe, page 133)
3 tablespoons extra virgin olive oil
3 large russet potatoes, baked until tender
3 tablespoons unsalted butter, cut into small pieces
Up to ¼ cup buttermilk
3 cloves roasted garlic

Kosher salt and freshly ground white pepper to taste
⅓ cup chopped toasted walnuts
3 large basil leaves, torn into pieces
3 large vine-ripened tomatoes, cut into ¼-inch-thick slices
3 anchovy fillets, drained of oil and rinsed
12 whole walnut halves
⅓ cup shaved Parmigiano-Reggiano

Preheat the oven and pizza tile, if you are using one, to 500°F. Evenly sprinkle a pizza peel or pizza pan with cornmeal.

To assemble the pizza: On a lightly floured surface, roll out the dough into a large round. Begin stretching the dough over closed fists to make a thin 14-inch round. Place the round on the prepared pan or peel. Let it stand in a warm place.

To prepare the topping: While the potatoes are still hot, carefully scoop out the flesh and put it into a mixing bowl. Add the butter and mash thoroughly. Slowly mash in the buttermilk until the potatoes are soft and somewhat creamy. Mash in the garlic cloves, then add the salt, pepper, and chopped walnuts and blend well. Set aside.

To assemble the pizza: Using your fingertips, dimple the entire surface of the dough. Then brush it with 1 tablespoon of the olive oil. Scatter pieces of fresh basil over the surface, then gently spread it with the mashed potato mixture, leaving about a ¼-inch-wide rim around the outside of the pizza. Place tomato slices over the mashed potatoes. Cut the anchovies into pieces and scatter them over the tomatoes. Tuck the whole walnuts into the exposed potato. Sprinkle evenly with the shaved Parmigiano-Reggiano and drizzle with 2 tablespoons of olive oil. Place the prepared pizza on the hot tile. Bake for 12 to 15 minutes, until rim of the pizza is browned and the cheese has melted. Serve at once.

MAKES A 14-INCH PIZZA

Greg Miller, Chestnut Doctor

Greg Miller grew up with a love of the woods. He and his family live on a farm near Carrolton, Ohio, where he grows and sells chestnuts. During our visit, the harvest was underway and his Empire Chestnut Company was having a very good year. He would gather and process more than thirty thousand pounds of chestnuts. Just a couple of years earlier he got only twenty thousand pounds, and when the cicadas came after their seventeen-year hiatus, he was able to market only six thousand pounds of chestnuts.

Greg's father was born on a farm but raised his family in Canton, Ohio. Still the lure of the farm was always there. In 1960, his father bought two parcels of wooded land in nearby Carroll County. His dad thought it was crazy that farmers there would clear out the woods to plant corn. Grow the corn in Iowa, he said. Let's do here what this area can do best, and he devoted himself to growing timber trees. Greg went off to Ohio State, and then to graduate studies at Iowa State, where he got his doctorate in forestry.

Greg, Diane, and their kids now live in a handsome house on the ninety-seven-acre plot. The other eighty-acre tract is just a few minutes away. With his dog Bingo, he took us first to a place where there were chestnut saplings, three or four feet high and two years old. But there were fledgling apple trees, too. He is working with other farmers to produce trees that will be more competitive and productive in that hilly environment. "The only trouble," he says, "is that it takes several years to find out if it worked."

A few hundred yards away is one of two twenty-acre orchards where he grows chestnuts. The trees are well placed and there is plenty of room between them. The older trees in this plot are from 1972, but he is getting good production from much younger trees as well. His commercial production comes from Asian trees, but he is fascinated with developing blight-resistant American chestnuts and works with the American Chestnut Foundation to get them reestablished in the woods.

He seems to know the history of every tree in the plot—when it was planted, who its mother was (he can't really know the daddy because the pollen floats free in the air and settles on the blooms of the mama), what kind of nuts it yields, what its prospects will be for forest life.

He has a small building where he prepares the chestnuts for shipping. He cleans the nuts and sizes them, and tosses out those that are cracked or otherwise damaged. If he sees evidence of a tiny hole where one of the chestnut-loving insects has bored through, he will dispatch that nut to limbo as well.

Then he puts them in a big mesh bag and gives them a hot bath, several minutes at about 49°C (about 120°F). That doesn't cook the nuts, but it does stop any insect or mold life dead in its tracks. He has developed a method for drying, cracking, and shelling the nuts. He sells them, whole or shelled, on the Internet and through his catalog. Off to the side are buckets of other chestnuts covered with water. These are seed nuts, which he sells to people who want to grow chestnut trees.

So for the livelihood of his family, Greg grows and sells the chestnut that came from Asia with the virus. But his work as a scientist is focused on helping to reestablish one of the noblest trees of the American forest. Little by little, some progress is being made. He stands looking at a straight, tall twenty-year-old hybrid chestnut tree. "It will resist the plague," he says. "And someday trees like it will grow in our woods again and live hundreds of years."

Marco's Piedmontese Chestnut Flour Gnocchi

Osteria della Rosa Rosso, in the small Piedmont hill town of Cherasco, is one of the regions most celebrated restaurants. The young chef who keeps it so is Marco Falco, whose passion for the foods of his region is palpable to all who have experienced his cooking. Luckily, our first visit was in the fall when the markets were filled with large and luscious chestnuts. He served us chestnut gnocchi two ways—tossed with browned butter and the other with rich, warm heavy cream. A day later, with the help of our mutual friend Nucci Russo, Marco not only shared some recipes, he also talked with us about his love for the foods of his childhood. When we asked which was best—gnocchi with chestnuts or gnocchi made with chestnut flour, he smiled and suggested we decide for ourselves.

2¼ pounds Yukon gold potatoes
Salted wated for cooking potatoes
1 cup plus 1 tablespoon
   unbleached flour
1 cup plus 1 tablespoon chestnut
   flour (see Sources, page 311)

2 teaspoons kosher salt
3 tablespoons grated Parmigiano-
   Reggiano, plus more for garnish
1 egg, beaten, if needed
12 tablespoons unsalted butter
⅔ cup heavy cream (optional)

Thoroughly cover the potatoes with salted water and cook until they are tender. Drain, cool slightly, then peel. Working in batches, press the potatoes in a ricer onto a large work surface.

Make a well in the center and pour in the two flours, salt, and cheese. Using a whisk, gently dry blend.

Gently work the flour and potato mixture together with your fingers, until the dough is smooth yet still a tad tacky. If the mixture just won't hold together, add half of the beaten egg and mix evenly into the dough.

With lightly floured hands, divide the dough into three equal parts, and shape each into a long rope about 1 inch in diameter. Cut each rope into pieces about ¾-inch long.

Using a long-tined fork, hold the fork with the curve at the bottom of the tines facing to the back. One at a time, with your index finger, gently press each small piece against the tines and let it drop. (This will make an indentation on one side and the fork-impressed lines on the other. This will ensure even cooking and little cups to hold the butter.) Repeat until all are shaped. Hold the gnocchi on a lightly floured cookie sheet in a warm place. Do not stack them on top of each other.

Just before serving, cook the gnocchi. Fill a large, wide soup pot with salted water and bring to a boil. At the same time, melt the butter in a small saucepan and carefully cook it until lightly browned. Pour it into a heated grain dish and keep it warm.

Working with small batches, drop the gnocchi into the boiling water and cook them until they rise to the top. Check the first one by cutting it in half to determine doneness (they are usually cooked once they reach the surface). Using a Chinese frying strainer or large slotted spoon, transfer the drained gnocchi to the gratin dish with the browned butter and toss. Repeat until all the gnocchi are cooked and coated with the butter.

If you wish to use cream as well as butter, heat the cream until very hot and pour it over the gnocchi. Add more salt and some freshly ground white pepper. Toss gently and serve in heated bowls. If you are only using butter, season with sea salt and freshly ground black pepper. Serve finely grated Parmigiano-Reggiano on the side.

SERVES 6

Nucci's Potato Gnocchi with Chestnuts

Linda has been making potato gnocchi ever since Marcella Hazan's first book, The Classic Italian Cookbook, *appeared in 1976. She has always heeded Marcella's admonition to avoid adding too much flour by adding it slowly, stopping when the mixture is soft and smooth yet a tiny bit sticky. So when our generous friend Nucci Russo sent us her own recipe for chestnut gnocchi, we were prepared. Her instructions are too lovely to ignore, "In principle the problem of gnocchi (I have not to teach to you, of course) is the quantity of flour. But my grandmother said that we have not to weight the flour because the potato says how much it wants, so I prepare about 250 grams of flour but I stop to add when I feel it is enough. This is a 'sure' recipe. I have just prepared for Flavio yesterday."*

1 pound 1½ ounces (500 grams)
   dried chestnuts (see Sources,
   page 311)
1 pound 7 ounces (650 grams)
   Yukon gold potatoes
Up to 2 cups plus 2 tablespoons
   unbleached flour
Generous pinch sea salt

1 beaten egg, if needed
12 tablespoons (1½ sticks)
   unsalted butter
⅔ cup heavy cream (optional)
Freshly ground black or white
   pepper
Freshly grated Parmigiano-
   Reggiano

In a heavy saucepan, cover the chestnuts generously with slightly salted water. Boil with lid slightly ajar, adding water as needed, until the chestnuts are very tender, at least 1½ hours. When they easily mash in your fingers, they are ready. Working in two batches, purée the chestnuts in a food processor or food mill. Keep them warm.

When the chestnuts have been cooking for 60 minutes, cover the potatoes with lightly salted water and boil them until they are tender. Drain, cool slightly, then peel.

Mash the potatoes in a large bowl. Combine them with the chestnuts and mix lightly. Working again in batches, process this mixture through a food mill, creating a mound on a clean work surface. Make a well in the center and pour about 1⅔ cups flour and a generous pinch of salt in the well. Quickly work the flour and chestnut mixture together with your fingers, adding more flour only as needed. You can tell that you have added enough flour and the mixture is ready when the dough is smooth yet just a tad tacky. If the mixture just won't hold together, add half of the beaten egg and mix evenly into the dough.

With lightly floured hands, divide the dough into three equal parts, and shape each into a long rope about 1 inch in diameter. Cut each rope into pieces about ¾-inch long.

Using a long-tined fork, hold the fork with the curve at the bottom of the tines facing to the back. One at a time, with your index finger, gently press each small piece against the tines and let it drop. (This will make an indentation on one side and the fork-impressed lines on the other. This will ensure even cooking and little cups to hold the butter.) Repeat until all are shaped. Hold the gnocchi on a lightly floured cookie sheet in a warm place. Do not stack them on top of each other.

Just before serving, cook the gnocchi. Fill a large, wide soup pot with salted water and bring to a boil. At the same time, melt the butter in a small saucepan and carefully cook it until lightly browned. Pour it into a heated gratin dish and keep it warm.

Working with small batches, drop the gnocchi into the boiling water and cook them until they rise to the top. Check the first one by cutting it in half to determine doneness (they are usually cooked once they reach the surface). Using a Chinese frying strainer or large slotted spoon, transfer the drained gnocchi to the gratin dish with the browned butter and toss. Repeat until all the gnocchi are cooked and coated with the butter.

If you wish to use cream as well as butter, heat the cream until very hot and pour it over the gnocchi. Add more salt and some freshly ground white pepper. Toss gently and serve in heated bowls. Serve freshly grated Parmigiano-Reggiano on the side.

SERVES 6

Surprise Tagliatelle with Escarole, Ricotta, and Pine Nuts

An experienced Italian cook is able to hide a raw egg yolk in escarole-and-cheese-filled ravioli and cook them so skillfully that the yolk stays runny, forming a delicious sauce for the filling inside. Since we are still trying to master the timing, we have managed an alternative that is almost as spectacular, and a whole lot easier to prepare. The perfect finish comes from the toasted pine nuts. We really enjoy their rich flavor and crunch.

Kosher salt
⅓ cup cider vinegar
8 medium-sized eggs, each cracked
   and in a small dish
1 pound trimmed escarole, cut in
   2-inch lengths
1½ sticks (12 tablespoons)
   unsalted butter
½ cup toasted pine nuts

1½ pounds tagliatelle (fettuccine)
1 cup fresh whole-milk ricotta
   cheese, brought close to room
   temperature
Sea salt and freshly ground black
   pepper to taste
Freshly grated Parmigiano-Reggiano
   for garnish

Fill a large soup pot with water. Salt it generously and place it over high heat to boil. Fill a large sauté pan with water, add several tablespoons of salt and the vinegar, then cover and bring to a boil. At the same time, fill a shallow bowl with warm water and place nearby.

Poach the eggs, 2 to 4 at a time, lowering heat as you put them into the water. With the water at a slow bubble, use a large spoon to bring the egg whites up and over each egg. You can increase the heat somewhat after you have "shaped" each egg into a neat package. When the whites are cooked and the yolks are still very runny, about 3 minutes, use a slotted spoon to transfer the eggs to the water bowl. (Using kitchen scissors, trim jagged pieces and shape each poached egg.) Or, if you have one, use a multiple egg poacher.

Keep the poaching water bubbling even after the eggs are cooked. Try to skim away any lingering egg white. Blanch the escarole in the bubbling water. Transfer the escarole to a large, heated bowl without draining any water clinging to it.

Pour the water from the sauté pan off, then add the butter and nuts. Cook over medium heat until the butter begins to brown. While the butter is browning, cook the pasta according to the package directions. Reserving ¾ cup of hot water, drain the pasta and transfer it to the escarole bowl. Add the butter and nuts to the escarole, along with the ricotta; add sea salt and pepper to taste. Toss well. Slowly add some of the reserved pasta water to make a thin sauce for the pasta.

Divide the pasta among 6 warmed soup plates (not bowls). Place a trimmed egg on top of each plate; make certain that each plate gets enough escarole, browned butter, and nuts. Sprinkle with grated Parmigiano-Reggiano.

Tell your guests to break the yolks at once to make additional sauce for their serving.

SERVES 6 TO 8

Bucatini with Lusty Lamb Ragout

The distinctive flavor of lamb blends beautifully with this marvelously flavored sauce. Long, slow cooking is what makes this an unusually rich sauce. Crunchy hazelnuts add another exciting layer of flavor and texture. The addition of garlic butter at the end gives the dish an extraordinarily silky texture. We first wrote about D'Amico Cucina in our first book back in 1990, when we picked it as one of the Best of the Midwest: to this day it is still one of the hottest restaurants in Minneapolis. Former Clevelanders, the brothers D'Amico, Larry and Richard, sent us more recipes than we could handle then. Now is the right time to share this one.

¼ cup olive oil

2 pounds lean ground lamb

1 cup finely chopped onion

½ cup finely chopped carrots

½ cup finely chopped celery

½ cup finely chopped parsnips

½ cup finely chopped leeks, whites and tender green parts

12 plump garlic cloves, minced

8 cups tomato purée

3 dried chile peppers, crushed

Kosher salt and freshly ground black pepper to taste

1½ pounds bucatini (long narrow hollow pasta)

4 tablespoons butter, at room temperature

3 plump garlic cloves, pressed

⅔ cup toasted chopped hazelnuts

3 tablespoons minced fresh herbs (basil, thyme, flat-leaf parsley)

1¼ cups freshly grated Parmigiano-Reggiano

Sea salt

Fresh herbs and edible flowers for garnish

In a large sauté pan, heat the olive oil. Add the lamb, onion, carrots, celery, parsnips, leeks, and garlic. Stir over medium heat until the lamb is lightly browned. Add the tomato purée and peppers and barely simmer over low heat for 2 hours. Skim off the surface fat. Stir in salt and pepper to taste. Increase the heat and simmer briskly for 3 to 5 minutes to thicken.

Cook the pasta according to the instructions. Then drain and add the pasta to the sauce in the sauté pan. Toss well, then add the butter, garlic, nuts, herbs, and cheese. Toss thoroughly.

Divide among heated soup plates. Sprinkle with some sea salt and garnish with fresh herbs.

SERVE 6

Pasta with Lemon, Walnuts, and Garlic

In our house, this is comfort food. When we are hungry but too tired to cook, we always know we can pull together a marvelous sauce for pasta just using a few simple ingredients. Nothing could be simpler, or more delicious, than walnuts, butter, lemon, and cheese. These are ingredients that are always available as well.

1 pound pasta, such as linguine, or
 spaghettini
1 tablespoon olive oil
3 tablespoons unsalted butter
1 dried chile, crumbled
⅔ cup finely chopped toasted
 walnuts

3 plump cloves garlic, pressed
Zest and 1 tablespoon juice from
 1 lemon
½ cup freshly grated Parmigiano-
 Reggiano, plus more for garnish
Kosher salt and freshly ground black
 pepper

Cook the pasta according to the package directions.

As the water comes to a boil, in a small skillet combine the olive oil, butter, and crumbled chile. Melt over low heat. Add the walnuts and sauté, stirring often, for 3 to 4 minutes. Add the garlic and lemon zest; stir for 30 seconds. Set the pan aside while the pasta is cooking. Reheat very carefully just before serving.

Drain the al dente pasta. Toss with the lemon juice, then with the walnut mixture and salt and pepper. Then toss with half the cheese.

Serve in heated bowls with more cheese on the side.

SERVES 4 TO 6

A Little Nut Music

Lyricist Arthur Swanstrom was trying to be romantic. In a song written for a 1933 Broadway musical, he had his hero proclaim that apple pie would tire him, ice cream would bore him, but peanuts and kisses, experienced together, would make him want more of both. (It sure didn't sound very appetizing to us.)

Singer and pianist Michael Feinstein, who knows as much about the American popular song as anyone, found "Peanuts and Kisses," for us. It is from the Broadway musical, *Hold Your Horses*, which opened in September 1933 at the Winter Garden in New York. It had a very modest run of just eighty-eight performances before slipping quietly away.

In his research, Michael found a total of twenty-eight nut songs, but only two, "I've Got a Lovely Bunch of Coconuts" and "The Peanut Vendor," are widely known. In addition to "Peanuts and Kisses," there were thirteen other songs with peanuts in the title. Coconuts came in second with seven. There were three chestnut songs, and one each for almonds, pistachios, and Brazil nuts. He also remembered that the late Rosemary Clooney had performed a song called "Love, Nuts, and Noodles" in his New York nightclub. It was written in 1932 by jazzman Red Nichols.

We remembered a singing commercial that told you to "ask your mummy to fill your tummy with Grape-Nuts," a cereal that contained neither, and a Civil War era song about "Eating Goober Peas," or raw peanuts right out of the ground.

Not a lot of nuts in our music. On the other hand, a surprising number of musical groups have saluted the nut in selecting a name. Cocktail Nuts is a Florida based combo that plays jazz, swing, and blues. Want them for a wedding? Check them at their Web site: *www.neverglades.com/cnuts*. Mixed Nuts is a popular Quebec punk band, trying, at last report, to get a CD on the market. Squirrel Nut Zippers is a swing band in Chapel Hill, North Carolina. The musicians in that group do other things, but music is a passionate hobby. One Groovy Coconut is a versatile band from Amityville, New York. Go-Nuts, Ginger Nuts, and Loose Nuts are also interested in playing for you.

And one of the key members of Kraftwerk, the cerebral German rock band of the sixties and seventies, has reentered the music scene as Mr. Coconut in a Chilean-based group that puts a South American twist on the austere minimalist music of his earlier career.

light meals, sauces, and relishes

Blintzes with Goat Cheese, Smoked Salmon, and Toasted Walnuts

Strudel Rolls with Curried Couscous, Pistachios, and Root Vegetables

Wayne's Supper Salad with Macadamia Nuts

Thai Shrimp and Noodle Salad with Peanut Sauce

Curried Chicken Salad with Toasted Black Walnuts

A New Look at Pesto

Minted Pesto with Pistachios

Romesco Sauce

A Green Nut Sauce

Rémoulade Sauce with Almonds

Lemon Pecan Mayonnaise

Confederate Relish with Pecans

Coconut Chutney

Blintzes with Goat Cheese, Smoked Salmon, and Toasted Walnuts

Blintzes are really a kind of crêpe, or very thin pancake, that are filled and fried. Traditional blintzes are filled with cottage cheese. Ours are filled with chèvre studded with smoked salmon and crunchy walnuts and will be served as a light supper or a lovely celebratory luncheon. A little green salad tossed with walnut oil is all you need on the side. Start with a simple tomato soup and finish with some luscious fruit. You will have some very happy guests for sure. One further note, we fry our blintzes in clarified butter (ghee) so they will not burn as easily.

1 stick (8 tablespoons) unsalted
   butter

BLINTZ BATTER

3 eggs

1¼ cups water

¼ teaspoon salt

½ teaspoon freshly ground white
   pepper

3 tablespoons unsalted butter,
   melted

1 cup unbleached flour

2 tablespoons pastry flour

THE FILLING

8 ounces soft goat cheese (chèvre)

¾ cups whole-milk ricotta

1 egg

2 teaspoons minced fresh dill

1 tablespoon minced shallot

½ to 1 teaspoon salt

½ teaspoon freshly ground white
   pepper

½ cup finely diced smoked salmon

½ cup finely chopped toasted
   walnuts

Sour cream, fresh dill, salmon caviar,
   thinly sliced smoked salmon, and
   more chopped toasted walnuts
   for garnish

To clarify the butter: Melt the stick of butter and pour it into a glass measuring cup and chill. When the butter has solidfied, gently transfer it to a clean dish and discard the milky residue. Reserve the clarified butter for frying the blintzes.

To make the blintz batter: In the bowl of a food processor fitted with a metal blade, combine the eggs, water, salt, pepper, and 2 tablespoons of the butter. Pulse to mix well. Add the flours and pulse until well blended. Scrape the sides and pulse about 4 times. Pour the batter into a bowl and refrigerate for 30 minutes. If the mixture is too thick to pour easily into a skillet, thin with some more water. (The density depends upon your flour.)

To make the filling: In the bowl of a food processor, combine the chèvre, ricotta, egg, dill, shallot, salt, and pepper. Pulse until thoroughly blended. Scrape the mixture into a bowl. Using a spatula, blend in the salmon and nuts. Cover with plastic wrap and chill until needed.

To prepare the blintzes: Prepare a stack of about 18 small squares of wax paper, so you can stack the little crêpes without their sticking to one another.

With the clarified butter, lightly butter and heat over high heat a well-seasoned crêpe pan that is 6 inches in diameter. When hot, add a scant 2 tablespoons of batter to the hot skillet. Quickly tilt the pan to distribute the batter evenly around it. Reduce the heat to medium and cook for about 1 minute. Turn the blintz gently with your fingers or a spatula and cook for about ½ minute on the other side. Turn out on a tea towel; repeat until all of the batter is used. Put strips of waxed paper between the blintzes. Add more butter to the pan only if necessary. Arrange the blintzes browned-side up.

Place a heaping tablespoon of filling in middle of each blintz, just a bit closer to you than the center. Roll the short end over the filling, fold the sides over, and roll. Each package should be about 3½ inches long and 1½ inches wide. Arrange the blintzes seam-side down on a large tray, cover with plastic wrap, and keep chilled until 30 minutes before serving time.

When you are ready to serve, melt some clarified butter in a cast-iron skillet over medium-high heat. Fry the blintzes until browned on both sides, about 5 minutes total.

Arrange 3 blintzes on each of 6 heated plates. Garnish with dollops of sour cream, dill, some salmon caviar, and a slice or two of smoked salmon. Sprinkle lightly with chopped toasted walnuts and serve.

SERVES **6**

Strudel Rolls with Curried Couscous, Pistachios, and Root Vegetables

Couscous piqued by a zesty mélange of curried root vegetables and lightly toasted pistachio nuts makes a satisfying filling for our crunchy phyllo. It is a dish that is enjoyed by meat eaters and vegetarians alike. Phyllo is easy to handle as long as you are not stingy with butter—a trade-off worthwhile from time to time. You can even prepare these early in the day, keeping them covered with plastic wrap and refrigerated for several hours before baking. Just be sure that the rolls are well buttered all over. We made our first savory strudel roll after reading about a lamb roll in The Splendid Grain *by Rebecca Wood (Morrow, 1997).*

1 cup vegetable stock
2 sticks (16 tablespoons) unsalted
   butter, melted

½ package instant couscous
3 tablespoons olive oil
1 cup finely chopped yellow onion

¾ cup finely chopped turnips

¾ cup finely chopped yams

2 plump garlic cloves, minced

2 tablespoons minced fresh ginger

½ cup finely diced dried apricots

1 tablespoon good-quality curry
  powder

1 dried chile, crumbled

1 cup lightly toasted pistachio nuts

Kosher salt and freshly ground
  white pepper to taste

1 package frozen phyllo dough,
  defrosted

In a medium-sized saucepan, bring the stock and 1 tablespoon of the butter to a rolling boil. Stir the couscous into it, remove the pan from the heat, cover, and let it stand for 15 minutes. Using a fork, stir it vigorously to keep clumps from forming.

In a medium-sized sauté pan, heat the oil over medium heat. Stir in the onion, turnips, and yams. Cover and cook over low heat until the yams are tender, 10 to 15 minutes. Then combine with the couscous in a large bowl.

Melt 2 additional tablespoons butter in a small skillet over medium heat. Add the garlic, ginger, apricots, curry powder, and chile. Stir until the aroma is warm and wonderful. Remove the pan from the heat and stir the contents into the couscous mixture along with the pistachios. Season to taste with salt and pepper.

Melt the remaining butter over low heat.

Preheat the oven to 400°F.

Unroll the phyllo dough, long side parallel to your body, on a dry surface. Using a sharp knife, cut the stack of sheets in half. This should make at least 32 small sheets. Immediately cover the sheets with some plastic wrap and a damp towel.

Remove 4 sheets of phyllo, 1 at a time. Brush each with melted butter, carefully stacking each over the other. Spread a rounded ½ cup of filling along 1 end of the short side, about 1 inch from the end, leaving ½ inch on either side free of any filling. From the end with the filling, roll 1 or 2 turns to totally enclose the filling. Then fold in the 2 long edges of the phyllo, and tightly roll to the end of the strip. Butter the outside thoroughly. Place the package on a large, well-buttered baking sheet, loosely covered with a sheet of waxed paper. Repeat with the remaining phyllo. If you are not baking it immediately, be sure to cover it tightly with plastic wrap.

Bake the packages until golden brown, 15 to 20 minutes. Remove them from the oven. Serve as whole packages, or cut in half on a diagonal before serving.

SERVES 6 TO 8

Wayne's Supper Salad with Macadamia Nuts

Celebrated cooking teacher and author Lydie Marshall and her husband, Wayne, spend most of their time in the Provençal town of Nyons now, but they used to celebrate Thanksgiving with us here in Cleveland. One of the nights of their stay here, or during our visits there, Wayne and Fred prepared a "supper" salad, using leftover turkey. In summer we often make it with good canned Italian tuna, or some grilled chicken or flank steak. Work on this book led us to adding nuts as well. Macadamias are the best; they make something wonderful, sublime.

3 tablespoons olive oil

1 plump garlic clove, pressed

2 to 4 slices country bread, cut into cubes

1 cup cooked white, brown, or wild rice, or

2 cups quartered, cooked new potatoes

4 hard-boiled eggs, sliced

4 carrots, finely chopped

1 generous chunk celery root, grated

Bunch of radishes, sliced

1 medium-sized red onion, thinly sliced

1 large red bell pepper, cut into medium dice

1 fennel bulb, trimmed and thinly sliced

⅔ cup quartered and cooked green beans

⅓ cup sliced pitted Nyons, Niçoise, or Kalamata olives

Mixed salad greens, 1 to 3 cups

2 or 3 vine-ripened tomatoes, coarsely diced (only in season)

3 cups diced cooked chicken, turkey, or thinly sliced flank steak

8 anchovy fillets, preferably from rinsed salt-dried anchovies

1 tablespoon Dijon mustard

½ cup good plain yogurt

1 plump garlic clove, pressed

¼ cup rich red wine vinegar

¼ cup extra virgin olive oil, plus more if needed

⅔ cup coarsely chopped macadamia nuts

½ cup minced fresh herbs, such as thyme, basil, lemon verbena, and chives

Kosher salt and freshly ground black pepper to taste

Heat the olive oil in a large skillet over high heat. Add the pressed garlic and bread cubes and toss in the oil until the cubes are golden. Set aside.

In a large salad bowl, combine the rice (or potatoes), sliced eggs, carrots, celery root, radishes, onion, bell pepper, fennel, green beans, olives, greens, tomatoes, whatever meat you are using, and the anchovies. Set aside.

In a small bowl, combine the mustard, yogurt, garlic, and vinegar. Blend thoroughly with a whisk. Slowly add the olive oil, whisking vigorously. Taste; if the dressing is too tart, slowly add more oil.

Pour the dressing over the salad. Sprinkle the nuts and herbs over the top. Season lavishly with salt and pepper. Gently toss until dressing is evenly blended, place in the center of a large dinner plate, and serve at once.

SERVES 4 TO 6

Thai Shrimp and Noodle Salad with Peanut Sauce

The mélange of hot chile sauce and the lovely sweet and crunchy peanut butter make a really dynamic duo. The supporting players include ginger, limes, garlic, and Nam Pla, the sour and mellow fish sauce of Thailand. Add shrimp and noodles and you have a great luncheon main dish, or a prelude to dinner. If you have leftover sauce, store it in a tightly closed, clean container in the refrigerator for up to two weeks.

5 to 6 ounces Thai rice noodles
    (available in Asian markets and
    some supermarkets)
2 tablespoons sesame oil
1 cup boiling water
2/3 cup chunky peanut butter
2 tablespoons chile sauce
2 tablespoons minced fresh ginger
Juice of 3 limes
3 plump garlic cloves, pressed
1/4 cup sweet soy sauce
1/4 cup dark sesame oil

1 tablespoon Nam Pla (fish sauce;
    available in Asian markets and
    some supermarkets)
1 cup shredded napa cabbage
1 large sweet onion, grated
4 medium-sized carrots, grated
1 1/2 to 2 pounds peeled and
    cooked large shrimp
1/3 cup minced fresh cilantro
1/2 cup coarsely chopped roasted
    peanuts
6 wedges fresh lime

Prepare the noodles by filling a large bowl with warm water and soak the rice noodles for 30 minutes, then drain thoroughly. Next fill a large saucepan with water and bring to a boil. Drop the noodles into the pot. Using chopsticks, gently separate the noodle strands to prevent clumping. When the water begins to boil, drain the noodles at once and plunge them into a bowl of ice water. Thoroughly drain, then toss them in a bowl with 2 tablespoons of sesame oil. Reserve at room temperature, stirring and lifting the strands with chopsticks from time to time to prevent clumping.

In the bowl of a food processor, combine 1 cup boiling water and the peanut butter. Pulse to blend. Add the chile sauce, ginger, lime juice, garlic, soy sauce, sesame oil, and fish sauce. Blend thoroughly and set aside.

In a large mixing bowl, combine the noodles, peanut sauce, cabbage, onion, and carrots. Toss to blend thoroughly. Add half of the shrimp and toss again.

Divide the mixture among 6 plates. Garnish with the remaining shrimp. Sprinkle with cilantro and chopped peanuts and serve with a wedge of lime.

SERVES **6**

"I Brake for Boiled Peanuts"

—A South Carolina bumper sticker

Justin, the Forager

Justin Rashid grew up in a family that understood and treasured the bounty of the woods. As a kid he was a forager in the Michigan forests. In the fall, he gathered black walnuts and dried them on the basement floor. Then in the winter he cracked them in ways that would drive OSHA crazy.

He collected all of the wild nuts, fiddlehead ferns, and wild berries. He also knew where to find morels. (Rule one of the forager: Never tell anyone where you got your morels.) They became the first forest food that he sold. New York chef Larry Forgione became a customer.

Eventually they became partners in American Spoon Foods, which collects and distributes the rare wild foods of the forests. During the long run of Forgione's restaurant, An American Place, you would always find these great, but almost unknown, treasures featured in dish after dish.

Justin will buy any wild nuts that a forager will collect, but they are always expensive. Forgione once asked for some beechnuts. They are delicious, but they are very tiny and hard to handle. Despite the fact that it had been a "mast" year—a year with a lot of forest activity—it still cost $32 just to produce a cup of shelled beechnuts.

American Spoon Foods (see Sources, page 311) is one of the few places in the country where you can still find the great wild nuts of the forest for sale. However, forest stewardship, saving the woods and replacing the forests we have destroyed, is Justin Rashid's biggest passion. He understands that the health of the planet is at stake.

Curried Chicken Salad with Toasted Black Walnuts

We always have black walnuts in the freezer. Toasted, they are delicious with a good chicken or turkey salad, especially when the mayonnaise is made from scratch. This is a very flavorful preparation. The combination of zesty curry works magically with the pungent toasted black walnuts—especially when there is a sparkling of sweetness from the dried cherries. Yes, Hellmann's is fine, but the truth is that homemade is even better.

THE MAYONNAISE

2 egg yolks

Zest of 1 lemon

1 teaspoon dry mustard

2 tablespoons fresh lemon juice

1 tablespoon fruit vinegar

½ cup extra virgin olive oil

½ cup organic canola oil

1 tablespoon good-quality curry
    powder, preferably Madras-style

2 teaspoons kosher salt, plus more
    if needed

1 teaspoon freshly ground white
    pepper, plus more if desired

½ teaspoon ground cayenne, plus
    more if desired

THE SALAD

6 cups cooked diced chicken, cut
    in ½-inch cubes

1 cup medium-diced sweet onion
    (or Spanish)

2 stalks medium-diced celery

½ cup dried cherries

2 hard-boiled eggs, sliced

⅓ cup minced fresh flat-leaf parsley

¼ cup minced fresh tarragon

¾ cup chopped toasted black
    walnuts

Leaf lettuce for garnish

To make the mayonnaise: In the bowl of a food processor combine the egg yolks, lemon zest, mustard, lemon juice, and vinegar. Pulse to blend well; scrape down the sides. With the motor running, very slowly add the oils to make a thick emulsion. Scrape down the sides and pulse in curry powder, salt, pepper, and cayenne. Transfer the mayonnaise to a small bowl and reserve.

To assemble the salad: In a large bowl, combine the chicken, onion, celery, and cherries. Add most of the mayonnaise; toss to coat well. Blend in the eggs, parsley, and tarragon. Taste and adjust the seasonings; add more mayonnaise if you desire.

Cover the salad and any remaining mayonnaise with plastic wrap and chill for 2 to 4 hours.

To serve, divide the lettuce among 6 plates. Then mound the chicken salad on the lettuce. Add a dollop of the remaining mayonnaise to the top of the chicken salad mound.

Sprinkle each lavishly with toasted black walnuts and serve with warm bread.

SERVES 6 TO 8

A New Look at Pesto

Fred Plotkin's Recipes from Paradise *is a mouthwatering collection of recipes and lore about one of Italy's most glorious regions—Liguria. His enthusiasm for our project was palpable. "You have to go and eat there," he said. "The Ligurians do glorious things with nuts, even though the nuts may come from Piedmont." Then he began to wax rhapsodic about the chestnuts, hazelnuts, and walnuts of Piedmont and the exceptional dishes the Ligurians make with them. This simple walnut pesto is adapted from his book. Among the wealth of information offered by Fred Plotkin is that the Ligurians would not use large-leaf basil, preferring the delicate flavor of small-leafed plants. This is something every cook can experiment with— substituting lemon basil or the "globe basil" sometimes called "Greek basil," instead of our most commonly grown large-leaf one. Please try to make this by hand with a mortar and pestle. The flavor difference is really worth the effort. We searched two continents until we happily schelpped home a twenty-pound stone mortar we found in San Francisco's amazing secondhand cookware store, Cookin' (located on Divisadero Street). Use your pesto at room temperature. Do not cook it.*

¼ teaspoon kosher or sea salt

½ cup packed small fresh basil leaves, preferably globe basil, or a mixture of lemon and globe basil, stems removed

½ cup loosely packed large fresh basil leaves, stems removed

1 plump garlic clove

½ cup coarsely broken, very lightly toasted walnut meats

3 tablespoons freshly grated Parmigiano-Reggiano

1 tablespoon freshly grated Pecorino Romano

Up to 4 tablespoons extra virgin olive oil, preferably from Liguria

In a mortar, combine the salt with about ¼ of the basil, leaves torn. Pound them together using a rocking motion all over the mortar, gradually adding more and more torn leaves until they are all used. Add the garlic and pound it until it releases its juices. Then pound in the nuts until they form a paste. Combine the ingredients well, then add the cheese and blend it together with the paste. Slowly stir in the oil until the pesto is very creamy.

(If you are using a food processor or a blender, start by processing the salt and basil until they are finely chopped. Add the nuts and pulse until pasty. Add the cheese and blend it all together. With the motor running, slowly add the oil until the desired creaminess is achieved.)

Scrape the pesto into a clean bowl, cover tightly, and chill in the refrigerator until several hours before using. Bring it to room temperature before serving.

MAKES ABOUT **1** CUP OR **6** SERVINGS

Minted Pesto with Pistachios

Our organic gardens yield a plethora of herbs every summer. What began as one small lemon verbena plant sent Federal Express by our Memphis cousin, Susan Cavitch, is now three enormous shrubs that winter yearly in an area greenhouse. Lemon verbena adds a sensational flavor to just about everything, so one day we decided to try it with basil and mint—and then we thought, hmm, pistachios! Then some cheese, and that led us to California Press's sensational pistachio oil (see sources, page 311). Now we have a superlative pesto that cannot only be used with pasta, but is marvelous under prosciutto on pizza, or pushed under the skin of butterflied chickens.

1 teaspoon sea salt

1 cup fresh basil leaves, preferably lemon basil

½ cup fresh fruit mint leaves

½ cup fresh lemon verbena or lemon balm leaves

3 plump garlic cloves

Zest of 1 lemon

½ cup shelled pistachio nuts, very lightly toasted

¼ cup grated Parmigiano-Reggiano

4 tablespoons unsalted butter, softened

½ teaspoon freshly ground white pepper, plus more if needed

⅓ cup pistachio oil (or extra virgin olive oil)

In a mortar, combine the salt with about ¼ cup of the basil leaves, torn. Pound them together using a rocking motion all over the mortar, gradually adding more and more of them and the other torn herb leaves until they are all used. Add the garlic and pound it until it releases its juices. Then pound in the zest and nuts; pound until they form a paste. Pound in the cheese, then the butter and pepper. Slowly stir in the oil until the pesto is very creamy.

(If you are using a food processor or blender, start by processing the salt and herbs until finely chopped. Add the nuts and lemon zest; pulse until they are pasty. Add the cheese and butter, blending well. With the motor running, slowly add the oil until the desired creaminess is achieved.)

SERVES 6 TO 10

Romesco Sauce

According to Penelope Casas, premier American author of things Spanish, romesco sauce comes from the ancient city of Tarragona, just south of Barcelona. This Catalan city was attractive to many invaders over the centuries. In fact, the ancient Romans left many monuments there long before the Arabs left theirs. Arab influence can easily be seen in this sauce, which was at first made only with almonds. In Tarragona, romesco accompanies seafood or is a sauce in which the seafood is cooked. Over the years the sauce's lively flavors have increased its popularity and the dishes with which it is served. Today's romesco is a heady blend of sweet and hot peppers with nuts, garlic, and olive oil, usually made into a silken sauce with the help of a mortar and pestle. Not only do we serve it with Bacalà Cakes (page 65), but we also use it with a spicy stuffed Rolled Flank Steak (page 207). The possibilities are endless. If you wish to use a food processor, we suggest that you first grind the nuts and garlic in a spice grinder. This helps to approximate the texture achieved by the mortar. The sauce keeps for several weeks.

¼ teaspoon kosher salt

7 plump garlic cloves, smashed and peeled

10 toasted almonds, chopped

10 toasted hazelnuts, chopped

1 small slice country bread, crust removed

1 dried chile pepper, seeded and crumbled

2 tablespoons minced fresh flat-leaf parsley

1 large sweet red pepper, roasted, peeled, seeded, and chopped

⅓ cup extra virgin olive oil, plus more if needed

3 tablespoons good sherry vinegar

In a large mortar, combine the salt and garlic. Pound vigorously with a pestle until smooth. Then pound in the nuts, bread, and dried chile. Continue to pound vigorously, gradually adding the parsley, then the roasted pepper. When the mixture is very smooth, slowly add the olive oil, then the vinegar. If the mixture is too thick, thin it slowly with more oil. (If you are using a food processor, pulse in the same order.) Store the sauce in the refrigerator for up to 1 month. Bring it to room temperature before serving.

MAKES ABOUT **1** CUP

A Green Nut Sauce

Our list of ingredients might appear to be strange bedfellows, but ground together their individual flavors blend to make a piquant whole that works as a dip for fresh vegetables. This tangy sauce is an outstanding accompaniment to beef, poultry, and fish that are cooked on a grill. It would also be a neat sauce for a plate of grilled vegetables. It will keep for a few days if refrigerated in a tightly covered container. If you are skilled with a mortar and pestle, use it; the sauce will be even more delicious.

1 teaspoon sea salt
4 plump garlic cloves
¼ cup fresh basil leaves
¼ cup fresh flat-leaf parsley
¼ cup fresh mint leaves, preferably fruit or spearmint
15 whole toasted almonds

15 toasted hazelnuts
1 teaspoon dry English mustard
2 teaspoons rich red wine vinegar
⅓ cup extra virgin olive oil
Freshly ground black pepper to taste

In a mortar, combine the salt and garlic. Pound until thoroughly broken and somewhat creamy. Gradually pound in the herbs, then slowly add the nuts, mustard, and vinegar, pounding it into a paste. Slowly add the olive oil. Season with pepper and more salt if desired.

Let sauce stand at room temperature for several hours before serving.

MAKES ABOUT ¾ CUP

Rémoulade Sauce with Almonds

This almond-tinged sauce is outstanding with cooked shrimp, stuffed hard-boiled eggs, and even as a dressing for chicken salad. It also stores very well in the refrigerator. If you don't wish to make your own mayonnaise, use Hellmann's or Best Food's.

⅓ cup slivered, blanched, and toasted almonds
1 hard-boiled egg
1 cup homemade mayonnaise (see recipe page 153)
¼ cup chili sauce, preferably Bennett's
¼ cup prepared white horseradish

2 teaspoons dry mustard
2 tablespoons minced onion
2 tablespoons fresh flat-leaf parsley leaves
1 rounded tablespoon anchovy paste
1 tablespoon fresh lemon juice
Kosher salt and freshly ground black pepper

Pulse the almonds and egg in a food processor until finely ground and combined. Add the remaining ingredients and run the motor until all are puréed together. Season, scrape the sides and bottom, and pulse again. Taste and adjust if necessary.

Scrape the sauce into a clean container, cover tightly, and store in the refrigerator until needed.

MAKES 1 1/2 CUPS

Lemon Pecan Mayonnaise

A mayonnaise that boasts the nutty flavors of both roasted garlic and pecan oil has to be delicious with just about everything—and this one is. We enjoy it with shellfish or cold chicken dishes—just about anything that might call for mayonnaise. You can store this in a clean, tightly sealed container in the refrigerator for at least one week. If you use a Cuisinart processor, take a look at the container that fits into the tube on the top. There is a tiny hole in it; that's for making mayonnaise! It allows oils to dribble into the eggs at just the right speed. It is just wonderful. By the way, feel free to "kick the heat up a notch" by using a tad more cayenne.

3 large egg yolks

4 cloves roasted garlic
   (see Basics, page 53)

1/2 teaspoon ground cayenne, plus
   more if you wish

1 tablespoon Dijon mustard

3 tablespoons fresh lemon juice

1 tablespoon champagne or pear
   vinegar

1/4 cup roasted pecan oil

1/4 extra virgin olive oil

1/2 cup organic canola oil

Kosher salt and freshly ground
   white pepper to taste

1 tablespoon minced fresh chives

In the bowl of a food processor, combine the egg yolks, garlic, cayenne, mustard, lemon juice, and vinegar; pulse several times, then keep adding oil to the tube container, so it will very slowly add the oils to the eggs, making a thick emulsion. Add salt, pepper, and chives. Chill until needed.

MAKES ABOUT 1 1/3 CUPS

Confederate Relish with Pecans

We are blessed with two splendid sources for organic, heirloom tomato seedlings, so we usually grow several dozen different varieties. At least twice what two people require! Come fall, our harvest of green ones is enormous. This dark, lusty relish, a jewel adapted from Marion Flexner's Out of Kentucky Kitchens, *includes cucumbers, onions, hot and mild peppers, crunchy pecan pieces, as well as seasonings ranging from horseradish to allspice and mace. It's similar in taste to a really good chili sauce. Serve it with dishes ranging from grilled fish and chicken to burgers, hash, corned beef, or any leftover meat. It makes a fine gift.*

15 green tomatoes, ends removed

9 medium yellow onions

2 English cucumbers, ends trimmed

2 large green bell peppers, seeded

2 hot fresh chile peppers

1 red bell pepper

½ cup kosher salt

3 cups cider vinegar

⅔ cup prepared white horseradish

3 tablespoons dry mustard

1 tablespoon freshly ground black pepper

1 tablespoon ground ginger

2 teaspoons ground cloves

2 teaspoons ground turmeric

1 teaspoon ground mace

1 teaspoon freshly grated nutmeg

4 packed cups dark brown sugar

1½ cups broken and toasted pecan pieces

Either through a grinder or a food processor, carefully process the tomatoes, onions, cucumbers, and peppers so they are in tiny pieces, not puréed. Combine the ground vegetables in a large crockery or non-aluminum bowl and mix with salt. Cover the bowl tightly and let it stand at room temperature overnight.

In batches, thoroughly drain the mixture the next day. It also helps to turn it into the center of a very heavy bath towel and squeeze the moisture out. Reserve.

Pour the vinegar into a heavy soup pot and bring it to a boil over high heat. At the same time, in a small bowl, combine the horseradish, dry mustard, black pepper, ginger, cloves, turmeric, mace, and nutmeg. Moisten the seasoning mixture with ¾ cup hot vinegar. Blend well, then add it to the vinegar pot. Stir in the brown sugar. When the mixture comes to a boil again, add the chopped vegetables.

Cook, stirring often, until the mixture begins to boil. Cover, reduce the heat to very low, and simmer for 3 to 4 hours, or until the mixture is the consistency of marmalade. Stir in the broken pecan pieces. If there is a lot of liquid, simmer, uncovered, for about 15 minutes to reduce it.

Let it cool and spoon into sterilized jars. Seal tightly and store it in the refrigerator. Serve the relish heated, or at room temperature, as a side sauce.

MAKES ABOUT **5** PINTS

Coconut Chutney

This simple chutney combines the basic ingredients of Kerala to make a robust relish, or chutney. It stores well and will add a zesty touch to any dish that suggests India. In Nimmy Paul's home it might also be served as a snack. "Spread some between two salted biscuits," she wrote. "It makes a perfect snack for short eats." Most organic markets sell young coconuts. Be sure to drink the water before you open it for the flesh.

1 cup freshly grated coconut,
   preferably young coconut
2 fresh green chiles

1 tablespoon minced fresh ginger
2 plump shallots
Kosher salt to taste

Grind the coconut, chiles, ginger, and shallots together to make a thick paste. If it is too dry, mix in a little coconut milk (see Basics, page 50). Season with salt. Store in a clean container in the refrigerator. Serve with prawns, shrimp, biriyani, and other spicy Indian dishes.

SERVES **6**

fish and shellfish

Nut Meal Pan-Fried Oysters on Toast with Lemon Pistachio Mayonnaise

Tamarind's Baked Lobster with Macadamia and Shellfish Stuffing

Clam Stew with Garlic and Almonds

Keralan Prawns with Cashews and Chiles

Vietnamese Shrimp in Caramel Sauce with Peanuts

Shrimp Cantonese with Salted Peanuts

Thai-Style Shrimp with Peanuts and Lettuce

Sautéed Soft-Shell Crabs with Hazelnuts

Pan-Fried Trout with Turkish Pine Nut Sauce

Red Snapper Amandine

Baked Sole with Lemon Walnut Crust

Pan-Braised Halibut in Garlic Hot Sauce with Peanuts

Lacquered Hazelnut Salmon

Roasted Bluefish with Shredded Horse-radish Pecan Crust

Georges Bank Cod in Spanish Sauce with Almonds

Baked Cod with Garlic, Vinegar, and Toasted Pine Nuts

Nut Meal Pan-Fried Oysters on Toast with Lemon Pistachio Mayonnaise

Fried oysters have always been one of Linda's favorites. Oysters breaded with finely chopped pistachios blew both of us away, when our friend, Paul Minnillo served them to us at his celebrated Cleveland restaurant, The Baricelli Inn. This dish is great for a small gathering of seafood lovers. Start with a raw bar, then finish with nut-crusted pan-fried oysters on grilled slices of bread, generously topped with a homemade mayonnaise. We suggest pistachios here, but you can use any nut and nut oil you wish.

LEMON PISTACHIO MAYONNAISE

¼ cup pistachio oil

½ cup vegetable oil

½ cup extra virgin olive oil

2 egg yolks

3 tablespoons lemon juice, plus
   more if needed

Sea salt and freshly ground white
   pepper to taste

1 plump garlic clove, chopped

Zest of 1 lemon

1 teaspoon Tabasco sauce

THE OYSTERS

36 large shucked oysters, with
   liquor

1 cup buttermilk

3 eggs

½ teaspoon ground mace

¼ teaspoon ground cayenne

1 cup finely chopped pistachios

½ cup unbleached flour

Up to 3 cups vegetable oil

6 thick slices bread

Sea salt and freshly ground white
   pepper to taste

Fresh minced parsley for garnish

2 lemons, cut into wedges

To make the mayonnaise: Combine the three oils in a large measuring cup and set aside.

Place the yolks, lemon juice, sea salt, and pepper in the bowl of a food processor. Pulse until blended. Scrape down the sides.

With the motor running, very slowly add the oils to the egg mixture. (If you use a Cuisinart processor, take a look at the container that fits into the tube on the top. There is a tiny hole in it; that's for making mayonnaise! It allows oils to dribble into the eggs at just the right speed.)

Scrape the sides, then again with motor running, add the garlic, lemon zest, and Tabasco. Taste and adjust the seasonings. If the mayonnaise is too thick, add more lemon juice. Scrape it into a serving bowl, cover, and refrigerate until needed.

To make the oysters: Drain the oyster liquor into a large, shallow bowl. Whisk in the buttermilk, eggs, mace, and cayenne. Add the oysters and toss to coat well in mixture.

In another shallow bowl blend together chopped nuts and flour; season with salt and pepper. Draining excess buttermilk mixture, coat oysters evenly in the nut mixture, placing them then on a large cake rack.

Heat ⅔ cup of the oil in a large cast-iron skillet over high heat. When the oil is hot enough to brown a cube of bread, begin to fry the oysters. Working in batches, and adding more oil as needed, fry until nicely brown on both sides, 3 to 5 minutes. Drain on paper towers and keep warm. While oysters are frying, toast or grill the slices of bread.

Place the toasts on warm serving plates. Slather with mayonnaise. Pile the oysters over the coated surface. Add a generous dollop of mayonnaise on the side. Sprinkle with salt, pepper, and parsley, and garnish with lemon wedges.

SERVES **4** TO **6**

Tamarind's Baked Lobster with Macadamia and Shellfish Stuffing

This is probably a rather sinful indulgence, but it is also exquisitely delicious. The silky texture of sea scallops and the rougher texture of crabmeat are in comfortable contrast to the nutty crunch of rich macadamia nuts. We were fortunate to have made two exceptional trips to Kenya in the mid-1980s. Our days in Nairobi were crowned by several delicious meals at The Tamarind, a restaurant with a Mombassa clone. There they served large Indian Ocean lobsters (no claws) with an utterly decadent stuffing that inspired this recipe.

1 stick (8 tablespoons) unsalted
    butter
1 crumbled dried chile
    pepper
1 medium-sized yellow onion,
    minced
2 plump garlic cloves, minced
6 (2-pound) lobsters
1 pound sea scallops, cut into
    medium dice
1 pound crabmeat, carefully picked
    over for pieces of shells, cut into
    medium dice

1½ cups coarsely chopped
    macadamia nuts, lightly toasted
1 cup soft bread crumbs
1 tablespoon fresh minced tarragon
Grated zest and juice of 1 lemon
Kosher salt and freshly ground
    white pepper to taste
1 cup heavy cream, plus more if
    needed
1 cup grated Gruyère cheese
Lemon wedges
Melted butter with lemon for
    dipping

In a small saucepan, combine the butter and chile. Cook over medium heat until the butter begins to bubble. Add the minced onion and garlic. Stir well and cook for 1 more minute. Let it cool.

To split the lobsters, place them shell-side down on a work surface. Insert a sharp knife into the abdomen and cut through thin shell toward tail. Pry the halves apart with your hands. Discard the stomach and intestines. Scrape the runny tomalley and coral roe, if any, into a large mixing bowl.

Add the sea scallops, crabmeat, nuts, crumbs, tarragon, lemon zest and juice, salt, and pepper. Blend the mixture thoroughly, then add the melted butter mixture. Gently blend again, then carefully stir in the cream and cheese.

Arrange the lobsters on baking sheets. Divide the stuffing among the lobsters, mounding it in each cavity. (You can refrigerate the lobsters for several hours at this point.)

Preheat the oven to 375°F. Bake the lobsters for 20 to 25 minutes, or until the shells are red and the stuffing is lightly browned. If baked straight from the refrigerator, you might want to insert a knife into the center of the stuffing and touch it to your lower lip to determine if the center is hot enough or needs a bit more cooking.

Place the lobsters on serving plates and serve with lemon wedges and melted butter for dipping.

SERVES **6**

Shakespeare on Nuts

In Shakespeare's work, you will find no cashews or Brazil nuts, no peanuts, pistachios, pecans, or pine nuts—and it is unlikely that the bard ever heard of a macadamia or a coconut. There were, however, a few nuts that made it into the great man's work.

In *Troilus and Cressida* it was said that "The parrot will not do more for an almond." In *Macbeth,* "A sailor's wife had chestnuts in her lap, and munch'd and munch'd." And in *Taming of the Shrew* we read that "Not half so great a blow to hear as will a chestnut in a farmer's fire." If you have roasted chestnuts on an open fire, you can relate to that one. In *As You Like It,* a comment on beautiful hair, "Your chestnut was ever the only colour."

Shakespeare's characters wax rhapsodic about the hazelnut. Petruchio in *Taming of the Shrew* says, "O sland'rous world! Kate like the hazel-twig is straight and slender, and as brown in hue as hazel-nuts, and sweeter than the kernels." In *The Tempest,* we are given this one, "I'll bring thee to clustering filberts."

The walnuts gets a couple of mentions. In *Merry Wives of Windsor* we learn that a jealous Ford, "searched a hollow walnut for his wife's leman." In *Shrew* we have this description, " 'Tis a cockle or a walnut-shell, a knack, a toy, a trick, a baby's cap."

There are some generic nuts as well. From *A Comedy of Errors,* "A hair, a drop of blood, a pin, a nut, a cherry-stone." Here are two from *As You Like It,* neither very complimentary, "Sweetest nut hath sourest rind. Such a nut is Rosalind." And "I do think him as concave as a covered goblet or a worm-eaten nut." Shakespeare sweetens up a little in *A Midsummer Night's Dream,* "I have a venturous fairy that shall seek the squirrel's hoard and fetch thee sweet nuts."

So the Bard did four of our twelve with some generic nut mentions. Certainly, had any of those other eight been around in the markets or eating houses of London or Stratford upon Avon, they would definitely have been immortalized in his work.

Clam Stew with Garlic and Almonds

Almonds, garlic, and tomatoes are among our most favorite combinations. Two roasted poblano peppers add just another flavor note to make the sauce particularly tasty. Combined with fish stock and clams these make a lusty sauce for our lovely clams. (Keep in mind this is a stew, not a soup.) We've become very fond of the aqua-cultured littleneck clams we get from Boston's Steve Connolly Seafood Company. They eliminate virtually all of the sand one invariably used to find when eating even the best-washed clams in the past.

Up to ½ cup extra virgin olive oil, plus more if needed

10 plump cloves garlic

2 large slices country bread, heavy crust trimmed

½ cup slivered almonds, lightly toasted

1 teaspoon kosher salt

½ cup minced white onion

2 roasted poblano peppers, peeled, seeded, and julienned

3 cups tomato purée

2 cups rich fish stock or clam broth, plus more if needed

Freshly ground black pepper

10 pounds aqua-cultured littleneck clams, rinsed

2½ to 3 cups steamed and buttered jasmine rice

⅓ cup minced fresh flat-leaf parsley

In a large sauté pan, heat the olive oil and garlic over medium heat. Stir and toss garlic until it turns golden, 5 to 8 minutes. Using a slotted spoon, transfer the garlic to a small dish. Adding more oil if needed, toast the bread on both sides until it is golden, then remove from the heat. Set the sauté pan aside as well.

In a large mortar, combine the almonds and 1 teaspoon salt. Using a pestle, smash and mash almonds as thoroughly as possible. Add the garlic cloves and continue. Gradually add the toasted bread as well. Mash these until they make a thick paste, then reserve.

Adding a bit of oil if needed, heat the onions and peppers in the reserved skillet, stirring frequently, until the onions have wilted. If the peppers do not have some heat to them, add 1 crumbled dried chile pepper. Then add the tomato purée, pepper, and stock.

Bring to a boil over medium heat. Gradually whisk in the garlic/almond paste until it is all absorbed into the tomato stock. Cook until simmering, adding more stock if sauce is too thick. Add the clams and cover tightly. Cook over medium heat until clams open, 5 to 7 minutes.

Spoon some rice into each of 6 large, heated soup plates. Ladle the clams and sauce over the rice and dust with parsley.

SERVES 4 TO 6

Keralan Prawns with Cashews and Chiles

Whether you use prawns or large shrimp, you will thoroughly enjoy another authentic South Indian recipe from our friend Nimmy Paul. She thought it would be of interest because it is a dry curry that incorporates raw cashews as an important flavor and texture in the "sauce." We use long, skinny green chiles for this. Nimmy's recipe called for double the number, in case you would like to try more. Do use a generous amount of salt. If you don't have tamarind, use a tablespoon of red wine vinegar. Serve with rice, some Indian pickles, and Kallappam (Coconut Rice Pancakes) (page 95).

1 cup raw cashews, soaked in
water for 2 hours
½ cup thinly sliced shallots
2 rounded tablespoons minced
fresh ginger
1 tablespoon minced garlic
4 long green (hot) chiles
1 rounded teaspoon ground
cayenne

¼ teaspoon ground turmeric
A generous amount of Kosher salt
12 curry leaves (optional)
Up to ⅓ cup coconut oil
½ cup thinly sliced red onion
1½ pounds large shrimp, peeled
and deveined
1 tablespoon puréed tamarind
dissolved in 2 tablespoons water

Two hours ahead of preparing the "sauce," place the cashews in a bowl and cover with water. Soak for 2 hours, then drain and reserve.

Combine the shallots, ginger, garlic, and chiles in a large bowl or a mortar. Using a heavy pestle, crush and pound until the ingredients are thoroughly "chopped." Pound in the cayenne, turmeric, salt, curry leaves, and drained raw cashews. When the mixture is almost smooth, set it aside.

Heat 2 tablespoons of the coconut oil in a wok over medium-high heat. Add half the red onions and cook, stirring, until the onions are golden. Transfer the onions to paper towels and repeat with the remaining onions.

Add more oil if needed, then stir shallot/cashew mixture vigorously over medium heat. Cover and cook over low heat for 10 minutes, stirring occasionally.

Raise the heat, and add more coconut oil if needed. Add the shrimp, fried onions, and the dissolved tamarind into the wok. Cook, stirring constantly, until the shrimp are cooked and "sauce" is dry, 3 to 5 minutes. Serve with rice, sides, and some Indian pickles.

SERVES 4 TO 6

Vietnamese Shrimp in Caramel Sauce
with Peanuts

This dish has almost all of the elements that one could possibly want in a successful Asian dish: sweet-and-sour, tender and crunchy, and heat and cool. Its inspiration comes from a small and understated San Francisco restaurant we've been enjoying a lot over the last, perhaps, half dozen years. And now the word is out across the country about Charles Phan's extraordinary food at The Slanted Door. We've been dining there since not long after it first opened and enjoy the flavors so much, we usually eat there twice during each visit. Even if we're off the mark approximating Phan's sublime shrimp in caramel sauce, at least this particular version is also quite delicious.

THE SAUCE

1 cup granulated sugar
1/3 cup nuoc mam (Vietnamese fish sauce)
4 plump shallots, cut in half and thinly sliced

THE SHRIMP

3 tablespoons peanut oil, plus more if needed
1/2 cup raw peanuts
6 plump garlic cloves, smashed and minced
1 crumbled dried chile
1 small fresh chile, thinly sliced
1 1/2 pounds large shrimp (22–24 count), peeled and deveined
Kosher salt and freshly ground black pepper to taste
4 scallions, trimmed with 1-inch green, thinly sliced
2 tablespoons minced fresh cilantro
Steamed jasmine rice

To make the sauce: Place the sugar in a small caramel pot, or heavy saucepan, and cook over medium heat, stirring constantly, until the sugar has melted and the liquid has become a dark, rich brown. Remove it from the heat and carefully, to avoid burning splatter, stir in the nuoc mam. Cook over low heat, stirring constantly, until the mixture is thoroughly blended. Stir in the shallots and reserve.

To make shrimp: Heat the oil in a wok over high heat. Add the peanuts and stir for 30 seconds, or until golden. Transfer to a bowl and reserve. Add more oil if needed, then the garlic and chiles to the hot wok. Stir vigorously for 30 seconds. Add the shrimp and cook, stirring, over medium-high heat until shrimp are opaque, 2 to 4 minutes. Add salt, pepper, and caramel shallot sauce. Stir until the shrimp mixture is thoroughly coated and the sauce is reduced.

Stir in the scallions, peanuts, and cilantro. Serve over rice.

SERVES 4 TO 6

Shrimp Cantonese with Salted Peanuts

Normally made with lobster, this wonderful shrimp version will be less daunting to those reluctant to kill a live lobster. In this version our large shrimp are cooked in a rich, garlicky sauce with ground pork, fermented black beans, and soy—eat this once and you will fall in love. Linda first tasted Lobster Cantonese at Joyce Chen's eponymous restaurant early in its first incarnation—in Belmont, Massachusetts, in the mid-1950s. Somewhat later, she adapted Joyce Chen's recipe to shrimp, then more easily available in the Midwest. The addition of salted peanuts came about the same time, and the added crunch is particularly pleasing. With thanks to the late, great Joyce Chen, we think we have developed a fairly simple recipe that all will enjoy.

THE FLAVORINGS
2 tablespoons minced garlic
3 scallions, minced
1 tablespoon minced fresh ginger

THE PORK
¾ pounds ground pork
1 tablespoon soy sauce
2 teaspoons rice wine
2 teaspoons water

THE SAUCE
1⅓ cups chicken stock
3 tablespoons soy sauce
3 tablespoons fermented black
   beans, thoroughly rinsed and
   minced
2 tablespoons rice wine
2 tablespoons dry sherry
2 teaspoons sesame oil

THE THICKENING
2 tablespoons cornstarch
3 tablespoons water
2 eggs

2½ pounds large shrimp, peeled
   and deveined, partially
   defrosted
3 tablespoons peanut oil
⅓ cup minced scallions
¼ cup minced fresh cilantro
⅔ cup coarsely chopped roasted
   salted peanuts

To prepare the flavorings: In a small dish, blend together the garlic, scallions, and ginger. Reserve.

To prepare the pork: In a small bowl, combine the pork, soy, rice wine, and water. Using your fingers in a beating motion, blend together to make a light mixture. Reserve.

To mix the sauce: In another bowl, combine the chicken stock, soy sauce, fermented beans, rice wine, sherry, and sesame oil.

To mix the thickening: In a small dish, blend together the cornstarch and water. Beat the eggs in another dish. Set both aside.

To cook: Assemble the ingredients in order of use within reach while cooking. Heat the oil in the wok until it's very hot. Add **the flavorings** and stir until fragrant, 20 to 30 seconds. Add **the pork** and stir vigorously until the color changes, about 1 minute. Add the shrimp. Toss vigorously until the meat mixture is evenly distributed with the shrimp, 30 seconds to 1 minute. Add **the sauce** and stir over high heat until boiling. Cover and cook until the shrimp are firm and opaque, 4 to 7 minutes.

While the shrimp are cooking, quickly restir **the thickening** mixture, to blend the cornstarch with the water. When the shrimp are ready, stir the thickening into the shrimp mixture, blending vigorously to avoid lumps. Stir until the sauce thickens, about 1 minute.

Using a chopstick for mixing, add the eggs in a slow stream moving over the surface, beating them into thin strands. Stir in the scallions and cilantro. Transfer to a heated serving bowl, sprinkle evenly with the peanuts, and serve.

SERVES **4**

Thai-Style Shrimp with Peanuts and Lettuce

Spicy shrimp with saucy peanuts spooned into lettuce cups—how could this dish not be delicious? To add more flavor and texture, we sprinkle the dish with a crunchy topping of finely chopped roasted peanuts. A final spritz of lime juice finishes this dish perfectly. Serve this with some pan-fried noodles or spicy fried rice.

⅔ cup roasted peanuts

2 pounds large shrimp (21–24 count), peeled and deveined

5 plump garlic cloves, minced

2½ tablespoons minced ginger

1 bulb-lemongrass, minced

3 tablespoons peanut oil, more if needed

1 fresh small hot chile, preferably red, seeded and minced

1 tablespoon granulated sugar

1 tablespoon Nam Pla (fish sauce)

¼ cup sweet soy sauce (or hoisin)

¼ cup rice wine

Zest and juice of 3 limes

3 large leaves Thai or regular fresh
   basil, torn

2 tablespoons minced fresh cilantro

12 large leaves Boston or Bibb
   lettuce

Wedges of lime and thinly sliced hot
   chile for garnish

Place the peanuts in a food processor and pulse until fine but not powdery. Set aside.

In a medium-sized bowl, combine the shrimp, garlic, ginger, and lemongrass. Toss to coat well and let stand in refrigerator for 1 hour.

Heat the oil in a wok over high heat. Add the shrimp with the seasonings and stir vigorously for 1 minute. Add the minced chile, sugar, fish sauce, soy sauce, rice wine, lime zest and juice. Continue to cook, stirring constantly, until the shrimp are cooked and fully coated with sauce, another 1 to 2 minutes. Remove the wok from the heat and stir in half the peanuts, and all the basil and cilantro.

Quickly arrange lettuce cups on dinner plates. Divide the shrimp among them. Sprinkle lavishly with the remaining nuts and the chiles.

Serve with lime wedges on the side.

SERVES **6**

Sautéed Soft-Shell Crabs with Hazelnuts

While we have never met a soft-shell crab preparation we didn't enjoy, this is one of the best. Hazelnuts lend a particularly rich, mellow flavor to any dish. Here hazelnut flour is the perfect counterpoint to the crab's briny tang. The combination is really satisfying, and the final nutty crunch is a delightful extra. Keep in mind that the smaller soft shells are far more flavorful than the big ones. Avoid those called "whales," at 5½ to 6 inches across—they are the largest ones sold, but the least prized by those in the know.

12 fresh medium-sized soft-shell
   crabs

1¼ cup hazelnut flour

½ cup unbleached flour

1½ sticks (12 tablespoons)
   unsalted butter

½ cup dry white wine

Juice and zest of 1 medium
   lemon

1 teaspoon minced shallots

¼ cup heavy cream

⅔ cup chopped toasted
   hazelnuts

¼ cup finely chopped fresh flat-leaf
   parsley

Watercress and lemon wedges for
   garnish

Clean the crabs by removing the lungs, eyes, and intestines (or ask your fishmonger to do this for you right before you buy the crabs). First lift up the sides of the upper shell and remove the gills. Place the crab on a wooden board and, using a sharp knife, cut off the head immediately behind the eyes. Use a butter knife to scrape out the lungs and intestines through this opening. Rinse well under running water. Then turn the crab over and pull open the "apron" and cut it off with a sharp knife or scissors. Dry the crabs with paper towels.

Combine the flours in a pie plate and dredge the crabs to lightly coat them on both sides. Place the coated crabs on a rack.

Heat a 12-inch skillet over medium heat until hot. Add 2 tablespoons of the butter. Place 4 crabs in the skillet, shell-side down, and sauté until brown, about 3 minutes. Turn with spatula or tongs and cook until the other side is brown. Transfer crabs to a warm platter, add more butter as necessary (reserving 1 stick of butter for the sauce), and repeat the process until all the crabs are done. Keep them warm. Cut the remaining butter into pieces and reserve.

Drain the skillet of excess butter. Add the wine, lemon zest and juice, and shallots. Cook over medium heat until the liquid is reduced to 2 tablespoons. Slowly whisk in the heavy cream and cook over medium-low heat until the mixture is reduced and thickened. Lower the heat, whisk in the butter pieces, and whip until smoothly blended. Remove the pan from the heat.

Place 2 crabs shell-side up on each of 6 heated plates. Drizzle each plate with some lemon butter. Garnish with hazelnuts and parsley. Add some watercress and lemon wedges and serve.

SERVES **4** TO **6**

Claire Lowenfeld in Britain's Wild Larder: Nuts *(1957) waxes rhapsodic. "A hazelnut may in a way be regarded as a miniature egg. Weight for weight, one handful of hazelnuts (about 42 nuts) weighs about as much as the average egg. The nuts contain about 50 percent more protein, are seven times richer in fat and five times richer in carbohydrates. Their caloric value is five times higher and they are more than four times richer in calcium and nearly twice as rich in phosphorous."*

Nut's Many Meanings

Hnutu: There, that's the earliest English spelling of nut that anyone could find. Or at least anyone at the *Oxford English Dictionary.* That is an Old English reference from the Erfurt Glossary of 875, back when our mother tongue was very young.

As the English language evolved, our nut got spelled in all kinds of different ways: nyte, nute, note, noote, nott, nutte, nutt, nuete, neut, and not—not to mention the plural of each of those forms. Those who could read knew what was meant—"a fruit which consists of a hard or leathery (indehiscent) shell enclosing an edible kernel; the kernel itself." Finally "nut" became the standard, but it took until 1526 before today's spelling finally appeared on paper.

Nut meanings occupy three pages (in very small print) in the *OED*, and they run the gamut. "Nut" has meant a person's head, a madman, a crank, an effete fop or snob, and, as early as 1300, something of trifling value. Nuts can mean testicles, nonsense, or rubbish. If you say "it's the nuts" it can mean something is really excellent. If you are "nuts about somebody" you really like them. If you are simply "nuts" it means you are crazy. Carl Sandberg was one of the earliest writers to use the word that way; in 1928 he wrote, "There was a screw loose somewhere in him, he had a kink and he was a crank, he was nuts and belonged in a booby hatch."

The nut's toughness lead to a writer in 1545 to say that a certain hard-to-solve problem "was a tough nut to crack." And "nuts and bolts" means the basics of any subject.

A "nut" can be part of a clock mechanism, part of the lock on a crossbow, part of a printing press, part of the lower end of a violin bow, part of a ship's anchor, the central part of a potter's wheel, a cello player's maneuver to make a very high note, the money needed for a business venture, something that holds the wheels on the car, and small lumps of coal.

To bring it back to the culinary world, a nut can mean the pancreas (sweetbread), a small knob of meat, or a small rounded biscuit or cake.

Nut as verb? Yes, both transitive and intransitive. To gather nuts, to curry favor with someone, to think, to use one's head, and that goes both ways—to butt with the head and to be hit by a blow to the head—and, sorry to say, it can mean to castrate.

There are also the combinations: nuthouse, nut wood (usually meaning walnut), nuthatch, nut boy, nut butter, nut milk, nut steak, nut cut, nut meat.

So what we are dealing with in this book, the hnutu, is a rich and venerable subject charged with many meanings.

Pan-Fried Trout with Turkish Pine Nut Sauce

The wonderful combination of cornmeal and corn flour as a coating for our trout is very much a Southern thing. We first tasted this combination a decade ago prepared at a Louisiana fishing camp. Here we exchange the Louisiana-style flavors for some from the Eastern Mediterranean. The end results are the same—heavenly fish, simply treated with just a bit of nutty garlicky lemon sauce at the end.

THE SAUCE

½ cup pine nuts

3 plump garlic cloves

2 small slices of country bread,
  crusts removed

3 tablespoons extra virgin olive oil,
  plus more if needed

Juice of 1 lemon

Kosher salt and freshly ground black
  pepper to taste

THE FISH

¾ cup finely ground
  cornmeal

½ cup corn flour

1 teaspoon kosher salt

1 teaspoon white pepper

2 eggs

2 tablespoons water

6 trout (about 12 ounces each),
  filleted

Up to 1 cup vegetable oil

3 tablespoons unsalted butter

Juice of 1 lemon

Lemon wedges for garnish

To make the sauce: In a mortar and pestle, or in a spice grinder or blender, crush together the pine nuts and garlic. Soak the bread in water then squeeze dry, and slowly beat it into the nut mixture. Working slowly, beat in the olive oil to make a smooth paste. Beat in the lemon juice. Season with salt and pepper. If the sauce is too thick, thin it slowly by beating in more olive oil. The sauce should be quite creamy. Let it stand at room temperature until needed.

To make the fish: In a large, shallow bowl, blend together the cornmeal, corn flour, salt and pepper. In a large soup plate, beat the eggs with 2 tablespoons water. Pat the trout dry, then dip them in the egg mixture, then their coat thoroughly with the cornmeal mixture. Place on cooling racks.

In 1 large—or 2 smaller—skillets, preferably cast-iron, pour enough oil to cover the bottom about ¼-inch deep. Place over medium heat until smoking. Add the fish and fry until golden, about 4 minutes per side.

Drain the fish on paper towels. Drain the oil from the skillet. Return the skillet to the heat and add the butter. When it begins to brown, remove the skillet from the heat and whisk in the lemon juice, then pour it into the pine nut sauce and blend thoroughly.

Serve the fish with a lemon wedge and some sauce spooned over it. Serve the remaining sauce on the side.

SERVES 6

Red Snapper Amandine

One of the simplest ways to finish fish like trout and snapper is to sauté thinly sliced almonds, blanched or not, in a lot of melted butter and finish them with some fresh lemon juice. A fish "amandine," the French word for a dish with almonds (it is some times misspelled almondine) has long been a popular way of serving delicious fresh fish. The sauce enhances the delicacy of the fish and does not overwhelm it. While trout is most commonly served this way, really fresh authentic red snapper is even better. Treat your fishmonger well and you will be on his list when this lovely fish is available.

6 tablespoons unsalted butter
½ cup slivered almonds
1 egg, beaten
⅔ cup milk
⅔ cup unbleached flour
1 teaspoon kosher salt
1 teaspoon freshly ground black
  pepper

1 teaspoon dried thyme, crushed
  between your fingers
2½ pounds red snapper fillets, ⅔
  to ¾ inches thick
3 tablespoons olive oil, plus more if
  needed
¼ cup minced fresh flat-leaf parsley
Zest and juice of 2 lemons

Melt 3 tablespoons of the butter in a skillet over medium-high heat. Add the almonds. Stir until the almonds are golden, about 3 minutes. Using a slotted spoon, transfer the nuts to a bowl. Pour the remaining butter into a small bowl and set aside.

Combine the egg and milk in a soup plate and blend well. Mix the flour with the salt, pepper, and thyme. Spread evenly on a plate. Cut snapper fillets into a 6 portions.

Heat the olive oil in a large (12-inch) nonstick skillet over medium-high heat. Dip the fish portions first in the egg mixture, then in the flour. Place on a cake rack near the stovetop. Repeat until remaining pieces are coated. When the oil is very hot, place the snapper fillets skin-side down in the skillet. Fry until the bottom is golden, about 2 to 4 minutes. Turn and fry for about 3 minutes, or until golden and fish is done. To check for doneness: Insert the tines of a fork into the thick part of the fish to check the appearance of the flesh, which should be firm and almost opaque.

Transfer the fish to heated plates. Wipe the saucepan with paper towels. Add all the remaining butter and cook over medium heat until the butter has melted. Add the lemon juice to the skillet and stir vigorously to deglaze the pan. Stir in the parsley and lemon zest. Remove the pan from the heat.

Season the fish with additional salt and pepper. Sprinkle with slivered almonds. Spoon the browned lemon butter over the nuts and serve.

SERVES 6

Baked Sole with Lemon Walnut Crust

Ground walnuts, lemon zest, and impeccably fresh sole are perfect companions in this simple preparation. We happen to love grey sole and lemon sole, but any one will do as long as it's perfectly fresh. You can dredge the fish in the nuts and pan-fry them in butter, adding the lemon juice at the end, along with some minced parsley. We had pan-fried hake served this way at a small restaurant in the French hill town of Venasque. Served with potatoes gratin, lunch was sublime. So was the view of the valley below as seen from our table at the mountain's edge.

½ cup ground walnut meal

Zest and juice of 2 lemons

3 pounds very fresh sole
fillets, preferably lemon or grey
sole

Kosher salt and freshly ground
pepper to taste

3 tablespoons unsalted butter, cut
into small pieces

Lemon wedges for garnish

Preheat the oven to 450°F.

In a small bowl, mix together the walnut meal and lemon zest. Set aside.

Arrange the fish in a single layer, skinned-side down, in a shallow baking dish. Drizzle the lemon juice over the fish, then sprinkle with salt and pepper. Spread the ground nut mixture over the top as evenly as possible. Scatter the butter bits over the nuts.

Bake for 6 minutes, or until fish is done. To check for doneness, gently insert the tines of a fork into the flesh; when flakes are opaque, the fish is done.

Divide fish the among 6 heated serving plates and garnish with lemon wedges.

SERVES 6

Pan-Braised Halibut in Garlic Hot Sauce with Peanuts

While this spicy dish has its roots in China, we also incorporate some Thai touches as well. The richly flavored sauce makes a fine background for the crunchy peanuts as well as the chile-piqued garlic and cilantro confetti.

3 plump garlic cloves, minced

3 tablespoons minced green onion

2 tablespoons minced fresh ginger

1 tablespoon minced fresh lemongrass

1 tablespoon chile sauce

⅓ cup rice wine

1 tablespoon sweet soy sauce

1 tablespoon Nam Pla fish sauce

6 halibut steaks, ½ inch thick

3 tablespoons plus 2 teaspoons cornstarch

3 tablespoons peanut oil, plus more if needed

1 small dried chile

⅔ cup raw peanuts

2 tablespoons water

¼ cup minced fresh cilantro

3 teaspoons minced garlic

1 small fresh red chile, minced

Combine the minced garlic cloves, green onion, ginger, and lemon grass in a small bowl and set aside. In another small bowl combine the chile sauce, rice wine, sweet soy sauce, and fish sauce. Set aside as well. Finally, dredge the fish fillets in 3 tablespoons of the cornstarch to lightly coat and place them on a rack. (Put all of these near your stove.)

Heat the oil and dried chile in a large skillet. When hot, add the peanuts and cook, stirring constantly, for about 1 minute, or until the peanuts become lightly browned. Using a slotted spoon, transfer peanuts to some paper towels to drain. Discard the chile.

Add 1 tablespoon more oil if needed, and reheat the skillet. Add the fish steaks in a single layer and brown on both sides, about 1 minute per side. Carefully transfer the fish to paper towels.

Over medium heat, add the garlic-scallion mixture and stir for 1 minute to wilt. Add the chile sauce mixture. Cook until hot, then slip the fish steaks into the sauce, spooning some over the top of the fish as well. Cook for 5 minutes over medium-low heat. To check for doneness: Gently insert the tines of a fork into the flesh. If they are done, the fish flesh should be opaque. Transfer the fish to a large, heated serving platter.

Quickly blend together the remaining 2 teaspoons of cornstarch and the water. In another bowl, blend together the cilantro, garlic, and fresh chile. Add the cornstarch mixture to the fish sauce and stir over high heat until the sauce has thickened. Spoon the sauce around the fish.

Sprinkle with the cilantro mixture and sautéed peanuts. Serve at once.

SERVES 6

Lacquered Hazelnut Salmon

You will love the heady spice aromas that waft through the kitchen as this salmon is roasting in the oven. Then, with every bite, there will be a mélange of Asian flavors that are deep and rich because of the wonderful hazelnut oil that gives our fish a very special personality. We serve this dish with some fried rice or even polenta.

½ cup teriyaki sauce

½ cup maple syrup

⅓ cup plus 2 tablespoons hazelnut oil

1 small shallot, peeled and cut up

3 garlic cloves, peeled

1 tablespoon minced ginger

1 teaspoon Chinese five-spice mix

3 teaspoons freshly ground black pepper

3 to 4 pounds salmon fillet, preferably 1 inch thick, cut into portions

Minced fresh cilantro for garnish

Fresh limes, cut into wedges

½ cup coarsely chopped toasted hazelnuts

One hour before cooking, prepare the lacquer: In the bowl of a food processor combine the teriyaki sauce, maple syrup, ⅓ cup hazelnut oil, shallot, garlic, ginger, Chinese five-spice mix, and pepper. Purée. Scrape the mixture into a bowl.

Arrange the fish, skin-side down, on a platter and paint generously with lacquer mixture. Refrigerate the fish, and paint at least three more times before cooking.

Preheat the oven to 400°F. Coat a large, shallow baking sheet with the remaining hazelnut oil.

Arrange the salmon fillets, skin-side down, on the baking sheet. Paint with lacquer one more time. Bake in the preheated oven for 18 to 22 minutes, or until fish flakes easily when tested with a fork.

Serve on heated plates garnished with cilantro, lime wedges, and hazelnuts.

SERVES **8**

Roasted Bluefish with Shredded Horseradish Pecan Crust

Linda was born and raised in Massachusetts and has always had a particular love for Cape Blues, the rich and full-flavored bluefish from the waters off Cape Cod. While this is a rather oily fish, we have found that a light coating of mayonnaise seems to actually reduce the oily nature of the bluefish. (We have no idea why.) In this recipe we use this coating to hold a mixture of shredded fresh horseradish and ground pecans. Baked together with the coating the fish acquires a wonderful flavor, and the crust is divine! By the way, if you don't have access to fresh horseradish root, combine 3 tablespoons ground white horseradish with the mayonnaise before it is spread. Then just use the seasoned nuts.

Olive oil for baking dish
2 teaspoons kosher salt
2 teaspoons freshly ground white pepper
1/3 cup finely grated fresh horseradish root
1/3 cup freshly ground pecans
2 large bluefish fillets, each about 1 1/4 pounds

2/3 cup Hellmann's or Best Foods mayonnaise, or homemade mayonnaise (see recipe page 153)
3 tablespoons unsalted butter, cut into tiny pieces
1 lemon, cut in half

Preheat the oven to 425°F. Lightly coat a large, shallow baking dish with olive oil.

In a small bowl, blend together the salt, pepper, horseradish root, and pecans. Set aside.

Arrange the bluefish fillets, skin-side down. Coat the fillets evenly with mayonnaise. Sprinkle evenly with horseradish pecan mixture, then, using your fingers, press the coating into the mayonnaise. Scatter the butter bits over the top.

Bake in the preheated oven for 15 to 20 minutes, or until the fish flakes easily when tested with a fork. If the whole fillets weigh less than 1 pound, test them after 16 minutes. If the coating is not browned, place the fish under a hot broiler for 1 minute.

Squeeze lemon juice over the fillets, divide into portions, and serve on heated plates.

SERVES 4 TO 6

Georges Bank Cod in Spanish Sauce with Almonds

While there are severe limitations on cod fishing in the North Atlantic, there are some areas that are no longer in jeopardy and fishermen are, again, bringing this meaty fish to market. One of the best of them is the display auction of Gloucester, Massachusetts, where high-quality, well-handled fresh fish get the responsible fisherman a higher price for his catch than at other auctions. This flavorful fish deserves the kind of preparation that enhances its taste and does not mask it. Our recipe provides a savory Catalonian-style tomato sauce that is somewhat thickened by ground almonds. Accompanied by a saffron rice, this results in a superlative meal, one that we think does justice to our beautiful cod.

1 very large sweet onion, quartered

3 plump cloves garlic

3 scallions, trimmed with 1 inch
   tender green and cut in half

3 tablespoons olive oil

1 dried hot chile pepper

1 tablespoon hot paprika

½ cup dry white wine or vermouth

2 cups canned crushed tomatoes
   and their juice

1 teaspoon herbes de Provence

½ cup lightly toasted blanched
   almonds, ground

2 whole bay leaves

Kosher salt and freshly ground black
   pepper to taste

½ cup chopped fresh flat-leaf
   parsley

½ cup sliced green olives stuffed
   with pimiento

3 pounds cod fillets, skinned

Pinch of cayenne pepper

½ cup toasted slivered almonds,
   coarsely chopped

Combine the onion, garlic, and scallions in the bowl of a food processor. Pulse until finely chopped. In a heavy saucepan, heat the oil over medium heat. Add the chile pepper, paprika, and onion mixture. Cook, stirring often, for about 5 minutes, or until the onions are wilted. Stir in the wine, crushed tomatoes, and herbes de Provence. Bring to a boil, then reduce heat to low and simmer for 15 minutes.

Stir in the ground almonds, bay leaves, salt, pepper, and ¼ cup each of the parsley and olives. Pour the sauce into a skillet large enough to hold the cod in a single layer. Season the fish with salt, pepper, and a bit of cayenne. Arrange fish, skinned-side down, in the skillet. Spoon some sauce over the top. Cover tightly. Place the skillet over high heat until the liquid begins to bubble. Reduce the heat and braise the fish until a thin-bladed knife passed through the fillet encounters little resistance, about 20 to 30 minutes.

Remove bay leaves, and sprinkle with the remaining olives, parsley, and the toasted slivered almonds.

SERVES 6 TO 8

Baked Cod with Garlic, Vinegar, and Toasted Pine Nuts

This fish dish is, indeed, a delightful mélange of contrasting flavors and textures. The caramel sweetness from the garlic is a pleasing contrast to the light, tart sauce. The tender cod flesh makes a great background for our crunchy pine nuts, while the lovely garnish of herbs and olives add still other interesting notes. This is a dish of contrasts inspired by a recipe in Flavors of Greece *by Rosemary Barron.*

½ to 1 cup extra virgin olive oil
2 garlic bulbs, broken apart and
   peeled (about 20 plump cloves)
4 large branches of fresh oregano
3 to 3½ pounds fresh cod fillets,
   skinned
Kosher salt to taste
4 whole bay leaves

¼ cup rich red wine vinegar
3 tablespoons water
Freshly ground black pepper to
   taste
¼ cup minced fresh flat-leaf parsley
¼ cup minced Kalamata olives
⅓ cup toasted pine nuts

Preheat the oven to 450°F.

In a small skillet, heat 3 tablespoons of the olive oil. Add the garlic cloves and cook, stirring, over medium heat, turning often, until garlic is golden and tender, about 20 minutes.

Using some of the remaining olive oil from the skillet, thoroughly coat a large oven-proof baking dish. Scatter the oregano branches on the bottom of the dish. Scatter the garlic cloves evenly over the oregano. Arrange the fish fillets in a single layer over the garlic. Sprinkle with salt. Break the bay leaves into pieces and scatter them over the fish.

Add the remaining olive oil and vinegar to the now-cooled skillet. Vigorously whisk in the 3 tablespoons of water. Pour the mixture over the fish. Follow with some freshly ground pepper.

Cover the baking dish with foil and bake for 10 minutes. Uncover, baste with pan juices, and bake for another 10 minutes, or until the fish flakes easily when pierced by a fork.

Transfer the fish to a heated platter. Spoon the garlic cloves around the fish. Garnish with pan juices, parsley, olives, and pine nuts.

SERVES 6 TO 8

poultry

Honeyed Roasted Young Chickens with Ground Almonds and Spices

Crisply Roasted Chickens with Asian Flavors and Peanuts

Butterflied Lemon Chicken with Thyme, Garlic, and Pine Nuts

Fried Chicken Kerala-Style

Fricasséed Chicken with a Ligurian Nut Sauce

Minted Yogurt and Pistachio-Crusted Chicken Breasts

Coconut Chicken with Potatoes and Lime

Exotic Chicken and Peanut Stew

Crispy Duck with Candied Apples and Marrons

Roasted Turkey with Chestnut Stuffing and Zinfandel Gravy

Honeyed Roasted Young Chickens with Ground Almonds and Spices

While roasting chickens are more commonly available in supermarkets, we now only use birds that are a little bigger than Cornish hens and far more delicious. These small chickens, weighing between 2¹/₂ and 3 pounds, are usually available in specialty markets and from butchers. Our maven of meats and poultry calls them "baby chickens" or "Italian fryers" (there is no answer to why Italian). These are really moist and delicious; and one is a perfect size for two guests. The nuts, apricots, and spices frequently appear together in Sephardic Jewish dishes. We think they have a particular affinity for poultry and we use them together in a wide variety of ways. This is one of our favorites. If you prefer, you can certainly use two 3¹/₂-pound fryers—just roast them for about 10 minutes longer.

3 small chickens (2 to 3 pounds each)

Kosher salt and freshly ground black pepper to taste

2 lemons—1 thinly sliced and seeded for garnish

¹/₂ cup finely chopped almonds

¹/₄ cup finely chopped pistachios

¹/₄ cup finely minced dried apricots

3 plump garlic cloves, minced

1 tablespoon minced fresh cilantro

1 tablespoon minced fresh ginger

1 teaspoon freshly ground cinnamon

1 teaspoon ground coriander

¹/₂ teaspoon ground mace

²/₃ cup honey

¹/₄ cup coarsely chopped pistachios

Place chickens on a clean work surface, breast-side down. Season with some salt and pepper. Turn birds over and gently loosen skin from flesh by carefully moving your fingers under the skin. Set aside.

Carefully zest 1 lemon, placing the zest in a medium-sized mixing bowl. Set the remaining lemon aside. Add the almonds, pistachios, minced apricots, garlic, cilantro, ginger, cinnamon, coriander, and mace. Blend thoroughly.

Gently spread spice mixture under the skins of the hens. Be sure to get some all the way down to the legs and thighs, too. Then season the skin with additional salt and pepper. Place hens, breast-side up, on a large, shallow baking sheet.

Preheat the oven to 450°F. Place an oven rack in the upper third of the oven.

In a small bowl blend together the honey with the juice of the lemon. Spoon some honey mixture over the top of each bird. Let them stand for 30 minutes at room temperature.

Roast the prepared chickens for 30 minutes. Spoon any pan juices over the skin, rotate the pan, and continue to roast until they are done, another 15 to 20 minutes.

Transfer the birds to a carving board and quarter. Serve on heated plates garnished with chopped pistachios and lemon slices.

SERVES **6** TO **8**

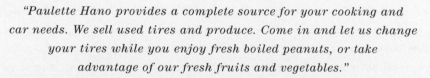

"Paulette Hano provides a complete source for your cooking and car needs. We sell used tires and produce. Come in and let us change your tires while you enjoy fresh boiled peanuts, or take advantage of our fresh fruits and vegetables."

—from a Web site for a multifaceted company in Amity, Lousiana

Mrs. Lambert's Nutmeato

She knew her nuts. In fact, the earliest nut cookbook we found in our research was hers. The *Guide for Nut Cookery* by Mrs. Almeda Lambert was published in Battle Creek in 1899. A strange book, really, with recipes for making a roast goose, or a turkey, or even a good-sized fish, out of nuts.

"Nutmeato" is the word she invented for the process in which a nut butter, dried bread crumbs, nut meal, eggs, grated onion, appropriate herbs and spices, and salt to taste are patted into a the shape of the desired creature, then roasted until golden brown. She believed passionately that "the purest and most easily digested of all meats is the meat of nuts." She also believed and hoped that "nuts will fully take the place of animal flesh, fats, and products."

"Nutora" was another word she coined, to describe a mixture of nut butter, flour, or cornstarch, and a perhaps a fruit for flavor, that was steamed and canned for later use. "Nutgrano" was her word for concoctions of ground nuts with various grains.

Mrs. Lambert could get nuts into anything. Even her oatmeal gruel, she assures us, is made better with the addition of some nut butter.

Her preoccupation with nuts made sense. In 1890, Almeda West married Joseph Lambert of Battle Creek. Originally a carriage maker, his skills as a machinist lead him into making equipment for various trades. In the mid-1890s he invented a grinder for making peanut butter. By the end of the decade, he had designed a home version and developed a business making and distributing nuts and nut products. An article in his hometown paper reports that after announcing plans for a new factory, he went to Virginia and bought twenty carloads of peanuts. His wife wrote the book that would encourage cooks to put nuts in any food.

The company stayed strong and healthy well into the new century, until in 1930 it, like so many other American enterprises, fell victim to the Great Depression.

A few copies of Mrs. Lambert's fascinating book are still around, handsomely designed and printed, with her insights into the history of nuts, the role they can play in keeping us healthy, and the endless and creative ways they can be brought to the table.

Crisply Roasted Chickens with Asian Flavors and Peanuts

We've learned from our meat and poultry "guru," Mr. Brisket, that if you want to add flavor to chicken, you put the seasonings under the skin. Otherwise, all you are doing is flavoring the skin, not the flesh. Here we roast chicken with some assertive Asian flavorings. While this is a simple recipe, the mélange of flavors is very exciting. You can adjust them however you wish, using a number of flavorings such as lemon grass, Thai basil, and/or kaffir lime leaves. You could also use cashew butter, or even hazelnut butter, instead of the peanut.

6 plump garlic cloves, minced

4 scallions, trimmed with 1-inch green, minced

2 large shallots, minced

1 fresh hot chile, seeded and minced

½ cup peanut butter, creamy preferred

2 packed tablespoons dark brown sugar

1 rounded teaspoon Chinese five-spice powder

3 tablespoons soy sauce

1 teaspoon sesame oil

2 small chickens (about 3 pounds each)

Kosher salt and freshly ground black pepper to taste

¼ cup minced fresh cilantro

2 limes, quartered

In a mortar or wooden bowl, or in a food processor, pound together the garlic, scallions, and shallots to make a paste. Then pound in the chile, peanut butter, brown sugar, Chinese five-spice powder, soy sauce, and sesame oil.

Carefully loosen the skin of each chicken with your fingers. Rub the seasoning paste under the skin and over the breasts and thighs. Rub some paste over the chickens as well. Cover and refrigerate for at least 3 hours, or up to 24. Bring the chickens to room temperature before cooking.

Preheat the oven to 425°F. Place the chickens, breast-side up, on a large, shallow-sided pan. Roast for 30 minutes. Season lightly with salt and pepper, baste with any pan juices, and roast for another 30 minutes, or until the skin is crisp and juices run clear when a thigh is pierced with a knife.

Let the chickens rest for 5 minutes before serving. Cut into quarters. Serve lavishly garnished with cilantro and a lime wedge.

SERVES 4 TO 6

Butterflied Lemon Chicken with Thyme, Garlic, and Pine Nuts

When you combine olive oil, garlic, lemon, and thyme you have guaranteed success for any kind of chicken. This recipe is no exception. Adding some good extra virgin olive oil and toasted pine nuts for the finish makes something delicious positively exciting. That added toasty crunch is a perfect contrast to the meltingly tender chicken. To make certain you miss none of the pan juices, you just might want to serve this accompanied by some yummy mashed potatoes. Then, too, you may want to try it the next day—this time using basil.

6 plump garlic cloves, minced

2 plump shallots, minced

1 small dried chile, crumbled

1 tablespoon fresh thyme leaves (or 2 teaspoons dried)

Zest and juice of 3 lemons

½ cup olive oil

3 small chickens (2½ to 3 pounds each), backbone removed and butterflied

Kosher salt and freshly ground black pepper to taste

½ cup high-quality extra virgin olive oil

2 tablespoons minced fresh flat-leaf parsley

⅓ cup toasted pine nuts

Sea salt

In a small bowl, blend together the garlic, shallots, crumbled chile, and thyme. Whisk in the lemon juice and zest. Then whisk in the olive oil.

Place the chickens, skin-side down on a work surface. With a heavy object such as a meat pounder, smash each chicken flat. Cut small slashes into the thigh and wing joints, so that they flatten too. Season the underside with salt and pepper. Turn the chickens over. Carefully loosen the skin with your fingers. Gently work the garlic mixture under the skin, coating the flesh even down to the thighs. Rub some over the outside of the chickens as well. Reserve the remaining garlic mixture. Cover and refrigerate the chickens for at least 1 hour, or up to 24 hours. Bring the chickens to room temperature before cooking them.

Preheat the oven to 425°F. Place the chickens, skin-side down, on a shallow pan. Roast for 30 minutes. Turn, season lightly with salt and pepper, baste with any pan juices and garlic mixture; then roast for another 30 minutes, or until the skin is crisp and the juices run clear when a thigh is pierced with a knife.

Let the chicken rest for 5 minutes before serving. Whisk together any remaining garlic mixture, the extra virgin oil, parsley, and pine nuts.

Carve the chickens into quarters. Transfer the pieces to heated plates and spoon some pine nut mixture over each serving. Sprinkle each with a bit of sea salt.

SERVES 6 TO 8

Sonny's Farm

Who grows these cashews? In America, only six thousand farmers produce our entire almond crop, but in India millions of farmers grow cashews. Sonny Matthew is one of them. His family has been farming in this beautiful part of India's Malabar Coast for generations. A governmental order limits the acres of cashews that any farmer can grow. Because they have a large family, Sonny and his brothers and sisters were able to keep most of their traditional family holdings. While his siblings went off to other things, he chose to maintain the tradition and the farm. He now grows cashews on nearly two hundred acres of land.

He does not need to be at the farm all the time. He lives with his family in the city of Kochi, where he has other interests. When the trees need him, however, he is there. He has an employee who handles three rounds of spraying as the nuts develop. When weeds need to be cut, usually twice a summer, he hires six women who live nearby to do the work. They also handle the fertilizing and pruning.

"When I see nuts falling," he says, "I send in the workers."

Sonny, like so many in this part of India, is fluent in English as well as Malayalam and Hindi. He thinks a lot about the problems Indian farmers have to face, and, like any farmer, he has his ups and downs; his last harvest was much smaller than he had expected. He is concerned about India's loss of market share. He worries that while newer, more productive cultivars are available, most small farmers cannot afford to plant them. Neither can they afford the pesticides or the quality fertilizers. He told us about new, well-financed cashew farms in Australia that use some of the newer varieties. Their harvesting methods are modern and efficient, and they can send their crop to China for processing, bring it back to Australia to package and market it, and sell it at a hard-to-match price.

"But," he says with a smile, "we are thinking about it. We understand the problems. We're working on it. We'll be all right."

Fried Chicken Kerala-Style

This is one of our absolute favorite recipes! One of the lessons we learned cooking with our Indian friend Nimmy Paul is that while her cuisine may contain a lot of hot peppers, the end result yields a flavorful warmth, not a searing burn. This chicken dish is incredibly tasty, but despite the amount of cayenne, it will not turn your mouth into a fiery inferno. We have to point out that curry leaves are important players in Keralan cuisine, yet they are tough to find in the U.S. Their distinctive flavor is just wonderful, but very difficult to define, though author Maya Kaimal suggests it is like a combination of "green pepper and citrus peel." It is worth trying to locate them. On the other hand, this dish will still be quite delicious without them. Just slightly different. Finally, try to prepare meaty chicken wings this way. Buffalo wings are nothing by comparison!

2 small chickens (2½ to 3 pounds each), cut into 2 legs, 2 thighs, 2 wings, 2 drumettes, 4 breast pieces for each chicken

5 plump shallots, thinly sliced

1½ inches peeled ginger

8 plump garlic cloves, peeled and smashed

1½-inch cinnamon stick

½ teaspoon whole black peppercorns

3 sprigs fresh curry leaves (often available in local Indian markets)

3 tablespoons ground cayenne, plus more if needed

½ cup water, plus more if needed

Up to 3 cups organic canola or vegetable oil

1½ cups thinly sliced red onions

1 tablespoon unbleached flour

1 tablespoon red wine vinegar, plus more to taste

Kosher salt to taste

½ cup fried cashews, chopped to the size of pine nuts

Cut the chickens into medium-sized pieces. Marinate for 1 hour in a large bowl with the shallots, ginger, garlic, cinnamon stick, peppercorns, curry leaves (if available), and cayenne.

Transfer the mixture to a large sauté pan. Add ½ cup water, cover, and cook over medium heat for 10 or 12 minutes, or until somewhat tender. If the mixture becomes dry, add more water.

Transfer the chicken to a large bowl. Carefully, using tongs, transfer shallots and garlic cloves to a small bowl. Pour the pan juices into another bowl and chill.

Shortly before cooking the chicken, pour 1½ cups of the oil into a wok and heat. Add the red onions and stir constantly until they are browned and crisp. Transfer to paper towels.

Working in batches and adding oil as needed, fry the chicken pieces until all are thoroughly browned and tender. When all are done, keep them warm in a large bowl or on a large platter.

Pour off all but a few tablespoons of oil and heat. Using a slotted spoon or Chinese frying strainer, transfer the shallots and garlic to the wok and fry them well. Then add the flour and stir until the flour turns golden. Gradually whisk in marinade/braising juices and cook until the sauce is thick and very hot. Stir in the vinegar and salt. Taste and adjust seasonings.

Pour the sauce over the chicken and toss to coat evenly. Serve with fried onions and cashews scattered evenly as a garnish.

SERVES 4 TO 6

Fricasséed Chicken with a Ligurian Nut Sauce

Early in our research for this book we discovered that Liguria's use of nuts for sauces went way beyond the pesto for which this beautiful Italian region in noted. Adapted from a Fred Plotkin recipe for rabbit, this casserole of chicken is enhanced by a luscious tomato and wine sauce flavored and thickened by a combination of almonds, hazelnuts, and pine nuts. Please try to use a mortar and pestle when making this sauce; use a grinder or food processor as a last choice. Serve this with something very American—some really rich mashed potatoes.

2 chickens (3½ pounds each)
2 plump garlic cloves
1 tablespoon sea salt
2 teaspoons dried rosemary leaves
2 teaspoons dried thyme leaves
¼ cup minced fresh flat-leaf
    parsley
1 teaspoon freshly ground white
    pepper
⅓ cup olive oil, more if needed
3 tablespoons unsalted butter
¼ cup extra virgin olive oil

1 large yellow onion, finely
    chopped
⅛ teaspoon freshly ground nutmeg
1 cup tomato purée (see Basics,
    page 52)
2 cups dry white wine
3 cups rich chicken stock
⅔ cup whole peeled almonds,
    coarsely chopped
⅓ cup toasted hazelnuts, coarsely
    chopped
⅓ cup pine nuts, coarsely chopped

Cut each chicken into 8 pieces and reserve.

In a mortar and pestle, grind together the garlic and salt, then add the herbs and pepper, and pound until they make a nice paste. Set aside.

Heat the olive oil in a large sauté pan over medium heat. Working in batches, brown the chicken pieces on all sides, 10 to 15 minutes total. Pour off the oil.

Add the extra butter and virgin olive oil to the sauté pan, cook over low heat until the butter has melted. Add the onions and nutmeg and cook, stirring often, until the onions are transparent, about 4 to 8 minutes.

Add the reserved herb paste. Stir thoroughly to mix ingredients well. Increase the heat to medium, adding the tomato purée, wine, and stock. When the sauce begins to bubble, slide the browned chicken pieces into it. Cover and cook until liquid bubbles. Reduce the heat and cook over very low heat for 1 hour.

While the chicken is cooking, prepare the nut paste: In a mortar and pestle combine the nuts. Pound vigorously until they are well pulverized. Add several tablespoons of stock or wine to facilitate the paste preparation.

After the chicken has cooked for 1 hour, test for tenderness. Stir in the nut paste and continue cooking the chicken for another 5 minutes, or until the chicken is tender. Taste and adjust the seasonings before serving.

SERVES 4 TO 6

Minted Yogurt and Pistachio-Crusted Chicken Breasts

This dish has it all—tantalizing aromas, superlative textures, and a luscious complexity of flavors! Yogurt, mint, garlic, and pistachios are four of the most loved ingredients in cuisines all over the Arab Crescent. While the yogurt, mint, and garlic lend an aromatic tenderness to the chicken, they also serve as a delectable bonding agent between the chicken and the nuts. Simple and delicious, this chicken dish makes a great addition to any buffet table; it is also marvelous for brunch.

Butter to grease pan
1½ cups whole-milk yogurt
3 plump garlic cloves, pressed
2 teaspoons dried mint
2 teaspoons kosher salt
1¼ teaspoons freshly ground white
    pepper

1 cup finely chopped pistachios
⅔ cup dry bread crumbs
5 chicken breasts, skin and bones
    removed, split
Juice and zest of 2 lemons
6 tablespoons unsalted butter,
    melted

Preheat the oven to 375°F. Lightly butter a shallow baking pan just large enough to hold the chicken breasts in a single layer.

In a large, shallow soup plate, gently blend together the yogurt, garlic, mint, salt, and pepper. In another, combine the nuts and crumbs. Working with breast halves one at a time, gently coat both sides of a breast piece with the yogurt mixture, then roll it in the nut mixture. Place each breast, skin-side down, in the prepared pan; take care that the pieces do not touch.

Combine the lemon juice and zest with the melted butter. Drizzle the butter mixture evenly over the chicken. (The pan can be covered and refrigerated for up to 6 hours at this point bring it back to room temperature 1 hour before baking.)

Bake for 20 minutes, then turn very carefully, spooning pan juices over the top of each piece. Continue baking until the chicken is browned and firm to the touch, about another 30 minutes. Serve immediately.

SERVES **6** TO **10**

Coconut Chicken with Potatoes and Lime

To our taste, anything cooked with coconut milk is absolutely delicious—especially in combination with the spices and herbs one associates with Indian cuisine. Add a touch of heat, some lime, onion, and garlic and you have the best combination possible for this delicious chicken and potato stew. You can make this dish ahead and reheat it, but please don't cut the potatoes until you are ready to cook—if the cubes are first soaked in water, it takes forever to get them to brown.

Up to 1/3 cup canola or peanut oil

4 large russet potatoes, peeled and cut into large chunks

1 1/2 frying chickens

1/2 cup cornstarch

1 hot red chile, minced

1 bulb lemongrass, trimmed and minced

2 tablespoons minced fresh ginger

3 plump garlic cloves, minced

1 1/2 cups finely chopped white onion

1 1/2 tablespoons good-quality Madras-style curry powder

Zest of 2 limes

2 tablespoons fresh lime juice

Up to 3 cups coconut milk (See Basics, page 50)

1/4 cup minced fresh cilantro

Heat 3 tablespoons of the canola oil in a large sauté pan over high heat. Add the potato chunks, reduce heat to medium, and cook, turning often, until the potatoes are browned on all sides, about 10 minutes.

While the potatoes are cooking, cut the chickens into quarters. Then separate the legs from the thighs, separate the wings from the breasts, discard the wing tips, and cut the breasts in half. Combine the chicken and cornstarch in a plastic bag and toss to coat evenly. Transfer the chicken pieces to a rack.

When the potatoes are browned, transfer them to a platter with a slotted spoon. Add more oil to the pan and heat. When hot, add the chicken pieces and brown thoroughly on all sides, 5 to 10 minutes. Transfer the browned chicken to the platter with the potatoes.

Add more oil if needed to the sauté pan and heat until hot. Add the chile, lemongrass, ginger, and garlic. Stir until the aromas are released. Then stir in the onions and cook until wilted, about 3 minutes. Stir in the curry powder; then add the lime zest and juice. Cook for a few minutes, then stir in 2 cups of the coconut milk. When the coconut milk begins to bubble, slip in the potatoes and chicken. Spoon some sauce over them, adding more coconut milk if needed.

Cover and cook over medium-low heat until the chicken is tender, about 45 minutes. Serve on heated plates garnished with cilantro.

SERVES 4 TO 6

Exotic Chicken and Peanut Stew

Peanuts appear in various cuisines—from Southeast Asia to Africa to the Caribbean. This particular recipe includes lemongrass, kaffir lime leaves, and basil more commonly found in Thai food than in African or Caribbean. Nevertheless, a lusty chicken stew is found throughout the Caribbean. You'd find peanut butter included in dishes in all these regions. While one would expect to serve this with rice, we happen to really love it with polenta.

2 frying chickens, each cut into 8 pieces, breasts then cut in half

Kosher salt and freshly ground pepper to taste

½ cup unbleached flour

6 plump garlic cloves, peeled and smashed

2-inch chunk fresh ginger, peeled and chopped

1 bulb lemongrass, coarsely chopped

2 fresh chiles, seeded

⅓ cup peanut oil, plus more if needed

1 cup thinly sliced shallots

2 small dried chiles, crumbled

Juice of 2 limes

1 cup creamy natural peanut butter

3 cups canned crushed tomatoes

⅔ cup coconut milk, canned or fresh (see Basics, page 50)

2 cups rich chicken stock, plus more if needed

2 kaffir lime leaves

2 cups yams, cut into ¾-inch dice

½ cup coarsely chopped fresh basil, preferably Thai

FOR GARNISH: wedges of lime, thinly sliced fresh hot chiles with minced cilantro, diced fresh pineapple, shredded coconut, fried peanuts, and raisins

Rub the chicken pieces with salt and pepper, then dredge them lightly in flour. Let the chicken stand while making the seasoning paste.

In the bowl of a food processor, combine the garlic, ginger, lemongrass, fresh chiles, and 2 teaspoons additional salt. Pulse until a thick paste is achieved. Set aside.

Heat half the oil in a very large cast-iron skillet over medium-high heat. Brown the chicken pieces on all sides, about 20 minutes total. As pieces are browned, transfer them to a large platter; add oil as needed to the skillet.

Then add the shallots to the skillet and stir over medium heat until all of the browned bits have been loosened. Cook until golden, 8 to 12 minutes. Add the seasoning paste and crumbled chiles. Stir for 1 minute, or until fragrant. Stir in the lime juice and peanut butter, then blend in the tomatoes. Add the coconut milk, 1 cup of the chicken stock, and the lime leaves. Cook, stirring often, until the mixture is bubbling.

Slip chicken pieces into the hot sauce, cover, and cook over low heat for 30 minutes, adding up to another cup of stock if sauce is too thick. Then add the yams and cook, covered, until yams and chicken are tender, about another 30 minutes. Stir in the fresh basil.

Carefully transfer the stew to large, handsome serving bowl. Garnish with wedges of lime. Surround with small bowls of cilantro with sliced chiles and scallions, pineapple, coconut, peanuts, and raisins.

SERVES **6** TO **8**

Crispy Duck with Candied Apples and Marrons

The combination of duck, chestnuts, and apples is a very traditional autumn one. As much as we love duck, we never seem to prepare it just for ourselves. Yet our recipe is very simple, yielding ducks with very crispy skin, as well as richly flavored chestnuts and apples. The addition of vanilla is really delightful. This makes a fantastic company dinner. Or, if you are tired of turkey, you just might want to serve this for Thanksgiving!

THE CHESTNUTS
24 cooked whole chestnuts
2 whole cloves
2 teaspoons pure vanilla
  extract
⅔ cup maple syrup

THE APPLES
4 tablespoons butter
3 large tart apples, peeled, cored,
  thinly sliced, and tossed in
  lemon juice
Juice of 1 lemon
¼ cup dark brown sugar

THE BASTING SAUCE
¼ cup hoisin sauce
1 cup apple cider (some will be
  used for the pan sauce)
1 teaspoon ground cardamom
1 teaspoon ground ginger

THE DUCKS
3 roasting ducks (4 to 6 pounds
  each)
Kosher salt and freshly ground black
  pepper to taste
2 tart apples, quartered
2 lemons, quartered

THE PAN SAUCE
⅔ cup rich duck or chicken stock

Preheat the oven to 450°F. Place a large rack inside a large roasting pan.

To prepare the chestnuts: In a small saucepan, combine the chestnuts, cloves, vanilla extract, and maple syrup. Cook over medium heat until the syrup begins to bubble; reduce heat to very low and simmer, partially covered, for 1 hour. Reheat just before serving.

To prepare the apples: In a skillet or sauté pan, melt the butter over medium heat. Add the apple slices, lemon juice, and brown sugar. Stir over medium heat until the apples are just tender, about 10 minutes. Reheat just before serving.

To prepare the basting sauce: In a small saucepan, combine the hoisin sauce, ½ cup of the cider, cardamom, and ginger. Bring to a boil and stir well to blend. Remove from heat.

To prepare the ducks: Remove any visible chunks of fat. Season the duck cavities with salt and pepper. Divide the apples and lemons among the them. Using a sharp-tined fork, prick the ducks all over, but especially in fatty areas. Place the ducks, breast-side up, on the rack, keeping some space between the ducks. Roast for 30 minutes.

Drain all fat from the pan. Turn ducks, back-side up, prick all over again. Then generously coat with basting sauce and roast for another 30 minutes.

Drain any accumulated fat again. Turn ducks breast-side up again. Baste thoroughly. Reduce the heat to 350° and roast for another 20 minutes. Test for doneness by piercing the fleshy area with the tines of a sharp meat fork. If juices are not yellow and the flesh tender, roast for another 10 to 15 minutes. Otherwise remove the pan from the oven and let the birds rest for 10 minutes on a carving board.

Reheat the chestnuts and apples over low heat.

To make the pan sauce: Pour off any duck fat. Add the remaining cider and the stock to the roasting pan and cook over high heat, scraping loose all browned bits. Blend in the remaining basting sauce and 1 tablespoon each of the sauces from the apples and the chestnuts; cook over high heat to reduce somewhat. Taste and adjust seasonings.

Cut the ducks into halves or quarters. Distribute the duck pieces, apples, and chestnuts among heated serving plates. Drizzle with pan sauce. Serve the remaining pan sauce on the side.

SERVES 6 TO 8

Roasted Turkey with Chestnut Stuffing and Zinfandel Gravy

We've been using kosher turkeys for the last five or six years. They are totally delicious and stay very moist. They can be found in most supermarkets at holiday times. Just remember, they do not need any additional salt. Cooking is simple; we only baste this turkey to achieve some good pan drippings for the gravy. So, if you wish, you don't have to baste it at all. Just start with a really good bird; the juices will stay inside. Calculate the roasting time by multiplying nine minutes times the weight of the unstuffed bird. Remove it from the oven when an instant-read thermometer inserted into the meaty part of the breast reads 160°F. Or use a Polder Cooking Thermo Timer with a thermometer probe inserted into the thigh and a cable also attached to a monitor that stays outside the oven. Place turkey on a heated platter and let it rest 30 to 40 minutes, uncovered, before carving.

THE STUFFING

2 pounds challah or another egg
    bread, torn into chunks

Water to cover

4 large eggs, beaten

3 to 4 cups coarsely chopped
    roasted chestnuts

4 slices smoked bacon, diced

1½ sticks (12 tablespoons)
    unsalted butter

1 cup chopped shallots

¾ cup finely chopped celery

3 large tart apples, peeled, cored,
    and coarsely chopped

3 plump garlic cloves, minced

1 dried chile, crumbled

½ cup minced fresh flat-leaf parsley

¼ cup minced fresh tarragon

1 tablespoon fresh thyme leaves

Kosher salt and freshly ground black
    pepper to taste

THE TURKEY GRAVY

1 set turkey giblets and neck

2 pounds chicken backs

3½ quarts water

2 carrots, scrubbed

2 large yellow onions; studded with
    1 clove each

1 whole bay leaf

4 sprigs fresh Italian parsley

6 black peppercorns, bruised

½ cup vegetable oil

⅔ cup unbleached flour

2 cups dry red wine, preferably
    (red) Zinfandel

THE TURKEY

18-to-24-pound kosher turkey

Kosher salt and freshly ground
    pepper to taste

Olive oil

Garlic powder to taste

2 cups rich chicken stock

3 carrots, scrubbed and broken in
    half

3 medium-sized onions, quartered

The day before, prepare the chestnuts and stuffing: Place the bread in a large bowl and cover with water. Soak for at least 1 hour. Drain well, pressing out as much water as possible. Return the bread mixture to the bowl and blend in the eggs and chestnuts.

Place the bacon in a large skillet and cook over medium heat until it begins to crisp. Using a slotted spoon, transfer the bacon to a cutting board and chop into small pieces. Add to the bowl with the bread and chestnuts. Add ½ stick (4 tablespoons) butter to the bacon fat and melt over medium heat. Add the shallots, celery, and apples; sauté, stirring often, until the celery is somewhat tender. Add the garlic, chile, and herbs; stir until garlic has wilted, about 2 minutes. Pour the mixture over the bread and chestnuts and blend thoroughly. Season with salt and pepper.

Melt the remaining butter in skillet over low heat. Add the prepared stuffing to the skillet and stir constantly until most of the liquid is gone. Remove from the heat and let cool. Store in the refrigerator until needed.

To begin the gravy: The day before, combine giblets, neck, chicken backs, and water in a 6-quart soup pot. Bring to a boil, reduce heat, and simmer briskly for 30 minutes, skimming off any scum that forms on the surface. Add the carrots, onions, herbs, and peppercorns and continue to simmer, covered, for 2 hours. Remove the giblets, slice, and set aside. Strain the stock and measure; there should be 10 cups of stock. If there is more, uncover, and continue simmering until it is reduced. Discard the remaining solids. Reserve and reheat just before finishing the gravy.

To finish the gravy: In a very large cast-iron skillet heat oil, add flour and whisk over medium heat until flour is very dark brown, 4 to 6 minutes. Reduce heat to very low and carefully whisk in wine. Whisk thoroughly until mixture is smooth and well-blended. Then whisk in 1 cup of turkey stock. Slowly, over 1½ hours, add the remaining 9 cups of stock, always cooking the mixture over the lowest heat possible and whisking frequently.

When all of the stock is incorporated, add the sliced giblets and set aside until the turkey is roasted and pan drippings are ready to add to this gravy.

To prepare the turkey: Preheat oven to 450°F.

Just before it is time to put the turkey into the oven, pat it dry. Lightly season the cavities and stuff with dressing. Skewer and lace (with string) the cavities shut. Bake the remaining stuffing in a well-buttered casserole.

Rub the bird with some olive oil and lightly season with only pepper and garlic powder if you are using a kosher turkey. Truss the turkey, if you like, and place it on a rack in a roasting pan. Place onions and carrots in roasting pan, too.

Roast the turkey for 45 minutes. Reduce the heat to 400°F and baste with some of the chicken stock. Turn the roasting pan (only cover turkey with some foil if the turkey is getting too brown). Baste the turkey at least three times more, rotating the pan at least once again.

Insert an instant-read thermometer into the fleshy part of the breast; when it reads 160°F remove the turkey from oven and place it on a heated platter in a warm place for 30 to 45 minutes. Do not cover the bird during this time or it will steam.

While the bird is resting, degrease the drippings that remain in the roasting pan; discard the onions and carrots. Add the prepared gravy and cook over medium-high heat, stirring vigorously until all of the crisp particles adhering to the roasting pan have been loosened and gravy has come to a boil.

Carefully scoop the stuffing from the turkey cavities and place in a heated serving bowl. Carve the turkey and place it on a heated serving platter. Serve with gravy on the side.

SERVES 12 TO 14

meat

Smothered Burgers with Almonds

Meat Loaf with Hazelnut Crunch

Grilled Tenderloin with Crunchy Asian Apple Radish Slaw

Rolled Flank Steak with Colorful Stuffing and Romesco Wine Sauce

Turkish-Style Meatballs with Nuts and Currants

Grilled Hanger Steak with Pecan Bourbon Butter

Braised Stuffed Eggplants with Beef and Walnuts in Tomato Sauce

Long-Bone Veal Chop Milanese with Ground Walnuts and Lemons

Hazelnuts and Root Vegetable—Stuffed Veal Brisket with Simple Pan Gravy

Lusty Italian Veal Stew with Green Beans and Pine Nuts

Braised Veal Short Ribs in Thai-Style Coconut Curry Sauce

Middle East Meets West Baked Veal and Eggplant

Peppered Pistachio-Crusted Rack of Lamb

Boneless Leg of Lamb Stuffed with Tapénade, Pine Nuts, and Kale

Lamb Ragout with Chestnuts, Onions, and Sage

Grilled Lamb Kabobs with Hard-Boiled Eggs and Pistachios

Wedad and Helen's Baked Kibbee with Pine Nuts

A Kerala Lamb Biriyani: Spicy Lamb Stew and Rice with Cashews

Pan Asian Pork Roast with Peanut Crust and Orange Sauce

Grilled Pork Tenderloins with Walnuts, Shallots, and Prunes

Asian-Style Barbecued Spareribs with Peanut Dipping Sauce

Braised Stuffed Pork Chops with Chestnuts and Apples

Heavenly Hash with Pine Nuts and Tangy Fruited Tomato Sauce

Smothered Burgers with Almonds

Philadelphia's Mrs. Rorer, the late nineteenth century's prolific American writer on matters of food, clearly enjoyed nuts. She not only included them in virtually all of her books, but also in numerous delightful pamphlets, including a gem titled "Dainty Desserts," written for Dunham's Cocoanut for the Dunham Manufacturing Company. The late James Beard included Mrs. Rorer's Almond Hamburg Steak in his book on American Cookery. We are also intrigued with a recipe called "Bobotee" in Mrs. Rorer's Philadelphia Cookbook, *published in 1896. In addition to fried onions and curry powder, she also included ground almonds with her ground meat. This is our adaptation.*

3 tablespoons unsalted butter

1 tablespoon curry powder

1 teaspoon ground cayenne

2 pounds ground flank steak

1 pound ground chuck

⅔ cup grated yellow onions

½ cup bread crumbs

3 plump garlic cloves, minced

⅓ cup finely chopped toasted almonds

Kosher salt and freshly ground black pepper to taste

2 eggs, beaten well

½ cup milk

5 tablespoons olive oil, plus more if needed

2 jumbo sweet onions, cut in half and thinly sliced

1 tablespoon sweet Hungarian paprika

Melt the butter in a small skillet. Add the curry powder and cayenne and stir over medium heat for 1 minute. Pour into a large mixing bowl. Add the ground meats, grated onions, bread crumbs, garlic, and almonds and blend thoroughly. Add salt and pepper, beaten eggs, and milk. Blend thoroughly again. Next form into half-pound burgers that are about 1 inch thick. Chill.

Heat 3 tablespoons of the olive oil in a large skillet over medium heat. Add the onions and sauté, stirring often and adding more oil if needed, until golden brown, about 30 minutes. Stir in the paprika and set aside.

Thoroughly clean your grill, spray with vegetable oil, and heat until hot. Reheat onions and keep warm. Grill the burgers for 5 minutes on one side, turn, and finish grilling on other side to the desired degree of doneness.

Serve the almond burgers with the onions on top.

SERVES 6

John Lagier's Value-Added Almonds

If you ate an almond today, a bee made it possible. In March tens of thousands of acres of almond trees in the great central valley of California are thick with the bloom; there is little in the agricultural world as beautiful, or as fragrant. In every orchard, bees are ready to go to work, pollinating the trees.

John Lagier is a third-generation farmer near Escalon. We walked his thirty-six acre almond orchard. (AM-en is the way you say it if you are a California almond grower.) The trees, about 103 per acre, were in full bloom and waiting for the bees. The beehives, essential for pollination, had just been deployed all around the orchard by itinerant bee-keepers. But it was a bit cool and the bees were staying at home. When the temperature hits 54°F and it isn't windy or raining, the bees will go to work. John loves this aspect of his work; he was a "bee boy" who early on learned the secrets of how these little honey-making creatures contribute so much to our lives.

For a while after college he worked for a mega-food operation, but he was drawn back to the farm. He started growing white wine grapes, then almonds, cherries, berries, table grapes, blood oranges, mandarin oranges, tangerines, and pomelos. Everything he grows is certified organic.

The challenge for farmers is to make a living in the complex agriculture economy. John Lagier believes in "value-added products." We sampled the almonds he takes every week to the Embarcadero market. He roasts and sugars them and flavors them with various herbs and spices—like cinnamon, tamari, and cayenne—and puts them in neat packages. He makes packaged products from the other special organically grown fruits as they come into season. That helps, too, as more and more consumers look for foods that are free of chemical fertilizer and pesticides. His creativity helps him make a good living on a relatively small farm.

As he waits for the bees to set to work, John Lagier looks at the beautiful sweep of almond blossoms. "This is a perfect place," he says. "I can't imagine working anyplace else."

Meat Loaf with Hazelnut Crunch

While we often prepare very elegant dinner parties, meat loaf is one of the most popular dishes at our table and most requested. We make a wide variety of them, varying both the meats and the flavorings. The constants are garlic and plenty of onion. This particular recipe has a lot of toasted hazelnuts, as well as a generous amount of dried mint. The flavors they add are quite pleasing, and there is the subtle crunch from the nuts. We also include shredded carrots and some evaporated milk for moisture.

4 pounds ground beef and veal

4 plump garlic cloves, smashed and minced

1 cup finely chopped onion, preferably sweet

1/3 cup minced fresh flat-leaf parsley

2 tablespoons fresh minced mint (or 1 tablespoon dried)

2 teaspoons fresh thyme leaves (or 1 teaspoon dried)

2 small dried chiles, crumbled

4 plump carrots, finely grated

2/3 cup evaporated milk, plus more if needed

4 large eggs

3/4 cup finely chopped toasted hazelnuts

1 tablespoon kosher salt

2 teaspoons freshly ground black pepper

4 strips smoked bacon, cut in half

2 bay leaves

2 cups canned crushed tomatoes

In a large mixing bowl, combine the ground meats and blend together well. Add the garlic, onion, parsley, mint, thyme, chiles, and carrots. Blend again. Then add the evaporated milk, eggs, hazelnuts, salt, and pepper. Vigorously mix all together. If too dry, slowly add more evaporated milk.

Turn the mixture into a large baking pan. Form it into a loaf that is about 2½ inches high and about 5 inches across. Make certain it is firmly packed. Place the bacon strips over the top of the loaf and the bay leaves over the bacon. Cover with plastic wrap and chill for several hours.

Preheat the oven to 400°F.

Bake the meat loaf for 45 minutes. Remove the fat from the pan and pour the crushed tomatoes over the meat loaf and bake for another 30 minutes. To test for doneness: In the center of the loaf, insert a knife halfway down. Quickly touch the knife to your lower lip. If the knife is hot, the meat is done; otherwise, continue roasting until it is done. Then remove it from the oven, place the pan on a rack, and let the meat rest for 10 minutes before slicing.

Carefully skim the fat from the pan sauce. Slice the meat loaf and serve it on heated plates with sauce spooned onto the top.

SERVES **6** TO **8**

Grilled Tenderloin with Crunchy
Asian Apple Radish Slaw

Tenderloin marries so well with all kinds of sauces. This cold and crunchy slaw with its Asian flavors and peanut crunch may be the best yet. It is a perfect summer party dish. The slaw can be prepared early in the day and kept cold. The tenderloin is a breeze to prepare on a grill. Don't freak at the grilling time and do not worry about a thermometer. Just follow the advice of those who cook and grill it covered for 10 minutes per side. Let it stand for at least 15 minutes. It will be medium-rare, except on the ends. This is especially delicious served with potatoes gratin.

THE BEEF

2 teaspoons minced fresh ginger

3 plump garlic cloves, smashed and minced

1 teaspoon hot mustard

⅓ cup soy sauce

2 tablespoons hoisin sauce

1 tablespoon Nam Pla (Asian fish sauce)

2 teaspoons dark sesame oil

¼ cup fresh lime juice

1 totally trimmed and tied beef tenderloin, about 4 to 4½ pounds

THE SLAW

½ cup cider vinegar, more if needed

¼ cup fresh lime juice

3 tablespoons granulated sugar

2 tablespoons crunchy peanut butter

1 tablespoon Nam Pla

3 teaspoons dark sesame oil

1 teaspoon whole celery seed

1 tablespoon whole mustard seed

2 teaspoons kosher salt

1 teaspoon freshly ground white pepper

2 large tart apples, peeled and finely shredded

⅓ cup finely grated fresh horse-radish root

½ red bell pepper, finely minced

1½ cups grated daikon radish

½ cup watermelon radish (if available)

4 cups finely grated napa cabbage

¼ cup minced chives

1 cup roasted peanuts, coarsely chopped

To prepare the beef: In a small bowl, combine the ginger, garlic, mustard, and soy sauce. Blend vigorously. Then blend in the hoisin sauce, Nam Pla, sesame oil, and lime juice. Blend thoroughly. One hour before grilling, rub the seasoning mixture over the meat and let rest at room temperature. Meanwhile make the slaw.

To prepare the slaw: In a small bowl, combine the vinegar, lime juice, sugar, peanut butter, Nam Pla, sesame oil, celery seed, mustard seed, salt, and pepper. Blend thoroughly and reserve. In a mixing bowl, combine the apples, horseradish, bell pepper, daikon radish, watermelon radish, and cabbage. Pour the vinegar mixture over the vegetables and blend thoroughly. Taste and adjust seasonings. Cover slaw and refrigerate for at least 4 hours.

Thoroughly clean the grill and heat until hot. Place the seasoned tenderloin, fat-side down, on the grill. Cover and cook for 10 minutes. Using tongs, carefully turn meat and grill for another 10 minutes for medium-rare. Transfer the meat to a large carving board and allow to rest for 10 to 15 minutes.

While beef is the resting, stir the chives and peanuts into the slaw. Slice the meat into ½-inch-thick pieces. Then arrange 2 slices, somewhat overlapping, on each dinner plate. Spoon slaw somewhat over and to the side of the beef.

SERVES 6 TO 8

Rolled Flank Steak with Colorful Stuffing and Romesco Wine Sauce

The Spanish "romesco" sauce is a heady blend of sweet and hot peppers with nuts, garlic, and olive oil, usually made into a silken sauce with the help of a mortar and pestle (although, one can certainly make it in a food processor). Here we take a butterflied flank steak, slather it lavishly with romesco sauce, cover it with a colorful mixture of ground veal, strips of omelet, roasted peppers, and herbs, and braise it into tenderness in a tasty bath of romesco-piqued tomato sauce. When cooked and sliced, it reveals its colorful filling. Served hot or at room temperature, it is best when dabbed with some of its delicious pan juices. We've made many stuffed flank steaks over the years, but this recipe is particularly inspired by Paula Wolfert's in Mediterranean Cooking *(Ecco Press, 1985).*

A 2-to-2½-pound flank steak
1 recipe Romesco Sauce (page 156)
1½ pounds ground veal
Up to 4 tablespoons olive oil
3 eggs, beaten thoroughly
2 large roasted bell peppers, peeled, seeded, and cut lengthwise into ¼-inch-wide strips
½ cup minced fresh flat-leaf parsley
2 teaspoons fresh thyme leaves

Kosher salt and freshly ground black pepper to taste
2 tablespoons unbleached flour, plus more if needed
1¼ cups finely chopped white onion
1 dried chile pepper, crushed
⅔ cup canned crushed tomatoes
½ cup red wine, as needed
Sprigs of fresh thyme

Open the flank steak on your work surface, short end facing you. Using a sharp knife, butterfly the steak, cutting it open like a book. Keep one long side intact. Once you are finished, open the steak. The meat's grain will be perpendicular to edge of the shorter sides. If the meat is too irregular, trim it somewhat.

Leave a ½-inch border around the meat, and cover the surface with 3 tablespoons Romesco Sauce. Spread evenly with ground veal. Let it rest for a few minutes.

Heat 1 tablespoon oil in a large skillet and add the eggs. Drag fork through mixture several times, as if you were making an omelet. Cook until it's firm. Turn it out onto the work surface and slice it into long strips, ⅓ inch wide.

Arrange the omelet strips over the ground veal. Then add strips of red pepper. Sprinkle with half of the parsley and thyme leaves. Season generously with salt and pepper.

Working at the short end, *roll the meat with the grain* (then when you slice it, you carve across the grain) into a firm cylinder. Cut 5 10-inch lengths of kitchen twine. Tie the meat securely. Then rub generously with flour and season with salt and pepper.

Pour the remaining oil into a large skillet over medium-high heat until hot. Add the meat and brown on all sides, adding more oil if needed, about 7 minutes. Transfer beef roll to an ovenproof casserole with a tight-fitting lid.

Preheat the oven to 350°F.

Add the onions and crushed chili to the skillet and stir over medium heat until wilted. Stir in the tomatoes, ¼ cup of wine, the remaining Romesco Sauce, and thyme. Season with salt and pepper. Bring to a boil, then pour over the meat.

Cover the casserole tightly and bake for 1 hour. Baste, adding more wine if needed. Cover again and reduce the oven temperature to 325°. Braise for another hour, or until the meat is tender.

Transfer the beef roll to a carving board. Let it rest for 15 minutes. Meanwhile, place the casserole over medium-high heat (or pour the gravy into a large skillet) and bring to a boil. Reduce the heat and simmer briskly until sauce has thickened somewhat.

Cut the strings and remove them from the beef roll. Cut the meat into ½-inch-thick slices and serve with some sauce over one side of the slices and dust lightly with some of the remaining parsley.

SERVES 6

Turkish-Style Meatballs with Nuts and Currants

Nuts and ground meat appear in a variety of guises throughout the Middle East. This particular version combines beef and veal, which is strictly a Griffith preference. The combination of more than one variety of nuts in a single meat dish, however, is not unusual in the Eastern Mediterranean. A dish such as this might often appear as one of many meze *dishes in Turkey. We enjoy these and the Spicy Sauce as a main dish, served along with a big bowl of Fatoush (see recipe page 110)*

2 tablespoons olive oil

2 pounds mixture ground beef and
  veal

2 teaspoons kosher salt

1 teaspoon freshly ground pepper

2 plump garlic cloves, minced

3 tablespoons unsalted butter,
  melted

2 teaspoons dried oregano

2 teaspoons ground cumin

½ teaspoon ground cayenne

1 medium yellow onion, minced

¼ cup finely chopped walnuts

¼ cup finely chopped hazelnuts

½ cup dried bread crumbs

2 large eggs

½ cup water

⅓ cup dried currants

⅓ cup toasted pine nuts

⅓ cup minced fresh parsley

1 tablespoon dried mint

SPICY SAUCE

½ English cucumber chopped

½ medium-sized sweet onion
  chopped

½ cup fresh cilantro leaves

½ cup fresh flat-leaf parsley leaves

¼ cup fresh mint leaves

10 drops Tabasco sauce

Kosher salt and freshly ground
  white pepper

To make the meatballs: Preheat the oven to 450°F.

Using olive oil, lavishly coat a large shallow-sided baking sheet.

In a large bowl, combine the ground meat, salt, pepper, garlic, butter, oregano, cumin, cayenne, onion, walnuts, hazelnuts, bread crumbs, and eggs. Blend together thoroughly. Add water and blend well. If the mixture appears to be too dry, gradually mix in more water.

In a small bowl, combine the currants, pine nuts, parsley, and mint.

Form meat mixture into walnut-sized balls. Then, one at a time, make a hole in the center, stuff with a bit of the currant mixture, then carefully close hole and place stuffed meatball on the baking sheet.

Bake the meatballs for 10 minutes. Using a spatula, carefully turn the meatballs. Bake for another 5 minutes or until meatballs are well browned and a thin knife inserted into the center of one comes out hot.

To make the spicy sauce: While the meatballs are in the oven, combine all sauce ingredients in a food processor and pulse them until they are puréed. Chill until serving time.

When the meat balls are done, place them on a platter and drizzle with the sauce.

SERVES 6

Grilled Hanger Steak with Pecan Bourbon Butter

Our preference in beef is for the cuts that may require a bit more chewing, but are really rich in flavor. Hanger steak, also known by its French name of onglet, or butcher's tenderloin, has historically been the cut saved by the butcher for himself—he knew a good thing. Marinated and grilled, this cut of meat is just sublime. You can, however, use this same preparation for skirt steaks, another delicious cut of beef that benefits from some hours in a delicious marinade. Both are quickly grilled on a hot fire, then glazed with a delicious slice of butter mixed with some bourbon and finely chopped pecans. Nothing could be better.

½ cup bourbon or whiskey

2 teaspoons dry mustard

4 plump garlic cloves, smashed

½ large red onion, cut into chunks

⅓ cup olive oil

⅓ cup pecan oil

1 tablespoon herbes de Provence (dried thyme, parsley, sage, basil, rosemary)

1 tablespoon coarsely ground black pepper

3 pounds hanger steak, cut into 6-inch-long pieces

6 tablespoons unsalted butter, softened

2 tablespoons finely chopped pecans

1 tablespoon bourbon or whiskey

Sea salt to taste

In the bowl of a food processor, combine the bourbon, mustard, garlic, onions, oils, herbs, and pepper. Pulse until puréed. Pour into a large plastic bag. Then add steak pieces, turning them in the marinade to coat on both sides. Refrigerate for at least 4 hours and up to 8, turning the meat several times.

Combine the softened butter, pecans, and whiskey in a mixing bowl. Blend together evenly. Then transfer mixture to a sheet of wax paper. Make a roll about 1 inch in diameter and refrigerate.

Thoroughly clean the surface of a gas or charcoal grill with a metal brush; then coat the surface evenly with vegetable spray.

Heat the grill to high. Remove the meat from the marinade and place it on the hot grill. Turn after 3 to 4 minutes and grill for another 2 minutes for rare, 3 minutes for medium. Transfer to heated plates, sprinkle generously with sea salt, and place slices of the nut butter on top of the steaks.

SERVES 6

Braised Stuffed Eggplants with Beef and Walnuts in Tomato Sauce

This delicious dish is our variation on a recipe given to us by Wedad and Helen Shaheen, our Syrian friends who live in Canton, Ohio. The mint-laced and garlic-piqued tomato sauce is so good, we just had to use it for other vegetable-based meat dishes. You can make these eggplants for a delicious summer weekend luncheon, or as part of a Middle Eastern buffet. Look for small, fresh-from-the-garden eggplants. We've used young white Japanese ones, as well as some small pink ones that are quite round.

6 to 8 small eggplants, about 6 inches long

Kosher salt

¼ cup olive oil

½ cup long-grain rice, rinsed in cold water

¾ pound coarsely ground beef

⅓ cup minced yellow onion

½ teaspoon ground allspice

1 tablespoon minced fresh flat-leaf parsley

⅔ cup lightly toasted coarsely chopped walnuts

⅔ cup canned tomato sauce

4 tablespoons unsalted butter, melted

Additional kosher salt

Freshly ground black pepper

1¼ cups Tomato Purée (See Basics, page 52) or canned crushed tomatoes

3 plump garlic cloves, minced

2 cups water

2 teaspoons dried mint

Middle Eastern yogurt for garnish

Cut the eggplants in half lengthwise. Carefully remove the flesh from each, leaving a shell that is about ⅙ inch thick. Reserve half of the flesh.

Salt the eggplants and the reserved eggplant flesh and let stand for 1 hour. Rinse thoroughly and pat dry. Finely chop the reserved eggplant flesh.

Heat the olive oil in a small skillet. Add the chopped eggplant and cook, stirring occasionally. When tender, transfer the cooked flesh to a mixing bowl. Add the rice, beef, onion, allspice, parsley, nuts, tomato sauce, butter, salt, and pepper. Stuff the eggplant about four-fifths full, leaving some room for rice expansion. Place the eggplants in a very large, heavy sauté pan.

Spoon a tablespoon of tomato purée evenly over each eggplant. Pour the remaining purée around the eggplants. Sprinkle garlic over the eggplants and into the saucepan purée. Then pour a tablespoon of water evenly over each one, and the remainder goes into the pan, itself. Finally, sprinkle with mint and more pepper.

Cover eggplants with a sheet of foil or parchment directly on them. Tightly cover and cook over high heat until liquid bubbles, 3 to 4 minutes. Reduce heat to low and simmer until tender, 30 to 45 minutes.

Serve on heated plates, generously napped with pan sauce. Pass yogurt on the side.

SERVES 6 TO 12

Long-Bone Veal Chop Milanese with Ground Walnuts and Lemons

This lightly nut-crusted veal chop is sauced by its lemon salad topping. It is totally delicious and one of our favorite treats. It's our version of a specialty of Cleveland's top restaurant, Johnny's Bar on Fulton—where the great and near great meet to eat. Be sure to have the cap removed from the chops; it makes a much finer presentation. If you have any preserved lemons, incorporate some in the salad topping.

THE CHOPS

6 long-bone rib veal chops, cut about 1½ inches thick

4 plump garlic cloves, pressed

Kosher salt and freshly ground black pepper to taste

½ cup unbleached flour, plus more if needed

2 eggs

Zest of 2 lemons

1 teaspoon water

¾ cup finely ground walnuts, plus more if needed

Up to ½ cup extra virgin olive oil

THE SALAD TOPPING

¼ cup extra virgin olive oil

1 teaspoon sugar

1 plump garlic clove, minced

2 tablespoons minced shallot

⅓ cup fresh lemon juice

2 tablespoons minced fresh basil

1¼ cups thinly sliced peeled English cucumber

⅔ cup currant tomatoes, halved (or cherry tomatoes, quartered)

Kosher salt and freshly ground black pepper to taste

To prepare the chops: Preheat the oven to 425°F.

Pound the veal chops to a thickness of ½ inch. Rub each side with garlic and season with salt and pepper. Pour flour on a large plate; beat eggs and lemon zest (reserving lemon juice for salad topping) in a soup plate with 1 teaspoon water; pour nut meal onto another plate. Dredge each chop first in flour, then in egg wash, and finally in the finely chopped nuts. Let chops rest on a cake rack for at least 15 minutes.

To make the salad topping: In a medium-sized salad bowl, whisk together 3 tablespoons extra virgin olive oil, sugar, garlic, shallots, lemon juice, and basil. Gently blend in cucumbers and tomatoes. Set aside.

To finish the chops: In ovenproof skillets large enough to hold 3 chops, each, pour enough olive oil to cover the bottom. Place over medium-high heat, add the chops, and sauté until golden on each side, 3 to 4 minutes total. Bake the chops in the oven until the chops feel firm when pressed with your fingers, 5 to 6 minutes.

Blot the chops on paper towel to remove excess oil, then place on heated plates. Spoon salad topping over each chop, season with more salt and pepper.

SERVES **6**

Hazelnuts and Root Vegetable–Stuffed Veal Brisket with Simple Pan Gravy

This aromatic winter dish is a much simpler version of the old-fashioned stuffed breast of veal; we've eliminated all the bones, excess fat, and gristle. Have your meat purveyor create a pocket by slicing an opening on one short side all the way through the middle of the brisket—just like a purse. The garlic-and-herb-piqued stuffing includes parsnips, turnips, celery root, and carrots. Chopped toasted hazelnuts add a deep, mellow flavor along with some pleasing crunch. Our simple red wine and onion pan gravy is quite delicious. You can, if you wish, make it more festive by finishing it with a cup of sautéed portobello mushrooms.

2 large turnips, cleaned and grated

2 large parsnips, scraped and grated

2 medium carrots, scrubbed and grated

2 medium yellow onions, grated

1 cup grated celery root

3 plump garlic cloves, pressed

2 large eggs

⅔ cup coarsely chopped toasted hazelnuts

¼ cup dry bread crumbs

1 tablespoon herbes de Provence

Kosher salt and freshly ground black pepper

2 veal briskets with pockets

1 tablespoon olive oil

¼ cup flour

4 cups finely chopped Spanish onion

2 medium carrots, finely chopped

1 cup dry red wine

1 cup dark brown veal or beef stock

2 tablespoons tomato paste

6 ounces cremini or portobello mushrooms, thinly sliced (optional)

½ cup chopped fresh flat-leaf parsley

Combine the turnips, parsnips, carrots, onions, celery root, and garlic in a large mixing bowl. Stir in the eggs, hazelnuts, bread crumbs, herbs, salt, and pepper. Mix thoroughly.

Divide the stuffing between the brisket pockets and close with skewers.

Preheat the oven to 350°F and lightly coat a large roasting pan with oil.

Rub the briskets with flour and season with salt and pepper. Scatter the chopped onions and carrots in the bottom of the roaster. Place the briskets on the onion mixture, fat-side up. Pour the wine and veal stock around them. Tightly cover the roasting pan with foil or a lid. Roast for 1¼ hours.

Carefully turn the briskets, baste, and cover. Roast until fork-tender, about another 1¼ hours.

Remove the briskets to a carving board and let stand for 10 minutes. Place roasting pan on the stovetop and bring to a rapid boil. Whisk in tomato paste. Reduce liquids in pan by a third, stirring from time to time. If using sautéed mushrooms, incorporate them at this time. Skim off any surface fat.

Cut the briskets across the grain into thick slices. Ladle some sauce on each heated dinner plate and place a slice of stuffed brisket on top. Add a generous dollop of sauce over each, sprinkle with parsley, and serve. Pour the remaining sauce into a heated gravy bowl and serve on the side.

SERVES 8 TO 10

Lusty Italian Veal Stew with Green Beans and Pine Nuts

This sublime stew is a perfectly balanced combination of flavors that make a luscious sauce for the small cubes of veal. We love the textural contrasts brought by the additions of green beans and toasted pine nuts. Don't be put off by the inclusion of anchovy fillets; they melt into the sauce, giving it a most pleasing savory flavor. If you cannot find peppers with some heat, roast a red bell pepper and add some dried hot pepper to the sauce. The heat should be there, but very subtle. To prepare the chile peppers: Char grill over flame or under broiler until skin is thoroughly darkened; sweat in a paper bag until cool, then peel and discard skin, slit open, and discard seeds and stem. We serve this over a soup plate of organic stone-ground Marino polenta from Piedmont (to order, see Zingerman's in the Sources, page 313).

2 roasted, skinned, and seeded red peppers that have some heat, such as ancho or poblano chiles

2 cups tomato purée (see Basics, page 52)
3 pounds boneless veal, cut into 1-inch cubes

1/3 cup unbleached flour, plus more
  if needed
1/4 cup olive oil, plus more if
  needed
1 cup finely chopped yellow onion
2 plump carrots, coarsely grated or
  chopped
8 plump cloves garlic, minced
7 anchovy fillets, preferably salt-
  packed, rinsed and chopped
2 cups red wine

2 cups rich chicken stock
1 fresh rosemary branch
Kosher salt and freshly ground black
  pepper
1/2 pound green beans, trimmed
  and cut into 1-inch lengths
1/2 cup toasted pine nuts

Polenta (as accompaniment)
Mascarpone cheese for garnish

Combine the peppers and 2/3 cup of the tomato purée in the food processor. Pulse until thoroughly puréed. Combine the mixture with the remaining tomato purée and set aside.

Dredge the veal cubes in flour. Heat 2 tablespoons of the olive oil in a very large, heavy sauté pan. Working in batches and adding oil as needed, thoroughly brown meat cubes on all sides over medium-high heat, about 20 minutes total. As the meat is browned, transfer the cubes to a large platter.

Add oil if needed, and combine the onions, carrots, and garlic in sauté pan. Lower the heat slightly and cook, stirring often, until the onions begin to change color and soften, 10 to 15 minutes. Stir in the anchovies and cook until melted into the onions.

Preheat the oven to 300°F.

Add the red wine to the sauté pan and cook over high heat until the liquid is reduced by half. Then add the tomato pepper purée, stock, and meat. Cook over high heat until the liquid bubbles. Add the rosemary branch, salt, and pepper.

Place the pan in the oven and cook until the meat is very tender, about 2 hours, stirring from time to time.

Transfer the pan to the stovetop. Add the green beans, cover, and cook over medium-low heat until beans are very, very tender, about 10 minutes. Stir in the pine nuts.

Spoon the polenta into heated soup plates. Add a generous dollop of mascarpone, then ladle stew over the polenta and serve.

SERVES 6

Braised Veal Short Ribs in Thai-Style Coconut Curry Sauce

When veal short ribs are slowly braised, the tough connective collagen breaks, down, making the meat meltingly tender. This sauce not only adds robust flavors to the meat, it also enhances its silken texture. Spicy flavors of onion and garlic, not to mention the various "curry" seasonings, all blend together to make this a superbly rich and delicious dish with the suggestion of tartness that comes from the use of both vinegar and Nam Pla. While you certainly can use beef short ribs, the veal is really preferable, at least to us. We suggest you ask for short ribs cut cross-wise, in what is commonly called the "flanken" cut.

½ cup unbleached flour

6 to 7 pounds veal flanken (bone in)

Up to ⅔ cup organic canola or
    vegetable oil, more if needed

2 cups thinly sliced yellow onions

6 plump garlic cloves, minced

2 tablespoons minced fresh ginger

1 bulb lemongrass, trimmed and
    minced

2 small dried red chiles, crumbled

1½ tablespoons good-quality
    Madras curry powder

1 teaspoon ground cardamom

1 teaspoon ground cayenne

Kosher salt and freshly ground
    white pepper to taste

2 kaffir lime leaves or zest of 1 large
    lime

1½ cups coconut milk, plus more if
    needed, canned or fresh (see
    Basics, page 50)

1¼ cups tomato purée, canned or
    fresh (See Basics, page 52)

1 tablespoon red wine vinegar

1 tablespoon Nam Pla (fish sauce)

½ cup finely chopped fresh cilantro

½ cup finely chopped roasted
    peanuts

6 wedges fresh lime

Steamed brown jasmine rice

Preheat the oven to 350°F.

Pour the flour onto a plate, then thoroughly dredge the short ribs in the flour to coat evenly. Place the ribs on a cake rack. Heat oil in a large, heavy sauté pan over medium-high heat. Add the short ribs and brown thoroughly on all sides, about 20 minutes total. Transfer the ribs to a large plate.

Reduce the heat to medium, adding oil if needed, then the sauté onions until they begin to caramelize, about 20 minutes. Add the garlic, and lemongrass. Stir often until the garlic is quite wilted, 3 to 5 minutes.

Stir in the chiles, curry powder, cardamom, cayenne, salt, and pepper; stir for a minute to release the aromas of the spices. Then add the lime leaves or zest, coconut milk, tomato purée, vinegar, and Nam Pla; stir until sauce is hot. Slip the browned short ribs into the sauce, spooning some over the tops of the ribs. Cover tightly and place into the oven.

Braise the short ribs until tender, about 2 hours. Baste several times, adding more coconut milk if needed. (You can prepare the ribs to this point and refrigerate overnight, reheating them, covered, very slowly over low heat.)

Serve the short ribs over rice, napping generously with the sauce. Sprinkle lavishly with cilantro and peanuts. Serve lime wedges on the side for spritzing.

SERVES **6**

Middle East Meets West Baked Veal and Eggplant

We have made a delicious eggplant gratin for years. Then in doing research for this book, we came across a Middle Eastern recipe for a creamy ground meat dish that got our taste buds all revved up. This is our creation, a totally delicious dish that makes a perfect addition to any buffet table, Middle Eastern or not. Don't be shocked at the amount of oil in the recipe. The more you fry eggplant, the better you will get and the less oil you will use. Also, use a fairly high heat and only turn the slices one time in the skillet. Then blot the fried slices as thoroughly as possible. Alternatively, you can use silpat nonstick baking sheets and a little bit of oil and broil the eggplant slices.

Kosher salt

2½ to 3 pounds eggplant, peeled and cut into very thin slices

1 to 2½ cups olive oil

½ cup pine nuts

3 plump garlic cloves, minced

½ cup finely chopped yellow onions

1 pound ground veal

¼ teaspoon ground allspice

Kosher salt and freshly ground black pepper to taste

1 teaspoon dried mint

1 cup unbleached flour, plus 3 tablespoons

4 tablespoons unsalted butter

3 cups whole milk, heated

1 teaspoon ground cinnamon

½ cup minced fresh flat-leaf parsley

1½ cups grated Gruyère or Beaufort or Swiss cheese

Sprinkle the eggplant generously with salt and drain in a colander for 1 hour, then rinse well and pat dry.

Preheat the oven to 400°F.

In a medium-sized skillet, heat 3 tablespoons of the olive oil over medium heat. Add the pine nuts and stir until lightly browned, 2 to 4 minutes. Transfer the pine nuts to a mixing bowl and reserve. Add the garlic and onions to the oil, reduce the heat, and cook until wilted, about 3 minutes. Add the ground veal and stir vigorously. When the veal has browned, stir in the allspice, salt, pepper, and mint. Transfer the veal mixture to the pine nuts and blend well.

Pour 1 cup of flour onto a plate. Dredge the eggplant slice in it and reserve. Pour $\frac{1}{2}$ cup of the olive oil into a very large skillet. If you can manage two eggplant slices at a time, do so. Heat until hot, then working in batches and adding oil as needed, fry the eggplant until golden, about 2 minutes per side. Drain well on paper towels.

Then make a béchamel sauce: Melt 3 tablespoons butter in a heavy saucepan over low heat, then whisk in 3 tablespoons of flour. Stir several minutes to cook flour a bit. Slowly add the hot milk, whisking constantly, to make a thick sauce. Stir in the cinnamon. Season with salt and pepper to taste.

Using the final tablespoon of butter, lightly coat a 3-quart baking dish. Layer eggplant, parsley, meat mixture, and 1 cup of the cheese. Sprinkle each layer with some salt and pepper. Repeat until you have three layers of meat and end with the fourth layer of eggplant only.

Pour the sauce over the prepared eggplant. Sprinkle with the remaining cheese. Bake, uncovered, in the preheated oven for 45 minutes, or until the mixture is tender when pierced with a long-tined fork and the top is bubbling and thoroughly browned.

Let it rest for a few minutes before cutting into servings.

SERVES **6** TO **8**

Walnut Catsup

Sorry, but walnut catsup may be against the law.

Not long ago, the United States government ruled that American Spoon Foods in Petosky, Michigan, could not refer to their delicious plum catsup as catsup.

Only sauces made with tomatoes can be called catsup, ruled the feds. Clearly the bureaucrats hadn't read early American recipes for walnut catsup and a host of other catsups made with almost anything *but* tomatoes.

Lettice Bryan wrote *The Kentucky Housewife.* Her famous compendium of southern cooking was published in 1839. In her book she offered a "catchup" made with walnuts, in addition to others made with oysters, lemon, rum, lobsters, mushrooms, anchovies, fish, and, yes, tomatoes.

Karen Hess edited the 1984 republication of *The Virginia Housewife.* In her wonderful notes in the book, she gives a definition of catsup. "The word comes from Amoy *kētsiap* or Malay *kēchap,* meaning brine of pickled shellfish; forms of the word appear in English by 1690, according to the Oxford English Dictionary. The English had long used anchovies and pickled oysters as condiments (hearkening back to the *garum* of ancient Rome), so that their swift adoption of the name and new variations is not surprising.

"Mrs. Rundell's recipe for Tomata Sauce in 1814 may be the earliest printed recipe for tomato catsup. Until nearly midcentury in America, *catsup* was generally understood to be based on mushrooms or walnuts."

Mushroom, oyster, and walnut catsups accompany the "tomata" in this book.

A "receipt" for a peach catsup came from Miss Fanny White of Milledgeville, Georgia, and is a part of *Tullie's Receipts,* a collection of plantation-style Southern cooking reprinted in 1976.

The fabled "Oscar of the Waldorf," Oscar Tschirky, published his classic cookbook in 1896. He includes five catsups—cucumber, mushroom, tomato, oyster, and this one, made with walnuts. "Put one hundred green walnuts into a mortar and beat them until well bruised, then put them into a jar with six ounces of chopped shallots, a head of garlic, one half pound of salt, and two quarts of vinegar. Stir the contents of the jar twice a day for a fortnight, then strain off the vinegar, put it into a saucepan with three anchovies, one tablespoonful of cloves, two tablespoonfuls of peppercorns, and one-fourth of an ounce of mace. Boil the vinegar for half an hour, then strain it off and leave it until cold. Pour the vinegar into bottles, being careful not to get any of the sediment mixed up in it. Cork the bottles tightly and keep them in a dry store-cupboard."

By 1965, when *Webster's Unabridged* was updated, the lexicographers had been co-opted, possibly brainwashed by the mega tomato catsup establishment; catsup, according to that dictionary, was "a sauce for meat" usually made with tomatoes.

Peppered Pistachio-Crusted Rack of Lamb

Nothing could be easier than coating lamb with some orange marmalade, then rolling it in a pepper-piqued mixture of crushed pistachio nuts and dry crumbs. A generous dash of ground coriander adds a pleasing, but mysterious note to the succulent meat. After high-temperature roasting the lamb will have a splendid flavor and superb texture. Try this when you are having dinner guests after a busy workday. It is simple and really elegant. Be sure to have the chine bone, cap, and all visible fat removed. This is one lamb dish that does not need any sauce, but a fig chutney on the side might be delicious. Serve with a purée of winter squash or yams mixed with a touch of vanilla extract and ginger.

½ cup dry bread crumbs
½ cup finely chopped pistachio
   nuts
2 teaspoons ground coriander
1 tablespoon finely ground black
   pepper
1 whole rack of lamb (2 pieces)

3 tablespoons pistachio nut oil (see
   Sources, page 311)
Kosher salt
1 tablespoon orange marmalade
   lightly beaten with 2 teaspoons
   water

On a large plate, blend together the crumbs, nuts, coriander, and pepper. Lightly rub the undersides of the meat with some oil. Generously season the underside of bones with salt.

Using a pastry brush, lightly paint the meat with the marmalade. Be sure to get the sides as well. Then roll the meat in the crumb mixture, pressing down gently. Use your hands to pat the coating evenly over the meat. Sprinkle the tops of the bones with any remaining crumbs as well. Place the lamb, top-side up, in a shallow pan. Drizzle remaining oil over the tops of the racks. Let stand at room temperature for 1 hour.

Preheat the oven to 475°F.

Place the meat in the oven and reduce the temperature to 450°. Roast for 22 minutes, or until an instant-read thermometer reads 125° for rare. Remove the meat from the oven and let it stand for 5 minutes. Carefully slice and arrange the chops on heated plates.

SERVES **4** TO **6**

Boneless Leg of Lamb Stuffed with Tapénade, Pine Nuts, and Kale

A combination of tapénade, braised dandelion greens, kale, and golden pine nuts add sensational flavors to this boned leg of lamb. Roasting at high heat adds enormously to its richness. Tell your butcher that this will be stuffed, rolled, and tied. That way he can make certain that it opens properly for stuffing. (You will need kitchen twine for this.) Serve with some richly flavored potatoes and you have a meal for kings.

TAPÉNADE

2 packed cups pitted Niçoise or
   Kalamata olives, thoroughly
   drained
8 oil-packed, or water softened,
   sun-dried tomatoes
5 plump garlic cloves
1 teaspoon dried oregano
1 teaspoon freshly ground black
   pepper
10 anchovy fillets, preferably salt-
   packed
Up to ¼ cup extra virgin olive oil

LAMB AND VEGETABLES

1 leg of lamb, 8 to 10 pounds,
   butterflied (final weight about 7
   to 9 pounds)
½ cup toasted pine nuts
1 pound chopped braised
   dandelion greens and kale
4 garlic cloves, thinly sliced
3 tablespoons olive oil
Kosher salt and freshly ground
   pepper
3 medium-sized onions, peeled and
   split
½ cup rich red wine
1 cup rich chicken stock
2 tablespoons minced fresh flat-leaf
   parsley

To make the tapénade: In the bowl of a food processor, combine the olives, sun-dried tomatoes, garlic, oregano, pepper, and anchovies. Pulse until puréed. With the motor running, gradually add just enough olive oil to make a thick paste. Scrape and process again. Set the tapénade aside.

To make the lamb: Place a rack in the lower third of the oven. Preheat the oven to 500°F.

Open the leg of lamb on a work surface, skin-side down. Spread the tapénade in a thick layer over the meat. Then scatter the pine nuts, then the greens evenly over the nuts.

Carefully bring all of the pieces together. You may want to have some skewers available. Then, using your twine, tightly tie the leg together in 4 or 5 places, making a nice package of the stuffed leg.

Working with the outside of the lamb, using a sharp knife, make about 20 slits all over. Insert pieces of garlic into each; rub the surface with olive oil, kosher, salt and freshly ground black pepper.

Place the leg, top-side up, in a shallow roasting pan. Rub the onion pieces with olive oil and scatter them around the lamb.

Roast for 1 hour 10 minutes (7 pounds, boned) to 1 hour 20 minutes (8 to 9 pounds, boned). Since the meat is of so many thicknesses, we seek three readings, from 125° to 135°F.

Remove the roast from oven and transfer it to a carving board. Let it rest for 10 to 15 minutes.

Meanwhile, pour the pan juices into a glass measuring cup. Pour off almost all the fat. Reserve. Deglaze the roasting pan with the red wine over medium-high heat. Discarding the burnt pieces, press the onions to mash into the sauce. Add the stock and cook briskly to thicken a bit. Taste and adjust seasonings. Spoon pan sauce into a serving bowl.

Slice the lamb and carefully serve on heated plates, spooning some stuffing over the slices that do not have it in the center. Garnish with the parsley.

SERVES 8 TO 12

Lamb Ragout with Chestnuts, Onions, and Sage

We've enjoyed a host of chestnut dishes during winter visits to France. One memorable one was a lamb and chestnut stew that was surprisingly delicate. While chestnuts could make the dish a tad too sweet, we find that a host of onions and diced bacon provide just the right flavor counterpoints. Hard to believe that something this simple could be so delicious.

1 pound dried chestnuts
1/2 cup unbleached flour, plus more if needed
3 pounds boneless lamb, cut into 3/4–1-inch cubes
3/4 cup diced bacon
3 tablespoons olive oil, plus more if needed
1 1/2 cups dry white wine
1 cup finely diced celery
18 small onions, peeled and blanched
2 1/2 teaspoons dried sage
Kosher salt and freshly ground black pepper to taste
1 3/4 cups rich chicken stock, plus more if needed
1/3 cup minced fresh flat-leaf parsley
Mashed Yukon gold potatoes as accompaniment

Cover the chestnuts with water and bring to a boil. Cover and simmer for 1½ hours, or until tender.

Preheat oven to 350°F.

Pour the flour into a plastic bag. Add the meat and toss to coat evenly and heavily. Combine the bacon and olive oil in a 5-quart cast-iron Dutch oven. Cook over medium heat until the bacon begins to release fat. Transfer the bacon to a small bowl. Add the lamb and brown well. Add 3 tablespoons more flour to the pot and stir until flour had darkened.

Slowly stir in the wine, then increase the heat to bring to a boil, stirring constantly. Add bacon and stir for a few minutes. Then add the drained chestnuts, celery, onions, sage, salt, and pepper.

Add stock just to cover meat. Cover tightly and bring to a boil. Place in oven and braise for 1 hour. Stir in parsley and add more stock if needed. Continue cooking for another 30 minutes, or until the meat is tender. Serve over mashed potatoes.

SERVES **6** TO **8**

Grilled Lamb Kabobs with Hard-Boiled Eggs and Pistachios

Ground lamb kabobs appear in cuisines throughout the Eastern Mediterranean and from the Middle East into India and Pakistan. Some traditions include nuts, others do not. Some regions use a lot of spices, and others prefer the kabobs to be more delicately flavored. We think that these are particularly satisfying, and we especially like the taste and texture of the pine nuts. Guests always smile when they find the wedge of egg inside. We serve these with a refreshing, somewhat spicy cucumber sauce on the side.

2 teaspoons whole cumin seeds

1 teaspoon whole anise seeds

1-inch cinnamon stick

1 dried red chile

1 teaspoon dried mint

½ cup minced white onion

2 plump garlic cloves, minced

3 pounds lean ground lamb

½ cup dry bread crumbs

½ cup coarsely chopped, toasted pistachio nuts

2 large eggs

¼ cup water, plus more if needed

Kosher salt and freshly ground black pepper

3 hard-boiled eggs, cut into 4 wedges each

SPICY SAUCE

½ English cucumber chopped
½ medium-sized sweet onion
  chopped
½ cup fresh cilantro leaves
½ cup fresh flat-leaf parsley leaves

¼ cup fresh mint leaves
10 drops Tabasco sauce
Kosher salt and freshly ground
  white pepper

Place the cumin, anise, cinnamon, and chile in a very small skillet and toast over high heat, stirring constantly until browned, about 1 minute. Transfer spices to a cold plate to cool, then grind them to a fine powder in a spice grinder or in a mortar with a pestle. Transfer the spices to a large mixing bowl. Add the mint, minced onions, garlic, lamb, bread crumbs, pistachio nuts, eggs, water, salt and pepper. Mix vigorously until the meat is thoroughly blended. If the mixture seems too dry, add a bit more water.

Divide the meat mixture into 12 balls. Shape each into a cylinder about 4 inches long. As you are shaping each, insert an egg wedge into the center, making certain that egg is totally covered with meat. Place kabobs on a platter, cover lightly, and chill for several hours.

Meanwhile, combine the sauce ingredients in a food processor and pulse until puréed. Chill until serving time.

Heat the kitchen broiler until hot (or prepare your grill). Broil the kabobs about 4 inches from the heat for 7 minutes on one side, turn and broil for another 7 minutes—the kabobs will be just a bit pink in the middle.

Place the kabobs on a serving platter and drizzle with sauce.

SERVES 6

Wedad and Helen's Baked Kibbee with Pine Nuts

Lamb, pine nuts, and bulgur wheat are the predominant flavors and textures in this very delicious dish. Aromas and flavors are both judiciously piqued by all-spice and cinnamon. This baked kibbee is particularly delicious, far from the heavy stuff often found in most Middle Eastern restaurants. Wedad and Helen Shaheen were taught cooking by their Syrian mother and grandmother. Their home has changed little since they were children when their father grew grapes and coosa squash in the garden. We have previously asked these talented women to share recipes with us. As in the past, not only does each recipe work perfectly, but the dishes taste exactly as they did when we were privileged to sample them in their Canton, Ohio, dining room.

THE STUFFING

2 tablespoons butter

⅔ pound ground lamb or beef

1 medium onion, finely chopped

¼ teaspoon ground allspice

Kosher salt and freshly ground black
   pepper to taste

¼ cup pine nuts

THE KIBBEE

1½ cups cracked wheat (*burghol*
   or bulgur), #1 grind

1⅓ pounds lamb or beef, ground
   twice

1 medium onion, finely grated

1 teaspoon ground allspice

⅛ teaspoon ground cinnamon

1 tablespoon kosher salt

¼ teaspoon ground black pepper

¼ cup olive oil

½ cup mixture of melted butter
   and extra virgin olive oil

Middle Eastern yogurt for garnish

For the stuffing: Melt the butter in a small skillet. Sauté the meat for 10 minutes, then add the onion, allspice, salt, and pepper. Cook until the onion is limp. Add the pine nuts and cook for another 5 minutes. Set aside to cool.

For the kibbee: (Remember to wash your hands first.) Rinse the cracked wheat three times. After the third rinse, squeeze out the remaining water by hand.

Transfer the wheat to a large mixing bowl. Add the meat, onion, spices, salt, pepper, and olive oil. Knead thoroughly. While kneading, rinse your hands in a bowl of ice-cold water to keep the kibbee soft. If you have a meat grinder, run the mixture through it several times to achieve a finer consistency. Or you can also pulse it in a food processor. Divide the kibbee in half.

Generously butter a 9×13-inch pan. Dip your fingers in a bowl of ice water and pat the first half of the kibbee into the pan. Smooth evenly. Dip your fingers again into the cold water and pat the layer, pressing gently. Carefully spread the stuffing mixture evenly over the first layer, also pressing gently.

Spread the remaining kibbee on top by making patties, then smooth them together with wet fingers. Patting with wet fingers helps to soften the kibbee. Loosen the edges with a sharp knife.

Using the knife, cut the kibbee into large squares, then cut each diagonally, dipping the knife into cold water periodically. Then, with the tip of a thin, sharp knife, poke holes into each triangular piece. Pour the butter and oil mixture evenly over the top.

Preheat the oven to 400°F. Bake the kibbee for 30 to 40 minutes, or until lightly browned. Then, if needed, place under a hot broiler for 5 to 10 minutes to further brown. Let it stand for at least 5 minutes before serving. Serve with a side dish of yogurt.

SERVES 6 TO 12

A Kerala Lamb Biriyani: Spicy Lamb Stew and Rice with Cashews

Biriyani is really a Northern Indian, or Mogul, dish featuring rice. While often incorporating meat, poultry, or anything from the sea, biriyani is really about rice, exquisitely seasoned. Since Indian food differs so much from one region to another, we were astonished but delighted when Kochi's Nimmy Paul said that we'd be preparing a lamb biriyani for dinner. And when we sat down to eat, we thoroughly enjoyed its classic textures, which were in perfect balance with traditional Kerala ingredients. This is all you need for the meal. Serve with papadums, sliced hard-boiled eggs, fried banana chips, and a variety of Indian pickles and chutneys, including Coconut Chutney (see page 160). The one modification we have made to Nimmy's recipe is to increase the amount of meat. While a long recipe, it is not a difficult one. You can prepare the various parts early in the day, assemble the biriyani in the afternoon, and finish it before serving time.

THE LAMB MARINADE

2½ pounds boneless leg of lamb, cut into ¾-inch cubes

½ cup plain yogurt

¼ teaspoon ground turmeric

THE RICE

1¼ pounds basmati rice, rinsed and soaked for 30 minutes

THE THICKENING

1-inch piece cinnamon stick

½ teaspoon ground mace

7 whole green cardamom pods, cracked

7 whole cloves

1 generous pinch nutmeg

½ teaspoon whole anise seed

¼ teaspoon whole caraway seeds, preferably black

10 large cashews

10 blanched almonds

3 tablespoons milk

THE LAMB SEASONINGS

8 plump shallots, thinly sliced

7 hot green chiles

2 tablespoons minced garlic

1 tablespoon minced ginger

¾ cup ghee (see Basics, page 50)

2 large, ripe tomatoes, finely chopped

⅓ cup very thinly sliced pieces of fresh pineapple

¼ cup puréed fresh mint

¼ cup puréed fresh cilantro

1 tablespoon fresh lime juice

THE GARNISH

1 medium-sized red onion, cut in half and thinly sliced

10 large toasted cashews

⅓ cup raisins

THE FINISH

1 generous pinch saffron

2 tablespoons milk

¼ cup minced fresh cilantro

To prepare the lamb marinade: The night before, in a large bowl, combine the lamb with yogurt and turmeric. Mix well and refrigerate, covered. Let it stand at room temperature for 1 hour before it will be cooked.

To prepare the rice: In a heavy-bottomed saucepan, combine the drained rice with water to cover by 3 inches. Bring to a boil and cook until it is partially cooked about 10–15 minutes. Drain and reserve.

To prepare the thickening: In a small skillet, combine the cinnamon, mace, cardamom, cloves, nutmeg, anise seed, and caraway. Stir over medium heat until very aromatic, no more than 2 minutes. While the spices are cooling, in either a good grinder or mortar and pestle, grind the nuts and milk to make a paste. Add the cooled spices and grind thoroughly. Reserve.

To prepare the lamb seasonings: In a mortar with pestle, one at a time, crush the shallots, chiles, garlic, and ginger until each almost looks finely chopped.

Heat the wok and melt 2 tablespoons ghee. Add shallots and chiles and stir until aromatic. Then stir in garlic and ginger. Cook until tender, adding more ghee if needed. Then stir in the tomatoes and cook until tomatoes are somewhat cooked. Add the lamb mixture, stir well, cover and cook until the meat is tender, 20 to 30 minutes. After meat has been cooking a while, stir in pineapple, puréed mint and cilantro.

When the lamb is tender, stir in the thickening mixture and cook, stirring often, until the nut mixture is thoroughly incorporated into the lamb mixture. Season with lime juice and blend. Set aside.

To prepare the garnish: Heat half the remaining ghee in a wok over medium heat. Add half the thinly sliced onion and cook, stirring often, until brown and crisp. Repeat with the remaining onions. Drain on paper towels and set aside in a small bowl. Add the cashews to the warm ghee and brown as well. Transfer to a paper towel while you fry the raisins for a minute. Drain and reserve, too.

To prepare the finish: Mix the saffron with the milk.

To assemble the biriyani: In a large, deep ovenproof casserole, 3 to 4 quarts in size, add half the rice and press lightly with your fingers. Cover evenly with the lamb mixture. Then press the remaining rice over that. Drizzle the top with saffron mixture, then dot with 2 tablespoons of the remaining ghee.

Preheat the oven to 350°F.

Cover the casserole with a tight-fitting lid or foil. Bake for 1 hour, or until the rice is tender.

To serve, scatter fried onions, cashews, and raisins over the top. Then dust with minced cilantro. Allow guests to help themselves to the biriyani and the garnishes.

SERVES **6** TO **10**

Skippy versus Peter Pan

Any list of classic television commercials will include the famous spots of the 1950s for Peter Pan Peanut Butter. Walt Disney produced a very popular animated movie version of *Peter Pan* in 1953. The following year Mary Martin was flying about the Broadway stage as Peter Pan. Written by Sir James Barrie in 1904, *Peter Pan,* in this musical revival, was one of the most successful shows in history, and every American had heard of it. So it made sense to have an animated version of the winged little boy who wouldn't grow up selling one of the world's most popular foods. Peter Pan, the peanut butter, had been around since 1920, but this connection with the famous movie and play gave it wings.

Head to head against Peter Pan in the fiercely competitive peanut butter market was the comic strip character Skippy. He was the prototypical American boy, with his sandy hair always falling into his eyes and uttering a boy's take on the issues of life as seen by his creator Percy Crosby. Skippy made his first appearance in a newspaper comic strip in 1923. He grew more and more popular with readers, and finally, in 1932, the makers of Rosefield Peanut Butter decided to change the name of their popular product to Skippy and use him in their advertisements.

Peanut butter had been around for a while when this marketing face-off began. Peanut butter had been used very early in West African and East Asian cuisines, but it still isn't clear who first made commercial peanut butter in the United States. In the 1890s Joseph Lambert invented a machine for making peanut butter in grocery stores and homes. By the turn of the century, it was on its way to becoming one of the country's most popular foods.

By the 1920s, there were dozens of brands on the market when Joseph Rosefield perfected a process to keep the oil from separating out of the peanut butter. His company was already a leading producer when he used Skippy and renamed his company. In 1955, Best Foods bought Skippy Peanut Butter, and five years later took up sponsorship of a TV series about another unpredictable boy, Dennis the Menace. Norman Rockwell made illustrations for Skippy. Annette Funicello did Skippy commercials in the late 1970s. However, by 1998, Skippy, the boy, wasn't hot enough any more, and the well-known shortstop Derek Jeter started selling peanut butter on TV.

ConAgra bought Peter Pan Peanut Butter and blended it into its Hunt Wesson group. Peter Pan is now a corporate cousin of catfish farms, chicken operations, cake mixes, feed mills, and scores of other mega food suppliers.

Skippy and Peter Pan are still very big brands, although it has been decades since either of those characters was truly active in the popular culture. There is a third major player in the peanut butter world: Jif, but no cartoon character and no legendary fairy leads this brand.

Who rules? No one at the big three would tell us, but the buzz in the peanut butter world is that it is Jif, just recently purchased from Procter and Gamble by Smuckers.

While a battle of the titans continues in a quest for the hearts and minds of the peanut butter lovers of America, a company called Krema in Columbus, Ohio, continues to do what it has been doing for over a hundred years. It makes fine nut butters for discerning customers across the country—and no comic book character need apply.

Pan Asian Pork Roast with Peanut Crust and Orange Sauce

Our seasoning paste includes scallions, shallots, and garlic mixed with fish sauce, peanut butter, and soy sauce. It makes a superb marinade for today's rather bland pork, not to mention a great addition to a flavor-filled onion-piqued orange pan sauce. Today's pork does not have to be cooked to death as it was in the past when parasites were a concern. In fact, longer cooking just makes a very dry piece of meat. We love our Polder Thermal Timer for pork. You insert a probe into the center of the meat and then close the oven door right over the fine cable line. The timer dial goes right on the oven door, easily read as you move about the kitchen. It's a great way to protect against overcooked meat (or turkey, for that matter).

8 scallions, trimmed with 1-inch green, coarsely cut

1 large chunk (1½ inches) fresh ginger, peeled

4 plump garlic cloves

3 plump shallots, quartered

1 dried chile, crumbled

⅔ cup crunchy peanut butter

⅓ cup dark soy sauce

4½ to 5 pounds boneless pork loin, silverskin removed

2 large yellow onions, finely chopped

1 tablespoon superfine sugar

2 teaspoons grated fresh ginger

1 teaspoon freshly ground black pepper

1 cup rich chicken stock

1 tablespoon plus 2 teaspoons cornstarch

Zest and juice of 2 large oranges

¼ cup minced fresh cilantro

In the bowl of a food processor fitted with a metal blade, combine the scallions, ginger, garlic, shallots, chile, peanut butter, and soy sauce. Pulse until well chopped, then purée until a paste is formed. Coat the pork loin with the paste and place it in a large baking dish. Cover the pork with plastic wrap and marinate it for at least four hours.

Preheat the oven to 350 degrees F. Lightly oil a shallow-sided roasting pan, then combine onions, sugar, ginger, and pepper in the pan and blend well. Gather the onion mixture in the middle to serve as a bed for the pork roast. Place the coated pork loin on the onion mixture.

Roast the loin for 50 minutes, or until an instant-read thermometer reaches 135° to 140°F. Transfer the pork to a heated carving platter and keep it warm, letting it rest for 10 minutes. (During this time the internal temperature of the pork will reach 145° to 150°F and the meat will be medium and juicy.)

While the meat is resting, place the roasting pan on the stove over medium heat. Add the chicken stock and stir, scraping up all of the browned bits that have adhered to the pan. Keep scraping until the mixture comes to the boil and begins to reduce. Quickly whisk the cornstarch and ¼ cup of the orange juice together to blend evenly. Add this and the remaining juice to the pan sauce. Stir over medium heat until the sauce thickens, then set aside off the heat. Adjust the seasonings, then blend in the orange zest and cilantro.

Carve the pork into ¼-inch-thick slices and serve with some sauce spooned over the top. Serve the remaining pan sauce as well.

SERVES 6 TO 8

Grilled Pork Tenderloins with Walnuts, Shallots, and Prunes

An herbal rub gives these tenderloins an earthy flavor. We especially like the note of mystery added by the Chinese five-spice powder. The real treat, however, is the delicious relish or sauce. We've been quite keen on the combination of prunes and walnuts ever since our first visit to the southwest of France. We think everyone will love this sauce. Folks seem to enjoy it with just about anything. By the way, if you like hash, prepare extra meat to use for the Heavenly Hash (page 234), which also includes any leftover Walnut Prune Sauce as a base for the sauce for the hash.

PORK SEASONINGS

2 teaspoons herbes de Provence	1 teaspoon white pepper
1 teaspoon ground marjoram	3 pork tenderloins (3 pounds total)
2 teaspoons Chinese five-spice powder	1 tablespoon walnut oil

WALNUT PRUNE SAUCE

4 plump shallots, peeled and cut in
half

1 tart apple, peeled, cored, and cut
in half

4 roasted garlic cloves (see Basics,
page 53)

3 tablespoons unsalted butter

1½ tablespoons granulated sugar

2 tablespoons rich red-wine, or
Banyuls, vinegar

1½ teaspoons ground ginger

Up to 2 cups rich chicken or veal
stock

Juice of 1 orange

A 12-ounce box pitted prunes,
coarsely chopped

¾ cup toasted walnuts, coarsely
chopped

Kosher salt and freshly ground
white pepper to taste

Minced fresh chives and other fresh
herbs garnish

To season the pork: In a small bowl, blend together the herbes, marjoram, Chinese five-spice powder, and pepper. Generously coat the tenderloins with walnut oil, then with the seasonings. Let them rest on a platter until you are ready to grill them. If you are doing this early in the day, cover them with plastic wrap and refrigerate, bringing the pork back to room temperature 1 hour before roasting.

Meanwhile make the walnut prune sauce: Preheat your broiler. When hot, broil the shallots and apple until they are browned on both sides. Allow them to cool, then chop finely.

In a cast-iron skillet or sauté pan, melt the butter. Add the roasted garlic cloves and stir, mashing them into the butter. Then add the shallots and apple. Cook over medium heat until everything is tender. Sprinkle with the sugar and cook, stirring well, for 2 minutes. Using a potato masher, press the apples and shallots; then add the vinegar and cook for 2 minutes, or until the vinegar appears to have been absorbed. Add the ginger, 1½ cups of the stock, the orange juice, and prunes. When the mixture is bubbling, reduce the heat just a bit to an active simmer. When the sauce has thickened, about 5 minutes, remove it from the heat and let it stand until needed.

Just before serving, reheat the sauce. If the liquid is all absorbed, gradually stir in the remaining stock. When the mixture is bubbling, add the walnuts, salt, and pepper.

To grill the tenderloins: Spray a clean grill with cooking oil and heat until hot. Grill the tenderloins over hot coals, covered, for 7 minutes. Turn and grill for 6 minutes, or until an instant-read thermometer inserted into middle reads 145°F. Remove the tenderloins from the heat and let them rest for 5 minutes in a warm place.

Slice on a slight angle and fan the slices on heated serving plates. Nap generously with sauce and sprinkle with herbs.

SERVES **6**

Asian-Style Barbecued Spareribs with Peanut Dipping Sauce

We frequently made conventional ribs outside in our barbecue pit/smoker during the summer, but we'd go through withdrawal symptoms through the winter. Nothing ever tasted as good when it was made in the oven, but we were tenacious, finally developing several recipes that would really satisfy us throughout the long Cleveland winters. Sure enough, by focusing on very different flavors from the summer ribs, we learned that using a combination of these Asian seasonings, one can roast the ribs in the oven and enjoy superlative flavor. The peanut sauce finishes them just perfectly.

THE RIBS

3 tablespoons minced fresh ginger

8 plump garlic cloves, minced

3 plump shallots, minced

2 bulbs lemongrass, minced

⅔ cup soy sauce

½ cup sweet soy sauce

⅓ cup black vinegar

½ cup rice wine

2 tablespoons Nam Pla (fish sauce)

¼ cup minced fresh cilantro

3 tablespoons dark sesame oil

2 rounded tablespoons Thai chile sauce

4 (3½-pound) slabs whole spare ribs, brisket, clip, and skirt removed (a trimmed 2-pound St. Louis rib)

Spicy Peanut Dipping Sauce (page 64)

To prepare the ribs: One day before cooking, in a large bowl blend together the ginger, garlic, shallots, lemongrass, soy sauces, black vinegar, rice wine, Nam Pla, cilantro, sesame oil, and chile sauce. Evenly coat the ribs on all sides and marinate them overnight in the refrigerator. Save the remaining marinade and store it in the refrigerator.

The next day, preheat the oven to 375°F.

Place the ribs, top-side down, on racks in a shallow roasting pan and baste with the marinade. Roast for 30 minutes. Carefully turn ribs, baste one more time, and roast for another 25 minutes. The ribs should be well-browned.

Cut the ribs into individual pieces and pile on a large platter, drizzling with Spicy Peanut Dipping Sauce as you stack them. Pour any remaining sauce over the very top layer.

SERVES 4 TO 6

Braised Stuffed Pork Chops with
Chestnuts and Apples

*Pork, cabbage, apples, and chestnuts have a wonderful affinity for one another.
Here we stuff the chops with chestnuts mixed with apples and onions. Then we
braise the stuffed chops on a bed of cabbage surrounded with more of the stuffing
mixture. It really is a sublime dish. At the end, if you wish, you can finish the sauce
by adding a little cream. It is a wonderful way to feed six hungry souls on a cold
winter's night. You might want to accompany these chops with some pan-fried
potatoes.*

1¼ cups peeled chestnuts

Water to cover

3 tablespoons butter

1 small onion, finely diced

1 plump clove garlic, minced

1 tart apple, peeled, cored, and
finely diced

1 teaspoon dried tarragon

Kosher salt and freshly ground
white pepper to taste

6 loin pork chops, 1½ to 2 inches
thick, with a pocket

¼ cup unbleached flour

3 tablespoons olive oil

2 cups shredded savoy cabbage

¼ cup Calvados or applejack

1½ cups rich chicken stock

½ cup heavy cream, plus more if
needed

Combine the chestnuts with water to cover in a small saucepan. Bring the water to a
boil, lower the heat to medium, and simmer until the chestnuts are tender, 35 minutes
to 1 hour. Drain and coarsely chop half of the chestnuts. Reserve both.

Preheat the oven to 325°F.

In a large skillet, melt the butter. Add the onions, garlic, apple, and tarragon. Cook
over medium-low heat, stirring occasionally, until the onions and apples begin to turn
golden, 10 to 15 minutes. Stir in the chopped chestnuts and salt and pepper to taste.

Carefully stuff the pork chops with the chestnut mixture, then lightly dredge in
flour. The stuffing is not bound together, so it will start to spill if you are not careful.
Save the extra stuffing.

Heat the oil in a very large cast-iron skillet or sauté pan. When the oil is hot, carefully brown the chops on both sides. Then transfer them to a large platter.

Add the cabbage and Calvados to the skillet and cook over medium heat until
browned bits are loosened. Add the chicken stock and bring the mixture to a boil.
Place the chops back in the skillet along with the remaining stuffing mixture and the
whole chestnuts. Season generously with salt and pepper. Cover tightly and place in
the oven.

Braise the chops for 1 hour 15 minutes, or until the chops are fork-tender. Transfer the chops to a heated platter and keep warm. Add the cream to the pan and bring to a boil over medium-high heat. Simmer for 5 minutes. Taste the sauce and adjust seasonings.

Serve the chops on heated plates napped with sauce.

SERVES **6**

Heavenly Hash with Pine Nuts and Tangy Fruited Tomato Sauce

Your guests will rave about this hash for days. We really plan and make both extra pork and extra kibbee, just to enjoy this particular combination. This is a colorful hash with little bits of red from the pepper and green from the herbs. Pine nuts add a marvelous crunch, while the Tabasco lends a very comfortable heat. Linda loves having a poached egg atop all forms of hash. You could also make them a bit ahead and just warm them with a bit of hot water. Meanwhile, the sauce also utilizes some leftovers—namely the Walnut Prune Sauce (see page 231). We suggest using some barbecue sauce as an alternative, but you could also use a fruited chutney just as well.

THE HASH

1½ pounds leftover (cooked) Pan Asian Pork Roast (page 229), finely chopped

1 pound leftover Baked Lamb Kibbee (page 224), finely chopped (or another cooked meat)

3 medium-sized cooked redskin potatoes, finely chopped

½ large sweet onion, finely chopped

2 stalks celery, finely chopped

1 red bell pepper, cored, seeded, and chopped

½ cup toasted pine nuts

¼ cup minced fresh flat-leaf parsley

1 tablespoon chopped fresh thyme leaves

1 tablespoon chopped fresh oregano leaves

1 tablespoon ground cumin

Kosher salt and freshly ground black pepper to taste

1 tablespoon Tabasco sauce

5 tablespoons unsalted butter, melted

THE SAUCE

2 cups canned tomato sauce

1 cup leftover Walnut Prune Sauce
(page 231) or 1 cup barbecue
sauce

Juice of 1 lemon

1 tablespoon minced fresh ginger

1 tablespoon minced jalapeño
pepper

1 teaspoon ground allspice

Kosher salt and freshly ground black
pepper to taste

THE EGGS

6 to 8 eggs

3 tablespoons cider vinegar

Kosher salt and freshly ground
pepper to taste

Preheat the oven to 425°F.

To make the hash: In a large bowl, combine the meats, potatoes, onions, celery, pepper, pine nuts, parsley, thyme, and oregano. Add the cumin, salt, pepper, and Tabasco. Blend really well.

To prepare the sauce: In a small saucepan, combine the tomato sauce, Walnut Prune Sauce, lemon juice, ginger, jalapeño, allspice, salt, and pepper. Cook over medium heat until bubbling. Stir and simmer for at least 15 minutes.

To finish the hash: In a 10- or 11-inch skillet, preferably cast-iron, melt the butter. Carefully cook until the butter begins to brown, about 1 minute. Tilt the butter around the skillet to coat the sides, then pour the browned butter into the bowl with the meat mixture and blend thoroughly.

Spoon the meat into the skillet and press it to pack it down evenly. One can cover this and store it in the refrigerator for up to 24 hours before baking, just bring it back to room temperature first.

Bake the hash until piping hot and crusty on top, 35 to 40 minutes.

To prepare the eggs: Shortly before hash is ready, prepare to poach the eggs. Break each egg into a small cup and place it within reach of the stove. Fill a large sauté pan with water. Add the vinegar and some salt. Bring to a softly rolling boil.

When the hash is ready, transfer the pan to the stovetop. Place heated plates nearby. Working in two batches, poach the eggs. Carefully tilt the eggs, one at a time, into the slowly bubbling water. Using a slotted spoon, quickly flip whites around the yolk, trying to keep each egg into an oval shape. Cook each egg for 2½ minutes. (Hold the cooked eggs in a bowl of warm water.)

To serve: Transfer the hash to warm plates. Place an egg in the center of each. Sprinkle the egg with a few grindings of pepper. Serve with some sauce on top of each portion, serving remaining sauce on the side.

SERVES 6 TO 8

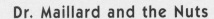

Dr. Maillard and the Nuts

In preparing the recipes for this book, we bought all kinds of nuts, but mostly raw, uncooked ones. Before testing a recipe, we would give the nuts of the day a toasting or roasting on the stove or in our oven. This brought them, whatever kind they were, to the peak of good taste before we used them. The byproduct of the process was always a beautiful aroma that could find its way to the corners of the house.

Of all of the world's creatures, only humans do things to food to make it taste better. A raccoon may wash his dinner, but no raccoon cooks. The first person who ever roasted a piece of meat over a fire learned a basic truth: Food tastes better cooked. If the lion knew what broiling a zebra could do for the flavor, there would be cooking fires all over the veldt.

Why cooking makes our food better is a question that has occupied scientists for over a century. Louis-Camille Maillard, a French biochemist and a physician, was the first person to study what actually happens when food browns on the fire. There was nothing in the taste of that raw potato that could predict how delicious it would be sliced and browned in goose fat. Maillard was intrigued by this and in 1912 he heated a sugar (glucose) with an amino acid (lysine). This experiment with two substances that are in all foods produced brown pigments and a pleasant aroma. It was the breakthrough; he had discovered the secret of browning. Variations of this basic chemical reaction are at the heart of the good taste of most of our cooked food.

Maillard died in 1936, well before modern flavor research got underway. In the early 1950s scientists revisited his work, and it became the starting point for almost all of our modern investigations into the chemistry of flavor and cooking. So important was his analysis of the so-called browning reaction, that by 1959 scientists in Europe and America were calling this universal culinary phenomenon the Maillard Reaction.

Food scientist Henry B. Heath is passionate about what he calls NEB, or nonenzymatic browning. "NEB," he says, "is responsible for some of the most pleasant flavors enjoyed by man. There is no question that freshly baked bread, a nice steak, a freshly brewed cup of coffee, [and] a piece of chocolate is appreciated by the consumer. Yet none of these flavors existed until the cook heated the product to develop the flavor."

So the pine nuts, pecans, almonds, and hazelnuts, so wonderful in the company of other foods, are even better when a little preliminary toasting causes the Maillard Reaction to kick in. Tasty nuts become delicious.

grains, potatoes, and vegetables

Creamy Lemon Grits with Roasted Peanuts

Pistachio Corn Cakes

Coconut Rice with Cardamom and Cloves

Braised Cabbage Rolls with Nutted Bulgur Stuffing

Spicy Red Potatoes with Garlic, Indian Spices, and Cashews

Marco's Chestnut Potato Gratin with Taleggio

Cream-Baked Chiles Rellenos with Black Beans, Goat Cheese, and Pine Nuts

Fried Baby Artichokes with Pistachio Crumbs

Theyal: A Coconut and Onion Side Dish

Baked Stuffed Artichokes with Carrots, Hazelnuts, and Greens

Mélange of Summer Squashes with Feta and Black Walnuts

Stuffed Herbed Tomatoes with Goat Cheese, Walnuts, and Garlic

Braised Savoy Cabbage with Virginia Ham and Browned Black Walnuts

Eggplant Gratin with Toasted Pine Nuts

Coconut Curried Winter Vegetables with Peanuts

Creamy Lemon Grits with Roasted Peanuts

Rich and creamy with a lemony zip. The best grits we have ever tasted, in fact, and we do know our grits. This is what happens when a French-trained chef decides to serve grits in his Charleston, South Carolina, restaurant. Chef Bob Waggoner of the Charleston Grill served them to us and we thought them sublime. Slow cooking and lots of cream are his "secrets." Sure they can be made with milk, but for the best results, go for the gusto and use cream. If you are preparing for company, you can make them a few hours ahead, then reheat them with more cream just before serving. In honor of Charleston's passion for peanuts, we add a generous portion of the roasted kind just at the last minute. These grits are outstanding with fried chicken or shrimp, as well as with rack of lamb, but you can also serve them as polenta, in a soup plate, and perhaps under some buttery lobster meat!

3 cups chicken stock
2 tablespoons unsalted butter
1 cup good quality stone-ground
  grits
2 to 3 cups heavy cream (not
  ultrapasteurized)

Kosher salt and freshly ground
  white pepper to taste
Juice and zest of 1 lemon
$\frac{2}{3}$ cup freshly roasted peanuts,
  coarsely chopped

Bring the stock to boil in a very heavy-bottomed large saucepan. Stir in the butter and grits; cook over low heat for 15 minutes, stirring from time to time. Add ½ cup of the heavy cream, stir, and cook over lowest heat, stirring often. As the cream is absorbed, add more, about ¼ cup at a time. The idea is to add as much cream as the grits will absorb. When they are done, they should be very thick and very creamy. Try to do this over a period of at least 1 hour and up to 1½ hours.

Just before serving, stir in salt, pepper, lemon juice, and zest. Serve in individual bowls garnished with a generous portion of chopped peanuts.

SERVES 6 TO 8

Professor of Nuts

Ted DeJong is the chairman of pomology (from the Latin *pommum*, or apple) at the University of California at Davis. His department is a center for the science and practice of fruit growing, and nuts are included.

Ted DeJong was not originally a tree man. He grew up on a California farm and early on was intrigued by the ecological aspects of farming. In his doctoral and postdoctoral work he concentrated on the flora of the beach and dune.

He came back to California to teach environmental ecology at UC Davis over twenty years ago. Fruit and nut trees kept looming up before him, and little by little he became an expert on how they live, how they relate to the environment, and how they can be made more productive. The department he now chairs is a major world center for the intense study of the trees that bear our nuts and fruits. He also understands the economics and marketing of agriculture.

The Central Valley of California is an ideal place for most of our tree crops. Almost all our almonds, pistachios, and walnuts are grown there. The weather is perfect with cool, moist winters with enough days of dormancy for the crops, and hot, dry summers with enough water to do the job. Besides, the soils of the region are nearly perfect for such crops, and not as many fungicides and pesticides are needed either.

DeJong has concerns about American agriculture. There is overproduction in all crops, and there are buying co-ops which effectively keep out the little guys. "Consolidation," he says, "is killing the little grower." He worries about the burgeoning growth of the walnut crop in China, which now has more trees than we have in the U.S. The walnut growers, he says, are afraid of what might happen. Cheap walnuts over there will mean trouble for walnut growers here. (The almond people are not so scared; China is just not right for almonds.)

It would be hard to find anyone who knows California's farmers better than Ted DeJong. He is proud of them and marvels at their creativity. He knows and understands their problems and challenges. He knows the scientific names of their tree crops. He knows the varietals that work best. He understands the mysteries of the almond orchards, when the bees start to work, what varieties complement each other in the pollination process. He knows the acreage of every crop, and he has a million stories about farmers and farming.

As we were leaving, Ted DeJong showed us around the pomology building, taking us into the labs where graduate students were toiling. In one place two Ph.D. candidates were cracking walnuts with claw hammers!

Pistachio Corn Cakes

Savory corn cakes make a good accompaniment to chicken and pork, or they can be the featured player in a vegetarian meal. This recipe combines corn and its meal with pistachio nuts to make a delicious cake that is gently enlivened by delightful splashes of onion and hot peppers. We like to serve these with some caramelized onions.

2 large ears of corn

¾ cup yellow cornmeal

⅔ cup pistachio flour (see Sources, page 311)

½ cup unbleached flour

2 teaspoons baking powder

Kosher salt and freshly ground white pepper to taste

2 tablespoons pistachio oil (see Sources, page 311)

2 tablespoons lemon juice

3 eggs, lightly beaten

1¼ cups whole milk, more if needed

2 tablespoons grated white onion

½ fresh red chile pepper, minced

⅔ cup lightly toasted pistachio nuts, coarsely chopped

2 tablespoons minced fresh chives

Caramelized onions for garnish

Olive oil or organic canola oil for frying

Spread a dishtowel on your work surface. Holding a corn ear upright on the towel and using a sharp knife, cut the kernels from the cob without going too close to the cob. Transfer the kernels to a small bowl. Repeat for the second ear. Then hold the cobs over the bowl and run the blunt end of the knife over each. This will dislodge any residual kernels and the corn milk. Reserve.

In a large mixing bowl, combine the cornmeal, flours, baking powder, salt, and pepper.

In a small mixing bowl, combine the pistachio oil, lemon juice, eggs, and milk. Beat vigorously to blend. Pour over the dry ingredients and blend thoroughly. Add the reserved corn mixture and blend thoroughly.

Then blend in the onion, minced chile, nuts, and chives. The mixture should be thick enough to make a good pancake, but if it is too thick, stir in a bit more milk.

Preheat the oven to 250°F.

Lightly coat a large skillet with oil. Heat it over medium-high heat until the oil begins to sizzle. Pour enough batter to make 3-inch round cakes, but do not crowd them. Fry until bubbles begin to appear on the surface, about 2 minutes. Turn and brown on the other side. Transfer the cakes to a cookie sheet lined with paper towels and hold in a warm oven until all corn cakes are made.

Serve on heated plates with a dollop of caramelized onions.

SERVES **6** TO **8** AS A SIDE DISH

Coconut Rice with Cardamom and Cloves

We serve this with just about any spicy meat or poultry done on a grill. The combination of soothing coconut and hot chiles is totally delightful. Even those who say they do not enjoy "curry" eat this with enthusiasm. We always use organic jasmine rice from Lowell Farms in El Campo, Texas (see Sources, page 313).

3 tablespoons unsalted butter

½ cup finely minced yellow onion

3 smashed and minced garlic cloves

1 tablespoon Madras-style curry powder

6 whole cloves

6 bruised whole cardamom pods

1 fresh hot chile, minced

2½ cups long-grain jasmine rice

2½ cups water

¾ cup unsweetened shredded coconut

2 teaspoons kosher salt

1 cup coconut milk (canned or fresh), plus more if needed

Melt the butter in a large, heavy saucepan. Add the onion and stir over medium heat until the onion has wilted, about 2 minutes. Add the garlic, curry powder, cloves, cardamom, and chile; stir for 1 minute. Then add the rice and stir for another minute. Stir in the water, coconut, and salt. Cover and bring to a boil. Add the coconut milk, reduce the heat, and cook, simmering but not boiling, until all the liquid is absorbed and the rice is tender and fluffy, about 15 minutes. If it's needed, add more coconut milk. Remove the pan from the heat, place some paper towels over the top, and then recover.

Allow the rice to rest at least 10 minutes before serving. Stir with a fork to fluff the rice before you serve it.

SERVES **6** TO **8**

Braised Cabbage Rolls with
Nutted Bulgur Stuffing

While this is a lengthy recipe, it really only takes about an hour of your time to pre-pare, and it is sumptuously delicious. Bulgur wheat and nuts go splendidly together, whether it is in a salad or as a side dish. Here we add greens and caramelized onions to the stuffing, as well as a hint of cinnamon. Braised in stock generously flavored by carrots, mushrooms, and caramelized onions, the rolls are immensely light and delicate, with a splendid pan broth. When prepared as a veg-etarian main dish, serve the rolls in a soup plate. They also make a marvelous side dish in a nonvegetarian meal. We then garnish them just with the vegetables from the sauce. You can prepare these in the morning, and save the broth ingredients to pour over the rolls just before braising.

¼ cup olive oil, plus more if needed

3 jumbo sweet onions, cut in half and thinly sliced

3 tablespoons unsalted butter

1 dried red chile, crumbled

3 plump garlic cloves, minced

1 pound baby spinach, washed and stemmed

½ pound dandelion greens, washed and coarsely chopped

2 cups coarse-grain bulgur wheat

4 cups chicken or vegetable stock, plus more as needed

2 teaspoons ground cinnamon

2 teaspoons kosher salt

1 teaspoon freshly ground black pepper

1 jumbo (5½ pounds) green cabbage, core removed

1½ cups fresh or frozen peas

1 cup coarsely chopped English walnuts, toasted

4 carrots, shredded

1 large portobello mushroom, finely chopped

⅓ cup mixed chopped fresh herbs (tarragon, fennel, parsley, lemon verbena, and garlic chives)

Heat the oil in a large, heavy skillet over medium heat. Add the onions and cook, cov-ered, for 20 minutes. Uncover and cook, stirring often and adding more oil if needed, until the onions are golden brown, about another 30 minutes. Set aside when done.

While the onions are cooking, melt the butter in a 3-quart heavy saucepan over low heat. Add the crumbled chile, garlic, spinach, and dandelion leaves and cook over low heat, covered, for 5 minutes. Stir in the bulgur, 2 cups of the stock, cinnamon, salt, and pepper. Cover and cook, stirring often, until the bulgur is tender, 20 to 25 minutes. Remove the pan from the heat and let it stand for 5 minutes.

Meanwhile, fill a large soup pot with water, salt generously, and bring to a boil over high heat. Add the cabbage, cover, and reduce the heat. Simmer briskly until the cabbage is softened, 10 to 15 minutes. Carefully separate the cabbage leaves and drain well. (You may have to return the cabbage to the hot water to soften the interior leaves.) There should be between 24 and 28 leaves.

When you are ready to stuff the cabbage, stir half the caramelized onions, the peas, and the walnuts into the cooked bulgur. Adjust the cinnamon, salt, and pepper.

Preheat the oven to 325°F.

Working with one cabbage leaf at a time, place a rounded ¼ cup of stuffing onto the center of the leaf. Trim away any coarse part of the stem and then close the sides of the cabbage leaf to make a neat package. Place the cabbage rolls, seam-sides down, close together in a wide 4-quart ovenproof casserole. Repeat until all of the leaves are stuffed, and the packages are stacked in only two layers.

Blend together the remaining onions, shredded carrots, mushrooms, and herbs. Sprinkle evenly over the cabbage rolls. Season with more salt and pepper. Pour the remaining stock over the rolls.

Cover and bake in the oven for 1½ hours, adding more stock as needed and basting several times. Let it stand for 10 minutes before serving.

SERVES **6** TO **8**

Mae West, being arrested in one of her movies, was told by a cop
that "anything you say will be held against you."
And she replied, "Nuts!"

Nuts in the Bible

We have long known that almonds were in bloom in the Holy Land when great events were taking place there, and the Bible bears this out. We know, for example, that when Moses was chosen to build and furnish a temple, he got some pretty specific instructions. When he started subcontracting, he made it very clear what was expected in every aspect of the job.

Bezaleel was given the assignment of creating the ark, including a candelabrum of pure gold. The language is still there, in Exodus 25:

"Three cups made like almonds, each. . . . And three cups made like almonds . . . itself four cups made like almonds. . . ."

Sounds like Moses wanted ten cups, but the translation is a little murky; cups, or bowls, to hold the lamp oil could hardly be shaped like an actual almond. Instead, it's likely that the craftsman was expected to shape the cups like the flower that is the almond blossom.

In Numbers, we find a magical transformation. "The rod of Aaron . . . was budded, and brought forth buds, and bloomed blossoms and yielded almonds." There is other talk of rods. In Jeremiah, "I see a rod of almond." In Genesis, ". . . Jacob took him rods of green poplar, and of the hazel and chesnut tree." And it is spelled that way in the Bible, with no middle "t." Also in Genesis, this reference to a nice sounding combination: "honey, gum, myhrr, pistachio nuts, and almonds."

In the Song of Solomon, the narrator says, "I went down into the garden of nuts to see the fruits of the valley, and to see whether the vine flourished, and the pomegranates budded." When the Bible just says "nuts," it is probably either walnuts or pistachios.

And finally this from Ecclesiastes, "The almond tree blossoms, the grasshopper drags." We are not sure what that means.

Spicy Red Potatoes with Garlic, Indian Spices, and Cashews

We never tire of the myriad spices typically found in the various cuisines of India. Perhaps it is because they marry so beautifully with onions and garlic as well as with nuts. This particular dish has a vivid personality, complemented by a generous garnish of cool cilantro and crunchy cashews. This makes a great vegetarian main dish when accompanied by some good greens and the Coconut Raita on the side.

COCONUT RAITA

2 teaspoons whole black mustard seeds (available in Asian markets)

2 teaspoons whole Tellicherry peppercorns (available in Asian markets)

½ cup unsweetened grated coconut

2 cups plain yogurt, preferably whole-milk

1 medium-sized sweet onion, cut in half and thinly sliced

2 teaspoons dried garden mint

1 teaspoon ground cayenne

2 tablespoons minced fresh cilantro

THE POTATOES

3 crushed dried chiles

3 teaspoons whole cumin seeds

2 teaspoons whole black mustard seeds

1 teaspoon whole anise seeds

2 teaspoons whole coriander seed

6 whole green cardamom pods, gently cracked

1 teaspoon whole Tellicherry peppercorns

¼ cup peanut oil, plus more if needed

1 jumbo onion, peeled, cut in half, and thinly sliced

1 tablespoon freshly grated ginger

7 garlic cloves, minced

18 medium-sized red potatoes, scrubbed, cut ¼-inch thick

Kosher salt

½ cup coarsely chopped toasted cashews

⅓ cup minced fresh cilantro

1 to 2 fresh red chiles, thinly sliced (optional)

To make the raita: In a small skillet, combine the mustard seeds and peppercorns. Stir until the aromas are released. Remove from the heat and cool, then grind into a powder. To the same skillet add the coconut. Stir over medium heat until lightly browned. Remove from the heat and cool.

In a medium-sized bowl, combine the yogurt, onions, mint, cayenne, cilantro, ground spices, and coconut. Stir thoroughly and spoon into a serving bowl. Cover and chill until serving time.

To make the potatoes: Heat a small skillet over medium heat. Add chiles, cumin, black mustard, anise, coriander, cardamom, and peppercorns. Stir until the aromas are released, about 1 minute. Remove from the heat and let cool, then grind into a powder.

Pour the oil into the wok and heat until hot. Add the onions and fry, stirring often, until the onions begin to brown. Add the ginger and garlic; stir for 1 minute more. Add potatoes, spices, and salt. Stir for 1 minute. If potatoes seem too dry, add a few more tablespoons of oil. Cover and cook, stirring several times, until the potatoes are browned and tender, 15 to 25 minutes. Stir in the cashews, cilantro, and fresh chiles.

Turn into a heated serving bowl. Serve with the Coconut Raita on the side.

SERVES **6** TO **8**

Marco's Chestnut Potato Gratin with Taleggio

Fortune smiled on us when we met Marco Falco, chef of Osteria della Rosa Rosso, in the small Piedmont hill town of Cherasco. With the help of our mutual friend Nucci Russo, a neighbor and fan of his, he told us about the food of the mountains of Piedmont where he grew up. This is one of Marco's favorite chestnut dishes prepared by his mother. Our instructions are detailed, but not difficult. The end result will be sublime and sinfully delicious. Ripe Tallegio cheese is very soft and runny, so slicing it is really more of a division of it into portions that you spoon over the gratin.

1½ cups dried chestnuts (2 cups cooked)

3 tablespoons olive oil

2 jumbo Spanish onions, cut in half and thinly sliced

3½ pounds yellow potatoes, peeled and sliced ¼ inch thick

3 cups whole milk

1 cup heavy cream, plus more as needed

4 large eggs

2 teaspoons minced fresh rosemary

Sea salt and freshly ground black pepper

1 cup freshly grated Parmigiano-Reggiano

8 to 12 ounces very ripe Taleggio cheese, at room temperature

Generously cover the chestnuts with salted water in a small saucepan. Cover and bring to a boil. Then reduce the heat and simmer briskly, adding more water if needed, until the chestnuts are very tender, 1½ to 2 hours. Transfer the chestnuts to a cutting board and chop very coarsely. Reserve.

While the chestnuts are cooking, heat the oil in a large sauté pan over medium heat. Add the onions and toss to coat well. Reduce heat to low. Cover and cook, stirring occasionally, until the onions begin to brown, 30 to 45 minutes. Uncover and increase the heat somewhat. Stirring often, continue to cook the onions until very golden, 5 to 10 minutes. Reserve.

In a heavy saucepan, cover the sliced potatoes with the 3 cups of milk, bring just to a boil, cover, and simmer until the potatoes are somewhat tender. This should take between 6 to 10 minutes. Carefully transfer the potatoes to a large plate. Pour the leftover milk into a large measuring cup.

Combine the heavy cream and 2 cups of the leftover milk in a saucepan. Heat until very hot. While the milk is heating up, beat the eggs vigorously in a medium-sized bowl. Slowly temper the eggs by beating in small amounts of the hot milk. Finally beat in all of the milk and reserve.

Preheat the oven to 350°F.

Oil a 3-quart shallow gratin dish. Arrange one-third of the potatoes in the bottom of the pan. Sprinkle half of the rosemary and the chestnuts evenly over the potatoes. Scatter one-third of the onions. Sprinkle with salt and pepper, then one-third of the Parmigiano-Reggiano. Repeat for a second layer. Finally, layer the remaining potatoes over the top. Season with salt and pepper. Scatter the remaining onions and cover evenly with remaining Parmigiano-Reggiano.

Pour the egg mixture over the potatoes. If more liquid is needed to partially cover the top layer, add more cream.

Bake for 1 hour. Then raise the temperature to 375°F. Bake for another 30 minutes, or until the gratin is golden and the potatoes feel very tender when pierced with a knife.

Carefully slice the Taleggio so there is one slice for each portion. Lay the cheese carefully over the top of the gratin so each person will have potatoes with some melted Taleggio.

SERVES 6 TO 12

Van Dyke's Walnuts

We had a vague recollection of a TV show where Mary Tyler Moore was caught up in a closet full of walnuts. It actually happened. Through The Walnut Times, a Web site for the Dick Van Dyke Show, one of early television's best, we were able to get a copy of the program. It was first broadcast on February 6, 1963.

Carl Reiner, the show's writer, had been fascinated by the film *The Invasion of the Body Snatchers,* in which "pods" from a planet called Twilo appeared and absorbed the Earthlings. He decided to write an episode called "It May Look Like a Walnut," in which he substituted walnuts for the pods, turned Danny Thomas into an alien from Twilo, and wrote a dream sequence in which Dick Van Dyke, playing a comedy writer, has his sense of humor and his thumbs taken away by the aliens—neither a very good thing for a comedy writer.

In 1963, television bedroom scenes were not like those on *NYPD Blue.* Dick Van Dyke and his TV wife, Mary Tyler Moore, slept in twin beds, and wore full-length pajamas, buttoned up to the chin. When they turned out the lights to sleep and dream about the great walnut threat, it was as bright with the lights off as it was when they were on. Hanky-panky was impossible—but other things were.

Both were swept up by pernicious and corrosive walnuts during a long night of dreams. It all culminates when Mary Tyler Moore becomes an alien with eyes in the back of her head and slides out of a closet on nine hundred pounds of Central Valley Walnuts bought especially for the filming of the episode.

Cream-Baked Chiles Rellenos with Black Beans, Goat Cheese, and Pine Nuts

Roasted poblano chiles make a piquant outer case for this both tender and crunchy filling. The cream sauce is a simple and refreshing change from the more complicated traditional Mexican red sauce. We've been making versions of these for many years. The combination of black beans and goat cheese was first brought to us by Minneapolis chef Mark Haugen when we wrote our first book, The Best of the Midwest. *We first baked chiles with cream when chefs Rick and Deann Bayless's book,* Authentic Mexican, *reached us in 1987. Handle the chiles carefully once they are roasted; you don't want to tear them.*

8 large poblano chiles	11 ounces goat cheese
2 tablespoons unsalted butter	Up to 1½ cups heavy cream
3 teaspoons ground cinnamon	1½ cups cooked black beans
2 teaspoons ground cumin	1 small tomato, finely diced
1 small yellow onion, finely diced	½ cup toasted pine nuts
2 plump garlic cloves, minced	⅓ cup minced fresh cilantro
¼ cup white wine	Kosher salt and freshly ground black
½ cup chicken stock, plus more if	pepper to taste
needed	1 cup sour cream

Either on a hot grill, or under a hot broiler, roast the chiles without burning, on all sides. Gently place them in a paper bag and close it tightly. When the chiles are cool, gently remove the skins. Slit each on one side and carefully rinse the seeds out of the inside of the chile. Place them on towels to dry.

Preheat the oven to 375°F. Thoroughly oil a large rectangular baking dish ample enough to hold the chiles in a single layer.

In a 3-to-4-quart sauté pan, melt the butter over low heat. Add 2 teaspoons of the cinnamon plus the cumin and onion. Raise the heat to medium and stir until the onion is wilted, about 3 minutes. Add the garlic and stir for another minute. Then add the white wine and chicken stock and bring it to a boil. Reduce the heat to low and simmer until the liquid is reduced by half. Stir in three-quarters of the goat cheese and 1 cup of the cream. Cook over low heat until the mixture is a thick sauce.

Transfer half of the sauce to a medium-sized bowl. Add the remaining teaspoon of cinnamon, the beans, tomato, and half each of the pine nuts and the cilantro. Season with salt and pepper; set aside.

Gently spoon the bean filling into the chiles one at a time. Carefully fold one open side over the other and place cut-side down in the oiled baking dish. Repeat until all of the chiles are stuffed.

Blend together the remaining sauce and the sour cream. If it is too thick, add more cream. Spoon the sauce evenly over the stuffed chiles. Sprinkle with the remaining goat cheese and some grindings of pepper. Bake until the top is bubbling and lightly browned, about 30 minutes.

Serve on heated plates lavishly garnished with the remaining pine nuts and cilantro.

SERVES 6 TO 8

Fried Baby Artichokes with Pistachio Crumbs

These are just so good! Nuts and artichokes seem to be made for one another. These little artichokes are perfectly delicious when battered and fried in olive oil. A drizzle of some pistachio oil adds a special little something to your enjoyment of them. We've served these as a small course on their own. Just remember, artichokes rarely go well with wine, so save it for the next course.

Juice of 2 lemons	1 teaspoon dried mint
Kosher salt	1¼ cup finely ground pistachios
12 baby artichokes	Freshly ground black pepper
2 eggs, beaten	Up to ½ cup olive oil
1 teaspoon Tabasco sauce	¼ cup pistachio oil (see Sources,
3 plump cloves garlic, pressed	page 311)
½ cup fine, dry bread crumbs	Lemon wedges
2 teaspoons dried thyme	

Fill a large bowl with water. Add the lemon juice and some salt.

To prepare the artichokes, cut each in half lengthwise, then trim the exterior of the stem and remove the tip. Place cut-side down on a work surface and, using a sharp knife, cut through, removing the top half of the globe. Remove the tough exterior leaves. If there is any sign of a choke inside, remove it with the point of the knife. Plunge the prepped half into the lemon water and repeat until all are prepared.

Drain the artichokes and pat dry. To the beaten eggs, blend in the Tabasco and garlic. In another bowl, blend together the bread crumbs, thyme, mint, pistachios, and salt and pepper to taste. Dip each artichoke piece in the egg mixture, then coat it well in the nut mixture. Place on a rack to dry. Repeat until all are coated.

To fry, generously coat the bottom of a very large frying pan with olive oil. Heat oil until almost smoking. Add half the artichokes, reduce the heat to medium-low, and cover. Fry, covered, for 4 minutes. Check and turn only if the bottom is well-browned. Otherwise, continue frying until the first side is done. Turn the artichokes and continue to fry, adding oil if needed, until the artichokes are tender and both sides are browned. Transfer to paper towels and keep warm. Repeat until all are fried.

Serve the artichokes with a dusting of salt, a drizzle of pistachio oil, and lemon wedges.

SERVES **6**

Theyal: A Coconut and Onion Side Dish

We thought we knew everything about cooking with coconut until we went to Kerala. Truthfully, most coconuts we find in our supermarkets are old and the flesh too dry for most dishes. What Keralans use for making milk and for grating are coconuts about 10 months old, some months younger than what gets to Midwestern markets. We are, however, able to get some seven-month-old ones, called "fresh" or "tender" coconuts (sometimes in the United States they are described as "water" coconuts). These are easy to puncture and drain, saving the water for only yourselves and your best friends! Once cut in half, the flesh can be scooped out with a spoon, then finely chopped in the food processor. This is the flesh we use for this dish and most others. This theyal is difficult to describe other than it is a very, very delicious combination of fried shallots and coconut, with some tang and some heat. While not like most conventional American side dishes, its refreshing flavors and aromas make it a satisfying partner to virtually any style of very spicy foods. While this traditionally is a Hindu recipe, our friend Nimmy Paul said that it was a very popular one among all Keralans, probably because it holds well in a cooler. That's because the coconut in this recipe is cooked and not raw.

1 tablespoon tamarind paste (available in Asian markets)	5 large shallots, finely chopped
⅓ cup hot water	2 fresh green chiles, finely chopped
3 to 4 tablespoons coconut oil	3 curry leaves (optional)
1 cup freshly grated young coconut	¼ teaspoon whole black mustard seeds (available in Asian markets)
1 teaspoon whole coriander seeds	
1 heaping teaspoon ground cayenne	2 red chiles, minced
Up to ¼ cup organic safflower oil	Additional curry leaves for garnish

Combine the tamarind paste and ⅓ cup hot water in a small bowl and blend until dissolved. Reserve.

In a medium-sized skillet heat 2 tablespoons of the coconut oil. Add the coconut and fry over low heat, stirring often, until the coconut becomes golden brown, about 15 minutes. Stir in the coriander and cayenne and fry for 1 or 2 minutes, or until the raw smell goes away.

Spoon the coconut mixture into a small grinder or processor. Add 1 tablespoon water and grind into a smooth paste.

Heat 3 tablespoons of the safflower oil in a large skillet over medium heat. Add the shallots, chopped chile, and curry leaves. Fry until the shallots are light brown, stirring often, about 10 minutes. Remove from the heat and stir in the coconut paste. Then add the tamarind, bring it to a boil, reduce the heat and stir it until the oil seems to bubble on the edges and the top. Reserve.

In another skillet, heat 1 more tablespoon coconut oil. Add the mustard seeds and stir. When they begin to pop, add the red chiles and curry leaves. Fry for 1 minute, then add to the coconut/onion mixture and blend.

Serve at room temperature.

SERVES 4 TO 6

Baked Stuffed Artichokes with Carrots, Hazelnuts, and Greens

Hazelnuts and carrots make a sweet combination. With the additions of chard and bread crumbs, we have a scrumptious stuffing for our plump artichokes. Then we braise them on a bed of onions and chard, making an aromatic and moist atmosphere that ultimately also becomes a marvelous sauce for them, too.

4 to 6 large artichokes

Juice of 1 lemon

6 tablespoons olive oil

3 cups thinly sliced red onions

3 cups chopped chard, blanched

2 teaspoons minced fresh thyme
   (1 teaspoon dried)

Kosher salt and freshly ground black
   pepper

4 plump garlic cloves, minced

1 cup fresh bread crumbs

1 cup finely chopped toasted
   hazelnuts

1½ cups grated carrots

½ cup dry white wine, plus more if
   needed

½ cup vegetable or chicken stock

To prepare the artichokes, fill a large mixing bowl with cold water. Add the lemon juice and reserve. With a sharp knife, remove the stem of the first artichoke. Cut off and discard top third of the artichoke, then remove and discard the tough lower leaves.

Finally, using sharp kitchen scissors, cut off the upper half of all remaining leaves. With a small spoon, remove the choke from the center and carefully scrape out all of the fuzz. Then immediately plunge the artichoke into the lemon water. Repeat until all the artichokes are prepared and soaking in lemon water.

Preheat the oven to 350°F.

Heat 3 tablespoons of the olive oil in a sauté pan over medium heat. Add the onions and chard, stir, and cover. Cook over low heat, stirring several times, until the onions begin to wilt. Transfer the mixture to an ovenproof casserole large enough to hold the artichokes standing upright. Stir in the thyme, salt, and pepper; smooth the onion mixture to make an even layer.

In a small mixing bowl, combine the garlic, bread crumbs, nuts, carrots, plus salt and pepper to taste. Blend in the remaining 3 tablespoons of the olive oil.

Put some stuffing into the center of the first artichoke. Then, using your fingers to pull the petals open, carefully insert some stuffing around the base of the artichoke leaves. Make certain that there is stuffing throughout the artichoke. Repeat until all are prepared.

Arrange the prepared artichokes over the onions. Add the wine and stock around the artichokes. Cover the casserole with a tight-fitting lid or cover tightly with foil. Braise in the oven until the artichokes are very tender, 1 to 1¼ hours. To test for doneness, very gently tug a lower artichoke leaf; when it needs the barest suggestion of pressure to come out, the artichokes are done.

Serve the artichokes on heated plates. Spoon some of the onion chard pan sauce over each.

SERVES 4 TO 6

Mélange of Summer Squashes with Feta and Black Walnuts

Our bags of freshly picked summer squash grown at Silver Creek Farm are always great treats. We have come to enjoy them best when simply braised in a little olive oil with thinly sliced sweet onions and a bit of dill weed. The rich, yet refreshing flavor of feta works well with a generous sprinkling of toasted black walnuts, adding a particularly pleasing crunch, as well as another contrasting flavor, which is really an additional harmonious note.

3 tablespoons olive oil, plus more if needed
1 large sweet onion, cut in half and thinly sliced

6 medium-sized summer squash, cut into ½-inch rounds
6 ounces feta (preferably sheep milk), crumbled

Kosher salt and freshly ground
white pepper

Fresh dill weed to taste

½ cup finely chopped, toasted
black walnuts

Heat the oil in a large sauté pan over medium heat. Add the onion and squash, cover and cook, stirring frequently. Add more oil if needed and cook until the squash rounds are tender, 6 to 10 minutes.

Remove the pan from the heat and stir in the feta, salt, pepper, and dill weed. Blend together gently but thoroughly. Stir in the nuts and serve.

SERVES 6 TO 8

Stuffed Herbed Tomatoes with Goat Cheese, Walnuts, and Garlic

This is a very simple way of serving baked tomatoes. The filling could be used for zucchini, too. Cheese, garlic, walnuts, bread crumbs, and oil work so well together in the summer. That's probably why they appear together so often in foods all over the Mediterranean.

6 large vine-ripened tomatoes

2 to 3 ounces of fresh goat cheese or feta, broken into small pieces

2 plump garlic cloves, pressed

2 tablespoons minced fresh herbs (tarragon, chives, thyme, oregano)

2 tablespoons dry bread crumbs

⅓ cup chopped walnuts, pieces the size of pine nuts

1 tablespoon good walnut oil

2 tablespoons extra virgin olive oil

Sea salt and freshly ground black pepper to taste

Preheat the oven to 450°F.

Slice the top off each tomato. Then remove the core and seeds. Trim the inside of the tomato to leave a thick wall.

In a small bowl, combine the cheese, garlic, herbs, crumbs, and nuts. Add the walnut oil and 1 tablespoon of the olive oil. Then add salt and pepper to taste. Blend well. Spoon some of the cheese mixture into each tomato. There should enough cheese to sprinkle over the top of each tomato as well.

Transfer the tomatoes to a small baking sheet and bake until the cheese is melted and the tops have browned, 15 to 20 minutes. Remove from the oven, transfer to an attractive serving plate and serve.

SERVES 6

Eggplant Gratin with Toasted Pine Nuts

We've been preparing this dish for many years with one variation or another. The many Asian eggplants in the markets make this a particularly delicious dish to serve both hot and at room temperature. Not only is the crunch of pine nuts quite pleasing, their toasty flavor is just perfect with the cheese and tomato sauce. For an additional treat, pour some heavy cream around the edges right before you put the gratin into the oven.

2½ to 3 pounds Asian eggplants, peeled and thinly sliced

½ cup unbleached flour

Up to 2 cups olive oil

½ cup finely julienned fresh basil

⅔ cup minced fresh flat-leaf parsley

1 cup coarsely chopped toasted pine nuts

1 heaping tablespoon minced fresh garlic

A 32-ounce can San Marzano tomatoes, drained and diced

1¼ cups grated Italian Fontina cheese

Kosher salt and freshly ground black pepper to taste

Extra virgin olive oil

Heavy cream (optional)

Preheat the oven to 400°F.

Dredge the eggplant slices in flour and place them on a cake rack. Shake off excess any flour before frying.

Pour ½ cup of the olive oil into a very large skillet and heat until hot. Working in batches, and adding oil as needed, fry the slices until golden on both sides. Drain on paper towels. Lightly oil a 2½- to 3-quart shallow ovenproof casserole.

In a small bowl, blend together the basil, parsley, and nuts. Arrange a layer of eggplant. Sprinkle evenly with some of the herb nut mixture, then some of the garlic, tomatoes, and cheese. Sprinkle lightly with salt and pepper, too. Repeat until you reach the last eggplant layer. Sprinkle that with only the Fontina, salt, and pepper. Drizzle with very good extra virgin olive oil just before baking.

Bake for 45 minutes, or until the top is golden and juices are bubbling around the edges. Let stand for 10 minutes before cutting into servings.

SERVES 6 TO 8

Wild Thing

For centuries *Juglans nigra*, the North American black walnut, was everywhere in the eastern United States. Gathering the nuts was a fall ritual for people who lived near the woods. But the walnut tree was also coveted for its wood, so much so that in 1927 the Kentucky Department of Agriculture warned that the black walnut was a disappearing species.

Luckily, reports of its demise were greatly exaggerated. In fact, there is a coalition of interests that is protecting the black walnut, encouraging limits on cutting and making sure that there are always new trees growing. Most important, it encourages people to collect and eat this great and tasty nut.

At Wheelersburg in the hill country of southern Ohio, Christina Gerlach is doing her part. Through her feed store, she buys any black walnuts that her neighbors collect when the nuts fall in October. In 2000, she bought fifty-two thousand pounds of hulled walnuts, paying $10 for each one hundred pounds. Some collectors bring as little as a bushel of nuts. One man over three weekends collected six thousand pounds, enough to fill his pickup six times.

Some collect nuts to add a little to the household income. There is a ninety-year-old woman who always brings in a few. It is what she has always done in those hills in October, and something she will continue to do as long as she is able. For some it is a family event, a celebration of the harvest, a Saturday outing that recalls earlier times for the grandparents and lets the grandchildren experience what it was like back then. Whoever shows up with black walnuts invariably has stained hands, a badge of their special toil.

Christina's rural feed store is one of 250 places in the thirteen walnut states of the East that gather these tough wild forest nuts for Missouri's Hammon Company, the world's only processor and marketer of black walnuts. That company started small way back in 1946. Today, it markets two million pounds of nutmeats a year. That is good news. After all, the black walnut is one of the richest nuts, and we all now know, the richer the nut, the better it is for us.

Braised Savoy Cabbage with Virginia Ham and Browned Black Walnuts

For whatever reason, braised cabbage is always a part of our Christmas table. With goose, we make a spicy red cabbage and apples; when the main dish is beef, we serve this marvelous savoy cabbage slowly braised with nuggets of smoky Virginia ham (see Sources, page 313) and chicken stock. The real treat comes at the end, when we add the buttery, slowly browned black walnuts, a treat taught us by Richard Perry, who as a young St. Louis chef was one of the national leaders of the renewed interest in American food. Don't save this dish for one meal a year; you'll enjoy it with any poultry, but it's also good as part of a buffet table with barbecued brisket or roasted pork. The browned nuts are equally delicious with shredded Brussels sprouts or steamed broccoli.

BRAISED CABBAGE

4 tablespoons unsalted butter

1 cup rich chicken stock, plus more
    if needed

1 heaping teaspoon kosher salt

1 rounded teaspoon freshly ground
    white pepper

2/3 cup thinly sliced shallots

5 pounds savoy cabbage, cored
    and shredded

1½ cups finely diced aged Virginia
    ham

BROWNED BUTTER BLACK WALNUTS

2 sticks (½ pound) unsalted butter

2 cups shelled black walnuts,
    coarsely chopped

To prepare the cabbage: Preheat the oven to 325°F. Thoroughly butter a 5-quart ovenproof casserole fitted with a cover. (You can also use heavy-duty foil as a cover.)

Combine the butter, stock, salt, and pepper in a small saucepan and heat until bubbling. Meanwhile, blend the shallots, cabbage, and ham together in the prepared casserole. Pour the hot stock mixture over cabbage, cover the casserole tightly, and place it in the oven. Braise for 1 hour, then uncover and stir. If the cabbage seems dry, add more stock. Then, cover again, and continue cooking until cabbage is meltingly soft, about another hour.

To prepare the nuts: At the same time the cabbage is cooking, combine the butter and nuts in a small, heavy saucepan and place over the lowest heat possible. Stirring often, cook as slowly as possible until the walnuts are very brown, but not burned. This should take at least 1 hour, sometimes even longer. Set the nuts aside until the cabbage is ready to serve, then reheat quickly.

To serve, remove the cover from the cabbage; taste and adjust the seasonings. Then pour the buttered nuts evenly over the cabbage.

Serve immediately.

SERVES 12

Coconut Curried Winter Vegetables with Peanuts

You will love this silky sauce of coconut milk piqued with the flavors of India in this dish. It's the perfect background for slowly braised winter vegetables. There is no particular heat in this dish, so if you wish some, add a diced fresh hot chile or two with the vegetables. Of course, you can substitute one vegetable for another. Finally, the roasted and salted peanuts make a cooling crunch at the end.

2 to 3 tablespoons organic canola or vegetable oil

1 dried red chile, crumbled

2 tablespoons good-quality Madras curry powder

½ teaspoon finely ground white pepper

3 plump garlic cloves, minced

1 tablespoon minced fresh ginger

4 cracked whole cardamom pods, preferably green

½ cup coarsely diced yellow onions

3 large sweet potatoes, peeled and cut into 2-inch chunks

3 medium parsnips, peeled and cut into 1½-inch lengths

3½ cups cauliflower florets

4 medium carrots, scrubbed and cut into thirds

3 or 4 turnips, scrubbed and quartered

Kosher salt

2½ cups canned coconut milk, plus more if needed

⅔ cup roasted and salted peanuts, coarsely chopped

¼ cup minced fresh cilantro

Combine the oil, chile, curry powder, and white pepper in a large, heavy Dutch oven. Cook over medium heat, stirring frequently, for 2 minutes to release the flavors of the seasonings. Add the garlic, ginger, cardamom, and onions. Stir until the onions begin to wilt. Add the sweet potatoes, parsnips, cauliflower, carrots, and turnips. Stir to blend with the seasonings. Sprinkle with salt and add the coconut milk. Cover tightly and cook until the coconut milk is hot but not boiling. Reduce the heat to low and cook, carefully stirring several times, for 30 minutes, or until the vegetables are tender. If necessary, add more coconut milk if the sauce reduces too much.

Transfer the vegetables to a heated serving dish. Sprinkle with nuts and cilantro just before serving.

SERVES 6 TO 8

desserts

Cashew Rum Raisin Ice Cream

Crème de Marron Ice Cream

Caramel Sundae with Peanut Butter
French Ice Cream and Spanish Peanuts

Ambrosia

Mélange of Pineapple and Other
Fruits with Coconut Curry Sauce

Bananas Foster with Caramelized
Pecans

A Fruity Tiramisù

Malabar Coconut Pudding with
Tapioca

Creamy Coconut Rice Pudding with
Mango

Divine Chocolate Mousse with
Amaretto

Pumpkin Coconut Crème Caramel

Our *Monte Bianco* Mont Blanc

Heavenly Chocolate and Pine Nut
Bread Pudding

Chocolate Amaretto Pudding Cake

Tracy's Carrot Cake with Walnuts and
Coconut

Chocolate Almond Cherry Torte

Karithopita: Greek Walnut Syrup Cake

Pineapple Cheesecake with Macadamia Nuts

Danièle's *Le Creusois* (Hazelnut Cake)

Sbricciolona: Crumbly Almond Cake

Sbricciolona: A Crumbly Hazelnut "Cake"

Apple Brown Betty with Toasted Hazelnuts

Blueberry Cobbler with Almonds

Freddie's Famous Phyllo Tart with Apples and Pistachios

Fresh Pear and Hazelnut Galette

Edgar's Pecan Pie

"My Pecan Pie" from John Thorne

Leona's Pecan Pie

McFarland Lunch Coconut Cream Pie

Chocolate Black Walnut Pie

Dutch Letters: Flaky Almond Pastries

Margaret Wine's Simple Strudel

Marzipan

Mexican Wedding Cookies

Grandma's Thimble Cookies with Pecan Meal

Kourabiethes: Greek Almond Shortbread

Hazelnut Biscotti

Roberta's Nut Bars

Texas Pralines

Cashew Rum Raisin Ice Cream

We keep our ice cream machine in a hard-to-reach cupboard. It's done for a very good reason, namely to reduce the frequency with which we make these delicious treats for ourselves. Once in a while, however, one just has to throw caution to the wind. If you like nuts and you like raisins, you will thoroughly enjoy this very flavorful and crunchy ice cream. Scooped into a dish or on a cone, it's bound to please, but do keep in mind it's even better with some warm fudge sauce drizzled over the top. By the way, nut butters are easily obtained in organic and natural food markets today.

2 cups whole milk
1 vanilla bean, slit down the middle
2/3 cup dark raisins
1/4 cup Myers's Rum
6 egg yolks
2/3 cup superfine sugar

1/4 cup roasted cashew butter
3/4 cup crème fraîche (see Basics, page 50)
2/3 cup coarsely chopped toasted cashews

Combine the milk and vanilla bean in a small, heavy saucepan. Bring to a boil, remove from the heat, and cover. Let stand for 30 minutes.

Combine the raisins and rum in a small bowl. Stir often while soaking. Drain raisins just before using.

Combine the egg yolks and sugar in the bowl of an electric mixer fitted with a whip; beat at high speed until the yolks are pale and form a ribbon when dropped from the beater. Remove the vanilla bean from the milk and scrape the seeds into the pot. With the motor running, gradually pour the milk into the egg-and-sugar mixture, then pour into a heavy-bottomed saucepan.

Put the cashew butter into a large mixing bowl. Fill a larger mixing bowl with ice and set it aside.

Place the saucepan with the egg mixture over low heat, stirring constantly, until it forms a very thick custard (about 180°F on a candy thermometer). Remove the saucepan from the heat and place it on the bed of ice. Gradually combine the cashew butter and the custard base. Stir in the crème fraîche. Keep stirring until the mixture cools, about 5 minutes. Then chill in the refrigerator for about 45 minutes.

Freeze the mixture in an ice-cream maker according to the manufacturer's directions. As the mixture begins to thicken, add the drained raisins and the cashews. Complete the freezing process.

Spoon the ice cream into a large, clean container and store it in the freezer, tightly covered. Let it soften somewhat before serving.

SERVES **8**

Crème de Marron Ice Cream

A French custard ice cream of any kind is one of life's greatest food treasures. It is richer, silkier, and just much more wonderful than any other style. Add to it the lush flavor of crème de marron, a sweetened chestnut paste ever so slightly marked by vanilla, and we have a totally memorable dessert. To gild the lily one might have some marron glacé as a garnish. The crème de marron, as well as the unsweetened chestnut paste, are available in many supermarkets now and are produced in France by Clement Faugier.

3 cups whole milk
1 vanilla bean, slit
7 large egg yolks
1 cup superfine sugar
½ teaspoon ground cinnamon

A 17½-ounce can crème de marron
1 cup crème fraîche (see Basics, page 50)

Combine the milk and vanilla bean in a small, heavy saucepan. Bring to a boil, remove from the heat, and cover. Let stand for 30 minutes.

Combine the egg yolks and sugar in the bowl of an electric mixer fitted with a whip; beat at high speed until the yolks are pale and form a ribbon when dropped from the beater. Remove the vanilla bean from the milk and scrape the seeds into the pot. With the motor running, gradually pour the milk into the egg-and-sugar mixture, then pour into a heavy-bottomed saucepan.

Fill a large mixing bowl with ice and set it aside.

Place the saucepan with the egg mixture over low heat, stirring constantly, until it forms a very thick custard (about 180°F on a candy thermometer). Working with about one-quarter of the can at a time, stir the marron crème into the hot custard. When the custard mixture is smooth, remove the saucepan from the heat and place it on the bed of ice. Stir in the crème fraîche. Keep stirring until mixture has cooled.

Then chill it completely in the refrigerator. Freeze the mixture in an ice-cream maker according to the manufacturer's directions.

Spoon the ice cream into a large, clean container and store it in the freezer, tightly covered. Let it soften somewhat before serving.

SERVES 6 TO 8

Relanghe

Roberta Ceretto had invited us to see her family's winery on a beautiful hilltop just outside of Alba in Northern Italy. In our hours with her, we learned that her father and uncle, the two owners of the place, bought a vineyard in Piedmont and, quite by accident, got a few acres of hazelnuts as a bonus.

The hazelnuts of Piedmont are said by some to be the best in the world, and as Roberta Ceretto says, their orchard was a limited and very prestigious one, "like a 'cru' for hazelnuts." So the wine family had several options: sell the orchard, get someone to harvest the nuts and sell them, or gather them and make something out of them. The Cerettos love wine, but candy ranks high with them, too. So they decided to go into the candy business.

They set up a small company called Relanghe, named after the orchard where their hazelnuts grow. They built a factory in Alba, perhaps the most important of the small cities of Piedmont, hired some skilled confectioners, and started to make by hand and market a hazelnut-filled nougat, which is a tradition of the region. The delicious candy is 50 percent *nocciole Piemonte* (the great local hazelnuts), white cane sugar from Cuba (the best in the world, says our host), honey, a little vanilla, and some glucose.

The honey and sugar are cooked together for eight hours for the crunchy nougat and four hours for the soft. The hazelnuts are roasted, bagged, and chilled. They are kept cold until it is time to add them to the soft nougat. The cooked candy is spread and allowed to set, and then in one of the few machine operations in the factory, the candy is cut and packaged.

The company also produces a few other candies with hazelnuts, but nougat rules. The company produces about one hundred tons of candy a year, and they say with little fear of contradiction that it is made with the best hazelnuts in the world. Their confections can be obtained in the United States through Corti Brothers (see Sources, page 311)

Caramel Sundae with Peanut Butter French Ice Cream and Spanish Peanuts

It's decadent, sinful—and totally irresistible! A rich, custard-based ice cream is the perfect background for this peanut-lover's delight. Make the crème fraîche for both the ice cream and the sauce the night before. Force yourself to eat this one slowly; revel in the rich flavors and salty crunch.

THE ICE CREAM
3 cups milk

1 vanilla bean, slit lengthwise

7 large egg yolks

1 cup sugar, preferably vanilla
   sugar*

¼ cup creamy peanut butter

¼ teaspoon freshly ground nutmeg

1¼ cups crème fraîche (see Basics,
   page 67)

THE CARAMEL SAUCE
1½ cups crème fraîche, plus more if
   needed

1¼ cups superfine sugar

THE GARNISH
Up to 1 cup Spanish peanuts

To make the ice cream: In a small saucepan, combine the milk and vanilla. Bring just to a boil, cover, and remove from the heat. Let stand for 30 minutes. Slit vanilla bean open and scrape seeds into the milk.

Combine the egg yolks and sugar in the bowl of an electric mixer fitted with a whip (if mixing by hand, use a large-bulbed whisk). Beat at high speed until the yolks are pale and form a ribbon when dropped from the beater.

With the motor running, gradually pour the milk into the egg-and-sugar mixture, then pour into a heavy-bottomed saucepan.

Spoon the peanut butter into a large mixing bowl. Fill a larger mixing bowl with ice and set it aside.

Cook the egg mixture over low heat, stirring constantly, until it forms a very thick custard that will thickly coat a wooden spoon (about 180°F on a candy thermometer). Remove the pan from the heat and gradually whisk the hot custard into the peanut butter to incorporate it thoroughly. Whisk in the nutmeg. Place the bowl on the bed of ice. Stir in the crème fraîche. Keep stirring until the mixture cools, about 5 minutes. Then chill in the refrigerator, about 45 minutes.

Freeze the mixture in an ice-cream maker according to the manufacturer's

*Note: We use deseeded vanilla beans to make vanilla sugar. In a quart container, combine the slit and scraped vanilla beans with 4 cups granulated sugar. Mix occasionally and store in a cool place. Always replace the sugar as you use it.

instructions. Spoon it into a plastic container and store it in the freezer until serving time.

To make the caramel sauce: Heat the crème fraîche to just below boiling and set it aside. Put the sugar in a caramel pot or small saucepan. Slowly heat, stirring over medium to medium low heat, until the sugar has dissolved and turned a beautiful golden brown.

Remove the pan from the heat and carefully pour in half of the warm crème fraîche. Stir until the mixture is smooth. Whisk in the remaining crème fraîche, a bit at a time, until the sauce becomes the texture of hot fudge. Let it cool.

Just before serving, stir the sauce well. If it is too thick, thin it with some of the remaining crème fraîche. Store the leftover caramel sauce in a clean container in the refrigerator and bring it to room temperature, or heat slightly, just before using.

To make sundaes: Arrange generous scoops of ice cream in each serving bowl. Spoon warm Caramel Sauce over the top and garnish lavishly with Spanish peanuts.

SERVES 6 TO 8

Ambrosia

A dessert right out of America's Old South, this simple and delicious combination of fresh coconut and oranges is perfect after any rich meal. Purists would tell you that there should be only four ingredients: fresh grated coconut, diced orange segments, sugar, and wine. They would also tell you that this is traditionally served at Christmas. The truth is that something this good should be served more often than that.

8 large navel oranges, peeled, pith
removed, broken into segments
1½ cups fresh grated coconut
(about a 2-pound coconut)

½ cup granulated sugar, plus more
if desired
¾ cup berry or dessert wine
Fresh mint leaves for garnish

With a sharp knife, cut each orange segment into small pieces. In an attractive serving dish, scatter a layer of orange pieces across the bottom. Distribute some of the coconut and sprinkle with some sugar. Repeat, ending with some coconut and sugar. Pour the wine over the top and allow to stand for 1 hour. Mix the ingredients gently and allow to stand for another hour before serving.

Garnish with mint and serve.

SERVES 6 TO 8

Mélange of Pineapple and Other Fruits with Coconut Curry Sauce

This recipe is cool, refreshing, and totally satisfying. It is also quite flexible. We have added blood orange in season, musk melon is also marvelous, and garden-fresh strawberries are sublime. Feel free to experiment because the coconut curry sauce is heavenly with any fruit. If you wish, a simple butter cookie or gingersnap would be lovely on the side.

1 ripe pineapple, cut into quarters, peeled, and thinly sliced

½ ripe honeydew, cut into wedges, peeled, and thinly sliced

1 ripe mango, peeled and cut into small pieces

2 ripe kiwi, peeled and thinly sliced

2 cups seedless grapes

1 pint fresh berries

2 seedless oranges, peeled and thinly sliced

Juice of 2 limes

⅛ teaspoon freshly grated nutmeg

3 cups whole-milk yogurt, preferably maple or vanilla

2 teaspoons Madras-style curry powder

⅓ cup richly flavored honey

¾ cup unsweetened coconut (grated fresh is best)

In a large bowl, combine the pineapple and honeydew. Add the mango, kiwi, grapes, berries, orange slices, lime juice, and nutmeg. Gently toss to blend.

In another bowl, blend together the yogurt and curry powder. Stir in the honey and coconut. Mix vigorously to blend evenly.

Serve the fruit in small bowls garnished with a generous dollop of coconut curry sauce.

SERVES 6 TO 8

Bananas Foster with Caramelized Pecans

This is the signature dessert of Cleveland's Johnny's Bar on Fulton from the night they first served dinner, about twenty years ago. It continues to be Linda's absolutely most favorite dessert in the world, with or without pecans. If you are serving this to more than 6 people, do make it in stages. No one minds waiting for something this delicious.

2 sticks (½ cup) unsalted butter

⅛ teaspoon ground cinnamon

⅓ cup extra-light brown sugar, firmly packed

½ cup pecans (optional)

6 ripe bananas, peeled and cut in half lengthwise

¼ cup crème de banane liqueur

3 tablespoons Myers's dark rum

1 quart top-quality vanilla ice cream

In a large sauté pan or chafing dish, over medium heat, whisk together the butter, cinnamon, brown sugar, and pecans until the ingredients are thoroughly mixed and the contents begin to boil. Do not actually caramelize. Add the bananas and sauté them on each side, about 1 minute.

Add the liqueur and rum to the pan, ignite, and let the flame burn off.

Scoop the ice cream into serving bowls. Distribute the bananas and sauce among the dishes and serve.

SERVES 6

A Fruity Tiramisù

The contrasting layers of tender fruit and silky creams are in pleasing contrast to the crunchy pieces of delicious amaretti cookies made in Italy. There is also the surprise of tasty bits of dried apricots. To satisfy the chocoholics among us we have incorporated a suggestion from a dear Cleveland friend, Virginia Maver. There is something for everyone in this.

1 to 2 teaspoons almond oil

1 cup crushed amaretti cookies

¾ cup finely diced dried apricots

½ cup amaretto, or another kind of liqueur or a brandy

2 cups mascarpone cheese

½ cup superfine sugar

Zest and juice of 1 lemon

2 cups heavy cream (not ultrapasteurized)

1 cup grated bittersweet chocolate

5 cups fresh raspberries, blueberries, and/or sliced strawberries (or sliced oranges and/or peaches, seedless grapes)

½ cup chopped toasted almonds

Thoroughly oil a pretty 3-quart serving bowl and chill until needed. In a small bowl, combine the crushed amaretti, apricots, and liqueur; blend and set aside.

In a large bowl, whisk the mascarpone with sugar and lemon juice. In the bowl of an electric mixer fitted with a whisk, whip the cream until it forms soft peaks. Lighten the mascarpone mixture by vigorously blending it with about a quarter of the cream. Then gently fold the remaining cream into the mascarpone mixture.

Spoon a third of the mascarpone mixture into the serving bowl. Sprinkle with about a third of the grated chocolate. Cover the cream with half the berries. Then repeat again, ending with the cream and chocolate. Cover tightly with plastic wrap and chill for at least 1 hour. This can be prepared in the afternoon and kept chilled, however.

Sprinkle with the toasted nuts just before serving.

SERVES 12

Malabar Coconut Pudding with Tapioca

This dessert totally wowed our guests! Like us, most had not had a tapioca pudding in years. The coconut flavor really shines here, but we enhance it with the addition of some good vanilla. Our "Indian daughter" Nimmy Paul served it to us spooned into handsome dessert cups and garnished with slices of the best papaya we have ever tasted. We've served it with mango and some delicious pitted fresh cherries, but the best way may be with thinly sliced pineapple. As we were to hear many times during our Kerala visit, pineapple and coconut have a real love for one another. One variation you might want to make is to cook the pudding with a split vanilla bean, discarding it after the cooking is finished. Finally, you can use all canned coconut milk in this recipe. While the pudding does not totally set up in the bowl, you will enjoy its light and silky texture.

1 cup tapioca "beads"
3 cups water
⅓ cup superfine sugar

½ teaspoon kosher salt
5 cups coconut milk
Fresh fruit for garnish

Combine the tapioca and water in a medium-sized saucepan; soak for 2 hours.

Then stir in the sugar and salt. Next add 4 cups of the coconut milk and blend well. Cook the pudding over medium-low heat, stirring frequently, until the beads virtually disappear and the pudding is very thick, 30 to 40 minutes.

Add the remaining coconut milk and stir over low heat until the mixture is very hot, 15 to 20 minutes. Do not, however, allow the pudding to boil. Pour the pudding into a 2-quart soufflé dish and refrigerate for at least 6 hours, but preferably overnight. Serve in small bowls with fresh fruit on top.

SERVES 6

Amelia's Almonds

American Cookery was published in Hartford in 1796. Written by Amelia Simmons, who identified herself as "an American orphan," it was the first American cookbook.

The full title of her little forty-six-page book, as was so often the case in those times, is long: *American Cookery, or the Art of Dressing Viands, Fish, Poultry and Vegetables, and the Best Modes of Making Pastes, Puffs, Pies, Tarts, Puddings, Custards, and Preserves, and All Kinds of Cakes, from the Imperial Plumb to Plain Cake Adapted to this Country, and All Grades of Life.*

The tree nuts of the New England forests were readily available to Amelia Simmons and other cooks of the time, but none of her recipes involved the local chestnuts, walnuts, hickories, chinkapins, or beechnuts. They were undoubtedly just taken for granted and not deemed important enough to go into a recipe book.

The only nut Amelia mentions was an obvious import—the almond—and it turns up three times. She suggests a "plumb" cake, a boiled custard, and this one for a cream almond pudding, "Boil gently a little mace and half a nutmeg (grated) in a quart cream; when cool, beat 8 yolks and 3 whites, strain and mix with one spoon flour, one quarter of a pound almonds; settled, add one spoon rose-water, and by degrees the cold cream and beat well together; wet a thick cloth and flour it, and pour in the pudding, boil hard half an hour, take out, pour over it melted butter and sugar."

Later she would amend this "receipt," calling for 8 whole eggs, 8 spoons of flour instead of one, and increased the boiling time to an hour and a half. Still, despite her dissatisfaction with how it came out, this stands as the first recipe ever published in America that called for a nut of any kind.

Here is an earlier almond encounter, not from an American cookbook, but from *The Ladie's Handmaid or a Compleat System of Cookery,* published in London in 1758, but widely used in the Colonies. It is for what was called "jumbals," a kind of cookie.

"Let a pound of fine flour, and as much sugar, be made up into a paste with beaten whites of eggs; then add thereto half a pint of cream, half a pound of fresh butter, and a pound of blanch'd almonds well stamp'd; knead all together thoroughly with a little rose water, and cut out jumbals into what figure you please, in order to be baked in a gentle oven."

Creamy Coconut Rice Pudding with Mango

This wonderfully creamy dessert can be served as is, or with a fruit topping. In keeping with the rather exotic nature of the coconut, we like to serve it with sliced mangoes or diced, fresh pineapple. Slow cooking in the steamy atmosphere of a double boiler enhances the aroma and flavor of the pudding. It also insures its creamy texture. We always use exceptionally delicious, organically grown jasmine rice, which comes from Lowell Farms in El Campo, Texas (see Sources, page 313), where Linda and Lowell Raun long ago taught us about making rice pudding in a double boiler.

1 cup jasmine rice
½ cup superfine sugar
½ teaspoon salt
4 cups coconut milk, preferably
  fresh (see Basics, page 50)
2 cups whole milk

¼ teaspoon freshly grated nutmeg
1 teaspoon ground cinnamon
⅓ cup lightly toasted unsweetened
  coconut
Diced mango or pineapple for
  topping

Combine the rice, sugar, salt, 4 cups coconut milk, and 1 cup of the whole milk in the top of a double boiler. Cover and cook, stirring frequently, over simmering water for 1 hour. Stir in the nutmeg; cover again. Cook for another hour, or until the rice is soft and the mixture is thick but creamy. Stir in the cinnamon.

Remove the double boiler from the heat.

If you are serving the rice pudding as soon as it has cooled, stir in the remaining cup of milk now. Then keep rice covered and let stand, over the water, for another 20 minutes. Serve warm, garnished with toasted coconut and fruit.

If you are serving the rice pudding chilled, remove the pot from the water, uncover, and continue to cool. Stir in the remaining milk after the pudding has cooled, then pour it into a 1½-quart serving dish, sprinkle with toasted coconut, and chill. Serve with fruit topping.

SERVES 6

Divine Chocolate Mousse with Amaretto

There is a marvelous restaurant in Lisbon, Pap'Açorda, that serves the best choco-late mousse in the entire world. At dessert time you will see waiters rushing around with huge stainless mixing bowls filled with it. They stop and offer a gar-gantuan spoonful to each guest. If you eat with gusto, they will offer you seconds. We think lovers of Pap'Açorda will enjoy ours, too. Because everyone seems to love chocolate and amaretto together.

6 ounces bittersweet chocolate, chopped
4 tablespoons unsalted butter, cut into small pieces
6 large eggs yolks
1 tablespoon plus ¼ cup superfine sugar

⅓ cup amaretto liqueur
¼ cup water
5 large egg whites
Whipping cream, berries, or candied violets for garnish

Melt the chocolate in a heavy-bottomed pan. Whisk in the butter, a bit at a time. Set aside to cool.

Combine the yolks, 1 tablespoon of the sugar, and the amaretto in another heavy-bottomed saucepan and whisk over very low heat until the mixture forms a custard. Remove the pan from the heat and keep stirring until the mixture cools. (If you do not have a heavy-bottomed pan, do this step in the top of a double boiler over hot water.)

In a small saucepan, combine the water and the remaining sugar; cook over medium-high heat until the mixture becomes syrupy. In the bowl of a mixer fitted with a whisk, beat the egg whites just until opaque. With the motor on high, add the hot syrup in a steady stream, then keep beating until the whites are stiff and shiny like meringue.

Gradually stir the chocolate mixture into the custard, then blend thoroughly. Add the chocolate mixture to the meringue and beat on low until the mixture is evenly blended.

Spoon the mousse into serving dishes and chill. Garnish just before serving.

SERVES 6 TO 8

Pumpkin Coconut Crème Caramel

Ever since we discovered that this dessert is even lighter than the pumpkin meringue pie we used to serve, this has become our primary dessert for Thanksgiving. Linda has had many fans of her conventional crème caramel, some going back nearly thirty years. Now we've discovered something better than the best—just by including coconut milk and pumpkin purée. If you wish, fill the center with whipped crème fraîche (see Basics, page 50) and berries.

2½ cups superfine sugar

7 large eggs plus 2 yolks

1 cup fresh roasted pumpkin purée

1 cup canned coconut milk

5 cups half-and-half

1 tablespoon Myers's Rum

2 teaspoons vanilla extract

2 teaspoons ground ginger

¼ teaspoon freshly ground cinnamon

Melt 1 cup of the sugar in a caramel pot, stirring until it becomes a nice, rich brown. Pour the sauce into a 12-cup ring mold and carefully coat the sides. Be sure to use oven mitts to do this because the mold gets very hot. Set the mold aside to cool.

Combine the eggs in the bowl of an electric mixer and beat well. Add remaining 1½ cup sugar and beat thoroughly.

In a small mixing bowl, beat together the pumpkin purée and coconut milk. When thoroughly blended, pour it into the egg mixture. Add the remaining ingredients. Beat again. Let the mixture rest for 1 hour.

Preheat the oven to 350°F.

Pour the egg mixture through a fine strainer into the mold. Fill a large baking pan with hot water, place the filled ring mold in the center, and carefully place the pan in the preheated oven. Bake for 1¼ hours, or until a long knife inserted into the custard comes out clean. Transfer the crème caramel to a cooling rack. When very cool, chill in the refrigerator. To serve, carefully loosen the sides of the custard by pressing a finger gently around the outer and inner edges. Invert the mold on a large serving platter and shake gently. Remove the ring.

SERVES 10 TO 12

Baci di Cherasco

One day Nucci and Flavio Russo took us from their little Hotel Al Cardinal Mazzarino in Cherasco to their favorite candy store.

Their friend Giancarlo Torta had been a chef in Rome, but he grew up in this little Piedmont town, and as a child he had been in love with this shop. He had always hoped that someday he would be able to buy it.

That opportunity came when the two sisters who owned it decided to retire and they sold him Barbero di Cherasco. For a year and a half he and his wife, Carla, worked with the sisters as they phased themselves out of a business that had been in their family since 1880. Then he started making those hazelnut-rich candy kisses, the Baci de Cherasco.

Roberto Donna, the chef-owner of Galileo in Washington, D.C., grew up in nearby Asti. He knew that store, too. His friends, Nucci and Flavio, told him about Giancarlo Torta's return. Ever since, Donna has been trying to persuade Torta to sell him Baci de Cherasco for the people who dine at his famous restaurant.

Giancarlo resisted. He says he doesn't make enough of it. It costs too much to ship it. It doesn't travel well. Still, hope springs eternal; every time Roberto Donna comes home to Italy, he visits the shop, enjoys a few of Giancarlo's great candies, and tries again to get him to send some to Washington.

If it happens, someday after a world-class dinner at Galileo, your check will come with Baci de Cherasco, and you will know that Donna has pulled off a remarkable culinary coup.

Our *Monte Bianco* Mont Blanc

When the weather is right, one can see the snow-capped Alps from most places in Piedmont. This very simple chestnut dessert, traditionally served at New Year's, is named for that high Alpine peak, Mont Blanc. Some make this dessert with chocolate added to the purée, sometimes not. We asked our Piedmontese friend, Nucci Russo, how she makes hers and she said, "We cover the peeled chestnuts with fresh milk with vaniglia. I cook slowly for about 50 minutes, then I add the sugar and I prepare a purée . . . pass then in the special tool for purée and I form the mountain that I cover with the cream. I add also the rum but I think that also a good cognac (or Armagnac) could be OK." It is more than OK, dear Nucci! Prepare all but the whipped cream several hours ahead. Just keep the mountain itself in a cold place, adding the snow before serving.

1½ pounds fresh chestnuts
    (or 1¼ pounds peeled or dried)
Up to 6 cups milk
4 teaspoons vanilla extract
2 tablespoons unsalted butter
½ cup superfine sugar, more if
    needed

½ cup rum, brandy, or Armagnac
4 ounces melted unsweetened
    chocolate (optional)
2 cups heavy whipping cream, plus
    more if needed
Sweet cocoa powder for dusting
    (optional)

Cover the chestnuts with milk in a heavy-bottomed saucepan and cook until the milk is nearly boiling. Reduce the heat, add 3 teaspoons of the vanilla, and simmer until the chestnuts are very soft, 50 to 60 minutes. If the milk is absorbed before the chestnuts are soft, add more milk and continue simmering. To determine tenderness, press half a chestnut with the side of a knife. When it mashes easily, it is done. When chestnuts are ready, stir in the butter and sugar. Purée the chestnuts in a food processor. Add the rum and chocolate (optional). Pulse and add more milk as needed to make a fairly stiff but tender mixture. It must be firm enough to keep its "string shapes" as it passed through the small holes of a food mill or potato ricer.

To create the "mountain," hold a food mill fitted with a medium-holed disk, or a potato ricer, above a serving platter, fill with the chestnut mixture, and slowly turn. Let the "strings" fall onto the platter, creating a small, loose mound, drawing the mountain higher by raising your food mill ever higher. (Keep it cold at this point.)

In a mixing bowl, combine the cream and remaining vanilla. Beat until firm peaks form. Carefully coat the upper part of the mountain with whipped cream; it does not have to be evenly coated, but rather with varying depths of "snow," carefully coming together in a peak of cream at the very top. Dust with cocoa if you wish and serve immediately.

SERVES **6** TO **8**

Heavenly Chocolate and Pine Nut Bread Pudding

Creamy chocolate, pillows of bread, sweet and nutty pine nuts—all are the stuff that dreams are made of. You can prepare it in the morning and bake it at night. Your guests will never forget how wonderful it is. Although it is a big caloric splurge, it is also something that creates lasting food memories.

1 tablespoon unsalted butter, softened

2 tablespoons plus 2 cups superfine sugar

2 cups heavy cream

1 quart half-and-half

10 ounces bittersweet chocolate, chopped

5 eggs

2½ teaspoons pure vanilla extract

1 loaf (at least 2 pounds) challah bread, torn into chunks

1 cup currants

1 cup toasted pine nuts

½ cup finely chopped candied orange peel (optional)

Whipped cream or vanilla ice cream for garnish

Thoroughly butter a 3-quart baking dish. Add 2 tablespoons of the granulated sugar and toss to coat evenly. Reserve.

Preheat the oven to 375°F.

Combine the cream, half-and-half, and chocolate in a large saucepan and heat to near boiling. Remove from the heat and stir until the chocolate has melted. Set aside to cool.

In a large mixing bowl, thoroughly whisk together the remaining sugar, eggs, and vanilla. Tear the bread into small pieces and put them into a large mixing bowl. Pour the chocolate cream mixture over the bread and toss until very well coated. Add the sugar-and-egg mixture and toss again. Put half of the bread mixture in the prepared baking dish.

Evenly distribute currants, pine nuts, and orange peel over the surface, then add the remaining bread mixture. (You can refrigerate it at this point, but allow it to stand for 1 hour at room temperature before baking.)

Bake for 1 hour, or until firm. Let the pudding cool for about 20 minutes on a cake rack. Serve with whipped cream or ice cream.

SERVES 6 TO 10

Chocolate Amaretto Pudding Cake

Chocolate and almond are a much-loved dynamic duo. This is the perfect dish for chocolate lovers who are looking for a splendid sugar fix. It's wonderfully gooey as well as positively seductive. Fred insists that it should be topped with ice cream to make it perfect.

1 tablespoon unsalted butter, softened

2 tablespoons plus 1 cup superfine sugar

1 cup whole wheat pastry flour (available at organic markets)

½ cup Dutch cocoa

2 teaspoons baking powder

½ teaspoon baking soda

Pinch of salt

3 tablespoons unsalted butter, melted

½ cup buttermilk

2 teaspoons vanilla extract

¾ cup firmly packed dark-brown sugar

⅓ cup amaretto liqueur

⅔ cup water

Vanilla ice cream (optional)

Preheat the oven to 350°F. Butter and sugar a 1½-quart soufflé dish with 1 tablespoon of butter and 2 tablespoons of superfine sugar.

In a cake sifter, combine the flour, ⅔ cup of the sugar, 3 tablespoons of the cocoa, the baking powder, baking soda, and salt; sift into a medium-sized bowl. Add the butter, buttermilk, and vanilla. Stir well and spread in the prepared soufflé dish. Mix the remaining cocoa and sugar with the brown sugar. Sprinkle the mixture evenly over the flour mixture in the soufflé dish. (This can be prepared in advance to this point.)

Just before baking, combine the amaretto and water; sprinkle evenly over the top of the sugar mixture. Bake the pudding cake in the preheated oven for 35 to 38 minutes. The top will feel firm and crisp; there will be sauce in the bottom. Serve warm.

Scoop portions into serving bowls, spooning bottom sauce over each. If you wish, garnish with a scoop of ice cream.

SERVES **6** TO **8**

Tracy's Carrot Cake with Walnuts and Coconut

Carrots, walnuts, and coconut are the primary flavors of this scrumptious cake. When Tracy married Linda's son, Rob Myers, she was not a cook, but she knew how to make this cake, and it became her regular contribution to family dinners. It is simple and lasts well (if there are uneaten pieces). Best of all, virtually everyone has seconds.

1 tablespoon unsalted butter, softened

THE CAKE
2 cups unbleached flour
2 cups superfine sugar
1 cup sweetened shredded coconut
2½ teaspoons ground cinnamon
2½ teaspoons baking soda
1 teaspoon salt
4 large carrots, grated
1¼ cups organic vegetable or canola oil

2 teaspoons pure vanilla extract
11-ounce can Mandarin oranges, finely chopped including juice
4 large eggs
1 cup coarsely chopped toasted walnuts

THE FROSTING
8 ounces cream cheese
1 tablespoon melted butter
1 teaspoon pure vanilla extract
Minced zest of 1 orange
3 cups confectioners' sugar

Preheat the oven to 350°F. Thoroughly butter a 13×9-inch baking pan.

To make the cake: Combine the flour, sugar, coconut, cinnamon, baking soda, salt, carrots, oil, vanilla, oranges, eggs, and walnuts in the bowl of an electric mixer. Using the paddle attachment, blend for 2 minutes at low speed. Pour the batter into the prepared pan and smooth the top. Bake for 45 to 55 minutes, or until a toothpick inserted into the middle comes out clean. Remove the cake from the oven and cool on a rack.

To make the frosting: Combine the cream cheese, butter, vanilla, zest, and sugar in the bowl of an electric mixer. Beat on medium speed until the mixture is smooth and creamy, then spread it on the cake. If you wish, just before serving, garnish the cake with slices of orange.

MAKES A 13×9-INCH CAKE

Chocolate Almond Cherry Torte

We doubt there is anyone who does not love the combination of chocolate and almonds. Add cherries to the mix and you have a marvelous dessert indeed. We do prefer using fresh, pitted cherries, but since they have such a short season we do use ones from a can in winter. Finally, we use just a tad of pure almond extract to enhance that special almond aroma it provides.

2 tablespoons unsalted butter, softened

¼ cup fine amaretti cookie crumbs

1 tablespoon plus 1 cup superfine sugar

3 large eggs

1 tablespoon kirsch or framboise

1 stick (8 tablespoons) unsalted butter, melted

1 teaspoon vanilla extract

⅛ teaspoon pure almond extract

5 tablespoons Dutch cocoa

½ cup unbleached flour

1½ to 2 teaspoons baking powder

½ cup finely chopped almonds

2 cups drained pitted sweet cherries

⅓ cup plus 1 tablespoon confectioners' sugar

1 cup crème fraîche (see Basics, page 50)

10 candied violets (or fresh Johnny jump-ups)

Place an oven rack above the middle of the oven and preheat the oven to 325°F. Butter a 9-inch springform cake pan. Combine the cookie crumbs and 1 tablespoon of the sugar, then turn the mixture into the pan and shake well so that the cake pan is evenly coated. Shake out excess and set the pan aside.

Place the eggs and remaining sugar in the bowl of an electric mixer; beat until mixture is very thick. Add the kirsch. Then, with the motor on low, stir in the butter, vanilla, almond, and cocoa. Remove the bowl.

Combine the flour and baking powder in a small bowl. Carefully fold the mixture into the batter. Gently blend the almonds into this.

Distribute the cherries evenly in the prepared pan, then pour the batter over them and firmly smooth the cake with a rubber spatula. Bake in the preheated oven for about 50 minutes, or until the cake feels firm to the touch. Remove the cake from the oven and place it on a cooling rack for 10 minutes. Run a sharp knife around outer edge of the cake to loosen it from the sides, then release the spring.

Let the cake cool completely, then invert it and remove the bottom of the pan. Carefully turn cake over once more. Just before serving, sift ⅓ cup of the confectioners' sugar evenly over the top of the cake. Whip the crème fraîche with the remaining sugar until the soft peak stage. Distribute 10 generous dollops of cream evenly around the edge of the cake. If you are using violets, place one on each dollop. Serve.

MAKES A **9-INCH** TORTE

A Wild Nutella Ride

No one in the cosmos has bought more hazelnuts than Alberto Rosa Brunet. He is the purchasing director of Ferrero, the Italian-based maker of Nutella, a wildly successful chocolate hazelnut butter that is used across the world. Only in the United States does Ferrero find the going slow, but, then, we already have peanut butter.

Brunet, the purchasing manager of the company, gave us a lesson on the geography of the hazelnut. His company is greedy for every nut it can find. Most of what it uses comes from Turkey, the world's biggest producer. Italy is second, but there is a great deal of variation in the quality and size of Italian hazelnuts, and the northern nuts are just too costly.

Like so many big companies, Ferrero started small with a man and an idea.

Pietro Ferrero was a pastry maker who, after the war, found himself dealing with a cocoa shortage. He found he could stretch his supply by adding ground toasted hazelnuts that were abundant around his Piedmontese town of Alba.

He came up with a spread that he called *pasta gianduja*. People liked it, and records of the now giant company show that in 1946 he made 660 pounds of it. By 1949, he had made his product more easily spreadable and inexpensive. Then the name became *"Supercrema Gianduja."* In those days, neighborhood food stores would keep an open container on the counter, and for a penny or two, a child could bring in a piece of bread and have it "smeared" with the *Supercrema*.

Finally in 1964, the company came up with still another name, Nutella, and started to market it across Europe. Ferrero said then, and they say today, that it is better than peanut butter—and there seems to be no slowing down.

On the Internet we went on a wild Nutella ride. We learned that Nutella-maker Ferrero is the world's twenty-fifth largest advertiser; the company had an ad budget of $581 million in 1998.

"A food for divinity, and worthy of use in sexual play," writes one Nutella worshipper. Another called it, "The world's most wonderfully sinful food." We found an engraving of Adam and Eve, leering in anticipation at each other—and Adam was holding in his hand a jar of Nutella.

Nutella is made of sugar, hazelnuts, cocoa, skim milk powder, and "aromas." You can understand how it would work well with ice cream, but Nutella and salami? We found such a recipe!

We also learned that "The largest consumers of Nutella are Italian University students studying for finals. Some say they are 'nut-dependent.'"

There is, of course, a Nutella fan club—and a Nutella prayer:

Lo, I worship thee, O maiden of unending, chocolately, gooey joy!

Blessed are thee unto whom thy nutty visage has been revealed, for they shall inherit the richness of thy flavor, the silken, sticky softness of thy texture, and the eternal figure of thy vessel. Thou art the Alpha-bits and omelettes of thy chosen peoples.

If this grabs you, you can find Nutella in most American specialty stores and major supermarkets. Kobe Bryant of the Los Angeles Lakers will be looking at you from the label on the jar.

Karithopita: Greek Walnut Syrup Cake

We've never met a Greek pastry we didn't enjoy—probably because they almost always include walnuts, almonds, or pistachios. We know that everyone will applaud the combination of flavors in this deliciously nutty cake. After all, what could be better than nuts and honey! While there are myriad variations of the recipe, we think that ours is the best "take" on the subject. Some recipes include almonds with the walnuts; some use zwieback instead of flour; others call for rum instead of whiskey; and many do not call for butter at all. Many recipes use so much syrup that the cake is served with a spoon. Yet others omit the syrup entirely. Anyway, we think that this particular version is among the best, and, to be honest, it was a lot of fun reaching this conclusion.

2 tablespoons unsalted butter, softened

THE CAKE
3 cups cake flour
2 teaspoons baking powder
2 teaspoons ground cinnamon
Finely grated zest of 1 orange
1 pound English walnuts, finely ground
1 stick (¼ pound) unsalted butter

1¼ cups superfine sugar
10 eggs plus 1 egg white, separated
1 teaspoon vanilla extract
¼ cup whiskey

THE SYRUP
5 cups water
3 cups superfine sugar
1 cup honey
¼ cup orange juice

Preheat the oven to 350°F. Thoroughly butter a 13×9-inch baking pan.

To make the cake: In a large bowl, combine the cake flour, baking powder, cinnamon, orange zest, and ground walnuts.

In another bowl, cream the butter and sugar. Add the egg yolks and beat until mixture is very creamy and light in color. Beat in the vanilla and whiskey. Add the flour and nut mixture and blend thoroughly. Beat the egg whites until they form stiff, but not dry, peaks. Add a quarter of the egg whites to the nut mixture and blend thoroughly to lighten it. Then fold in the remaining egg whites. The batter is quite heavy, so be patient.

Spread the mixture evenly in the prepared baking pan.

Bake until firm and the cake has pulled away from the sides of the pan, about 30 minutes. The top will not be well-browned. Transfer to a cooling rack and, using a thin skewer, poke many holes in the cake.

While the cake is baking, make the syrup: Combine the water, sugar, and honey in a small saucepan. Bring to a boil, then reduce the heat and simmer until the mixture has some viscosity to it, about 20 minutes. Stir in the orange juice.

Slowly spoon the syrup evenly over hot cake. Let it stand for at least an hour before serving.

MAKES ABOUT **36** PIECES

Pineapple Cheesecake with Macadamia Nuts

Macadamia nuts marry beautifully with all fruits, but especially well with pineapple. In a cheesecake, piqued with ginger, the combination is delightful. While some of the instructions sound strange, they really prevent this cake from cracking. There is only one real problem with this recipe—the cake is so good it is tempting to eat it all at one sitting!

THE CRUMB CRUST

1 cup finely chopped unsalted
  macadamia nuts
¾ cup crushed zwiebacks
6 tablespoons unsalted butter,
  melted

2 teaspoons ground ginger
½ cup superfine sugar
Finely grated zest of 1 lime

THE FILLING

1 pound cream cheese

⅔ cup superfine sugar

1 tablespoon finely minced
   crystallized ginger

1 teaspoon ground coriander

2 tablespoons Myers's rum

5 eggs

1½ cups thoroughly drained
   crushed pineapple

1 tablespoon fresh lime juice

THE TOPPING

2 cups sour cream

2 tablespoons Myers's rum

4 tablespoons superfine sugar

½ cup coarsely chopped toasted
   macadamia nuts

Preheat the oven to 375°F.

To make the crumb crust: Combine the nuts, crushed zwiebacks, butter, ginger, sugar, and lime zest in a small mixing bowl and blend well. Press evenly and firmly in the bottom and around the lower sides of a very well-buttered 9-inch springform pan. Chill for 15 minutes in the freezer, then bake in the preheated oven for 10 minutes. Remove from the oven and cool.

To make the filling: In the bowl of a mixer fitted with a paddle, beat the cream cheese and sugar until thoroughly blended. Scrape the sides, then add the ginger, coriander, and rum. With the motor running, add the eggs, one at a time. Beat vigorously for 3 minutes. Then add pineapple purée and lime juice and blend well.

Pour the filling into the prepared pan and bake for 1 hour.

When the cake is done, remove it from the oven and place it on a cake rack while you prepare the topping.

To make the topping: Combine the sour cream, rum, and sugar in a small bowl and blend well. Spread the topping evenly over the cake, sprinkle with nuts, and return the cake to the oven and bake for 7 minutes. Transfer the cake immediately to the refrigerator until thoroughly cooled. Remove the ring from the pan just before serving.

SERVES **6** TO **12**

Danièle's *Le Creusois* (Hazelnut Cake)

Our dear friend Danièle Giusti arrived from Paris with this recipe and a bag of hazelnut flour among her belongings. A devotee of traditional French cuisine, Danièle was horrified at the suggestion that we could also make this with chestnut flour. "No, no, Leenda," she said. "This cake is a specialty from La Creuse, a small town not far from Limoges . . . and it is always made with noisette *flour." Its preparation is quite unusual in that the dry ingredients are slowly added to the egg whites and melted butter goes in last. Don't worry, while it's only about 2 inches tall, the cake is totally delicious with a subtle meringue crunch. (It is also quite delicious when made with chestnut flour—but, shh!) Traditionally this cake is served quite plain, but it is wonderful in summer with a bowl of berries on the side.*

2 tablespoons unsalted butter,
   softened
5 egg whites
1 cup plus 1 tablespoon granulated
   sugar

¾ cup unbleached flour
1 cup hazelnut flour (see Sources,
   page 311)
6 tablespoons unsalted butter,
   melted and cooled

Preheat the oven to 375°F. Lavishly butter a 9-inch springform pan. In the bowl of an electric mixer fitted with a whisk, beat the egg whites until they hold very firm peaks.

Using a wooden spoon, very lightly stir in the sugar, then the unbleached flour, then the nut flour, scraping the sides of the bowl several times. Finally stir in the butter.

Scrape the batter gently into the prepared pan and smooth the top. Bake until the top is nicely browned and a toothpick inserted into the center comes out dry, 40 to 50 minutes.

Transfer the cake to a cooling rack. After 5 minutes, remove the sides of the pan. After 30 to 40 minutes, gently remove the bottom.

To serve, cut into wedges and serve on attractive plates accompanied by fresh berries.

SERVES **6** TO **8**

Nocino

After a great four-hour lunch at Trotteria la Bucca in Zibello, Miriam Bonafè, the owner, brought us little glasses of nocino, a dark, bittersweet nut liqueur that her family has served for ages from the cellar of their remarkable restaurant.

This liqueur rarely makes it to the United States. Most of it is sold and consumed in Northern Italy. Later in Modena, better known for Ferrari cars and balsamic vinegar, we learned how it is made.

Dr. Pietro Aggazzotti, like so many Italian business executives, was wearing a nifty suit with a beautiful tie. Not appropriate garb, one would think, for toiling among the messy crushed green walnuts that are the key to this liqueur. His family owns the company, which in an adjacent building also produces the highest-quality balsamic vinegar.

The company has its own walnut orchard, about twenty acres, which they planted in 1988 with trees from an old nursery in the mountains. Younger and lower trees are easier to harvest. They are delicate and are treated like fruit trees. Harvesters will not even lean a ladder against one of them. Traditionally the walnuts are carefully picked by hand on the twenty-fourth of June, some weeks before they would have ripened, and the farmers have a traditional celebration, and possibly quaff some of last season's nocino. The nuts will not have developed their hard shell and the nut pulp inside is still undefined.

The green nuts are quickly sliced to release the juices, and placed in large glass jars, demijohns, probably ten gallons in size, with the small opening on top covered with a red plastic lid. The process gets a jump-start with the addition of a little alcohol. The demijohn rests in a plastic basket, and maybe two hundred of them are lined up on the floor and on low shelves of a brightly lit building. The light enhances the oxidation and development of the dark color as the fermentation process starts.

Walnuts, even green walnuts, have a lot of color clout. Working with them can turn your hands brown. And the liqueur, slowly aging in the large jars, is the color of chocolate. The demijohns are stirred three times in the eleven months that it takes for appropriate fermentation; then, in May, the liqueur is poured off and the remaining fluid is pressed out of the nut pulp. The liqueur is strained and then given a year's rest in large stainless tanks before bottling.

Not much is likely to come to the United States. Even if there were some available for export, the red tape that would have to be cut makes it unlikely that they would try to send any nocino to the Americans. So if you want some, go to Northern Italy. And give us a call; we'll go with you.

Sbricciolona: Crumbly Almond Cake

According to Marcella Hazan, these crumbly cakes have their roots in Ferrara, where almonds are the featured nut. But we've also enjoyed versions in other parts of Emilia-Romagna made with pine nuts, hazelnuts, or both. This crumbly cake does looks more like a cake than a cookie, but its texture is still drier than that of a traditional cake. We first tasted it at Trattoria La Bucca, in the village of Zibello, a short distance from Parma. The much celebrated owner/cook Miriam Bonafè had served us an exceptional parade of delectable specialties, but would not allow us to decline at least a small wedge of something sweet. We were delighted that she had insisted. In our enthusiasm for nuts, we confess enjoying this with a bowl of zabaglione (a light foamy custard) made with some nocino, the region's popular green walnut liqueur.

12 tablespoons (1½ sticks) unsalted butter, softened, plus more for greasing the pan

2 tablespoons olive oil

¾ cup superfine sugar

1 cup toasted slivered almonds, well-chopped

½ teaspoon kosher salt

½ cup fine semolina

2 cups unbleached flour

2 large eggs

2 teaspoons vanilla extract

2 teaspoons almond extract

2 tablespoons confectioners' sugar for garnish

Preheat the oven to 350°F. Place one rack in the upper third of the oven. Lavishly butter a 10- or 11-inch tart pan with a removable bottom.

Beat the butter and oil with an electric mixer on medium speed until the mixture is light and fluffy. Scrape the sides and beat in the sugar. Scrape the sides and with the motor on low, beat in the nuts, salt, semolina, and flour. Scrape again and beat in the eggs. The mixture will be crumbly. Then blend in the vanilla and almond extracts.

Turn the dough out into the prepared pan. Distribute the dough evenly over the pan, patting it until evenly filled. Bake on the upper rack for 35 to 45 minutes, or until the cake is lightly browned, firm in the middle, and dry when tested with a toothpick.

Transfer the pan to a rack to cool, then remove the cake from the pan.

Serve at room temperature, garnished with confectioners' sugar.

MAKES AN **11-INCH** CRUMBLY CAKE (SERVES **6** TO **12**)

Sbricciolona: A Crumbly Hazelnut "Cake"

While it's more like a pizza-sized cookie, this totally delicious hazelnut-filled dry cake is usually served on a large platter in the middle of the table. It is another version of sbricciolona, *the dry nut cakes so popular in the Emilia-Romagna region of Italy. Guests get a big kick out of breaking off chunks as they wish. Linda likes to serve it with bowls of fresh fruit compote and sorbet. Fred, of course, prefers the accompaniment to be large dishes of creamy ice cream and fudge sauce.*

12 tablespoons (1½ sticks)
    unsalted butter, softened, plus
    more for the pan

2 tablespoons hazelnut oil (see
    Sources, page 311)

¾ cup superfine sugar

1 cups hazelnuts, toasted, skinned,
    and finely chopped

½ teaspoon kosher salt

½ cup fine yellow cornmeal

Finely grated zest of 1 lemon

2 cups unbleached flour

1 large egg, plus 1 yolk

2 teaspoons vanilla extract

2 tablespoon confectioners' sugar
    for garnish

Preheat the oven to 350°F. Place one rack in the upper third of the oven. Lavishly butter a 14-inch round pizza pan.

Beat the butter and oil in an electric mixer on medium speed until light and fluffy. Scrape the sides and beat in the sugar. Scrape the sides and with the motor on low, beat in the nuts, salt, and cornmeal, lemon zest, and flour. Scrape again and beat in the eggs. The mixture will be crumbly. Then blend in the vanilla.

Turn the dough out into the prepared pan. Distribute the dough evenly over the pan, patting the dough into a 14-inch circle. Bake on the upper rack for 30 minutes, or until the cake is lightly browned and firm when touched lightly in the center.

Transfer the pan to a rack to cool. To serve, carefully slide the cookie onto an attractive platter and shake confectioner's sugar through a fine strainer over it.

MAKES A 14-INCH COOKIE (SERVES 6 TO 8)

Apple Brown Betty with Toasted Hazelnuts

Chopped apples, soft challah bread crumbs, and honey water don't sound like much, but wait until you taste our updated version of a very old dessert. The black walnuts make for an outstanding crunch and burst of flavor that really enhances the apples. This dessert is adapted from a superlative little book, The Airline Honey Cookbook, *published by the A. I. Root Company, Medina, Ohio, in 1915. Filled with charming recipes and honey lore, the book is a treasure trove of simple treats made with honey that the company used to produce. Today A. I. Root is still the major manufacturer of beekeeping supplies in the country.*

2 tablespoons unsalted butter, softened

2 cups good-quality honey

1⅓ cups hot water

8 to 9 cups finely chopped peeled cooking apples

1¾ cups raisins

1 cup coarsely chopped toasted hazelnuts

3½ to 4 cups soft challah bread crumbs (preferably Linda's Challah with Raisins and Hazelnuts, page 90)

3 tablespoons cinnamon sugar

6 tablespoons unsalted butter

1½ cups heavy whipping cream

Preheat the oven to 375°F. Thoroughly butter a deep 3-to-4-quart ovenproof casserole.

In a medium-sized bowl, blend together 1¼ cups of the honey with the hot water and reserve.

Sprinkle a quarter of the apples in the prepared dish, follow with a quarter of the raisins and nuts, then sprinkle with a quarter of the crumbs. Pour a quarter of the honey water evenly over the crumbs. Sprinkle with cinnamon sugar and a bit of butter. Keep layering until dish is full, ending with a layer of crumbs, honey water, butter, and cinnamon sugar.

Cover tightly and bake for 1 hour. Remove it from the oven and let it cool slightly.

Beat the cream until thick, then combine it with the remaining honey. Serve the Brown Betty with this sauce ladled over it.

SERVES 6 TO 10

Blueberry Cobbler with Almonds

Blueberries and almonds make a very pleasing combination. This is one of our most popular deserts, especially when we flavor the topping with some really good quality almond flour and oil. The sprinkling of chopped almonds on top adds a nifty crunch.

1½ cups superfine sugar

Zest from 2 lemons

⅛ teaspoon freshly grated nutmeg

1¾ cups unbleached flour

8 cups fresh blueberries

½ cup almond flour (see Sources, page 311)

2½ teaspoons baking powder

½ teaspoon salt

8 tablespoons unsalted butter, cut into small pieces

1 tablespoon almond oil

1 large egg plus 1 egg yolk, lightly beaten

⅓ cup chopped toasted silvered almonds

2 tablespoons cinnamon and sugar (vanilla sugar or plain sugar)

Vanilla ice cream

Preheat the oven to 375°F.

In a large mixing bowl, combine 1 cup of the sugar, lemon zest, nutmeg, and ¼ cup of the flour. Add the blueberries and toss gently. Pour the mixture into a 3-quart well-buttered baking dish.

In a shallow bowl, combine the remaining ½ cup sugar, 1½ cups flour, almond flour, baking powder, and salt. With your fingers, a pastry blender, or a fork, blend in the butter and almond oil until the mixture looks like coarse cornmeal. Pour the beaten eggs over the pastry mixture and, using a long-tined fork, mix just until it holds together; it will be coarse and lumpy. Distribute this dough evenly over the berries. Sprinkle the cobbler with chopped almonds, then the cinnamon sugar mixture.

Bake for about 1 hour, or until the top is nicely browned and crusty and the berries are bubbling. Transfer to a rack and let cool.

Serve warm with vanilla ice cream.

SERVES 8

Freddie's Famous Phyllo Tart with Apples and Pistachios

This delicious fruit dessert, baked on a large pizza pan, makes a handsome appearance as part of any dessert table. The combination of crisp pastry, meltingly tender apples, and crunchy nuts has made this one of Fred's favorite desserts for years. It is especially wonderful when made in September with a mixture of heirloom apples. It also sure tastes good in the cold winter when made with Granny Smiths. Always one to gild the lily, Fred prefers to see this accompanied by both whipped crème fraîche with honey and homemade cinnamon ice cream. One note about phyllo: It's a lot easier to handle if you keep it in the freezer until the night before you plan to make the tart, then transfer it to the refrigerator.

½ cup raisins

¼ cup Grand Marnier or Cointreau

5 pounds mixed tart apples, peeled, cored, and thinly sliced

½ cup superfine sugar

⅓ cup packed dark-brown sugar

1 teaspoon ground ginger

1 teaspoon ground cinnamon

¼ teaspoon ground cloves

¼ teaspoon freshly grated nutmeg

⅓ cup cornstarch

⅔ cup shelled pistachios, very lightly toasted

1 pound package phyllo dough (defrosted)

2 sticks (½ pound) plus 4 tablespoons unsalted butter, melted

Confectioners' sugar for garnish

Combine the raisins with the Grand Marnier in a small bowl and let them stand while you peel the apples.

In a large bowl, combine the apples, sugars, spices, cornstarch, and nuts. Gently mix until the apples are evenly coated. Add the raisin mixture and blend thoroughly.

Preheat the oven to 350°F.

Butter the surface of a large pizza pan (14 inches in diameter), or a large, rimless cookie sheet. Open the phyllo and cover it with a slightly damp towel to keep it from drying out.

Quickly butter and fold two sheets of phyllo and place them in the center of the pan as a base for the tart.

Keeping a circular shape, but making certain that the center of the pan is always covered by one end of the phyllo sheet, begin to butter and layer the phyllo. Use a broad pastry brush for the buttering. Go clockwise around the pan. Work quickly but don't panic. When there are only 2 sheets left, set them aside, keeping them covered with the towel.

Place the filling in the center of the prepared pan. It looks best if the apples are somewhat mounded in the center. Then quickly, one at a time, bring the phyllo leaves over the top to cover, buttering what had been the underside of the leaves as you flip them up. When the leaves are all in place, generously butter the whole tart. Slice the 2 remaining sheets of phyllo into 1-inch-wide strips, and roll some of these strips into curls and gently tie some into knots. Toss all of these on the top of the tart, pour the remaining butter evenly over the top.

Bake for 1 hour, but check the tart to make certain that it doesn't burn during the last half hour. If it gets too brown, reduce the heat slightly.

Transfer the pan to a cooling rack and let it cool for 10 minutes, then carefully transfer the tart to a rack. When it's cool, dust it with confectioners' sugar.

Serve at room temperature with whipped cream or crème fraîche or ice cream, if desired.

SERVES 12

Fresh Pear and Hazelnut Galette

This combination of pears and hazelnuts with a thin and flaky pastry is a perfect end to a heavy meal. It's just so light and fruity! There's a big thanks here to dear friend and superlative teacher of matters culinary, Lydie Marshall. After celebrating more than a dozen Thanksgivings together, she has dramatically enhanced our comfort in making pâte brisée. There is always a fruit galette on the holiday table.

THE PASTRY

8 tablespoons unsalted butter, cut
    into pieces
1 cup unbleached flour
Pinch of salt
2 to 3 tablespoons ice water,
    depending on the weather

THE FRUIT TOPPING

1/3 cup toasted hazelnuts or pecans
4 tablespoons superfine sugar
2/3 cup warm orange or apricot
    marmalade
5 juicy pears, peeled, cored, and
    cut into 8 wedges each
Freshly grated nutmeg to taste
1 cup sour cream mixed with 3
    tablespoons honey for garnish

To make the pastry: Place the butter in the freezer for 5 minutes.

In the bowl of a food processor, combine the flour, salt, and butter. Process for 10 seconds, then add 2 tablespoons water in humid weather or 3 in dry. Process for another 10 seconds, or until the mixture looks like cornmeal.

Dump the mixture onto a table or counter and bind a small amount at a time with the heel of your hand, using a sliding motion to incorporate the butter and flour smoothly.

Gather the dough into a ball and flatten it. Wrap it in wax paper and refrigerate it for 15 minutes, just long enough to firm up the butter.

Flour a work surface and rolling pin. Roll the dough into a 13- to 14-inch circle, always making sure there is flour under the dough and on the rolling pin; otherwise the dough will stick. Transfer the dough to a large pizza pan, carefully folding the edges over to make about a 1-inch border.

Chill the dough while you prepare the pears.

Preheat the oven to 450°F, with a rack on the bottom shelf of the oven.

To prepare the fruit topping: Combine the nuts and sugar in a food processor and pulse until the nuts are finely chopped. Reserve.

Lightly brush the pastry center with marmalade. Sprinkle with half of the nut mixture. Arrange pears decoratively over the surface, wedges slightly overlapping.

Gently draw the pastry rim slightly over the edge of the pears. Paint the entire surface of the tart with a little more than half of the remaining marmalade. Sprinkle with the remaining nuts. Lightly grate some nutmeg over the top.

Place on the lowest oven rack, immediately reducing the heat to 400°. Bake for 30 minutes, or until the bottom crust is golden (peek by gently lifting tart with a long, narrow spatula.)

Transfer the tart to a cooling rack. Paint with the remaining marmalade.

Serve with a dollop of the sweetened sour cream.

SERVES **8** TO **10**

*"Let us be many sided. Turnips are good,
but they are best mixed with chestnuts and these two
noble products of the earth grow far apart."*

—*Von Goethe in* Prose Maxims.

Pecan Pie Scholars

Was there pecan pie before the invention of commercial corn syrup? Some food historians have said that the pecan pie that most of us knew in our youth never really existed before Karo hit the scene. John Thorne in his book *Outlaw Cook* says that in pecan pie history, "B.C." means "before corn syrup." It was in 1902 that the Corn Products Refining Company of Chicago and New York first produced a syrup from corn and took it to market as Karo (possibly named after Caroline, the wife of the researcher who perfected the product). In advertisements they called it "the great spread for daily bread." But there is no early evidence of its use in pecan pies.

In 1910, Emma Churchman Hewitt produced the first *Karo Cook Book*, with 150 recipes. Pecan pie was not one of them. It wasn't until the early 1930s that a recipe for a Karo pecan pie was published by the wife of a Karo salesman. It called for Karo syrup, sugar, eggs, vanilla, and pecans in a pie shell, and since that time, most recipes for pecan pie followed that formula. That recipe swept the nation.

At the McFarland Lunch in downtown Charleston, West Virginia, fifty years ago, pecan pie was one of the most popular desserts. Myrtle Long was the head cook of the Griffith family's long-running restaurant. (We didn't use the word chef back then.) She literally threw things together; there were no recipe files in her kitchen. She used the same lard-based flaky crust in all of her pies—fruit pies with whatever was in season; mile-high meringue pies with coconut, lemon, or chocolate; simple custard pies; mincemeat pies in the winter; and her pecan pie. We called Fred's mom to get her recollection on Myrtle's pecan pie. "Just Karo syrup and eggs," she said, "and some pecans"—typical of the detail you get when you ask a restaurant person for a recipe. (Actually, we pressed her to refine it a little, and she said "a cup of sugar, a cup of Karo, light or dark, it doesn't matter, and a cup of pecans. And some eggs, of course." How many? "Three or four, and maybe some vanilla if you have any.")

Even before the ready availability of commercial corn syrup, cooks in the South made pies with pecans. Many of the older recipes call for a darker commercial sugar syrup, and some used molasses. A northern variation involved maple syrup. We found one in *The Congressional Club Cook Book,* published in Washington in 1929. Mrs. John Moore, wife of a Kentucky congressman, used no syrup at all in her pecan pie—just milk, sugar, pecans, and eggs. James Beard wrote about nineteenth-century puddings made with pecans that could have been the pie's lineal ancestor. As far back as Roman times, Apicius, while he had no pecan trees available to him, also mentioned nut puddings. Nevertheless, very few recipes showed up in cookbooks until the Karo revolution.

Kathy Herrlich of the Schlesinger Library at Harvard, after checking several cook-books from 1885 to 1903, finally found a pecan pie recipe published in New Orleans in 1900. The book's plastic binding indicates that the Harvard copy was probably a reprint. Still, this is very likely a recipe from that period. It calls for "Louisiana syrup," which Bar-bara Haber, a culinary historian at the Schlesinger, believes was a pre-Karo version of corn syrup.

Edgar Rose is a food lover and retired nautical engineer whose work building ocean-going yachts took him to all kinds of places. His travel fired his passion for food, and he is now a noted collector of rare food books and not a bad cook. And one of his greatest passions is for pecan pie. Like John Thorne, he fears a lack of character in a pie made with corn syrup.

He believes that there were versions of pecan pie, B.C., but he does not know of any recipe in a cookbook.

When Rose cooked and tested, he did it like an engineer. He would bring two dif-ferent versions of pecan pie to work and serve both to ten or more people. For their treat they had to fill out a questionnaire, commenting on the texture of the filling, the nuts used, the crust, etc. Then he would make a second try with two more pies, addressing the short-comings that his coworkers noted. (Too sweet. Not sweet enough. The molasses over-powers the pecans, etc.)

He found that there were two basic groups: those who loved the sweet and sweeter vs. those who thought the pies were way too sweet. It turns out that the four tasters who always wanted a sweeter pie were from south of the Mason–Dixon line. "If it isn't so sweet that it hurts the fillings in your teeth," said one, "then it isn't sweet enough." This process ultimately led to "the best possible pecan pie." No Karo. Just eggs, butter, brown sugar, salt, vanilla, rum, and pecans.

We give you here, three pecan pies—one by Edgar Rose, another from John Thorne with the dark sugar and Lyle's Golden Syrup, and Leona Griffith's ad-lib recipe that is typical of the Karo syrup pies that were America's standard for half a century.

Edgar's Pecan Pie

9-inch pie crust, fully prebaked
4 tablespoons unsalted butter
4 extra-large eggs
1 pinch salt
1 teaspoon vanilla extract

1 teaspoon dark rum
1½ cups light-brown sugar
1¼ cups chopped pecans
Whipping cream, whipped and
 flavored to taste

Preheat the oven to 350°F.

Melt the butter. Beat the eggs in a mixing bowl with a fork until uniform in color. Add the salt, vanilla, and rum. Mix. Add the sugar gradually while mixing. Add the melted butter and mix.

Spread three-quarters of the nuts on the bottom of the crust. Pour the filling into the crust and sprinkle on the remaining nuts. Bake at 350°F for 20 minutes. Reduce the heat to 250°F and bake until the center of the filling has just barely stopped jiggling when you shake the pie pan.

Serve with slightly sweetened, slightly vanilla-flavored whipped cream.

Note: If you like your pecan pie very sweet, increase sugar to 2 cups.

"My Pecan Pie" from John Thorne

1 well-packed cup full-flavored
 brown sugar
Scant ⅔ cup Lyle's Golden Syrup
 (see Sources, page 313)
2 tablespoons Myers's dark rum
4 tablespoons unsalted butter

3 eggs
¼ teaspoon salt
2 cups broken pecan meats
9-inch unbaked pie shell
Whipped cream

Preheat the oven to 350°F.

In a large saucepan, heat the brown sugar, Lyle's Golden Syrup, rum, and butter to the boiling point. Stirring constantly and scraping back any foam that clings to the side of the pan, let this mixture boil for about 1 minute. Remove it from the heat and let it cool while, in a separate bowl, beat the eggs until creamy.

When the boiled syrup has cooled, beat in the eggs, salt, and pecan meats. Pour the mixture into the 9-inch unbaked pie shell. Bake for about 50 minutes, or until a skewer inserted into the center of the pie comes out clean.

Cool the pie on a rack. Serve at room temperature with plenty of unsweetened whipped cream.

Leona's Pecan Pie

1 cup Karo syrup (can be either
    light or dark)
1 cup granulated sugar
3 or 4 eggs

1 cup pecans, broken
Pinch of salt
A little vanilla extract
9-inch unbaked pie shell

Preheat the oven to 350°F.

Mix the syrup and the sugar in a saucepan. Heat until the sugar has dissolved. Let it cool.

Beat the eggs until smooth. Add them to the cooled sugar and syrup and mix. Add the pecans, salt, and vanilla and mix. Pour into a 9-inch unbaked pie shell. Bake for about 45 minutes or until the pie is firm in the center.

Leona didn't mention it, but here, too, whipped cream could enhance the experience. Some may want to use their own pie crust recipe, but just in case, we offer an excellent and versatile one under Basics (see page 51).

McFarland Lunch Coconut Cream Pie

Linda happens to have a real weakness for coconut cream pie. Unfortunately, she never had a chance to taste the ones made by Myrtle Long, a cook in Fred's dad's Charleston, West Virginia, restaurant. Fred has always described them, calling them "mile-high" because of their fabulous meringues! We've experimented with many fillings, but have come to prefer the flavor of this particular recipe. Virtually all recipes for cream pies call for cooking the filling even after the custard thickens, and thanks to the doyen of such things, Shirley Corriher, author of the much-acclaimed book CookWise, *we now know why. It is to kill certain enzymes in yolks that could cause the filling to thin as the pie cooled. That our not-quite-mile-high meringues no longer weep is also because of Shirley's brilliant book.*

1 cup granulated sugar
3 tablespoons unbleached flour
1/3 cup cornstarch
1/4 teaspoon Kosher salt
5 eggs, separated, yolks beaten
3/4 cup whole milk
3 cups canned coconut milk (not
    Lite)
2/3 cup heavy cream

1 cup sweetened flaked coconut
3 tablespoons unsalted butter
1 1/2 teaspoons pure vanilla extract
1 baked 10-inch pastry shell (see
    Basics page 51)
6 egg whites
1/2 teaspoon of cream of tartar
3/4 cup superfine sugar

Preheat the oven to 400°F.

Combine the sugar, flour, cornstarch, and salt in a heavy-bottomed saucepan. Whisk to blend well.

In a medium-sized bowl, beat the egg yolks, then whisk in whole milk, coconut milk, and heavy cream. Whisk the egg mixture into the dry ingredients in the saucepan. Whisk vigorously to eliminate any lumps.

Cook over medium heat for 5 minutes, whisking occasionally. Then, cook for another 7 minutes, stirring constantly (use a whisk occasionally to eliminate any lumps). The mixture will become very thick. When it reaches a boil, you will see big bubbles slowly coming up to the surface between stirs. Once you see those bubbles, stir constantly for another minute.

Remove the saucepan from the heat. Stir in ¾ cup of the coconut, the butter, and 1 teaspoon of the vanilla. Stir until the butter has melted.

Pour the mixture into the pie shell and immediately make the meringue. In a clean mixing bowl, combine the 6 egg whites. Beat until frothy, then add the cream of tartar. Continue beating until the egg whites form soft peaks. With the motor on high, add the superfine sugar, 1 tablespoon at a time. When meringue is very stiff and shiny, beat in the remaining ½ teaspoon vanilla.

Spread at least a third of the meringue evenly over the entire pie, making certain it covers the edges well. (It will be difficult to do this, just be patient.) Then add the remaining meringue, and mound it attractively. Sprinkle with the remaining ¼ cup coconut. Bake in hot oven until very well browned, 10 to 15 minutes.

Cool on a rack, then refrigerate until serving time.

MAKES A **10-INCH PIE**

Chocolate Black Walnut Pie

Lucky is the forager who has a pet black walnut tree. West Virginia has historically been a region rich in foraged treasures. While best known for the ramps, or wild leeks, found in most Appalachian forests, the black walnut tree is also highly prized. Many years ago Black Walnut Cookery, *a little jewel of a pamphlet, was compiled by the Little Kanawha (pronounced ka-NAW-uh) Council and published by the West Virginia Department of Agriculture. We were especially intrigued by a pie recipe from Mrs. W. B. Parrish of Spencer that is the inspiration for this pie.*

4½ ounces unsweetened
chocolate, finely chopped
6 tablespoons unsalted butter

2½ cups plus 5 tablespoons
superfine sugar
6 large eggs

⅔ cup unbleached flour

Pinch kosher salt

2 teaspoons fresh lemon
juice

1½ cups lightly toasted black
walnuts, chopped into small
pieces

10-inch unbaked pie shell (see
Basics, page 51)

2 cups heavy (not ultrapasteurized)
cream

5 tablespoons sour cream

⅓ cup finely chopped black
walnuts for garnish

Preheat the oven to 375°F.

In a large, heavy-bottomed saucepan, melt the chocolate and butter over low heat. Remove from the heat and beat in 2½ cups of the sugar. One at a time, vigorously whisk in the eggs.

Whisk in the flour, salt, and lemon juice. Blend in the nuts and pour into the prepared pie shell. Bake for 35 to 40 minutes, or until the filling is firm to the touch. Transfer to a cooling rack. Then chill in the refrigerator until just before serving.

To serve, combine the creams in the bowl of an electric mixer. Add the remaining sugar and beat until the mixture holds soft peaks. Spoon over the pie in an attractive fashion. Sprinkle with finely chopped nuts and serve.

SERVES 6 TO 10

Dutch Letters: Flaky Almond Pastries

Pella, Iowa, was founded by Dutch immigrants in 1847. In the town square, there is still a beautiful windmill that celebrates the town's history. In springtime it is surrounded by tulips. These scrumptious pastries used to be part of every household's holiday preparations. When we visited Pella back in the late 1980s there was only one bakery still making them. Thanks to the then manager of the Strawtown Inn, Roger Olson, we left with not only the recipe but also with a large box filled with these delightful treats.

1 pound unsalted butter, softened,
plus extra for greasing cookie
sheets

4 cups unbleached flour

1 cup water

1 pound almond paste

2 cups superfine sugar, plus more if
needed

3 eggs

1 teaspoon vanilla extract

2 egg whites, beaten

In the bowl of an electric mixer fitted with a paddle, cream the butter, scraping the sides several times. Gradually add the flour, then the water. Scrape the sides and, using your fingers, gather the dough into a ball. Wrap it in plastic and chill overnight.

Scrape the almond paste into the mixing bowl. On medium speed, beat until the paste is smooth. Scraping the sides several times, gradually beat in the sugar, then the eggs one at a time. Finally, beat in the vanilla. Cover this and chill for several hours.

Preheat oven to 400°F. Butter several cookie sheets.

Divide the dough into 14 equal portions. Also divide the filling into 14 portions (about 3 tablespoons each). (Use a kitchen scale for best results.)

On a lightly floured surface, roll each dough portion into a 14×4-inch strip. Spread a portion of the filling down the center of the dough strip. Fold one 14-inch side of dough over the filling, then fold the other side. Pinch the ends together.

Place the roll on the buttered sheet with seam-side down. Repeat with the remaining portions. You can probably place 3 rolls on each sheet, possibly 4.

Brush the tops of the rolls with the beaten egg whites and sprinkle with more sugar. Prick them with a fork every 2 inches so that steam can escape. Bake in the preheated oven for about 30 minutes, or until golden.

Gently transfer the pastry rolls to cooling racks, then cut into sections at the perforation marks.

MAKES 6 TO 8 DOZEN

Margaret Wine's Simple Strudel

She is our good friend Sanford Herskovitz's mother, and all of us who have had the privilege of knowing her are much the richer. No matter how bad her arthritis is, she manages to create endless platters of exquisite pastries for every occasion. Born in what was a part of Rumania and is now Hungary, Mrs. Wine came to this country as a young woman, with the world about to go up in flames. With courage and determination she has lived her life as a model for all of us, and when things are particularly tough, she bakes and bakes. We have tried to stay true to all of the recipes she has generously taught us; because we do not keep kosher, the only significant change we have made is to replace the margarine with unsalted butter. We have also measured the filling ingredients!

¾ cup orange juice, boiling hot
3 tablespoons superfine sugar
1 package dry yeast (1 scant
    tablespoon)
3½ cups unbleached flour

2 sticks (1 cup) unsalted butter,
    melted
3 egg yolks
2 tablespoons unsalted butter,
    softened

2 cups cherry preserves or
   raspberry jam
2 (20-ounce) cans crushed
   pineapple, thoroughly drained
2 cups raisins

1½ cups coarsely chopped pecans
   or walnuts (or 1 cup finely
   chopped)
¼ cup confectioners' sugar

Combine the juice and sugar in a small bowl, and stir until the sugar is dissolved. When it's cool enough, add the yeast. Blend thoroughly and let it bubble in a warm place.

In a large mixing bowl, mix the flour and butter. Add the egg yolks and the yeast mixture. Blend thoroughly. If too sticky, add more flour 1 tablespoon at a time.

Divide the dough into 6 balls, lightly flour, and wrap them well in plastic. Chill in the refrigerator overnight. Remove them from the refrigerator 1 hour before preparing.

Preheat the oven to 350°F. If you have 2 ovens, preheat them both. Lavishly butter 2 large shallow-sided baking sheets.

As you roll each ball, keep the board and rolling pin well floured, but as you roll this dough, be sure to turn it frequently and gently brush off any excess flour. Each piece should be rolled as a long rectangle, 16 inches by 8 inches. Have the long side parallel to you. Each should be quite thin.

Smear with one-sixth of the preserves, spreading them within an inch of the long sides. Then spoon one-sixth of the pineapple down the center, one-sixth of the raisins and one-sixth of the nuts over the pineapple. Lift the long end closest to you over the pineapple, then gently, but tightly, make a firm roll away from you. Place on a large baking sheet, then score on an angle, making each about 1¼ inches wide. Repeat until all the rolls are made.

Bake for 40 minutes, or until golden. Remove them from the oven and let them partially cool. Cut them into pieces while they are still warm. Transfer the pieces to a cooling rack, however. Sprinkle with confectioners' sugar when serving.

MAKES 5 DOZEN

Marzipan Madness

Wanna fight? Tell us who invented marzipan.

For a long time, confectioners in the North German city of Lübeck argued that this great paste of ground almonds and sugar was first made there during a famine in 1407. Some historians say the famine was not in Lübeck, but in Venice, and it was that city's cooks who pioneered new uses for almonds, grinding them to make a substitute for bread. Today, marzipan makers in Lübeck no longer make that claim. Records show that almonds were brought there from Italy as early as the thirteenth century and that by the sixteenth century they started working on creative ways to use them.

Somehow, what they made back then came to be known as a curative, and it could only be made and distributed by pharmacists. Sugar was enormously expensive and almonds were not much cheaper. The result was that pharmaceutical marzipan was only used by the well-to-do. It wasn't until the end of the eighteenth century, when cheap beet sugar came into the marketplace, that marzipan was industrialized and it became available to the ordinary person.

In 1845 Charlotte Erasmi started a company called Carstens Lübecker Marzipan, which still exists today. That company admits that marzipan was made elsewhere first. German law requires that the paste be 50 percent almonds and 50 percent sugar, but the tradition in Lübeck is to use a 70/30 mix and the finest, called Edelmarzipan is 90 percent almonds and only 10 percent sugar. It is great marzipan that confectioners color and shape into fruits and flowers.

Now, how about another scenario? Mary Taylor Simeti, who writes about the food of Sicily, makes the case that it was the Arabs who brought both almonds and sugar there, probably as early as the ninth century. Sicilians learned early how to combine the two into a commodity that was both exported in trade and used widely at home, often modeled into pastry decorations. It was often called "pasta reale." Some say the Arabs first took their culinary secrets to Spain and Portugal, and then to Sicily.

Others argue that almonds and sugar were both available in the Middle East, and that cooks there had very early made a paste of it and served it "at the sultan's table." Still others say that it was made as a snack for the women of the harem, sweets to the sweet ladies of the ruler.

The *Larousse Gastronomique*, which usually has the answer to every conceivable food question, blows off marzipan. "Marzipan is of very ancient order," it tells us. "It would seem that, as with most little cakes and sweets, it was made originally by some order of nuns." The writer Balzac agreed, and he was sure that they were French nuns.

There is some archeological evidence that marzipan, or something similar, was made four thousand years ago. Whenever it was first made, it was almost certainly the world's first candy.

The word marzipan, itself, is a mystery. No one really knows where it came from or what it originally meant. The *Oxford English Dictionary* in a two-page entry documents the confusion. Perhaps marzipan came from "mazaban" or "mahsaban," an Arab word for the small wooden box the sweet was sometimes stored in. Maybe it is from "Marci panis," or St. Mark's bread, dating from the time of the hypothetical Lübeck famine. The OED makes the strongest case for a connection with Martaban, the name of a Burmese port where glazed jars for the shipment of expensive and quality foods were made. The jars were called martabans after the town. The almond-sugar paste was often packed in them, and maybe someone mispronounced it marzipan.

Marzipan

There are dozens of ways to make marzipan. The traditional recipe in Simeti's book calls for equal amounts of sugar and ground almonds. She calls for a teaspoon of almond extract, made from bitter almonds, to give it its kick. Another we found calls for a two-to-one ratio of almond to sugar and specifies that for every 100 regular almonds there must be one bitter almond to provide that desired edgy taste. Most of the quality German marzipans call for an even larger proportion of almonds with some rosewater. Yet others call for egg whites or even whole eggs to provide the necessary moisture.

Here is a basic marzipan recipe with a two-to-one almond-sugar ratio that has worked well for us.

2 cups blanched almonds	1 teaspoon almond extract
1 cup superfine sugar	1 teaspoon pure vanilla extract
2 egg whites	Rosewater

In a food processor, pulverize the almonds until they are like a paste. Add the sugar, egg whites, almond extract, vanilla extract, and pulse until they form a ball. If it is too stiff to work, add a few drops of rosewater (or water if you don't have any). Sprinkle a work surface with powdered sugar and knead it until it is the consistency of a dense pie pastry. Save in the refrigerator, wrapped in plastic or foil, until you are ready to use it. The paste can be dyed with food color and then formed into decorations for pastries.

Mexican Wedding Cookies

These very buttery cookies, loaded with chopped pecans, get their name from a cookie description Linda read in the El Paso Chile Company catalogue. She decided to attach the name to this recipe—a cookie she has made for at least forty years that only bore the name "Butter Cookie with Pecans." There is one modification to that recipe, however. We use an outstanding organic Mexican vanilla bean from Zingerman's Deli in Ann Arbor, Michigan (see Sources, page 313).

½ pound unsalted butter, softened
1 cup superfine sugar
Scraped beans from 1 vanilla pod
1 teaspoon vanilla extract
1 egg yolk
2 cups unbleached flour, sifted

1 cup finely chopped toasted
  pecans
1 egg white, beaten
½ cup confectioners' sugar, plus
  more if needed

Preheat the oven to 250°F.

Cream together the butter and sugar. Scrape the bowl and blend in the vanilla, vanilla extract, and egg yolk. Add the flour and ½ cup of the nuts. Blend thoroughly.

Spread the mixture on a large cookie sheet 12×14 inches, and press to spread evenly to about ¼ inch thick. Brush with egg white and sprinkle evenly with the remaining nuts. Bake for 1 hour, or until the top is lightly browned and pastry is firm to the touch.

Remove from the oven and cut into strips that are 1½ inches wide. Cut crosswise, or on an angle, so that the cookies are 2½ to 3 inches long. Transfer to a rack to cool.

Using a strainer, dust generously with sugar. Then store in an airtight container.

MAKES **4** TO **5** DOZEN

Grandma's Thimble Cookies with Pecan Meal

These buttery cookies go back to Linda's childhood when her Grandmother Weller would have a container of these waiting for her visit. Linda uses pecans because that's how Grandma made them, but you can really use any nut you have on hand.

½ pound unsalted butter, softened
¾ cup superfine sugar
3 egg yolks
Pinch salt

2½ cups unbleached flour
⅓ cup raspberry or cherry jam
¼ cup finely ground pecans

Combine the butter, ½ cup of the sugar, the egg yolks, salt, and flour in a mixing bowl. Using your fingers, lightly mix the ingredients until well combined.

Preheat the oven to 325°F.

Form balls of cookie dough the size of quarters. Place them on nonstick cookie sheets about 2 inches apart. Using a thimble, or the handle end of a wooden spoon, make an indentation in the center of each cookie. Carefully fill this with some of the jam. Sprinkle the cookies with ground nuts.

Bake in the preheated oven until golden, 15 to 20 minutes. Remove the cookies from the sheets and let them cool on racks.

MAKES ABOUT 3½ DOZEN

Kourabiethes: Greek Almond Shortbread

Many countries have a version of this, a much-loved, melt-on-your-tongue, powdered sugar–covered shortbread cookie made with lightly toasted ground almonds. Even among the Greeks there are many variations: some include whiskey, some not; there are eggs in some, not in others, and baking powder is included by some cooks but most eschew it, just as some put a whole clove in the center, while others may include some fragrant rosewater in the dough or sprinkled over them when fresh out of the oven. Be careful with these. It is very difficult to stop after eating only one or even after four!

3½ cups cake flour, plus more if
   needed
1 teaspoon baking powder
1 pound unsalted butter, at room
   temperature
¾ cup confectioners' sugar, plus
   more for use after baking

2 egg yolks
¼ cup whiskey
2 teaspoons vanilla extract
1 cup lightly toasted ground
   almonds
2 to 3 tablespoons rosewater
   (optional)

Preheat the oven to 350°F.

Sift 2 cups of the flour and baking powder into a small bowl and set aside.

Cream the butter in the bowl of a cake mixer using a paddle. Beat until the butter is lightly and fluffy, about 5 minutes. Slowly add the sugar, scraping the sides several times. Add the yolks, whiskey, and vanilla. Beat for another 3 to 4 minutes. With the motor on low, gradually add the sifted flour to the butter mixture. Beat until thoroughly blended. Add the nuts and beat again, scraping the sides several times. Gradually add the remaining (unsifted) flour until the dough is soft but not sticky.

Turn the dough out on your work surface lightly dusted with cake flour. Knead for a minute or two. This dough should be very soft and silky and not stick to your hands. Pinch off about a walnut-size amount of dough and form into a small ball or crescent. Place on an ungreased, heavy-gauge cookie sheet and space all about 1 inch apart.

Bake until the tops are light sand colored and firm to the touch, 15 to 20 minutes. (If you are in doubt about doneness, break one in half to make certain that they are baked in the center.) When the cookies are done, transfer them to a cooling rack.

While the cookies are cooling, sprinkle an even layer of confectioners' sugar over a shallow platter or baking pan. After the cookies have cooled for 10 minutes, place them directly on the sugar. Spoon more sugar over the tops and sides, or fill a strainer with sugar and shake it evenly over the cookies. Place them back on the cooling rack until cold. Store in a large tin with a tight-fitting top.

Sprinkle generously with more sugar before serving.

MAKES 5 DOZEN

Hazelnut Biscotti

When one is lucky enough to have number 14 or 15 hazelnuts from Piedmont, this is the way to feature them. (These are the largest and the finest quality you can find.) However, you can still enjoy these with any other fresh, toasted hazelnuts as well. By the way, in early fall, try Esperya, the on-line source (www.esperya.com). We've been able to get the great Piedmontese nuts from them.

5 large eggs

3 cups unbleached flour

1 cup hazelnut flour

2 teaspoon baking powder

1 teaspoon salt

1⅔ cups superfine sugar

½ cup hazelnut oil (see Sources, page 311)

1 tablespoon Fra Angelica liqueur

1¾ cups toasted, coarsely chopped hazelnuts

Preheat the oven to 375°F.

Beat the eggs in a small bowl. Remove 1 tablespoon of the beaten eggs and put it into a small dish with 1 teaspoon water. Reserve both.

Combine the flours, baking powder, salt, and sugar into the bowl of an electric mixer fitted with a paddle. With the motor running, add first the large bowl of beaten eggs, then the oil and liqueur. Beat thoroughly.

If the dough is too sticky add more flour, 1 tablespoon at a time. Then add the nuts and blend thoroughly as well.

Butter two shallow-sided baking sheets.

Divide the dough into 3 pieces and shape each piece into logs that are about 7¾ inches by 3 inches by 1 inch high. Place the logs about 2 inches apart on the prepared baking sheet. Beat the reserved egg wash and brush it over the logs. Bake for 40 to 50 minutes, or until golden and fairly firm.

Remove the baking sheet from the oven. Let the logs cool for 15 minutes, slide them onto a cutting board. Using a very sharp knife, cut them—if you wish, on a diagonal—into ½-inch- to ¾-inch-thick slices. Arrange the slices on the baking sheets.

Bake for 10 to 12 minutes, or until golden on both sides. Transfer to wire racks to cool. Store in tightly covered tins.

MAKES 3 TO 4 DOZEN

Roberta's Nut Bars

Our friend and adviser on all things relating to herbs and esoteric culinary matters, Roberta Sunkle, brought us one of these bars and the recipe for Christmas. It was rich with nuts and fruits and absolutely delicious. It is an old recipe from a church in Kylertown, Pennsylvania, and the church still prepares vast quantities to sell as a holiday time fundraiser. Your friends will love it so much, you could even set a high price for the recipe! Just make sure to send the proceeds to Kylertown.

1½ cups unbleached flour
1½ cups superfine sugar
1 teaspoon baking powder
1 teaspoon kosher salt
5 large eggs
1 teaspoon pure vanilla extract

2 pounds pitted dates
1 pound shelled walnuts
½ pound shelled Brazil nuts
1 jar (10 ounces) maraschino
   cherries, drained and stemmed

Preheat the oven to 325°F. Fill a large pan with hot water and place it on the lower shelf while you prepare the bars. Oil a 9×13-inch pan and line it with parchment. Oil the parchment, too.

In a large mixing bowl, sift together the flour, sugar, and baking powder. Add the salt.

In a small bowl, beat together the eggs and vanilla. Set aside.

To the flour mixture add the dates, nuts, and cherries. Stir thoroughly to evenly coat the fruits and nuts with it. Then stir in the vanilla mixture. Again, make certain everything is coated.

Spoon the nut mixture into the prepared pan and spread evenly. Bake on a rack above the water pan for 1 hour 15 minutes. The nut bar mixture will be browned and fairly firm.

Transfer to a cooling rack and let cool for 15 minutes. Carefully transfer the cake from the pan to a cutting board. Using a large, sharp knife, cut it into 8 bars that are 9 inches long. Transfer the bars to a cooling rack and continue to cool.

When the bars are cold, wrap them in double layers of aluminum foil. Serve in thin slices.

MAKES **8** BARS

An old nut riddle: "First I am frosted, then I am beaten,
then I am roasted, then I am eaten.
What am I? A chestnut."

Pralines

The late Jamie Shannon in his book *Commander's Kitchen* says, "Walk through the French Quarter . . . and every so often you'll pass a doorway from which wafts the aroma of burnt sugar or molasses—not a bitter smell, but a sweet, intoxicating one. It can mean only one thing: pralines." Jamie cautions us that the word is PRAW-leens, and in his view they shouldn't be chewy or made with chocolate. His recipe: cup of sugar, cup of heavy cream, cup of pecans, and he adds a little orange zest.

It seems that every cook in the South had a personal version of this remarkable candy. Purists say it is just sugar and pecans. For example, in 1903, Celestine Eustis's book on Creole cooking calls for two cups of brown sugar, half a cup of water, and a cup of pecans. Diane Spivey, writing about the global migration of African cuisine, sings the praises of a much more complicated praline. Her version has butter, cream, white sugar, brown sugar, chocolate chips, vanilla, and, of course, pecans. Food historian John Edge favors a recipe with a helping of corn syrup. In Austin, Texas, the famous Lammes candy company makes chewy pralines with caramel, using a 108-year-old recipe. Another delicious version comes from our friend Nancy McAfee, who got it from her husband's Texas grandmother. (Yes, Georgia, they have pecans there, too. And yes, New Orleans, Texans know pralines.) She also uses Karo, plus a little salt, baking soda, butter, rum, and bourbon, along with the sugar and nuts.

In the old Picayune cookbook, the people who gathered the traditional Creole recipes at the beginning of the last century defined the praline more broadly as "a distinctive Creole sugar cake made of cocoanut and sugar or pecans and sugar." Sometimes the "cocoanut" pralines would be given a rose color with the addition of red food colorings like cochineal (made of dried insects!) or carmine. The children of the neighborhood were as fond of the white or pink coconut pralines as they were of the darker pecan version. So old-time pralines were either made of white sugar and shredded coconut or brown sugar and pecans. Confectioners sometimes used almonds or peanuts instead of pecans. And there was another version called La Colle, which was a molasses praline—just molasses and pecans.

Texts Pralines

This delicious Texas version comes from Nancy McAfee.

2 cups granulated sugar

¼ cup light Karo syrup

½ cup milk

¼ teaspoon salt

¼ teaspoon baking soda

4 tablespoons unsalted butter

1 tablespoon bourbon

1 tablespoon rum

2 cups pecans, broken slightly

Prepare a large work area by spreading some newspaper and covering them with wax paper. Reserve several places where you can put the saucepan down right there.

In a 3-quart saucepan, preferably one with a heatproof handle, combine the sugar, Karo syrup, milk, salt, baking soda, and butter. Bring to a boil over medium-high heat, reduce to medium-low or low, and cook, bubbling, until the mixture reaches soft-ball stage (240°F) on a candy thermometer, 20 to 25 minutes.

Remove the saucepan from the heat and quickly add the bourbon, rum, and pecans. Beat with a wooden spoon until it loses its shine, 2 to 3 minutes. Working very quickly, drop the mixture by spoonfuls onto the wax paper. We use a spoon that is not quite a tablespoon if leveled, but we overfill it somewhat. If the mixture gets too hard, stir it over the heat until it softens and then continue making the pralines.

When the pralines are cold, lift them carefully and place them on layers of wax paper or parchment in a large airtight container. Make certain you have set aside a few for yourself.

MAKES ABOUT 2 DOZEN

"Make the world better; eat more nuts."

—*A roadside sign in California.*

sources

GENERAL INFORMATION

American Chestnut Foundation
469 Main Street
Bennington, VT 05201
http://chestnut.acf.org
Tax-exempt foundation dedicated to restoration
of the American chestnut

Walnut Council
4545 Northwestern Drive
Zionsville, IN 46077
317-873-8780
www.walnutcouncil.org
Organization dedicated to preservation and
restoration of the black walnut; publishes
Walnut Council Bulletin

The Cracker
International Tree Nut Council
Boule, 2, E-43201
Reus, Spain
34-977 331 416
http://inc.treenuts.org
Trade journal for the ITNC

www.lindaandfredgriffith.com

**NUTS, NUT FLOURS, NUT CANDIES,
NUT OILS**

American Spoon Foods
1668 Clarion Avenue
Petoskey, MI 49770
888-735 6700
www.spoon.com
Hardwood North American tree nuts, and other
wild foods; on-line shop

California Press
6200 Washington Street
Yountville, CA 94599
707-944-0303
www.californiapress.com
Nut oils and flours: filbert (hazelnut), pistachio,
pecan, almond, and walnut

Corti Bros.
5810 Folsom Blvd.
Sacramento, CA 95819-4610
800-509-3663
Sheller almonds, Relange torrone, Spanish
paprika, Piment d'Espelette, and many other
nuts

Empire Chestnut Company (Greg Miller)
3276 Empire Road SW
Carrollton, OH 44615-9515
330-627-3181
www.empirechestnut.com
Fresh chestnuts, peeled chestnuts, dried
chestnuts, and chestnut flour

Easterlin Pecan Company
Highway 49N
Fort Valley, GA 31030
478-825-7731
Pecans and pecan products

Hammons Products
105 Hammons Drive
P.O. Box 140
Stockton, MO 65785
888-4bwnuts
www.black-walnuts.com
Black walnuts, and heavy nutcrackers

Hillson's Nut Company
3225 West 71st Street
Cleveland, OH 44102-0038
1-800-333-2818
nuts@hillsonnut.com
All kinds of nuts

King Nut Company
30725 Aurora Road
Solon, OH 44139
800-860-5464
www.kingnut.com
All kinds of nuts, wholesale and retail

Krema Nut Company
1000 West Goodale Boulevard
Columbus, OH 43212
800-222-4132
www.krema.com
Peanut, almond, and cashew butters, nuts, and
nut candies

Lagier Ranches
16101 S. Murphy Rd.
Escalon, CA 95320
1-888-353-5618
www.LagierRanches.com
Flavored and roasted almonds, organic almond
butter, spreadable organically grown fruit

The Lee Bros.
P.O. Box 315
Charleston, SC 29402
843-720-8890
www.boiledpeanuts.com
Boiled peanuts and other peanut products

Liston Pine Nuts
909 East 900 South
Orem, UT 84097
www.pinenuts.net
Collector and marketer of pine nuts

Peterson Nut Company
6133 Rockside Road
Independence, OH 44131
888-817-6887
www.fornuts.com
All kinds of nuts, wholesale and retail

Santa Barbara Pistachio Company
P.O. Box 21957
Santa Barbara, CA 93121
800-896-1044
www.santabarbarapistachios.com
Pistachios, including green, immature
pistachios

Savannah Candy Kitchen
225 East River Street
Savannah, GA 31401-1220
1-800-443-7884
www.savannahcandy.com
Pecans and pecan candy

Sunnyland Farms
Albany, GA 31706-8200
912-436 5654 or 1-800-999-2488
www.sunnylandfarms.com
Pecans and pecan products

MISCELLANEOUS NUT PRODUCTS

Laral Products
42050 Holden Creek Lane
Springfield, OR 97478-8656
541-896-0862
Source for the MacCrack Nutcracker

M. E. Heuck Company
P.O. Box 23036
Cincinnati, OH 45223
1-800-359-3200
Source for the Quackenbush nut set

Nut of the Month Club
P.O. Box 1028
Tualatin, OR 97062
1-888-NUT CLUB
nuts@nutclub.com

CHEESES, OTHER SPECIAL INGREDIENTS

Zingerman's Deli
620 Phoenix Drive
Ann Arbor, MI 48108
1-888-636-8162
www.zingermans.com
Artisanal cheeses, Spanish paprika, Marino's
organic stone-ground polenta from Piedmont,
other specialty items, too

Dean and DeLuca
560 Broadway
New York, NY 10012
800-221-7714
www.deandeluca.com
Wide range of artisanal food products used in
this book, including Spanish paprika

Esperya
1715 West Farms Road
Bronx, NY 10460
877-907-2525
www.esperya.com
Artisanal Italian products including hazelnuts
from Piedmont

Murray's Cheese Shop
257 Bleecker Street
New York, NY 10014
888-692-4339
info@murrayscheese.com
www.murrayscheese.com
Piedmontese and other artisanal cheeses

West Point Market
1711 West Market Street
Akron, OH 44313
800-838-2156
www.westpointmarket.com
Specialty foods including Lyle's syrup

Lowell Farms
El Campo, TX 77437
1-888-484-9213
lowellfm@swbell.net
Jasmine rice

MEATS AND POULTRY

Mr. Brisket
2156 South Taylor Road
Cleveland Heights, OH 44118
877-274-7538
www.misterbrisket.com
misterbrisket@earthlink.net
Prime beef, veal, lamb, pork and totally
sensational poultry

Jamison Farm
171 Jamison Lane
Latrobe, PA 15650
800-237-5262
www.jamisonfarm.com
sukey@jamisonfarm.com
French-style lamb products

S. Wallace Edwards and Sons
P.O. Box 25
Surry, VA 23883
1-800-222-4267
www.virginiatraditions.com
Smoked hams, bacon

SPECIALTY GARLIC, EXCEPTIONAL SHALLOTS

Bobba-Mike's Garlic Farm
P.O. Box 261
Orrville, OH 44667
www.garlicfarm.com
Garlic and shallots

Filaree Farms
182 Conconully Highway
Okanogan, WA 98840
509-422-6940
filaree@northcascades.net
Both seed and culinary garlic

Robison Ranch
P.O. Box 1018
Walla Walla, WA 99362
509-525-6589
robisonr@wwics.com
www.robisonranchfoods.com
Walla Walla sweet onions, jumbo shallots

bibliography

Almond Production Manual. Oakland: University of California, Division of Agriculture and Natural Resources, 1996.

Anderson, Jean. *Jean Anderson Cooks*. New York: William Morrow & Company, Inc., 1982.

———. *The Food of Portugal*. New York: William Morrow & Company, Inc., 1986.

Anderson, Jean, and Deskins Barbara. *The Nutrition Bible*. New York: William Morrow & Company, 1995.

Baker, H. G. "Comments on the thesis that there was a major centre of plant domestication near the headwaters of the River Niger," *Journal of African History*, III, 2. Cambridge, 1962.

Beard, James. *James Beard's American Cookery*. Boston: Little Brown & Company, 1972.

Bianchini, Francesco, and Corbetta, Francesco. *The Fruits of the Earth*. London: Bloomsbury Books, 1973.

Bitting, Katherine Golden. *Gastronomic Bibliography*. San Francisco: 1939. (Limited edition facsimile. Mansfield, Connecticut: Maurizio Martino Publisher.)

Bhagwandin, Annie. *The Chestnut Cook Book*. Onlaska, Washington: Shady Grove Publications, 1996.

Blake, Anthony. "The Cooking Chemist; The Chemistry of Good Taste," *The Chemical Intelligencer*. New York: Springer-Verlag New York, Inc., 1995.

Bridge, Fred, and Tibbetts, Jean F. *The Well-Tooled Kitchen*. New York: William Morrow & Company, Inc., 1991.

Brothwell, Don and Patricia. *Food in Antiquity: A Survey of the Diet of Early Peoples*. New York: Frederick A. Praeger, 1969.

Brown, Theresa C. *Modern Domestic Cookery: A Collection of Receipts Suitable for All Classes of Housewives.* Charleston, South Carolina: Edward Perry, 1871. (Facsimile. Williamston, South Carolina: The Journal, 1985.)

Bryan, Lettice. *The Kentucky Housewife.* Cincinnati, Ohio; Shepard & Stearn, 1839. (Facsimile. Introduction by Bill Neal. Columbia, South Carolina: University of South Carolina Press, 1991.)

Burn, Billie. *Stirrin' the Pots on Daufuskie.* Daufuskie Island, South Carolina: Billie Burn, 1985.

Cambridge World History of Food. Kiple, Kenneth F., and Ornelas, Kriemhild C., editors. Cambridge, UK: Cambridge University Press, 2000.

Casas, Penelope. *Delicioso!* New York: Alfred A. Knopf, 1996.

———. *The Foods & Wines of Spain.* New York: Alfred A. Knopf, 1996.

Classic Chestnut Cuisine. Citizen Forester Institute, Mancelona, MI, 1993.

Collquitt, Harriet Ross. *The Savannah Cook.* New York: Farrar & Rinehart, 1933.

The Congressional Club Cook Book. The Congressional Club, Washington, D.C., 1927.

Corriher, Shirley O. *CookWise.* New York: William Morrow & Company, Inc., 1997.

Dabney, Joseph E. *Smokehouse Ham, Spoon Bread, & Scuppernong Wine.* Nashville: Cumberland House, 1998.

David, Elizabeth. *Elizabeth David Classics.* New York: Alfred A. Knopf, 1980.

Davidson, Alan. *The Oxford Companion to Food. Oxford*: Oxford University Press, 1999.

DeDomenico, Anita. *My Macadamia Nut Recipes from Our Plantation House.* Honokaa, Hawaii: Hawaiian Holiday Macadamia Nut Company, 1980.

Digby, John and Joan, editors. *Food for Thought: An Anthology of Writings Inspired by Food.* New York: William Morrow & Company, Inc., 1987.

Drummond, J. C. *The Englishman's Food: A History of Five Centuries of English Diet.* London: Readers Union, 1959.

Dull, Mrs. S. R. (Henrietta Stanley). *Southern Cooking.* New York: Grosset & Dunlap, 1941.

Edge, John T. *A Gracious Plenty.* New York: G. P. Putnam's Sons, 1999.

Edgerton, John. *Southern Food.* New York: Alfred A. Knopf, 1987.

Edmonds, Anna G. *A Taste of Turkey.* Istanbul: Redhouse Press, 1972.

Elkort, Martin. *The Secret Life of Food: A Feast of Food and Drink History, Folklore and Fact.* Los Angeles: Jeremy P. Tarcher, Inc., 1991.

Eustis, Celestine. *Cooking in Old Creole Days.* New York: R. H. Russell, 1903.

Farb, Peter, and Armelagos, George. *Consuming Passions: The Anthropology of Eating.* Boston: Houghton Mifflin, 1980.

Farley, John. *The Art of Cookery.* London: Scatcherd and Letterman, 1807. (Facsimile. Edited by Ann Haly. East Sussex, England: Southover Press, 1988.)

Fisher, Abby. *What Mrs. Fisher Knows About Old Southern Cooking.* San Francisco: Women's Co-Operative Printing Office, 1881. (Facsimile. Edited by Karen Hess. Bedford, Massachusetts: Applewood Press, 1995.)

Fitz-Patrick, David G., and Kimbuna, John. *Bundi: The Culture of a Papua New Guinea People*. Nerang, Australia: Ryebuck Publications, 1983.

The First Texas Cook Book. Houston, TX: The First Presbyterian Church of Houston, 1883. (Facsimile. Austin, Texas: Eakin Press, 1986.)

Flexner, Marion. *Dixie Dishes*. Boston: Hale, Cushman & Flint, 1941.

———. *Out of Kentucky Kitchens*. New York: Franklin Watts, Inc, 1949.

Food and Fruit-bearing Forest Species. Food and Agriculture Organization of the United Nations. Rome. 1986.

Frank, Dorothy C. *Cooking with Nuts*. New York: Clarkson N. Potter, 1979.

Gay, Lettie, editor; Rett, Blanche S., recipe collector. *200 Years of Charleston Cooking*. New York: Random House, 1934.

Gerarde, John. *The Herball—the Gererall Historie of Plantes*. London, 1597.

Grammatico, Maria, and Simeti, Mary Taylor. *Bitter Almonds*. New York: William Morrow, 1994.

Gugino, Sam. "Go Nuts," *The Wine Spectator*. October 15, 1999.

Harris, Marvin. *Good to Eat: Riddles of Food and Culture*. New York: Simon & Schuster, 1985.

Hazan, Marcella. *Essentials of Classic Italian Cooking*. New York: Alfred A. Knopf, 1992.

Harvey, Adell, and Gonzalez, Mari. *Sacred Chow*. Nashville, TN: Abingdon Press, 1987.

Heath, Henry B., and Reineccius, Gary. *Flavor Chemistry and Technology*. Westport, CT: AVI Publishing, 1986.

Hess, Karen. *The Carolina Rice Kitchen: The African Connection*. (Featuring in facsimile the *Carolina Rice Cookbook*) Columbia, South Carolina: University of South Carolina Press, 1992.

Hirsch, Alan R. "Scents of Childhood," *Chicago Medicine*, May 21, 1995.

———. "Nostalgia, the Odors of Childhood and Society," *Psychiatric Times*, August 1992.

———. "The Good Old Smells." *The International Journal of Aromatherapy*, Autumn 1992.

———. "Nostalgia: A Neuropsychiatric Understanding," *Advances in Consumer Research*, Volume 19, 1992.

Hyman, Mavis. *Indian-Jewish Cooking*. London: Hyman Publishers (no date).

Jones, Evan. *American Food: The Gastronomic Story*. New York: Vintage Books, 1981.

———. *American Food: The Gastronomic Story*. Woodstock, NY: Overlook Press, 1990.

Journal of the American Chestnut Foundation. Morgantown, WV, 2000.

Kaimal, Maya. *Savoring the Spice Coast of India*. New York: HarperCollins Publisher, 2000.

Junior League of Nashville. *Nashville Seasons Cook Book*. Nashville, TN: The Junior League of Nashville, Incorporated, 1964.

Lambert, Almeda. *Guide for Nut Cookery*. Battle Creek, MI: Joseph Lambert & Company, 1899.

Lang, Jenifer Harvey, editor. *Larousse Gastronomique*. New York: Crown Publishers, Inc., 1988.

Leslie, Eliza (A Lady of Philadelphia). *Seventy-five Receipts, for Pastry, Cakes, and Sweetmeats*. Boston: Munroe and Francis, 1828. (Facsimile: Bedford, MA: Applewood Books.)

Lifshey, Earl. *The Housewares Story*. Chicago: National Housewares Manufacturers Association, 1973.

Longone, Janice Bluestein and Daniel T. *American Cookbooks and Wine Books, 1797–1950*. Ann Arbor: The Clements Library & The Wine and Food Library, 1984.

Lowenfeld, Claire. *Britain's Wild Larder, Nuts*. London: Faber and Faber, 1957.

Luard, Elisabeth. *The Old World Kitchen*. New York: Bantam, 1987.

MacDougall, Allan Ross. *And the Greeks*. New York: Near East Foundation, 1942.

Manaster, Jane. *The Pecan Tree*. Austin: University of Texas Press, 1994.

Marks, Copeland. *Sephardic Cooking*. New York: Donald I. Fine, Inc., 1992.

Marshall, Lydie Pinoy. *Cooking with Lydie Marshall*. New York: Alfred A. Knopf, 1982.

———. *Chez Nous*. New York: HarperCollins, 1995.

McCord, Holly. *The Peanut Butter Diet*. New York: St. Martin's Press, 2001.

McGee, Harold. *On Food and Cooking*. New York: Charles Scribner Sons, 1984.

Merrill, Fred B. *Marketing Black Walnuts*. Frankfort, KY: Kentucky Forest Service, 1927.

Midgley, John. *The Goodness of Nuts and Seeds*. New York: Random House, 1993.

Neal, Bill. *Southern Cooking*. Chapel Hill, NC: The University of North Carolina Press, 1985.

———. *Biscuits, Spoonbread, and Sweet Potato Pie*. New York: Alfred A. Knopf, 1990.

New Orleans Times-Picayune. *The Picayune's Creole Cook Book*. New York: Random House, 1987. (Originally published in 1901.)

Oxford English Dictionary. Oxford: Oxford University Press, 2000.

Pennington, Jean A.T., and Church, Helen Nichols. *Bowes & Church's Food Values of Portions Commonly Used*. Philadelphia: J. B. Lippincott, 1980.

Plotkin, Fred. *Recipes from Paradise*. Boston: Little, Brown & Company, 1997.

Porter, Mrs. M. E. *Mrs. Porter's New Southern Cookery Book*. Philadelphia: John E. Potter and Company, 1871. (Facsimile. Edited by Louis Szathmáry. New York: Promontory Press, 1974.)

Randolph, Mary. *The Virginia Housewife*. Baltimore: Plaskitt & Cugle, 1828. (Facsimile. Birmingham, AL: Oxmoor House, 1984.).

Robb, Peter. *Midnight in Sicily: On Art, Food, History, Travel & La Cosa Nostra*. Boston: Faber & Faber, 1996.

Robotti, Frances D., and Peter J. *French Cooking in the New World*. Garden City, NY: Doubleday & Company, 1967.

Rogers, Julia Ellen. *Trees Worth Knowing*. New York: Doubleday, Page & Company, 1917.

Root, Waverly. *Food*. New York: Simon & Schuster, 1980.

Rorer, Mrs. S. T. *Mrs. Rorer's Philadelphia Cook Book*. Philadelphia: Arnold and Company, 1986.

Rosengarten, Frederic, Jr. *The Book of Spices*. Philadelphia: Livingston Publishing Company, 1969

———. *The Book of Edible Nuts*. New York: Walker and Company, 1984.

Rutledge, Sarah. *The Carolina Housewife*. Charleston, SC: W. R. Babcock & Co., 1847. (Facsimile. Edited by Anna Wells Rutledge. Columbia, SC: University of South Carolina Press, 1979.

Scott, Natalie V. *200 Years of New Orleans Cooking*. New York: Jonathan Cape & Harrison Smith, 1931.

Shannon, Jamie, and Martin, Ti Adelaide. *Commander's Kitchen*. New York: Broadway, 2000.

Simmons, Amelia. *American Cookery, or the Art of Dressing Viands, Fish, Poultry and Vegetables, and the best Modes of Making Pastes, Puffs, Pies, Tarts, Puddings, Custards and Preserves, and all kinds of Cakes from the Imperial Plumb to Plain Cake, Adapted to this Country and All Grades of Life*. Hartford: Hudson & Goodwin, 1796. (Facsimile. Mineola, NY: Dover Publications, 1984.)

Smith, Herman. *Stina, the Story of a Cook*. New York: M. Barrows & Company, 1942.

Smith, J. Russell. *Tree Crops*. New York: The Devin-Adair Company. 1950.

Sokolov, Raymond. Recipes by Susan R. Friedland. *The Jewish-American Kitchen*. New York: Stewart, Tabori & Chang, 1989.

Soyer, Alexis. *Soyer's Cookery Book*. London: George Routledge and Sons, 1854. (Facsimile. Foreword by James Beard. New York: David McKay Company, 1959.)

Spivey, Diane M. *The Peppers, Cracklings, and Knots of Wool Cookbook*. Albany: State University of New York Press, 1999.

Tannahill, Reay. *Food in History*. New York: Stein and Day, 1973.

Thorne, John. *Outlaw Cook*. New York: Farrar Straus Giroux, 1992.

Thornton, Phineas. *The Southern Gardener and Receipt Book*. Newark, NJ: A. L. Dennis, 1845. (Facsimile. Birmingham, AL: Oxmoor House, 1984.)

Taylor, David. "Tasty Brazil Nuts Stun Harvesters and Scientists," *Smithsonian*, April 1999.

Thorne, Tony. *The Dictionary of Contemporary Slang*. New York: Pantheon, 1990.

"Tree Nuts, Health and the Mediterranean Diet." Oldways Preservation and Exchange Trust, 1995.

Tschirky, Oscar. *"Oscar" of the Waldorf's Cook Book*. New York: The Werner Company, 1896.

Tullie's Receipts. Atlanta: Atlanta Historical Society, 1776.

Ude, Louis Eustache. *The French Cook*. Philadelphia: Carey, Lea and Carey, 1828. (Facsimile. New York: Arco Publishing Company, 1978.)

The Virginia Hostess. Mansur, Caroline E, editor. Truro Parish, Virginia: Ann Mason Guild of Pohick Church, 1960.

Von Bremzen, Anya. "Peanuts: A view from the peoples of Asia and the Pacific Rim," *Peanuts and Health: Science, Culture and Cuisine*. Oldways Preservation and Exchange Trust, 1996.

Waller, George R., et al., editors. *The Maillard Reaction in Foods and Nutrition*. American Chemical Society, Symposium Series 215, Washington, DC, 1983.

Walnut Production Manual. Oakland: University of California, Division of Agriculture and Natural Resources, 1998.

Windham, Katheryn Tucker. *Treasured Tennessee Recipes*. Huntsville, AL: The Strode Publishers, 1972.

Wolfert, Paula. *The Cooking of the Eastern Mediterranean*. New York: HarperCollins, 1994.

———. *Couscous and Other Good Food From Morocco*. New York: Harper & Row, 1973.

———. *Mediterranean Cooking*. New York: The Ecco Press, 1977.

Wolf, Burton, et al. *The Cooks' Catalogue*. New York: Harper & Row, 1975.

Wright, Clifford A. *Cucina Paradiso: The Heavenly Food of Sicily*. New York: Simon & Schuster, 1992.

index

peppered, -crusted rack of lamb, 220

phyllo tart with apples and, 291–92

strudel rolls with curried couscous, and root vegetables, 147–48

tempura, 57–58

Pizza

dough, 133

with hazelnut sauce, Fontina, and truffle oil, 134

with tapénade, pine nuts, and basil, 135

with tomatoes, nutty potatoes, and anchovies, 136

Plotkin, Fred, 134, 154, 191

Podelak, Janet, 30

Pork

Asian-style barbecued spareribs with peanut dipping sauce, 232–33

braised stuffed, chops with chestnuts and apples, 233–34

grilled, tenderloin with walnuts, shallots, and prunes, 230–31

hash with pine nuts and tangy fruited tomato sauce, 234–35

pan Asian, roast with peanut crust and orange sauce, 229–30

shrimp Cantonese with salted peanuts, 169–70

Potato(es)

chestnut, gratin with Taleggio, 247–48

coconut chicken with, and lime, 193–94

coconut curried winter vegetables with peanuts, 259

gnocchi with chestnuts, 139–40

gnocchi, Piedmontese, 138–39

hash with pine nuts, 234–35

pizza with tomatoes, nutty, and anchovies, 136

spicy red, with garlic, Indian

spices, and cashews, 246–47

spicy, salad with cashews and tomato cucumber mint raita, 125

Wayne's supper salad with macadamia nuts, 149–50

Pralines, 309–10

Prunes, grilled pork tenderloin with walnuts, shallots, and, 230–31

Pudding

chocolate amaretto, cake, 278

chocolate and pine nut bread, 277

coconut rice, with mango, 272

Malabar coconut, with tapioca, 270–71

Pumpkin coconut crème caramel, 274

Purvis, William Herbert, 20

Radish, Asian apple, slaw, 206

Ragout

bucatini with lusty lamb, 142–43

lamb, with chestnuts, onions, and sage, 222–23

Raisin(s)

bacalà (salt cod) cakes with pistachios and, 67

cashew rum, ice cream, 263

challah with, and hazelnuts, 90–91

Provençale salad with nuts and, 108

Raita

coconut, 124, 246

tomato cucumber mint, 125

Rashid, Justin, 91, 152

Raspberries, strudel, 300–301

Raun, Linda and Lowell, 272

Recipes from Paradise (Plotkin), 134, 154

Red snapper amandine, 175–76

Relanghe company, Italy, 265

Relish, Confederate, with pecans, 159

Rellenos, cream-baked chiles, with black beans, goat cheese, and pine nuts, 250

Rémoulade, celery root with Brazil nuts and herbs, 114

Rhubarb and almond coffee cake with cinnamon and cardamom, 98–99

Rice

coconut, with cardamom and cloves, 242

coconut, pudding with mango, 272

Kerala lamb biriyani, 226–27

Rogers, Julia, 12

Romesco sauce, 67, 156, 207

Rose, Edgar, 295

Rosengarten, Frederic, xx, 37

Ruscalleda, Carme and Toni, 74

Russo, Nucci and Flavio, 138–39, 247, 275–76

Rye bread with nuts and currants, 88–89

Sage, lamb ragout with chestnuts, onions, and, 222–23

Salad(s)

autumn, with toasted hazelnuts, pears, and Gorgonzola, 121–22

celery root rémoulade with Brazil nuts and herbs, 114

classic, with warm chèvre and walnuts, 112

coconut raita, 124

curried chicken, with toasted black walnuts, 153

fattoush, 110–11

Finnish mushroom, with pine nuts, 116

green almond, 109–10

lemon fennel, with Parmesan and spicy candied walnuts, 116–17

minted peas with goat cheese and walnuts, 120

Provençale, with nuts and raisins, 108

roasted beets with walnuts, 115

salade à la Chipolata, 108–9

spicy potato, with cashews and tomato cucumber mint raita, 125

Thai shrimp and noodle, with peanut sauce, 150–51